AF511659

THE VĀKĀṬAKA-GUPTA AGE

(Circa 200-550 A.D.)

Edited by

RAMESH CHANDRA MAJUMDAR

ANANT SADASHIV ALTEKAR

MOTILAL BANARSIDASS PUBLISHERS
PRIVATE LIMITED • DELHI

Reprint: Delhi, 1986, 2007
First Edition: 1967

© MOTILAL BANARSIDASS PUBLISHERS PRIVATE LIMITED
All Rights Reserved

ISBN: 81-208-0026-5 (Cloth)
ISBN: 81-208-0043-5 (Paper)

MOTILAL BANARSIDASS
41 U.A. Bungalow Road, Jawahar Nagar, Delhi 110 007
8 Mahalaxmi Chamber, 22 Bhulabhai Desai Road, Mumbai 400 026
236, 9th Main III Block, Jayanagar, Bangalore 560 011
203 Royapettah High Road, Mylapore, Chennai 600 004
Sanas Plaza, 1302 Baji Rao Road, Pune 411 002
8 Camac Street, Kolkata 700 017
Ashok Rajpath, Patna 800 004
Chowk, Varanasi 221 001

Printed in India
BY JAINENDRA PRAKASH JAIN AT SHRI JAINENDRA PRESS,
A-45 NARAINA, PHASE-I, NEW DELHI 110 028
AND PUBLISHED BY NARENDRA PRAKASH JAIN FOR
MOTILAL BANARSIDASS PUBLISHERS PRIVATE LIMITED,

FOREWORD

In the middle of the 19th Century all the parts of India were united under one sceptre, and then began a change, almost revolutionary in its character, in the evolution of India's political life and thought. At exactly the same time a revolution also began in Indian historiography. Hitherto our historians' stock-in-trade had been only pious legends, age-worn traditions, laudatory poems in hyperbole, and very late compilations of blended fact and fiction. The Hindu period of our past, covering nearly two thousand years, was dark, and the darkness was often made more misleading by the false light of Sanskrit romances. Even in the Muslim period the current histories were mostly popular abridgements and not original sources.

But a new era in the study of Indian history had dawned shortly before the Sepoy Mutiny. General Alexander Cunningham had begun to dig down to the roots of our Buddhistic, Jaina and Hindu past, and Sir Henry M. Elliot had begun the monumental translation of the History of India as told by its own historians. His great work, destined to be completed in a vastly amplified form and by another hand in eight volumes in 1877, made its first appearance in 1849 under the title of *Bibliographical Index to the Historians of Muhammadan India*. The first author to utilise the vast material, thus made available in English, was Stanley Lane-Poole, whose *Mediaeval India under Muhammadan Rule* (1903), when read with Elphinstone's chapters on the same subject, illustrates the advance in our knowledge made in less than half a century.

In the Hindu period, the immense mass of raw materials, in the form of inscriptions, coins, architectural remains and antiquities, brought to light by our field archaeologists—both official and private, scattered all over this continent of a country, was pieced together for the first time in V.A. Smith's *Early History of India* (1904). Indian readers had, no doubt, had an earlier glimpse of this new material, though in a very compressed form, in Hara Prasad Shastri's *School History of India*. But Smith's work, occupying a much ampler canvas and full of details and exact references, can rightly claim to be called an epoch-marking book.

But our progress did not stop here. An army of Indian scholars, some trained, but most others amateurs, continued Cunningham's work in their own localities or subjected the discoveries of others to critical study, and thus built up a vast body of more exact knowledge about our past than was available to Vincent A. Smith. All this knowledge lies scattered over numberless learned journals, popular magazines, sometimes even daily papers, pamphlets and books, in many languages besides English. Our problem for several years now has been to concentrate all these scattered rays of light into one focus, to make a synthesis of all our special treatises and researches in Indian history. As Professor Patrick Geddes used to warn our scientific students, "We have plenty of spinners, who have produced fine threads. We now want a master weaver who will synthetise all these isolated facts. That the crying need of the modern world of science : weave ! weave !"

A new History of India embodying all this accumulated knowledge and abreast of the latest research must fill many volumes. Such a work, both by reason of its size and the diversity of its contents, can be produced only by a syndicate of scholars. The writing of such a co-operative History of India was first discussed by me with the late Mano Mohan Chakravarti in 1908 after the first volumes of the *Cambridge Modern History* had come out and shown us the way. The plan was discussed in great detail and even lists of chapters drawn up on two occasions in collaboration with the late Rakhaldas Banerji in 1918 and 1920. A fourth project, confined solely to the cultural aspects of India's past on the model of the "Heritage" series, was pondered over by me with the late Rev. J. Farquhar. But all of these schemes very soon came to nothing because we felt that the time was not yet ripe and we had not enough scholars to do equal justice to every part of the subject.

At last in 1937, Dr. Rajendra Prasad publicly broached the present scheme and we two inaugurated it at a meeting held in Benares on 28th December, 1937. He was to take charge of the administrative and financial side of it, and I was to be the chief literary manager or chairman of the Editorial Board. Prompt and generous donations were received from the Indian mercantile community whose liberality to all good causes is well-known : and we actively set ourselves to planning the details, making the preliminary arrangements and corresponding with various scholars whose aid or advice we sought. Just after the actual writing had started, came the Japanese invasion in 1941, and our scholars were scattered and public libraries closed or removed elsewhere, which made us lose four years. At last in 1945, two volumes (the Fourth and the Sixth) out of a projected series of twenty (see the list at the end) were ready for the press and a third (the Twelfth, on Akbar) half completed. Now that the ground has been fully prepared, our progress both in writing and in printing will be much quicker.

It has been my dream to produce these volumes at a price (say Rs. 4 each) which would place them within reach of all our people, as the volumes would be sold separately. With the knowledge of our land's storied past daily advancing, revised editions would be frequently called for, in order that this science may not be stereotyped ; but a low price would enable most purchasers of the old edition to scrap it up and buy its improved and corrected successor. But the economic disturbance caused by World War II has belied this hope.

This History is being written entirely by Indians. Lest this limitation of choice should cause its spirit to be suspect I invite the reader's attention to the following correspondence which makes our aim fully clear.

From Sir Jadunath Sarkar to Dr. Rajendra Prasad, 19th November, 1937—"National history, like every other history worthy of the name and deserving to endure, must be true as regards the facts and reasonable in the interpretation of them. It will be national not in the sense that it will try to suppress or whitewash everything in our country's past that is disgraceful, but because it will admit them and at the same time point out that there were other and nobler aspects in the stages of our nation's evolution which offset the former, that a "drain inspector's report" is not the whole truth about any nation. The first duty of our national historian will be to depict all the aspects of our nation's life in the past usually ignored by foreign writers, who merely give us an unrelieved picture of bloodshed and dynastic change. Social life and thought, art and culture, will have no less importance in the history to be written by us. In addition, we shall try to explain, with that sympathetic insight which only a native can possess,—or a rare foreigner like the gifted Sister Nivedita,—why things happened with our ancestors as they did actually happen. In this task......the historian must be a judge. He will not suppress any defect of the national character, but add to his portraiture those higher qualities which, taken together with the former, help to constitute the entire individual."

From Dr. Rajendra Prasad to Sir Jadunath Sarkar, 22nd November, 1937—"I entirely agree with you that no history is worth the name which suppresses or distorts facts. A historian who purposely does so under the impression that he thereby does good to his native country really harms it in the end

Much more so in the case of a country like ours which has suffered much on account of its national defects, and which must know and understand them to be able to remedy them."

Our thanks are specially due to Dr. Ramesh Chandra Majumdar and Dr. A. S. Altekar, who have edited this volume and written most part of it, Dr. Majumdar contributing eight chapters and Dr. Altekar ten out of a total of 23. We have been fortunate enough to enlist the co-operation of a number of other scholars, each eminent in his special subject : Rao Bahadur K. N. Dikshit has written on Archaeological Remains, Prof. K. A. Nilkant Sastri on South India, Dr. Dines Chandra Sircar on the Eastern Deccan, Dr. P. C. Bagchi on Chinese Contact, Dr. Paranavitana on Ceylon, Dr. C. Sivarama-murti on South Indian Art, and Dr. V. S. Agrawala on Gupta Art. We offer our sincere thanks to all of them and also to the Director-General of Archaeology, Government of India, the authorities of the Nizam's Archaeological Department and the Mathura Museum for permission to print illustrations of which they hold the copyright.

We also take this opportunity to thank Mr. S. K. Sarasvati, M.A., Lecturer, Calcutta University, who has helped the editors in seeing the book through the press and has rendered very useful service in many ways. Our thanks are also due to the Sri Gouranga Press for having undertaken the printing of this book in a time of exceptional difficulty and executed it with commendable promptitude.

JADUNATH SARKAR,

General Editor.

General scheme of

A NEW HISTORY OF THE INDIAN PEOPLE

IN TWENTY VOLUMES

VOLUME

I. The Land, the People and pre-History.
II. Aryan Colonisation and the Vedic Age.
III. The Earliest States,—Jainism, Buddhism.
IV. Nanda and Maurya Empires. 366-210 B.C.
V. Śuṅgas, Sātavāhaṇas and Śakas. 210 B.C.-c.200 A.D.
VI. The Age of Vākāṭakas and Guptas. c. 200-550 A.D.
VII. Later Empires. 550-916 A.D.
VIII. Close of the Hindu Age. 916-1194 A.D.
IX. Sultanate of Delhi and Provincial Dynasties. 1194-1325.
X. North Indian States. 1325-1556.
XI. Bahmani (1349-1526) and Vijayanagara (1349-1565) Empires. (Includes Portuguese Settlement).
XII. Age of Akbar (1556-1605). (Art and Literature, 1556-1657).
XIII. Seventeenth century in the North. 1605-1707. (Includes Sikh Gurus).
XIV. Deccan Sultanates (1526-1687) and Maratha Royal House (1624-1707).
Vol. XV Later Mughals and early Peshwas. 1707-1761. (Includes Anglo-French rivalry for empire of India).
XVI. Later Peshwas and Downfall of Delhi Empire. 1761-1798. (Includes Sikh misl. Age and Early British Administrative Organisation).
XVII. British Paramountcy. 1798-1818.
XVIII. Completion of British India. 1818-1858. (Includes Sikh Kingdom of the Panjab, 1799-1849).
XIX. Modern India, Political History. 1858-1940.
XX. Modern India, Cultural and Economic. 1800-1940.

EDITORIAL PREFACE

A FEW words are necessary to explain the scope and nature of the history narrated in the following pages. As planned by the General Editorial Board, this volume covers the period 200 to 550 A.D. and is called the Gupta-Vākāṭaka age. The title of the volume was selected for the sake of convenience only. It is not claimed that the political or cultural achievements of the Vākāṭakas were comparable to those of the Guptas and sufficiently important to justify their association with the name of the age. Although this volume is intended to cover the period from 200 to 550 A D., it has not always been possible to conform to these chronological limits. The history of the Western Kshatrapas commences with 160 A.D., as the death of Rudradāman I is a convenient starting point. The history of Ceylon begins with 66 A.D., as the dynasty that was founded at that time continued to rule practically to the end of our period. The history of the Maghas of Kauśāmbī is taken back to *c.* 150 A.D. when their house started its career, as it was found more convenient to deal with the whole history of the dynasty in one place. The careers of the Vishṇukuṇḍins and the Maitrakas began at about 500 A.D., and several independent kingdoms, notably those of Nepal and Assam, arose about the same time. Their early history is not discussed in this volume but reserved for full treatment in the next one dealing with the period when they played an effective part in Indian history. In the case of the Maukharis and Later Guptas, however, their early history to the end of our period is dealt with, as it was necessary to discuss it in connection with the decline of the Gupta empire. It has been recently suggested (*IHQ*. XXI, 19) that the kings of Assam were mainly instrumental in bringing about the downfall of the

Guptas, but hardly any convincing evidence has been adduced to support so novel a hypothesis.

The reader of the modern or medieval history, whether of India or Europe, will no doubt find the narrative of the political history in this volume rather meagre and sketchy. But in the present state of our knowledge it is not possible to give a fuller account. In spite of the discovery of a large number of coins, inscriptions and monuments, it has to be confessed that there are some dynasties in our period where even the names of most of its rulers are unknown to us. Such, for instance, is the case with the Nāgas of Mathura and the Ābhīras of northern Mahārāshṭra. Sometimes we know the names of the kings of a dynasty, but are ignorant of their dates and inter-relations, as for example, the Later Kushāṇas and the early Pallavas. Sometimes the evidence is so indecisive that the historian cannot state with certainty whether a particular event did or did not occur, or whether a certain personage, *e.g.*, king Rāma-gupta, is or is not a historical figure. Sometimes the evidence is so scanty and dubious that it lends itself of diverse interpretations and the historian finds it difficult to choose between two or more possible alternatives. Such, for instance, is the case with the history of the successors of Skanda-gupta. If, therefore, the picture appears at places to be hazy, the account scanty and the discussions inconclusive, the fault lies primarily with the original sources and not the writers who have attempted to reconstruct the history. As a matter of fact, the first part of the period dealt with in this volume, *viz.*, 200 to 300 A.D., is usually known to be the 'Dark Period' of ancient Indian history. An effort has, however, been made to elucidate it as best as possible.

On account of the paucity of evidence some of the dynasties, which ruled during our period, have only been incidentally referred to, but not treated in detail. As notable examples may be mentioned the Ābhīras and the Traikūṭakas. We possess some coins and a few inscriptions of the Traikūṭakas, but beyond the names of two or three kings we know hardly anything about them. The Ābhīras are known from a single inscription and a number of incidental notices. But though the foundation of the so-called Kalachuri era, commencing in 248-9 A.D., has been ascribed to them, and an attempt has been recently made (*ABORI.* XXV, 161) to show that they established an empire, our knowledge of them is still very meagre. The little that is definitely known about them will be found in the chapters dealing with the history of the Western Kshatrapas and the Vākāṭakas, with whom they had come into close contact (pp. 48, 121). This book, it should be remembered, is intended to be a general history, and not an encyclopaedic account of each and every dynasty that ruled in our period. This will also explain the absence of reference to some of the unimportant feudatories or obscure chieftains that belonged to our age.

In a co-operative work of this kind, based upon data so vague and uncertain, it is almost inevitable that different writes, including the two editors, will express or at least entertain different opinions. In spite of long discussions between the two editors it was not possible to eliminate these differences altogether. Among important points on which they could not agree may be mentioned 'the extent of the Vākāṭaka empire (pp. 98 ff.) and the view that Pravara-sena II of the main dynasty was the Kuntaleśa of the Kālidāsa tradition, (p. 110 fn. 1), the struggle for independence waged by the Yaudheyas and others against the Kushāṇas (pp. 28 ff), and the relation between Piro and Rāma-gupta and specially the inference drawn from the coins of Piro about his character (pp. 22-23), Nor did complete agreement become possible with reference to the views expressed about the abdication of Chandra-gupta I (pp. 137-8). the precise western boundary of the empire of Samudra-gupta (p. 144), the assumption by him of the title *Vikrama* towards the end of his reign (p. 155), and the nationality of Toramāṇa (p. 198).

A careful reader would come across other instances of this kind in the body of this work, clearly showing that where difference really exists, no attempt has been made, by dogmatic assertions, to accept one view as authoritative and final and reject the others.

We are fully conscious of the defects and imperfections of this volume. Most of its chapters were written during the unusual circumstances created by the Second World War, when some of our contributors were denied the facilities of good reference libraries, as many of them had removed important books for safety. The proofs also could not be sent to some of our contributors owing to want of time. The fact that this, the sixth volume of the series, had to be published before its predecessors has also created some peculiar difficulties particularly with reference to controversial points of the earlier periods, which have their bearing on our age as well. We could not also know how the earlier history of the various cultural movements treated in this volume would be dealt with by other writers in the preceding volumes. We have, however, tried our best to give as complete and comprehensive a picture of the political and cultural history of the age as was possible in a volume of 500 pages. The political history with its wars and conquests is not allowed to dominate the scene ; cultural history, describing the religion and philosophy, the social and economic condition, the literature and sciences, and the art and architecture of the age occupies almost equal space with the political history. Nor have we looked at the history of our country from the view-point of the isolationist. India's commercial, cultural and religious contacts with and influence upon its neighbours, both in the east and the west, have been adequately described.

We wish to express our thanks to our contributors for their promptness in sending their promised chapters. We are indebted to Prof. K.A. Nilkanta Sastri, M.A., for supplying us some data from the Tamil literature, which have been utilised in the chapters dealing with the cultural history of the age. Mr. S. K. Sarasvati, M.A., has been of immense help in seeing the volume through the press and we are thankful to him for his care and assiduousness. And finally we have great pleasure in expressing our indebtedness to Sir Jadu Nath Sarkar for his valuable advice and suggestions.

R. C. MAJUMDAR,
A. S. ALTEKAR.

TABLE OF CONTENTS

CHAPTER IV

EASTERN DECCAN

By Dr. Dines Chandra Sircar, M.A., Ph.D. Lecturer, Ancient Indian History and Culture, Calcutta University

CHAPTER V

THE VĀKĀTAKAS

By Dr. A. S. Altekar

CHAPTER VI

By Dr. R. C. Majumdar, M.A., Ph.D., F.R.A.S.B.,

Formerly Vice-Chancellor, Dacca University

CHAPTER VII

FOUNDATION OF THE GUPTA EMPIRE

By DR. R. C. MAJUMDAR

CHAPTER VIII

THE EXPANSION OF THE GUPTA EMPIRE

By DR. R. C. MAJUMDAR

CHAPTER IX

THE IMPERIAL CRISIS

By DR. R. C. MAJUMDAR

CHAPTER X

By DR. R. C. MAJUMDAR

CHAPTER XI

By DR. R. C. MAJUMDAR

CHAPTER XII

SOUTH INDIA

By PROF. K. A. NILAKANTA SASTRI, M.A., Professor of Indian History, Madras University

CHAPTER XIII

CHAPTER XIV

THE ADMINISTRATIVE ORGANISATION

By Dr. A. S. Altekar

CHAPTER XV

THE COINAGE

By Dr. A. S. Altekar

CHAPTER XVI

COLONIAL AND CULTURAL EXPANSION

I. Colonial Expansion in Isnul-India

By Dr. R. C. Majumdar

By Dr. P. C. Bagchi, M.A., Docteur es Lettres (Paris), F.R.A.S.B.
Director, Cheena Bhavana, Viśvabhāratī,
Formerly Lecturer, Calcutta University

CHAPTER XVII

By Dr. R. C. Majumdar

CHAPTER XVIII

SOCIAL AND ECONOMIC CONDITIONS

By. Dr. A. S. Altekar

I. Social Condition

II. Economic Condition

CHAPTER XIX

RELIGION AND PHILOSOPHY

By Dr. A. S. Altekar

CHAPTER XX

EDUCATION, LITERATURE AND SCIENCES

By Dr. A. S. Altekar

CHAPTER XXI

By Rao Bahadur K. N. Dikshit, M.A., F.R.A.S.B.,

Formerly Director General of Archaeology in India

CHAPTER XXII

FINE ARTS

I. South Indian Art

By Dr. C. Sivaramamurti, M.A., Ph.D., Archaeological Section, Government Museum, Madras

II. Art in the Gupta Period

By Dr. V. S. Agrawala, M.A., Ph.D.,

Curator, Provincial Museum, Lucknow

* The Index has been prepared by Mr. Sudhir Kumar Das, M.A.

LIST OF ILLUSTRATIONS

ABBREVIATIONS

ABORI.—Annals of the Bhandarkar Oriental Research Institute, Poona.
Aham.—Ahanānuṟṟu.
Aiyangar Comm. Vol.—S. Krishnaswami Aiyangar Volume.
AHD.—Ancient History of the Deccan by G. Jouveau Dubreuil. Pondicherry, 1920.
AIG.—Age of the Imperial Guptas by R. D. Banerji. Benares, 1933.
AIC.—Ancient Inscriptions of Ceylon by E. Muller. London, 1883.
ASC.—Archaeological Survey of India, Reports of Sir Alexander Cunningham.
ASI. (*ASR*).—Archaeological Survey of India, Annual Reports.
ASR. WC.—Archaeological Survey of India, Western Circle, Annual Reports.
ASWI. IV.—Reports on the Buddhist Cave Temples and their Inscriptions by J. Burgess (Archaeological Survey of Western India, Vol. IV). London, 1883.
Beal—*Records*.—Si-yu-ki. Buddhist Records of the Western World. Tr. from the Chinese of Hiuen Tsang by Samuel Beal. London, 1906.
BEFEO.—Bulletin de l'Ecole Française d'Extrême-Orient. Hanoi.
Bhandarkar Comm. Vol.—Commemorative Essays presented to Sir R. G. Bhandarkar. Poona, 1917.
Bhandarkar—*List.*—List of Inscriptions of Northern India (Appendix to *EI*).
CAI—Catalogue of the Coins of Ancient India (in the British Museum) by John Allan. London, 1936.
CGD.—Catalogue of Coins of the Gupta Dynasties and of Śeśāṅka, King of Gauḍa (in the British Museum) by John Allan. London, 1914.
CII.—Corpus Inscriptionum Indicarum. Vol. III. (Inscriptions of the Early Gupta Kings and their Successors by J. F. Fleet). Calcutta, 1888.
CJS.—Ceylon Journal of Science, Sec. G. Colombo.
DKA.—Dynasties of the Kali by F. E. Pargiter. London, 1913.
DL.—Descriptive Lists of Inscriptions in the Central Provinces and Berar by Rai Bahadur Hiralal. Nagpur, 1916.
DUS.—Dacca University Studies. Dacca.
EC.—Epigraphia Carnatica.
EDA—History of the Early Dynasties of Andhradeśa by B. V. Krishnarao. Madras, 1942.
EHAC.—Early History of the Andhra Country by K. Gopalachari. Madras, 1941.
EHI—Early History of India by V. A. Smith (4th ed.). Oxford. 1924.
EI—Epigraphia Indica.
EZ.—Epigraphia Zeylanica. Colombo.

Fahien—Record of the Buddhistic Kingdoms being an account of the Chinese Monk Fa-hien's Travels. Tr. by J. H. Legge, Oxford, 1886.

Farquhar-*Outlines*.—Outline of Religious Literature of India by J. N. Farquhar. Oxford, 1920.

HBR.—History of Bengal (Vol. I.) Ed. by R. C. Majumdar. Dacca, 1943.

HFA.—History of Fine Art in India and Ceylon by V. A. Smith. Oxford, 1911.

HIIA.—History of Indian and Indonesian Art by A. K. Coomaraswamy. London, 1927.

HIJ.—History of India, 150-350 A. D. by K. P. Jayaswal. Lahore, 1933.

Hist. Ins. of South India.—Historical Inscriptions of South India by R. B. Sewell.

HNI.—History of North-Eastern India by R. G. Basak. Calcutta, 1934.

Hyd. Ar. S.—Hyderabad Archaeological Series, No. 14 (Vākāṭaka Inscription in Cave XVI at Ajanta by V. V. Mirashi). Hyderabad.

IA.—Indian Antiquary. Bombay.

IC.—Indian Culture. Calcutta.

IHI.—Imperial History of India in a Sanskrit Text by K. P. Jayaswal. Lahore, 1934.

IHQ.—Indian Historical Quarterly. Calcutta.

Ind. Archit. Buddhist and Hindu.—Indian Architecture : Buddhist and Hindu by Percy Brown. Bombay, 1942.

JA.—Journal Asiatique. Paris.

JAHC.—Journal of Andhra History and Culture.

JAHRS.—Journal of the Andhra Historical Research Society. Rajahmundry.

JASB.—Journal of the Asiatic Society of Bengal. Calcutta.

JASB. NS.—Journal and Proceedings of the Asiatic Society of Bengal, New Series. Calcutta.

JBBRAS.—Journal of the Bombay Branch of the Royal Asiatic Society. Bombay.

JBBRAS. NS.—Journal of the Bombay Branch of the Royal Asiatic Society, New Series. Bombay.

JBORS.—Journal of the Bihar and Orissa Research Society. Patna.

JBRS.—Journal of the Bihar Research Society. Patna.

JGIS.—Journal of the Greater India Society. Calcutta.

JIH.—Journal of Indian History. Madras.

JISOA.—Journal of the Indian Society of Oriental Art. Calcutta.

J. Mad. Un. (Jl. Mad. Univ.)—Journal of the Madras University. Madras.

JNSI.—Journal of the Numismatic Society of India. Bombay.

JOR.—Journal of Oriental Research, Madras.

JRAS.—Journal of the Royal Asiatic Society of Great Britain and Ireland. London.

JRASBL.—Journal of the Royal Asiatic Society of Bengal : Letters. Calcutta.

JRAS. C.B.—Journal of the Royal Asiatic Society, Ceylon Branch, Colombo.

Journ. Assam Res. Society.—Journal of the Assam Research Society. Gauhati.

Kumara.—Kumārasambhava of Kālidāsa.

Malaviya Comm. Vol.—Malaviya Commemoration Volume. Benares.

MAR.—Mysore Archaeological Department Annual Reports. Bangalore.

MASI.—Memoirs of Archaeological Survey of India.

Mbh.—Mahābhārata.

MKSP.—Mahākośala Historical Society, Proceedings.

Narada.—Nārada-Smṛiti.

NGGW.—Nachrichten von der Kgl. Gesellschaft der Wissenschaften zu Goettingen, Philolog.-histor. Klasse.

Num. Supp. (*Num. Suppl.*)—Numismatic Supplement to *JASB* or *JRASBL.*

PASB.—Proceedings of the Asiatic Society of Bengal. Calcutta.

PHAI.—Political History of Ancient India by H. C. Raychaudhuri (4th ed.). Calcutta, 1938.

POC.—Proceedings of the Oriental Conference.

Porunar.—Porunār-āṟṟuppaḍai.

Puram—Puranānuṟṟa.

Raghu.—Raghuvaṁśa of Kālidāsa.

Satapatha Br.—Śatapatha Brāhmaṇa.

Sel. Ins.—Select Inscriptions bearing on Indian History and Civilisation by D. C. Sircar. Calcutta, 1943.

SIE.—(Annual Reports of) South Indian Epigraphy.

SII.—South Indian Inscriptions.

Suc. Sat.—Successors of Sātavāhanas in Lower Deccan by D. C. Sircar. Calcutta, 1939.

Thomas Commemoration Vol.—Prof. F. W. Thomas Commemoration Volume.

Watters.—On Yuan Chwang's Travels in India by T. Watters. London, 1908.

Winternitz-*History.*—History of Indian Literature by M. Winternitz (English Translation). Calcutta, 1927 and 1933.

Yaj.—Yājñavalkya-Smṛiti.

ZDMG.—Zeitschrift der Deutschen Morgenländischen Gesellschaft. Leipzig.

INTRODUCTION

The Vākāṭaka-Gupta age (*c.* 200 A.D. to *c.* 550 A.D.), which is covered by the present volume of the *New History of the Indian People,* is undoubtedly a very important epoch in Indian history. A new political consciousness was created in the country and national solidarity was restored after the lapse of nearly four centuries of political disintegration and foreign domination. At the commencement of our period (*c.* 200 A.D.) the Kushāṇas and the Western Kshatrapas were the leading political powers, more powerful than any other state in the country. It is true that they had become completely Hinduised at this time and were as zealous champions and admirers of Hindu religion and Sanskrit literature as any other indigenous dynasty. But probably it was still felt that they were ethnically different; at any rate the local states and powers whom they had subdued a century earlier were not prepared to reconcile themselves with their domination. As the third century advanced the Kushāṇas were gradually ousted from the U.P. and the eastern Punjab where the Maghas, the Nāgas, the Yaudheyas and the Kuṇindas re-established their own independence. The rise of the Sassanians in Iran further weakened the Kushāṇa power, till eventually it sank into insignificance towards the end of the 3rd century A.D.

The Śaka power also began to decline in western India. At the death of Rudra-dāman I in *c.* 170 A.D., the Sakas were the masters of northern Mahārāshṭra, Kathiawar, Gujarat, Malwa, Sindh and greater part of Rajputana. Very soon, however, the Sātavāhanas re-asserted themselves and reconquered Northern Mahārāshṭra during the reign of Gautamīputra Yajñaśrī Sātakarṇi. Rajputana revolted under the leadership of the Mālavas and re-asserted its independence in *c.* 225 A.D. The rise of the Vākāṭakas under the emperor Pravara-sena I (*c.* 275-330 A.D.) led to the further decline of the Śakas. Their rulers are seen reduced to the feudatory status during the first half of the 4th century, and though there was a temporary revival under Rudra-sena III, the family was eventually wiped out by the Guptas towards the close of the 4th century A.D.

The third century had succeeded in practically putting an end to foreign domination. Early in the fourth century A.D. the Guptas rose to power (*c.* 320 A.D.). Their great achievement was to secure as large a political unity and solidarity for the country as was practicable in those days. The Yaudheyas and the Nāgas, the Kuṇindas and the Mālavas had no doubt re-established their independence, but their political horizon did not extend beyond their own homelands. They did not aim at establishing a strong state that might become a bulwark against foreign aggression and secure peace and prosperity for the country as a whole. The great Gupta emperors definitely aimed at founding a powerful unitary state, which could achieve these goals. Traditional political philosophy no doubt recommended that a conqueror should permit the vanquished kings to rule as feudatories; but like Ajātaśatru and Chandragupta Maurya, the Gupta emperors showed scant respect to it and boldly proceeded to annex the territories of a number of kings that were then ruling in Bihar, Bengal, the United Provinces and Central India. In the days of Samudra-gupta, Magadha once more became the leading power of India after a lapse of 500 years. He, however, did not follow the annexation policy throughout; he permitted the Yaudheyas, the Arjunāyanas, the Madras, the Mālavas and a few others to rule as his feudatories and restored the kingdoms of the conquered kings in Chhattisgarh, Orissa and Andhra-deśa. Probably he realised that the means of communication being what they were, it would be impracticable for a power in Magadha to rule effectively over these distant provinces, and the very aim of a strong central power would be defeated if the impossible was sought to be achieved.

Chandra-gupta II, the son of Samudra-gupta, attempted to bring his father's ideal to greater fruition. His conquest of Malwa, Gujarat and Kathiawar resulted in a considerable expansion of the Gupta empire. And if we assume, as is very probable, that king Chandra of Meharauli inscription is none other than Chandra-gupta II, it would follow that he succeeded in extending his sphere of influence over the Punjab as well. When his son-in-law, the Vākāṭaka king Pravara-sena II, died a premature death, the administration of the Deccan also came and remained under his guidance and supervision for about twenty-five years during the regency of his daughter Prabhāvatī guptā. For a time at any rate the extensive territories between the Godāvarī and the Śutlej were welded together under his sceptre, and most of the neighbouring states were willing to recognise his leadership.

The Guptas were thus practically an all-India power towards the end of the reign of Chandra-gupta II. The unity, however, did not last long. It was dependent to a great extent upon the ability of the reigning emperor. Neither Kumāra-gupta I nor Skanda-gupta was as able as Chandra-gupta II or Samudra-gupta. They also suffered from a political blunder that had been already committed by their great predecessor Chandra-gupta II. He did not realise the vital necessity of keeping an effective control over the Punjab and the Khyber pass, if the political integrity of the rest of India was to be maintained. The Guptas showed in this respect less political insight than the Mauryas, who did not relax their efforts till they had secured an effective control over the Khyber and Bolan passes. Had the Guptas followed their example, country might not have suffered as much as it did from the Hūṇa invasions during the 5th and 6th centuries. Had they effectively garrisoned the Khyber pass, the critical battles with the Hūṇas would have been fought beyond the Indus and not in Malwa and Central India.

The overlordship of the Guptas in the political field did not last for more than a century (*c.* 360 to 460 A.D.). The later Gupta emperors were not so able as the earlier ones; local governors began to develop into semi-independent feudatories, and the great strength acquired by the alliance with the Vākāṭakas disappeared when that Deccan power began to decline towards the middle of the 5th century. In the first half of the 6th century, it was clearly realised that the days of the Guptas and the Vākāṭakas were over and there was a great scramble for the imperial position between the Later Guptas, the Maukharis, the Hūṇas, and the Aulikaras in northern India, and the Naḷas, the Kadambas and the Kalachuris in the Deccan. The history of India once more assumed the spectacle of interminable wars between rival powers which decimated national strength without benefitting any party. The time-honoured political philosophy, which maintained that local powers should not be sacrificed for establishing a strong central state, was mainly responsible for this state of affairs. The situation was worsened by the influx of the Hūṇas, whose invasions were facilitated by the failure of the Guptas to secure or keep control over the Khyber pass and the Punjab.

In the course of Indian history, north Indian powers are often seen to be trying to dominate over south India. During our period, the Guptas made one such attempt, but it was successful only for a short time. In a later period a Deccan power—the Rāshṭrakūtas—attempted to secure political domination in northern India; during our period, no such attempt was made by any Deccan or South Indian power.

The absence of an enduring political unity in the country was more than counterbalanced by an all-pervasive cultural uniformity that prevailed throughout the land. The administrative machinery was similar all over the country. The powers of the king, the items of taxation and the extent of local self-government did not show much variation, whether we consider the Gupta or the Vākāṭaka or the Pallava administration. The same three religions,—Hinduism, Buddhism and Jainism—met a foreign observer, whether he was travelling in Bengal or in Mahārāshṭra. New religious ideas and philosophical views were travelling from one end of the country to the other with lightning rapidity. There is no doubt that the missionary and religious activities of monks and preachers contributed a good deal towards the fostering of the cultural unity. A Vasubandhu from Peshawar would go to Ayodhyā to preach his Mahāyāna philosophy, a Dharmapāla from Kāñchī would settle down in Nālandā to preside over and guide its educational activities. Ceylonese monks were moving about in India preaching the gospel of the master in the land of his birth, and Indian monks like Buddhaghosha and Buddhadeva were settling down in Ceylon to start a new era in its literary and religious history. The effect of the new ideas and movements in Hinduism could also be seen all over the country. During the 3rd century A.D. the enthusiasm for Vedic sacrifices was as marked in Rajputana as it was in the Tamil country. A little later the *Bhakti* movement made as pronounced a headway in the south as in the north. It is needless to add that the family structure, the caste system and religious rituals were almost the same all over the country and further helped its cultural unification.

But perhaps the greatest force in this direction was the existence of a common *lingua franca* for cultural purposes. Till the 3rd century Prākṛits which still showed only slight variations served this purpose, but their place was soon taken more effectively by Sanskrit, which became the official language of administration, and the favourite medium of expression for poets, philosophers and scientists. It is interesting to note that even the Buddhists and the Jains gave up their predilection for Pāli and Prākṛits and began to write in chaste and classical Sanskrit during our period. Nay, Sanskrit became the *lingua franca* between India and her cultural colonies in Insul-

India. When it became the sacred language of the Buddhist also, it began to be studied by the Chinese as well.

The cultural unity that was thus secured by the popularisation of Sanskrit was more deep-rooted than the one that is secured today by English, the present official language. English is not understood by the masses. Such was not the case with Sanskrit ; for it could be followed by ordinary people, as the Prākṛit dialects they spoke were still fairly akin to Sanskrit during our period. This cultural unity secured by a common *lingua franca* did not, however, last much longer than our age ; for from about the 6th century Dravidian languages gradually began to displace Sanskrit in South Indian administrative documents. In Northern India the spoken dialects—Prākṛits and Apabhraṁśas—began to diverge more and more from the parent language, Sanskrit, and the latter ceased to be understood by those who spoke the former from *c.* 800 A.D. onwards.

The Vākāṭaka-Gupta age will be ever remembered by a grateful posterity for its successfull efforts to spread Indian religion and culture in eastern Asia. Hindu colonising activity was, no doubt, started long before our period, but it is after the beginning of the 3rd century A.D. that we are able to trace its definite course and achievements. Without getting any help from any state in the mother country, private merchants, captains and missionaries managed to spread Hindu religion and culture and establish Hindu institution in Java, Sumatra, Cambodia, Cochin, China, Annam and Borneo. In China the Buddhist missionaries made a strenuous effort to spread their religion and translated a number of important works in the language of that country. If there exists an appreciable cultural unity today between India on the one side and China on the other, if valuable monuments which are silent witnesses to the glory of Indian culture are seen scattered all over Indo-China, Java, Sumatra and Borneo, tbe credit must be given to the great impulse given by the Gupta age to the spread of Indian culture outside India. It must be added here that the contribution of South India in this respect was as great as that of Northern India. It is interesting to note that the Brāhmaṇas of the age had no objection to the sea voyage ; we find them going to and settling in distant islands like Java, Sumatra and Borneo and also marrying local women. Some of them are seen performing Vedic sacrifices in Borneo and others maintaining Hindu temples in western Asia down to the beginning of the 4th century A.D.

A comprehensive intellectual renaissance was another important feature of our age. It helped the rise of organised educational institutions and the endowment of *Agrahāra* villages, which gave a great impetus to the cause of higher education. New Indian Universities were beginning to acquire international status and reputation. The literary products of the age were numerous and varied, and some of the great masterpieces of Sanskrit literature like the *Śakuntalā*, the *Raghuvaṁśa* and the *Mṛichchhakaṭika* were composed in our period. The Purāṇas were remodelled and a number of important Smṛitis were composed. Philosophy was mostly critical in our period, but it was remarkably creative as well in the case of the Mahāyāna school of Buddhism. The most original, the most daring and the most far-reaching contributions of this school to the progress of Indian philosophy were made by its thinkers who flourished in our period.

But it was not only in the realm of literature, religion and philosophy that the intellectual renaissance manifested itself. It was equally active in the realm of science. The epoch-making discovery of the decimal system of notation with the place value of zero, which was to simplify the arithmetical processes all over the world, was made by the Hindus during our age. They had a lead over their contemporaries in the fields of algebra and arithmetic. Their progress in astronomy was also remarkable. The discovery that the earth rotates round its axis was made by Āryabhaṭa in the 5th century. The length of his solar year is nearer its true duration than that postulated by Ptolemy. A comparison of the astronomical constants of Hipparchus and Ptolemy on the one side and those of the Hindu astronomers like Āryabhaṭa on the other shows that Hindu results were not only independent, but also usually more accurate. The progress in physics, chemistry and metallurgy was also remarkable. The famous Iron Pillar by the side of the Qutb Minar near Delhi is an eloquent testimony to the striking metallurgical skill of the Gupta age.

If Samudra-gupta and Chandra-gupta II were typical representatives of the age—as seems very probable—it follows that intellectual vigour usually went hand in hand with physical prowess, and martial spirit was often harmonised with literary and artistic temperament, during our period. Its leaders could thus take a comprehensive view of culture in its widest sense and promote its all-round progress.

One important characteristic of the Hindu scholarship of our age was its complete freedom from self-complacency and narrowness of outlook. Hindu scholars were keen to ascertain and study the advances made by the *savants* of other countries. Greeks were no doubt regarded as Mlechchhas but were nevertheless respected as highly as the ancient sages for their proficiency in astronomy. Hindu scholars had realised that there was nothing wrong in studying the contributions made by other countries and utilising them, if necessary, for further advancement of knowledge and science.

The intellectual urge of the age naturally resulted in strengthening the rational attitude in society. Leaders of religious thought were not content merely to appeal to ancient texts, but they sought to evolve logical systems based upon rational grounds. The six systems of Hindu philosophy assumed their classical form in our age. Every one of them was constantly on the alert and anxious to examine the new theories that were being advocated in contemporary times, and to refute them, if necessary. Conflict of theories and ideas that we see in our age is indeed interesting and exhilarating. The followers of the different religions, however, lived in harmony and there was complete toleration. Hindu kings endowed Buddhist monasteries. Buddhist kings performed Hindu rituals. In the same family some members followed the Buddhist, and some the Vedic religion.

Hinduism still believed that its scheme of religion and philosophy was intended for the whole humanity, and successfully tried to spread it in Java, Sumatra and adjacent islands. In the mother country itself foreign tribes still continued to be absorbed in the Hindu fold. The Scythian kings were so completely Hinduised during our period that their princesses began to be married into orthodox families. The Hūṇas became staunch and zealous Śivaites within two generations of their settlement in India.

Dhārma (piety), *Artha* (economic prosperity), *Kāma* (pursuit of normal pleasures) and *Moksha* (spiritual salvation) are the four aims of life (*purushārthas*) recognised by Hinduism, and every individual is expected to pursue them in the different stages of his life. In the Gupta period, an even balance was kept among them. *Dharma* did not, as happened in a later age, mean an unending series of rituals and *vratas* to be performed all the year round. Society sought to realise the goals of *Artha* and *Kāma* as zealously as those of *Dharma* and *Moksha*. Hence our age made as remarkable a progress in philosophy as it did in the fine and useful arts The best sculptures and the best paintings of ancient India undoubtedly belong to the Gupta age. The artists succeeded in perfecting their technique and evolving a technical language quite adequate to express abstruse conceptions and spiritual idealism. Here, again, there was a perfect balance between the aesthetic and the spiritual. The best sculptures and paintings of our age strike us as vigorous as well as serene, lovely as well as spiritual. In the famous seated Buddha in the Sarnath museum, for instance, the artist, who did not care even to hand down his name to us, has wonderfully succeeded in depicting the feeling of confidence, composure, compassion and the inexpressible glow of boundless spiritual bliss that marked the features of the great teacher. Our age succeeded in evolving the classical phase of Indian art, characterised by restraint, dignity, naturalness, expressiveness and beauty, and its influence made itself felt in the sandy deserts of Central Asia and the far-off islands of the Indian archipelago.

The Hindus of that age were as successful in evolving new and bold systems of philosophy as in building large and sturdy vessels to carry goods over the sea. Foreign trade increased the national income. The ample gold currency issued by the Guptas and the large number of Roman gold coins found in South India show that the balance of trade was in favour of India and that the country was overflowing with the yellow metal. The surprising variety of gold and pearl ornaments that were popular in society make it clear that the people had enough money to spare for rich and costly ornaments. Most of the country's wealth was derived from trade and industry, which could make considerable strides owing to the existence of numerous and efficient guilds.

A few words are necessary here about the governments of our period. They were both efficient and popular, and their laws and measures, humane as well as effective. It is true that there was no central parliament to control the king and ministers, but we have to remember that government was remarkably decentralised, and most of its functions were exercised by the district administration. In the district headquarters, the officials of the Central Government were assisted and controlled by popular councils, whose sanction was necessary even if the state wanted to sell its own waste lands. Villages, had their own popular councils which administered almost all the branches of administration, including the collection of taxes and the settlement of village disputes. The poor and the sick were offered free relief in hospitals and charitable institutions. Governments were keen in guarding the roads, promoting trade and agriculture and extending patronage to learning and fine arts. People as a whole were rich and prosperous and had very little ground to complain against the administration either for high-handedness or for inefficiency.

We should also draw attention to some developments in our age that were eventually to lead to the decline of Hindu culture and civilisation. The *Upanayana* of the Kshatriyas and the Vaiśyas began to be discouraged in this age. As it disappeared in the course of a few centuries, the gap between the classes and masses increased, and the standard of culture and education was lowered in society as a whole, putting a severe handicap on the progress in trade, industry and useful arts. The marriageable age of girls was lowered down to 12 or 13 in our period. This practically put an end to female education and eventually lowered the marriageable age of boys also, rendering *Brahmacharya* impossible to the end of the educational course. Inter-dining and inter-marriages were still taking place in the society of our age, but the Smṛiti-writers has begun to frown upon them. This was to result in their stoppage a few centuries later, leading to greater cleavage among the different sections of society, and rendering the admission of foreigners within the Hindu fold impossible.

The above survey of the features and achievements of our age will show that it was undoubtedly a very important epoch of Indian history. It put an end to foreign domination and political disintegration and evolved a mighty state which could protect the country against foreign aggression for a long time. Governments of the age were both efficient and popular and secured peace and prosperity for the people. Indians of our period made successful but peaceful efforts to spread Indian culture in Central Asia, China and Indian Archipelago and thus created new and valuable bonds of common culture between India and several islands and states in Eastern and Central Asia. Indian intellect in our period was remarkably creative and its achievements were notable as much in the spheres of religion, philosophy and literature as in those of science, and the fine and useful arts. An even balance was kept between *Dharma*, *Artha*, *Kāma* and *Moksha*, which enabled society both to lead a pious and religious life and to secure the economic prosperity and political greatness. Different religions and sects lived in peace and harmony, and the standard of average education and culture was higher than in any other period of Indian history. An age characterised by the above features may well be called the Golden Age of Indian history.

CHAPTER I

THE PUNJAB, SINDH AND AFGHANISTAN

(*c.* 180 A.D. to *c.* 450 A.D.)

Owing to the dearth of original sources, the history of the Punjab, Afghanistan and Sindh, subsequent to the death of Vāsudeva I (in c. 180 A.D.), is shrouded in considerable obscurity. There are no contemporary inscriptions to throw light upon the events in the political history of these provinces during the 3rd century A.D. The Purāṇas no doubt refer to Śaka, Yavana and Tushāra rulers ruling in the north-west during this period, but do not give their names or the duration of their reigns. Foreign sources supply us with some more definite information, but it is meagre and often difficult to interpret. Coins of the kings ruling in these provinces and their contemporaries in Iran and Bactria are almost the only reliable source of information. These, however, are not dated, and their legends also are often incomplete or illegible. It will be thus seen that we can at present reconstruct the history of this period only in broad outline; subsequent discoveries may modify our present tentative conclusions.

1. Kanishka III

(*c.* 180-210 A.D.)

According to the chronology accepted for this history, the accession of Kanishka III took place in *c.* 180 A.D.[1] The coins

---

[1] The latest known date for Vāsudeva I is 98 (of the Śaka era). He was then on the throne for at least 24 years and so we may place the accession of Kanishka III in *c.* 102 or 180 A.D.

of this ruler are numerous, and so we can reasonably assume that he had a fairly long reign, and may have ruled for about 30 years down to *c.* 210 A.D. They are found in the Punjab, Seistan and Afghanistan, which must, therefore, have been included in his kingdom. It also extended over Kashmir and Bactria[1]; the latter province was the homeland of the Kushāṇas for several centuries. Towards the south-east the kingdom probably continued to include Mathura down to *c.* 200 A.D. But soon after that date the south-eastern Punjab and the United Provinces slipped out of the Kushāṇa control owing to the revolt of the Yaudheyas and the Nāgas. How these powers along with some of their neighbours succeeded in driving the Kushāṇas from their own homelands will be narrated in Chapter II.

Kanishka III governed his kingdom through the agency of Satraps or governors, the names of some of whom appear in abbreviated forms in Brāhmī characters on the obverse side of his coins. Vāsu(deva), Virū(pāksha) (Pl. I, 1) and Mahī (śvara) or Mahī(dhara) were some among them. Of these Vāsu(deva) was probably his son, who succeeded him as Vāsudeva II.[2] It is not unlikely that either Mahīśvara or Virūpāksha or both may have been brothers of Vāsudeva. Vāsudeva was ruling in Seistan, for

---

The existence of Kanishka III as distinguished from Kanishka I and II is proved by numismatic evidence only, which, however, is conclusive. The monogram on the coins of this ruler is that of Vāsudeva I and not of Kanishka I, and so he must have succeeded Vāsudeva I and not preceded him. The Greek script on his coins is quite corrupt; Brāhmī letters are introduced on them, which was not done on the coins of Vāsudeva I or those of any of his predecessors. It is, therefore, certain, that Kanishka, whose coins show corrupt Greek script and Brāhmī letters, was a successor of Vāsudeva I. He is, therefore, described as Kanishka III to distinguish him from the earlier rulers of the same name.

[1] The view that Vāsudeva I had loss his hold over Bactria and Afghanistan because his inscriptions are found only near Mathura is disproved by the findspots of the coins of his successor Kanishka III.

[2] Banerji distinguished Vāsu from Vāsudeva II (*JASB.* N.S. IV, 87-88), but without much justification.

the coins of Kanishka III with the name of this governor are obtained mostly from that province.[1] Virūpāksha and Mahīśvara were probably ruling parts of the Punjab and Afghanistan. Letters *Vi*, *Si* and *Bhṛi*, which appear on the obverse of the coins of Kanishka III to the right side of the standing king are also most probably the initial letters of other governors ruling some other parts of the extensive kingdom. The names of the Kushān emperor and most of his governors are all Hindu ; this shows that the Hinduisation of the Kushāns had become almost complete by this time.

Apart from the initials or portions of the names of the governors, there appear on the coins of Kanishka III some additional letters like *Pa*, *Na*, *Ga*, *Chu*, *Khu*, *Tha*, *Vai*, etc. whose exact significance is not yet known. It is, however, likely that some of these may stand for the initials of the names of cities from which the coins were issued, and others for the initials of the names of the provinces or tribes among whom they were current. Thus *Pa* may be standing for Purushapura (Peshawar), *Na* for Nagarahāra (Jalalabad), *Ga* for Gandhāra country, and *Chu* and *Khu* for the tribes of the Chutsas and the Kshudrakas living in the upper and the middle Indus valley.[2] If we had more accurate information about the history and the geography of the period, it would have been possible to propose more confident interpretations for these letters making their mysterious appearance on the coins of the later Kushāns and their successors.

Kanishka III issued coins of two types. The first of these is a continuation of the type of his predecessor, Vasudeva I, where we have Śiva by the side of his bull on the reverse. In the second type (Pl. I, 1) the Roman goddess, seated Ardoksho, takes the place of Śiva. The coins of the first type are usually found in Bactria and Afghanistan and those of the

[1] *Ibid.* 83-86.
[2] *Ibid.* 84

second type in Gandhāra, Seistan and the Punjab. It is important to note the provenance of these types, because it helps us to unravel some of the incidents of the history of the period.

The appearance of the initials or portions of the names of satraps or governors on the coins of Kanishka III is a new departure in the Kushāṇa coinage, for earlier emperors of the dynasty never permitted such liberty to their governors. It is clear that during the reign of Kanishka III, the provincial satraps were getting more assertive even in the Punjab, and that the Central Government found it necessary to appease them by allowing their initials on the imperial coinage. Many of them must have aspired to establish independent kingdoms at the occurrence of a suitable opportunity. That opportunity presented itself at the death of Kanishka III.

2. Vasudeva II

(*c*. 210 to *c*. 230 A.D.)

Kanishka III was succeeded by Vāsudeva II, who was probably his son, governing the important and turbulent province of Seistan. His existence also is known only from numismatic evidence.[1]

During the reign of Vāsudeva II, the Kushān empire seems to have been partitioned among the provincial governors, who were already aspiring for independence during the preceding reign. Coins of Vāsudeva II are rather rare and show only the Śiva and Bull type (Pl. I, 2), which was prevailing in Bactria and Afghanistan. It is thus probable that Vāsudeva II could control only these provinces and his governors in the Punjab and Seistan had become independent. Letters *Rada*, *Phri* and *Ha*

[1] Coins of Vāsudeva II have to be differentiated from those of Vāsudeva I, because they show greater degeneration in Greek script and permit the initials of the names of governors. The monogram is also different.

which appear on some of his coins may be portions of the names of some of his governors, who were still loyal to him.

The position of the Kushāns towards the end of the reign of Vāsudeva II became very critical. The Gangetic plain had been already lost[1] and provincial governors had become independent in the Punjab. A tribe named Jouan-Jouan was threatening them from the north-east from beyond the Oxus.[2] The Sassanians, who had now founded a powerful kingdom in Persia, were casting their covetous eyes on the fair valley of the Oxus, which used to form part of the Persian empire under the Achaemenians. Under such circumstances, therefore, it was but natural for Vāsudeva II to try to enlist help from outside quarters. We would not be, therefore, wrong in identifying him with P'o-tiao, the king of the great Kushāṇas, who is known to have sent an embassy to Chinese court to ask for help in *c.* 230 A.D. No outside help could, however, save the Kushāns. Their days were now numbered. They had to fight hard against the Jouan-Jouans, and were weakened by the struggle. They had lost their rich Indian provinces, which replenished their treasury. Ardeshir I took advantage of the situation and succeeded in establishing his own supremacy over Bactria in *c.* 238 A.D. He started the practice of sending the crown-prince as governor over the new province, as was often done by the Achaemenians also six hundred years earlier. The crown-prince so deputed had the privilege of issuing his own coins with the little *Kushān Shāh*, the king of the Kushāṇas. From 252 A.D. onwards this title was changed into *Kushān-Shahān-Shāh*, the King of the kings of the Kushāṇas.[3]

That the Kushāṇa prince overthrown by the Sassanians was Vāsudeva II is made fairly certain by the evidence of the

[1] Chap. II will show how the Yaudheyas and the Nāgas reasserted their independence in this region.

[2] *Num. Supp.* XLVII, 25.

[3] Herzfeld, *Kushāno-Sassanian Coins*, p. 33,

Kushāno-Sassanian coinage, which was issued by the royal governors of Bactria. The coins of this series have on the reverse Śiva and the Bull, which was the only type issued by Vāsudeva II, and which is known to have been current in Bactria. Following the usual practice of conquerors in ancient Bactria and India, the Sassanians imitated the coinage of the king whom they supplanted. He must, therefore, have been Vāsudeva II and none else.

3. The Period of Sassanian Ascendancy

The Kushāno-Sassanian coinage[1] issued by the Sassanian viceroys was current only in Balkh, Merv and Samarkand ; its specimens are not to be found in Afghanistan, Seistan or the Punjab (Pl. I, 3). It is, therefore, clear that for some time the Sassanians were content to occupy only the home provinces of the Kushāṇas. Their titles on the coins, 'the king of the Kushāṇas' and 'the king of kings of the Kushāṇas' would further indicate that the Sassanians did not drive the Kushāns out of Bactria, but only established their suzerainty over that province. Very probably some Kushāṇa chiefs may have continued to rule as their feudatories.

The conquest of some Indian provinces of the Kushāṇa empire was attempted and accomplished by the Sassanian emperor Varahran II. This ruler succeeded in annexing Afghanistan, North-Western Frontier Province, Seistan and Sindh to the Sessanian empire by *c.* 284 A.D. Varahran II now transferred the crown prince Varahran III to Seistan as its Governor with the privilege of issuing coins with the title *Śakān-Shāh*, the king of the Śakas. We can understand the significance of this title of the crown-prince when we remember that

[1] These coins are called Kushāno-Sassanian because the obverse is in imitation of the Sassanian coins and the reverse of the Kushāṇa coins. Cunningham had described them as Scytho-Sassanian, but Kushāno-Sassanian is no doubt a more accurate term.

Śaka chiefs were in power in Sindh and Seistan for about two hundred years. The Punjab was not conquered by the Sassanians ; their coins are but rarely found in that province.

Afghanistan and the Indus valley continued to be under the Sassanian rule for about 80 years down to *c*. 360 A.D. There were frequent wars of succession during this period and therefore it was at one time thought that the Sassanian rule in the Indus valley must have been very short-lived. Inscriptions recently discovered at Persepolis show, however, that even in 310-1, A.D., when the reigning Sassanian emperor Shapur II was only a baby, his elder brother continued to rule in Seistan enjoying the titles, King of Śakastān, Minister of ministers of Sindh, Śakastān and Tukhāristān. The Sassanian rule in these regions was well established and organised ; for the Persepolis inscription discovered by Herzfeld refers to a High Judge at Kabul and a Minister of Public Instruction in Śakastān (*Śakastān andarzpet*).[1]

We must, however, note that during the period of Sassanian ascendancy in Afghanistan and the Indus valley, some Śaka and Kushāṇa chiefs continued to rule as petty feudatories. Thus there was a feudatory Kushāṇa family ruling at Kabul; for the wife of the Sassanian emperor Hormuzd II (303-309 A.D.) was a Kushāṇa princess belonging to that family. It is quite possible that there may have been other Kushāṇa and Śaka feudatories in the Indus valley as well.

4. The Punjab During *c*. 230 to *c*. 340 A.D.

We have seen already that the Sassanian conquests in the east did not extend to the Punjab proper. The conquest of this province is not explictly claimed for any Sassanian ruler, nor does the coinage of the province of the 3rd century A.D. show any Sassanian influence. It is, however, difficult to state

[1] Herzfeld, *Op, cit*, pp. 35-6.

who precisely were the successors of Vāsudeva II in the land of the Five Rivers. There are no inscriptions to enlighten us on the point and coins again are our only source of information.

The numismatic evidence shows that the Western and Central Punjab was being governed during this period by three Scythian houses. The Western part of the province was being ruled by a dynasty, which may be described as the Shāka (not Śaka) dynasty, as the term Shāka appears on the obverse of most of the coins issued by its rulers. Peshawar was the capital of this house; a large hoard of its coins was recently discovered there. The coins of the rulers of the Shāka family so closely resemble those of Kanishka III and Vāsudeva II[1] that we may safely presume that it immediately succeeded Vāsudeva II in *c.* 230 A.D. Śayatha, Sita and Sena are either the names or portions of the names of three rulers of this house. *Pra*, *Mi*, *Bhṛi*, and *Bha* are probably the initials of four other members. The dynasty ruled for about 100 years and may well have consisted of seven kings thus known to us from its coinage.

The numismatic evidence shows that the Shīladas and the Gaḍaharas were holding sway over the Central Punjab at this time. Kings Bhadra, Bacharṇa and Pāsana of the former dynasty and Peraya and Kirada of the latter are known from coins. There may have been other rulers as well, whose coins may not have come down to us. Both these dynasties were ruling in the Central Punjab down to the days of Samudragupta ; for a Gaḍahara chief is seen putting the name of that emperor on his coins. They however lost a portion of their kingdom when the Madras re-established their republic at Sialkot sometime before 325 A.D.

From the Purāṇas we learn that 8 Yavana, 14 Tushāra and 13 Muruṇḍa chiefs ruled, presumably in the Punjab, after the fall of the Andhras.[2] It would appear that the Puranic

---

1 Cunningham, *Later Indo-Scythians*, Pl. II, 11.

2 *DKA*. p. 45.

writers had the Shāka, Shīlada and Gaḍahara dynasties in view when they wrote this account. *Prima facie*, it appears strange that the Purāṇas should have described one of these dynasties as Yavana ; Greek rule had become extinct long ago. It is however likely that the term may be referring to the tribe Jouan-Jouan of the Chinese writers, who were threatening the Kushāns in *c.* 320 A.D. and who may have eventually penetrated to the Punjab during the confusion subsequent to the overthrow of the Kushāṇas.

It may be pointed out that the coins of the above Scythian families (Pl. I, 4) are never found outside the Punjab. Coins and inscriptions on the other hand show that the Yaudheyas, the Arjunāyanas and the Mālavas had risen to power and become independent in the Eastern Punjab, Northern U. P. and Rajputana during the 3rd century A.D. There can, therefore, be no doubt that the Scythians were driven out from these territories early in the 3rd century A.D. The part played by Hindu chiefs in this episode will be discussed in chapter II.

5. The Kidāra Kushāṇas

The rule of the Shākas and the Shīladas came to an end in *c.* 340 A.D. with the rise of a tribe, which is sometimes described as the Little Kushāṇa and sometimes as Kidāra Kushāṇa. Its chief Kidāra,[1] whose capital was at Peshawar, was originally a feudatory of the Sassanians, who were then supreme in Afghanistan and the Indus valley. On his early coins, the bust of Kidāra is seen facing right, a convention which had to be followed by all the feudatories of the Sassanian empire. In course of time, however, Kidāra conquered Kashmir

---

[1] Cunningham had placed Kidāra in *c.* 425 A.D. (*Later Indo-Scythians*, p, 185) but Major Martin has now adduced fairly conclusive numismatic evidence to show that this chief must have flourished about a century earlier. See *Num, Supp*. XLVII, 30 ff.

and the Central Punjab.[1] He now felt himself strong enough to assume independence and began to issue coins with the bust facing to the front, which was the privilege of the Sassanian emperor only (Pl. I. 5). This step, probably taken in *c.* 355 A.D., evoked imperial anger and reprisal. We find Shapur II encamped at Kabul in 356-57 A.D. and pursuing operations against his rebellious feudatory.[2] He was successful in this venture, Kidāra was compelled to acknowledge his suzerainty. We find him sending assistance to his liege lord in 359 A.D. when he was engaged in his Mesopotamian campaign.

The closer association with the imperial army probably enabled Kidāra to realise its weak points and he began to mature plans for reasserting his independence. He secured the goodwill of Samudra-gupta, who had by this time extended his sphere of influence to the Punjab, by sending him presents along with professions of allegiance, and delivered his blows against Shapur II in 367-8 A.D. Kidāra was successful in his undertaking ; he annihilated one Sassanian army and drove away another, though it was being led by Shapur himself. These victories enabled Kidāra to consolidate his power in Gandhāra, Kashmir and the Western and Central Punjab. He appointed a number of Satraps to rule these provinces. Varo Shāhi, Piroch and Buddhabala, whose names are preserved on his coins,[3] were three among them ; there may have been others as well.

Kidāra was succeeded by his son Piro in *c.* 375 A.D. He must have naturally attempted to extend his power further eastward in the Punjab when the strong arm of Samudra-gupta was removed by death at about this time. To check this growing menace, Rāma-gupta, the successor of Samudra-gupta, seems

---

[1] The Purāṇas mention a Mlechchha king ruling over these territories contemporaneously with the Guptas ; *DKA.* p. 55. Most probably he is the Kidāra king.

[2] *Num. Supp.* XLVII, 31.

[3] *Ibid.* 41-2.

to have undertaken an expedition against him in the Punjab, but was signally defeated and compelled to conclude an ignoble peace, requiring the surrender of the Gupta crowned queen. A glance at the features of Piro[1] shows that he was a cruel and lascivious ruler, who could well have imposed the above condition on his vanquished adversary.

The success of Piro was, however, short-lived. Shapur III (383-88 A.D.) took steps to avenge the defeat inflicted upon his predecessor and broke Piro's power. He was compelled to acknowledge the Sassanian suzerainty and issue coins as a feudatory, with the bust facing to right instead of facing to front. Chandra-gupta II also seems to have hammered Piro from the east[2]; we do not know, however, whether his attack was before or after the defeat inflicted by Shapur III. The Gupta armies seem to have pursued him right up to the Indus,

The Guptas do not seem to have followed their victories in the Punjab to their logical conclusion by annexing the province and stationing their garrison in the Khyber pass. In fact we have very little evidence of the Gupta influence in the Punjab apart from that of the Shorkot inscription, which seems to have been dated in the year 83 of the Gupta era. Nor was the province under the Sassanian sphere of influence, for no coins of Sassanian emperors or their feudatories who ruled later than Shapur III have been found in the *stūpas* of the Punjab or Afghanistan.

Numismatic evidence shows that a number of petty rulers like Kṛitavīrya, Śilāditya, Sarvayaśas, Bhāsvan, Kuśalā and Prakāśa were ruling in the Punjab during the first half of the 5th century A.D. They were probably Kidāra Kushāṇa rulers, for the name Kidāra appears on their coins on the obverse.

---

1 *Num. Supp.* XLVII, Plates I and II, Nos. 15-21.

2 This is on the assumption that king Chandra of the Meharauli pillar inscription is Chandra-gupta II. This assumption is the most probable one, but it has not yet been accepted by a few scholars.

Their names would show that they had been completely Hinduised by this time. They were probably professing allegiance to the Guptas, when it became necessary to do so. It must be admitted that neither Chandra-gupta II nor Kumāra-gupta showed keen interest in securing an effective hold over the Punjab. The expedition of Chandra-gupta II to the Indus appears to have been a mere raid, for it does not seem that he took any steps to occupy the Punjab or to garrison the north-western frontier in an effective manner. The local Kidāra chiefs, referred to above were swept away easily and completely when the Hūṇa avalanche broke in its full fury by the middle of the 5th century.

CHAPTER II

NEW INDIAN STATES IN RAJPUTANA AND MADHYADESA

(*c.* 200 to *c.* 350 A.D.)

The history of the United Provinces during the 3rd century A.D. is still shrouded in considerable mystery. Kanishka was most probably ruling over Benares in 81 A.D. but no inscription of his successors has been found east of Mathura. It is, however, not unlikely that *Madhyadeśa* or the upper Gangetic plain continued to be under the Kushāṇa sphere of influence, if not under Kushāṇa administration, down to the death of Vāsudeva I in *c.* 180 A.D. ; for seventeen coins of Huvishka and a coin-mould of Vāsudeva were found at Bhita in the Allahabad district.[1] It was during the reign of Kānishka III, the successor of Vāsudeva I, that the upper Gangetic plain slipped out of the Kushāṇa control ; coins of neither this ruler nor those of any of his successors are found in this region.

There is, however, no unanimity of views as to the causes and circumstances that led to the disintegration of the Kushāṇa empire in its eastern portion. Which powers drove out the Kushāṇas from the United Provinces and Rajputana, what part did each of them play in this achievement, and where precisely they were ruling, are questions upon which there is a sharp difference of opinion among the scholars.

1. Did the Bhāraśivas drive out the Kushāṇas ?

The credit for the overthrow of the Kushāṇa power in the Gangetic plain was once given to the Guptas,[2] but this view

---

[1] *ASI.* 1911-12, pp. 63-5.
[2] Banerji, *The Age of the Imperial Guptas*, p. 5.

can no longer be upheld. There is no evidence to show that the Kushāṇa empire continued to include the Gangetic valley after *c.* 180 A.D. The Allahabad inscription of Samudra-gupta makes it certain that there was no Kushāṇa rule in Magadha or U.P. when the Guptas were laying the foundation of their empire. The kings of Āryāvarta, whom Samudra-gupta forcibly uprooted, were all Indians ; none of them was of Kushāṇa or Śaka extraction.

The late Dr. Jayaswal advocated the view that the Kushāṇa empire collapsed owing to the onslaughts of the Bhāraśivas, whose work in this connection was later completed by the Vākāṭakas under the leadership of the emperor Pravara-sena I.[1] It will be shown in Chapter V how the Vākāṭaka emperor never came into contact with the Kushāṇas. Nor is there any evidence to show that the Bhāraśivas were the leaders of the movement to emancipate the country from the foreign rule. They had no doubt celebrated ten horse-sacrifices, but these were often performed in our period by even small rulers with no claims to imperial achievements or conquests.[2]

According to Jayaswal, the Bhāraśiva family is identical with the Nava-nāga family of the Purāṇas and that its founder was king Nava, whose capital was at Kāntīpurī, modern Kantit, in Mirzapur District, U.P. There is nothing to indicate that any Nāga family was ever ruling at Kāntīpurī or that king Nava of coins was a Nāga ruler who belonged to it. His coins are not found at Kāntīpurī and bear no resemblance whatsoever

[1] Dr. Jayaswal's Bhāraśiva theory is based almost entirely on numismatic evidence ; the present writer has shown in details elsewhere how the numismatic data do not support the theory at all. See *JNSI.* V, 111-134.

[2] The Ikshvāku king Śāntamūla, who had performed an Aśamedha sacrifice in *c.* 225 A.D., did not rule over more than two or three districts. Kadamba king Krishṇa-varman, who had celebrated it in *c.* 450 A.D., was not even an independent king. The Vishṇukuṇḍin king Mādhava-varman I, who had performed 11 of them in *c.* 425 A.D. was ruling over a very small kingdom.

to any known Nāga coinage. Nāga rulers invariably attach the epithet *nāga* to their names on their coins, though they are very small; king Nava never does so, though his coins are relatively much larger in size. The assumption that Vīra-sena, the successor of Nava, was the real founder of the three Nāga families ruling at Kāntīpurī, Padmāvatī and Mathura, has yet to be proved. Since his coins are found in Mathura, it is quite likely that he was an independent Nāga ruler. But there is nothing to show that he had ousted the Kushāṇas from the eastern Punjab, for his coins are but rarely found beyond the Jumna. The view that the successors of Vīra-sena—Traya-nāga, Haya-nāga and Barhiṇa-nāga—pressed the Kushāṇas so hard that they were compelled to seek the protection of the Sassanian emperor Shapur I, has absolutely no shred of evidence to support it. The coins of these rulers are never found in the Punjab, which is said to have been the scene of their military exploits; nay, it is very doubtful whether we have got their coins at all, for the legends on the coins, attributed to them, are very blurred and cannot be read with certainty.

When considering the question of the disintegration of the Kushāṇa empire, we must therefore disabuse our mind of the notion that it was the Bhāraśivas of Kāntīpurī who annihilated the Kushāṇa empire. The riddle of the disappearance of the Kushāṇa power from the Gangetic plain can be solved only by carefully studying the coins and inscriptions of the contemporary powers. If we do so, we shall find that the Yaudhevas, the Kuṇindas, the Mālavas, the Nāgas and the Maghas[1], who began to strike coins as independent powers in the 3rd century, all played their own part in driving out the Kushāṇas.

Like most other dynasties in Indian history the Kushāṇas

[1] The Maghas asserted independence earlier in *c.* 160 A.D., as will be shown later in this chapter; but the Kushāṇas probably connived at their rebellion as the Magha homelands lay in the jungle tracts of Rewa, not easily accessible.

also began to decline after a career of about 150 years in *c.* 200 A.D. They had no doubt been indianised by this time, but nevertheless, it was probably felt that they belonged to a different ethnic stock and the Yaudheyas and their neighbours, with their age-long republican traditions, were not prepared to lose a golden opportunity to regain their political independence, when they detected that the imperial Kushāṇa power had become weak. Evidence available at present does not favour the view that any big federation consisting of all the above powers and working under a common leadership was formed in order to overthrow the Kushāṇa empire. The Yaudheyas were the strongest and probably the first to inflict an effective blow, perhaps in co-operation with their immediate neighbours, the Kuṇindas and the Arjunāyanas. The success of this move emboldened the Nāgas of Padmāvatī and the Mālavas of Rajputana to follow their example and to reassert their independence. We shall now proceed to narrate how all these events took place in the first half of the 3rd century A.D.

2. The Yaudheya, Kuṇinda and the Arjunāyana Republics

The credit of giving the first blow to the Kushāṇa empire really belongs to the Yaudheyas, and it is rather strange that their achievement in this connection should have escaped the notice of most of the modern historians. Before the rise of the Kushāṇa empire the Yaudheyas were a great power ruling over a wide stretch of territory covering northern Rajputana and the south-eastern Punjab.[1] Soon afterwards however the Kushāṇas under the leadership of Kanishka smashed their power and succeeded in penetrating right up to Benares, if not beyond.

The Kushāṇa power was at its zenith during the reigns of Kanishka and Huvishka, and so the Yaudheyas could not raise

[1] *Mbh*, II, Chap, 35, vv. 4 ff.

their head for about half a century. They were, however, too matrial and freedom-loving to brook the foreign yoke and raised their standard of revolt in *c.* 145 A.D. somewhere in the north-eastern Rajputana. The task of crushing their rising was entrusted to Śaka Mahākshatrapa Rudra-dāman I and he proudly states in his Junagadh record how he forcibly overthrew the Yaudheyas, who had become insubordinate owing to their pride due to their valour being respected by all the Kshatriyas. The Yaudheyas were not dismayed by this initial reverse. They bided their time for a few decades and made a second bid for independence towards the end of the second century A.D. This time they were successful in their venture and succeeded in freeing their homeland and ousting the Kushāṇas beyond the Sutlej.

Though the above view relies almost exclusively on the evidence of coins, yet it is fairly conclusive. It is true that there is no evidence directly referring to the conflict between the Yaudheyas and the Kushāṇas, but the evidence supplied by numismatics conclusively shows that the former could have succeeded in re-establishing their power only by overthrowing the later. The coins of Kanishka III (*c.* 180 to *c.* 210 A.D.) and Vāsudeva II (210 to 240 A.D.) are not found to the east of the Sutlej ; it is thus clear that they had lost all cis-Sutlej territories. On the other hand, the post-Kushāṇa coins of the Yaudheyas having legends in the characters of the 3rd or 4th century A.D. are found in large hoards between the Sutlej and the Jumna, the homeland of the Yaudheyas, in the districts of Saharanpur, Dehra Dun, Delhi, Rohtak, Ludhiana and Kangra.[1] It is therefore quite clear that they were ruling over this territory as an independent power from the beginnings of the 3rd century A.D., obviously after ousting the Kushāṇas who were previously holding it. The territory on the banks of the Sutlej

---

[1] *ASC.* II, 14, 77.

right up to the borders of the Bahawalpur state is still known as Johiyawar after the Yaudheyas ; it is therefore clear that the state of Patiala and the greater part of northern Rajputana must have been included within the dominions of the resuscitated Yaudheya republic.

The above achievement of the Yaudheyas was a remarkable one. It was no easy thing to challenge a power whose empire extended from Bactria to Bihar, whose resources were practically limitless, and whose kings enjoyed the prestige of being revered as the Sons of Heaven for more than a century. The Kushāṇas must have probably thrown all their select reserves from the North-Western Frontier and Central Asia in their effort to put down the Yaudheya rising, but they proved of no avail against the bravery and patriotism of the revolting republic.

The Yaudheya victory over the imperial Kushāṇas naturally increased their prestige and reputation. They were already known as Kshatriyas *par excellence* ; now it began to be believed that they possessed a mystic formula (*mantra*) ensuring victory in all circumstances and against all odds.[1]

The Yaudheyas naturally celebrated their independence by issuing a new currency (Pl. I. 6)[2]. As it was intended to replace the coinage of the Kushāṇas, it bore a striking resemblance to it in weight and general fabric. The foreign Greek and Ksharoshṭhī scripts were however replaced by the national Brāhmī one, and the legend, *Yaudḥeygaṇasya jayaḥ* proudly proclaimed the victory of the new republic. Kārtikeya, the generalissimo of the gods, occupies the place of honour on the coinage and naturally ; for he was also the tutelary deity of the Yaudheyas since the days of the *Māhābhārata*.[3]

---

[1] A Yaudheya clay-seal found near Ludhiana along with Yaudheya coins has the legend योद्धेयानां जयमंत्रधराणाम् ; *PASB*. 1884, p. 139.

[2] As to the dates of these coins, see Allan, *Catalogue of Indian Coins, Ancient India*, Introduction, para 184.

[3] *Mbh*. II, Chap. 35, vv. 4 ff.

The Yaudheyas very probably received valuable support and co-operation in their bid for independence from the Kuṇindas, their northern neighbours, who were occupying the region between the upper courses of the Sutlej and the Beas. The Kuṇindas, like the Yaudheyas, were an independent republic before the middle of the first century A.D., and they also had to submit to the Kushāṇa hegemony at *c.* 70 A.D. The coins of a Kuṇinda ruler Chhatreśvara bearing the titles *Mahātman* and *Bhāgavata* have been found with a legend in characters of *c.* 200 A.D. They bear close resemblance in type, fabric and size to the contemporary coinage of the Yaudheyas with Kārtikeya on the obverse.[1] This remarkable resemblance in coinage will, to some extent, support the hypothesis that Kuṇindas and Yaudheyas were contemporary powers and worked hand in hand in regaining their independence towards the beginning of the 3rd century A.D. As compared to the Yaudheyas, the Kuṇindas were a small state and it seems that they eventually coalesced with them. For, we do not find their coinage subsequent to *c.* 250 A.D. ; nor do they figure among the republics mentioned in the Allahabad inscription of Samudra-gupta.

To the south-east of the Yaudheya country lay the territory of another republic, the Arjunāyanas, who were occupying the Agra-Jaipur area. There is no doubt that they also rebelled against the Kushāṇas and established an independent state ; it continued to flourish down to the middle of the 4th century, as it figures among the tributaries of Samudra-gupta. It is rather inexplicable that we should have so far found no coins of the Arjunāyanas issued during the post-Kushāṇa period.

On some of the Yaudheya coins issued at this time, we have the mysterious words, *dvi* (two) and *tri* (three) after the legend *Yaudheyagaṇasya jayaḥ*. No satisfactory explanation of these

[1] Allan. *CAI.* Pl. XXIII, 11-16 with Pl. XXXIX, 22 & XL, 10-14.

terms can at present be proposed. According to the traditional belief, the Arjunāyanas and Yaudheyas were the descendants of the Pāṇḍava brothers, Dharma and Arjuna.[1] It is likely that this belief may have facilitated the formation of a kind of loose union between the two neighbouring republics. We have seen already how the Kuṇindas also appear to have coalesced with the Yaudheyas after *c.* 250 A.D. In course of time a kind of loose confederation seems to have been formed between these three republics, the move being also due to the realisation of the necessity of having a strong state which would effectively meet the Scythian menace, if it occurred again. The terms 'two' and 'three' occurring on some of the later Yaudheya coins, may perhaps refer to the second and third members of the Yaudheya confederation, *viz.*, the Kuṇindas and the Arjunāyanas.

The Yaudheyas continued to be a powerful republic down to the third quarter of the 4th century A.D. Their coins in the characters of the 3rd and 4th centuries A.D. are found in large numbers, in northern Rajputana and the south-eastern Punjab, thus showing that they continued to be a formidable power throughout this period. Unfortunately we possess no information about the details of their republican administration. As shown above, it was probably a confederation of three republics, the Yaudheyas, the Arjunāyanas and the Kuṇindas. The federating units, it seems, enjoyed complete autonomy and did not lose their separate existence. The foreign policy and the military operations were probably under the direction of a council of the presidents of the three republics, elected by the federating units. The presidents enjoyed the titles of Mahārāja and Mahāsenāpati. A fragmentary inscription of such a Mahārāja-Mahāsenāpati, elected by the Yaudheya republic, has been found in the Bharatpur state.[2] Had the name and the genealogy

---

[1] *Mbh.* I, Chap. 95. v. 75 (Bom. Ed.).
[2] *CII.* III, 252.

of this dignitary been preserved, we might have known whether the post was hereditary or depended on election.

3. The Madra Republic

Towards the beginning of the 4th century A.D. the Gaḍaharas lost a portion of their kingdom in the central Punjab to the Madras. Emboldened by the success of the Yaudheyas, the Madras also made a bid for independence at this time and eventually succeeded in establishing their independent republic in the Ravi-Chenab doab ; Sialkot was probably their capital. The Madras seem to have issued no coins ; at least none have been found so far. The successful establishment of their republican state is however proved by the evidence of the Allahabad inscription of Samudra-gupta in which the Madra republic appears as the most north-western one.

Before the rise of the Kushāṇa empire there was an Audumbara republic occupying the districts of Kangra, Gurudaspur and Hoshiarpur in the Punjab. Numerous coins of this republic have been found issued in the pre-Kushāṇa period but none in the post-Kushāṇa epoch. This circumstance may probably be explained on the assumption that the Audumbaras did not succeed in emerging as an independent state in the 3rd or the 4th century A.D. Probably they were merged in the Madra republic.

4. The Mālava Republic

The Mālavas, who were occupying the Ravi-Sutlej doab in the days of Alexander the Great, later moved southwards, probably due to foreign pressure. In course of time they occupied Ajmer-Tonk-Mewar area, where they flourished as an independent republic till about the end of the Ist century A.D. With the rise of the Kushāṇas and their feudatories, the Western

Kshatrapas, the power of the Mālavas was eclipsed for about a century. They were defeated and their territory was annexed to the dominions of the Western Kshatrapas.

The Mālavas, however, did not permit the Kshatrapas to rule over them peacefully. They were rising in rebellion or making furtive attacks on the allies of their conquerors. Nahapāna had to send his son-in-law Ushavadāta to relieve his allies, the Uttamabhadras, who were being molested by the Mālavas. The Mālavas, however, could not hold their own against the Śakas and had to submit to the Śaka rule till the end of the 2nd century A.D.

At this time there arose a prolonged war of succession in the Śaka kingdom between Jīva-dāman and his uncle Rudrasiṁha I, which considerably weakened the Kshatrapa power (see Chap. III). This gave a golden opportunity to the Mālavas to reassert their independence. A Mālava leader named Śrī (?)soma raised the standard of revolt and celebrated in *c.* 225 A.D. the Ekashashṭi sacrifice to proclaim the independence of his republic.[1] Curiously enough the record which describes this victory does not mention the name of the enemies defeated, but it is clear that they could have been none others than the Western Kshatrapas. Henceforward neither the Western Kshatrapas nor the Kushāṇas were able to impose their hegemony over the Mālavas.

From *c.* 225 A.D. the Mālavas continued to flourish as an independent republic down to the time of Samudra-gupta. Their rise was also due to national fervour, for we find Śrī (?) soma proudly referring to his descent from the Ikshvākus, probably in contrast to the pedigree of the foreign Śakas. Like the Yaudheya republic, the Mālava one also was administered by elected chiefs, who sometimes became hereditary. Śrī (?)soma,

[1] This statement is based on the evidence of Nāndsā Yūpa inscriptions, which are being edited by the present writer in the *Epigraphia Indica*. They may be published in 1946.

who liberated the Mālavas, is described as supporting the *ancestral* yoke of public administration. It is, however, noteworthy that neither he nor his father nor grandfather is given any royal or military title like Mahārāja or Senāpati. It is clear that the republican traditions were strong among the Mālavas; even the glorious hero who rescued their country from the foreign yoke did not dare to arrogate to himself any royal title, not even in the record which was primarily intended to proclaim his signal achievement.

The Mālavas issued a copious currency (Pl. I, 7) during the 3rd and the 4th centuries A.D. proving their continued existence as an independent state.[1]

It is usually held that the careers of the Yaudheya, the Madra, the Arjunāyana and the Mālava republics mentioned in Samudra-gupta's Allahabad inscription came to an end owing to the imperialistic ambition and expansion of the Guptas. There is, however, no definite evidence to support this view. Samudra-gupta only claims that these republics accepted his overlordship and paid him tribute. This is quite compatible with internal autonomy, and it is quite possible that the republics may have continued their existence during the reigns of Chandra-gupta II and Kumāra-gupta I. It is important to note in this connection that we have no evidence whatsoever to show that the homelands of these republics were ever annexed to the Gupta empire. The fact that no monuments of the Gupta rule have been found in Rajputana or beyond Mathura shows that the Guptas could hardly exercise any effective control over these republics. They may well have continued their semi-independent existence down to the middle of the 5th century

[1] It is held by some scholars that the names like Magaja, Mapojaya, Magajaya, etc., which occur on these coins, are the names of Mālava kings, proving their foreign extraction. The Mālavas were, however, claiming a descent from the Ikshvākus at this time. These mysterious legends cannot be satisfactorily explained at present.

A.D., when they appear to have been engulfed in the Hūṇa avalanche.

5. The Nāgas of Padmāvatī and Mathura

During the 3rd and the 4th centuries A.D. two Nāga families were ruling in Western U. P. and Gwalior state, the capital of the one was Mathura and that of the other, Padmāvati, now represented by the small village Padam-Pawaya in Gwalior state, about 125 miles to the south of Mathura. It is possible that the two Nāga houses ruling at these places were related to each other, but we have no definite evidence on the point.

According to the Purāṇas seven kings had ruled at Mathura and nine at Padmāvatī when the Guptas were rising to power by *c.* 325 A.D.[1] This would show that these houses started their career in the latter half of the 2nd century. The early rulers must have been the feudatories of the Kushāṇas.

Of the two Nāga families, the one ruling at Padmāvatī seems to have been the more important one, and its rulers were most probably known also as the Bhāraśivas. It is well known how the Bhāraśivas were very particular to carry always a *Śivaliṅga* on their shoulders ; the Nāgas of Padmāvatī give a prominent position to Śiva's emblem *Triśūla* and vehicle *Nandi*, on their coins. Bhava-nāga, the only individual Bhāraśiva ruler known to us, has a Nāga-ending name, suggesting his Nāga extraction. His coins also are known to be found along with those of the other members of the Nāga families of Padmāvati. Their palaeography shows that Bhava-nāga, the Nāga ruler of the coins, must have flourished in the first half of the fourth century ; the Vākāṭaka history shows that Bhava-nāga, the Bhāraśiva ruler, also must have flourished at exactly the same

[1] *DKA.* p. 53.

time. It is thus almost certain that the Bhāraśiva rulers, who are known to have conquered the territories right up to the Ganges and performed ten Horse-sacrifices, were none others than the Nāga kings of Padmāvatī.[1]

The Purāṇas state that there were nine rulers in the Nāga family of Padmāvatī, but do not give either their names or their order of succession. Coins disclose the existence of ten Nāga rulers, Bhīma-nāga, Vibhu-nāga, Prabhākara-nāga, Skanda-nāga, Bṛihaspati-nāga, Vyāghra-nāga, Vasu-nāga, Deva-nāga, Bhava-nāga (Pl. I, 8) and Gaṇapati-nāga ; the *Harshacharita* refers to an 11th ruler named Nāgasena, who also figures in the Allahabad inscription of Samudra-gupta, which possibly mentions further a 12th Nāga king, named Nāgadatta.[2] Padmāvatī and Mathura are separated by about 125 miles only ; it is therefore not improbable that some of the coins may belong to the Nāga family of Mathura as well. The coins of Gaṇapati-nāga are much more common at Mathura than at Padmāvatī, and he very probably belonged to the Mathura dynasty.

As the order of the above Nāga rulers is not known at present, it is futile to conjecture as to who among them were the feudatories of the Kushāṇas, and as to who were the distinguished heroes who got the Ganges water by their valour for coronation and performed ten Horse-sacrifices. These last-mentioned incidents must have occurred during the first half of the 3rd century A.D. when the Kushāṇas are known to have lost the upper Gangetic plain. The Maghas in the south and the Yaudheyas in the north were making successful efforts at about this time to reassert their independence, and the Nāgas or the Bhāraśivas also must have followed their example. The Kushāṇa empire was already reeling under the blows inflicted by the Yaudheyas, as shown above, and the Nāgas therefore

[1] See *JNSI.* V, 21-27 for a more detailed discussion of this topic.

[2] It is possible that Vīrasena, whose coins (Pl. II, I) are found at Mathura, may have been a 13th Nāga ruler.

could not probably have found it difficult to establish their authority right up to Mathura in the north and the Ganges in the east by displacing the local Kushāṇa governors. They celebrated their victory by performing as many as ten Horse-sacrifices. This large number of Horse-sacrifices need not, however, be taken as proving that they were the leading power to oust the Kushāṇas; for Horse-sacrifices were often performed by petty rulers in our period. The fact is that the Kushāṇa empire lost its eastern provinces by the almost simultaneous risings of the Yaudheyas, the Mālavas and the Nāgas ; the leading rôle however was played by the Yaudheyas, as already shown above.

Among the Nāga rulers of Padmāvati, definite historic information is available only of Bhava-nāga, who was ruling from *c.* 305 to *c.* 340 A.D. His daughter was married to the Vākāṭaka crown prince Gautamīputra in *c.* 300 A.D. The Vākāṭaka records never fail to mention that Bhava-nāga was the maternal grandfather of Rudra-sena I. Maternal grandfathers are usually introduced in royal genealogies either when they are distinguished rulers or when they happen to have rendered material assistance to their maternal grandsons. In the present case both the reasons seem to be operating. After a career of nearly a century, the Nāga kingdom of Padmāvatī had become a fairly strong power. Pravara-sena, therefore, naturally felt that he would strengthen the position of his rising dynasty by marrying his crown-prince to a daughter of Bhava-nāga. We do not know whether Bhava-nāga participated in any of the campaigns of Pravara-sena or the latter son Gautamīputra, but there is nothing improbable in his having done so.

Bhava-nāga's son-in-law Gautamīputra predeceased his father and so the crown passed on to the latter's son Rudra-sena I. The new king found himself in a sea of troubles soon after his accession and received material assistance from his experienced maternal grandfather, which enabled him to maintain his hold upon the throne. The situation will be fully elucidated in Chap. V.

At the death of Bhava-nāga in *c.* 340 A.D. the Nāgas had become fairly powerful in U. P. The successful help which Bhava-nāga had given to the Vākāṭakas had increased their prestige. The two Nāga houses, among themselves, were ruling over the territory which included Mathura, Dholpur, Agra, Gwalior, Cawnpore, Jhansi and Banda.

Nāgasena and Gaṇapati were the two Nāga rulers ruling by the middle of the 4th century. The first of them seems to have been the king of Padmāvatī and the second, of Mathura.[1] They could not maintain themselves against the rising power of the Guptas ; they were both defeated by Samudra-gupta, who annexed their kingdoms.

Padmāvatī, the Nāga capital, became a flourishing city under the Nāga rule. It was situated near the confluence of the Sindhu and the Pārā and thus had natural protection from three sides. It could boast of a number of magnificent places and temples. It was also a famous centre of culture and education. Its reputation in this respect did not diminish even after the fall of the Nāga dynasty ; we find ministers from Berar sending their sons for higher education to this city even during the 8th century A.D.[2]

A king named Achyuta had risen to power in Ahichchhatra (Rohilkhand) by the middle of the 4th century A.D. His coin-type (Pl. II, 2) bears a close resemblance to that of some Nāga

---

[1] The *Harshacharita* definitely states that Nāgasena was ruling at Padmāvatī ; but its commentator states that he lost his life and kingdom due to the machinations of a minister, and not owing to the invasion of an outsider. His coins also are not yet found in the hoards of Nāga coins. One cannot be therefore certain whether he was ruling at Padmāvatī. The coins of Gaṇapati are still very common in the markets of Mathura. I myself have seen hundreds of them there.

[2] *Mālatīmādhava*, Act IV. Bhavabhūti, no doubt, describes the city of the 8th century A.D., but the ruin and their stratifications show that it was flourishing from the 2nd century A.D. *ASI*. 1915-16, pp. 100 ff.

coins and it is not improbable that he was himself a Nāga ruler, perhaps a scion of a collateral branch of the Mathura family. He offered stubborn resistance to Samudra-gupta but it proved of no avail (see Chap. VII). His kingdom was incorporated in the Gupta empire.

To judge from the name, king Nāgadatta of Āryāvarta, overthrown by Samudra-gupta, was also a Nāga ruler. But where precisely he was ruling, we do not know. Probably he was a member of a collateral branch of the Nāga house of Mathura, ruling somewhere in the upper Doab.

The Guptas claim to have forcibly uprooted all the Nāga families. But some members of the old houses continued to exist either as Gupta feudatories or officers down to the decline of the Gupta empire. Samudra-gupta himself married his son Chandra-gupta II to the daughter of a Nāga chief in *c.* 370 A.D., and Śarva-nāga was the Gupta governor of the Doab about a century later.

6. The Maukharis of Baḍvā

At Baḍvā in Kotah state, about 150 miles to the west of Padmāvatī, the Nāga capital ; there was a small Maukhari principality during the first half of the 3rd century A.D.[1] Mahāsenāpati Bala[2] was at its head in 239 A.D. and he had three grown up sons to help him in the administration. At this time the title Mahāsenāpati usually denoted the status of a feudal chief, ruling over a district or so. The Maukharis of Baḍvā were, therefore, probably a feudatory power, owing allegiance either to the Western Kshatrapas of Ujjayinī or to the Nāgas

[1] See *EI.* XXIII, 42-52.

[2] According to the strict rules of grammar the title Mahāsenāpati has to be construed not with the father Bala but with his sons. But there is no doubt that we have an instance of *sāpeksha-samāsa* in the expression *Mahāsenāpateḥ Mokhareḥ Balaputrasya Somadevasya yūpaḥ*. It is very improbable that all the sons of Bala should have attained the status of Mahāsenāpati in 239 A.D.

of Padmāvatī. The family seems to have championed the Vedic religion ; each of the three sons of Bala had performed a Trirātra sacrifice in 239 A.D. The stone *Yūpas* (pillars) erected to commemorate these sacrifices have rescued the family from oblivion, for it is so far known only from the records inscribed on them. Its earlier or later history is quite unknown. It is therefore impossible to state whether the Maukhari families that subsequently rose to power in south Bihar and Kanauj were or were not connected with the Maukharis of Baḍvā.

7. The Maghas Baghelkhand and Kauśāmbī

To the south-east of the Nāga kingdom of Padmāvatī was the principality of the Maghas,[1] which was in the beginning confined to Baghelkhand alone. There is a great controversy about the dates of the rulers of this dynasty, but it seems most probable that the era they used was the Śaka era, rather than the Chedi or the Gupta one.[2]

Vāśishṭhīputra Bhīmasena is the earliest known ruler of this dynasty, and his son was Kautsīputra Poṭhasiri. The known

---

[1] This name is given to the dynasty by the Purāṇas ; four of the kings of the dynasty, known so far, have names ending in *magha*.

[2] Messrs. N. G. Majumdar and Krishna Deva think it very probable that the era used is the Chedi era, starting in 248 A.D. (*EI*. XXIV, 146 and 253); Rai Bahadur Daya Ram Sahni thinks that the era is the Gupta era (*Ibid*. XVIII, 159). Marshall, Konow and Dr. Moti Chandra opine that the era used is the Śaka era (*ASI*. 1911-12, p. 417 ; *EI*. XXIII, 247 ; *JNSI*. II, 95 ff). The most cogent argument in favour of the Chedi or the Gupta era is palaeographical ; there is no doubt that the characters of the Magha inscriptions are almost the Gupta characters. This argument however is not a convincing one ; for many of the Gupta forms of characters are to be seen in an inscription of Kanīshka, dated in the 14th year (92 A.D.); *see EI*. XXI, 2. The most fatal objection against referring the dates of the Chedi or the Gupta era is the contemporaneity of some of these rulers with the Imperial Guptas, which it renders inevitable. The Gupta feudatories even in the distant parts of the empire refer to their overlords in their records; is it likely that Samudra-gupta, who had forcibly uprooted the kings of the Gangetic valley, would have allowed Bhīma-varman to rule as an independent king at Kauśāmbī in the year 139-358 A.D.? No Gupta feudatory was ever permitted to mint any coins. Is it

dates for the father are 51[1] and 52[2] and for the son, 86, 87 and 88.[3] We may therefore place the reign of Bhīmasena from *c.* 120 to *c.* 140 and that of Poṭhasiri from *c.* 140 to *c.* 170 A.D.

During the greater part of the above period the Kushāṇa empire was at the zenith of its power, extending up to Benares, and it is therefore impossible that Kauśāmbī, which lay on the high road to that holy city, could have been under the sway of this house at that time. It is interesting to note that no inscriptions of Bhīmasena are found to the north of Ginja, about 40 miles south of Allahabad. The sealing of this ruler found at Bhita may have gone there with a letter ; it does not prove his sovereignty over that city. It is clear that the Kushāṇas, like the Mughals in later times, did not care to penetrate into the jungles of Baghelkhand and Rewa state and permitted Bhīmasena to rule there more or less as an independent ruler.

Mahārāja Kautsīputra Poṭhasiri, the son of Bhīmasena, is known to us from six unpublished records, all hailing from Bandhogarh in the heart of Baghelkhand.[3] His known dates are Śaka 86, 87 and 88; he therefore ruled from *c.* 140 to *c.* 170, when Huvishka and Vāsudeva I were the ruling Kushāṇa emperors. Poṭhasiri was an able ruler and his capital at Bandhogarh flourished under his fostering care. Merchants from even distant Mathura were visiting the place and making religious endowments.

Magha, the foreign minister of Poṭhasiri, must have been the guiding light in the planning and execution of the ambitious

---

possible that the Guptas would have permitted a feudatory family ruling at Kauśāmbī to issue its own coinage ? On the other hand, if we refer the inscriptions to the Śaka era, there will be a gap of more than 50 years between the Maghas and the Guptas. It will explain the independent status of the Maghas, as also the circumstance of the Magha coinage showing no influence on the Gupta copper issues.

[1] Supplied by a Bandhogarh inscription, not yet published.

[2] Supplied by the Ginja record, *EI.* III, 302.

[3] I am indebted to Dr. N. P. Chakravarti for kindly supplying me the summaries of these unpublished records.

foreign policy of the heir-apparent Bhadra-magha or Bhaṭṭadeva,[1] which aimed at taking advantage of the growing decay of the Kushāṇa empire under Vāsudeva I and extending the bounds of the kingdom northwards. By *c.* 155 A.D. Bhadra-magha had snatched away Kauśāmbī from the Kushāṇas ; we begin to get his inscriptions there from (Śaka) 81 or 159 A.D. We have got the rather strange phenomenon of finding the father Poṭhasiri ruling at Bandhogarh down to 166 A.D. and the son Bhadra-magha administering the affairs at Kauśāmbī from 159 A.D.[2] We can explain this riddle by the assumption that the Crown Prince Bhadra-magha managed to extend the kingdom beyond Kauśāmbī by his own valour or diplomacy and that the father permitted him to rule at the latter place as an independent ruler even in his own life-time. It was probably by diplomacy or a *coup*, rather than by an open rebellion against Vāsudeva I, that Bhadra-magha succeeded in getting Kauśāmbī ; Vāsudeva I connived at this aggression in a distant corner of his empire as did the Bijapur Sultan in the case of Shivaji at the beginning of the latter's career, probably for similar reasons.

As a corollary of the growing importance of the dynasty, Poṭhasiri seems to have started coinage near the fag-end of his rule.[3] It was however his son Bhadra-magha, who started the 'Magha' series of coins by determining the type which was to continue for several generations.

The duration of the rule of Bhadra-magha is not definitely known. His father probably died in 168 A.D. ; from this time his inscriptions begin to appear at Bandhogarh also. His inde-

---

1 Bhadra-magha of the Kauśāmbī records of the years 81, 86 and 87, Bhadradeva of one Bandhogarh inscription dated 90, and Bhaṭṭadeva or Bhaḍadeva of another record of the same place and date are obviously identical personages.

2 Bhadra-magha's records are dated in the years 81, 86, 87 and 90 and those of Poṭhasiri in the years 86, 87 and 88.

3 This assumption presupposes that the single blurred copper coin, found at Bhita, apparently bearing the legend Prashṭhaśriya, was issued by him. The legend is however indistinct. *ASI.* 1911-12, p. 66.

pendent reign did not last long and seems to have terminated before *c.* 175 A.D.

Gautamīputra Śiva-magha seems to have been the successor of Bhadra-magha. No date of this ruler is known, nor do we possess any definite information about his relationship with Bhadra-magha. We may however presume that he was his son, and ruled from *c.* 175 to 184 A.D.[1] No incidents of his reign are known.

The view that Gautamīputra Śiva-magha was a younger son of the Vākāṭaka emperor Pravara-sena I, ruling as a provincial viceroy at Kauśāmbī, cannot be accepted. It is true that the metronymic Gautamīputra lends some colour to this theory, for it was the metronymic of the eldest son of Pravara-sena. Siva-magha however clearly belonged to the 'Magha' dynasty, for his seal found at Bhita bears the same symbols as those found on the seal of Bhīmasena.[2] Śiva-magha issued a copious currency ; it would be strange that the Vākāṭaka kings themselves should have issued no coins whatsoever when one of their viceroys was doing so. The coins of Śiva-magha clearly belong to the Magha series and he cannot be separated from that dynasty and engrafted on the Vākāṭakas.

King Śiva-magha was succeeded by king Vaiśravaṇa some time before 185 A.D. The latter was the son of Mahāsenāpati Bhadrabala and so it is difficult to state the precise relationship between Śiva-magha and his successor. It is tempting to suggest

[1] 107 *i.e.* 185 A.D. is the earliest date for the next ruler Vaiśravaṇa. It is possible that Bhadra-magha may have continued to rule up to that year. But then we shall have to postpone the reign of Śiva-magha sometime after *c.* 230 A.D. This is rendered rather improbable by the very close resemblance between the seals of Bhīma-sena, who was ruling in *c.* 125 A.D. and that of Śiva-magha.

[2] The symbols are, to right woman standing, to left standing bull with crescent below its neck. The legend is below the symbols on the seal of Bhīmasena and above them on that of Śiva-magha. *ASI.* 1910-11, pp. 50-1. This point however can be conclusively proved when evidence becomes available to show that Śiva-magha was a son or a relation of Bhadra-magha.

that Mahāsenāpati Bhadrabala is identical with Bhadra-magha, the predecessor of Śiva-magha. In that case Vaiśravaṇa would be his younger brother. It is however more probable that Bhadrabala was a junior member of the royal family, whose son Vaiśravaṇa succeeded in usurping the throne by a *coup*.[1]

Vaiśravaṇa's reign extended from *c*. 185 to *c*. 205. It was probably during his reign that the kingdom was extended northwards at least up to Fathepur district. This was rendered easy by the growing decay of the Kushāṇa empire. The Maghas now became the certain neighbours of the Nāgas of Padmāvatī. The rulers of Kauśāmbī very often ruled over Mirzapur and Benares. Whether the Maghas did so in the heyday of their glory is not known. No Magha coins or antiquities are found in these districts. The southern limit of the Magha kingdom is but vaguely known. From the Purāṇas we learn that they ruled over (southern) Kośala, but the southern boundaries of this province also are but vaguely known. It is however not unlikely that the Magha kingdom may have extended about 150 miles to the south of Bandhogarh.

Like his predecessors, Vaiśravaṇa also issued a copious currency attesting to the prosperity and orderly government under his supervision. His rule terminated in *c*. 205.

The successor of Vaiśravaṇa was most probably king Bhīmavarman,[2] whose known dates are 208 and 217 A.D. He may therefore be presumed to have ruled from *c*. 205 to 225.

---

[1] In a Bandhogarh inscription of king Vaiśravaṇa his father Bhadrabala is called a Mahāsenāpati only and not a *Rājā* or a *Mahārāja*. Bhadra-magha, the predecessor of Śiva-magha, assumes the title Mahārāja in a number of his records. It is improbable that if Vaiśravaṇa was the son of Kauśikīputra Bhadra-magha, he would have designated his father by an inferior title like Mahāsenāpati, when he had assumed the higher title of Mahārāja in the latter part of his career. Mahāsenāpati Bhadrabala, the father of Vaiśravaṇa, thus appears to be different from Mahārāja Bhadrabala, the predecessor of Śiva-magha.

[2] It is possible that Vāsithiputa Siri Vichitasena, known from a fragmentary and undated inscription from Bandhogarh, may have ruled for a short period before Bhīma-varman. One and the same donor

We have so far referred to six kings of the Magha dynasty. The Purāṇas however state that there were nine kings in this family and two out of the three missing kings are obviously Śata-magha and Vijaya-magha, whose coins were published[1] by me in 1943. The coins clearly belong to the series started by Śiva-magha and we can therefore have no hesitation in assigning these rulers to the Magha dynasty. The dates of these rulers are unknown. They however cannot be placed anywhere amongst the six kings mentioned above. We must therefore place them after Bhīma-varman, between *c.* 225 and 265 A.D. It is possible that one or two more rulers may have followed, but it does not seem likely that the Maghas were in power after 300 A.D.

Numismatic evidence shows that a king named Nava succeeded the Maghas at Kauśāmbī. His coin type is an exact copy of the Magha coin type, tree in railing and three-arched hill on the obverse, and bull on the reverse. We may place his reign between *c.* 300 and 320 A.D. Who followed Nava we do not know, but by the middle of the 4th century A.D. a king named Pushvaśrī or Pushpaśrī was ruling at Kauśāmbī. I have recently published the coins of this ruler.[2] It is probably a successor of this ruler, who was ousted by Samudra-gupta.

Pushya is seen making a grant in the reigns of Poṭhasiri and Vichitasena.

[1] *JNSI.* IV, 10-11.

[2] *Ibid.* IV. 13-7

CHAPTER III

THE ŚAKA RULERS OF WESTERN INDIA

(*c.* 170 to *c.* 400 A.D.)

1. Dāmajada I, Jīva-dāman and Rudra-simha I

The Western Kshatrapas had reached the zenith of their power when their greatest ruler, Rudra-dāman I died about 170 A.D. His was a remarkable career ; starting almost without any patrimony he had succeeded in extending his kingdom in less than 25 years over Malwa, Gujarat, Kathiawar, northern Konkan, western Rajputana and Sindh. His son and successor Damaghsada or Dāmajada I[1] continued to rule over the whole of this extensive territory. He was associated with his father in the administration as a Kshatrapa, and very probably took an active part in some of his campaigns. The coins of Dāmajada as a Mahākshatrapa are very rare, and the portrait on them shows that he was an old man at the time of his accession. His reign, therefore, probably did not extend beyond 175 A.D. During this short rule of about five years the peace of the kingdom was most probably undisturbed. The Sātavāhanas were still reeling under the blows that had been inflicted by Rudra-dāman in *c.* 150 A.D., and the Kushāṇa emperors were getting weaker and weaker. The Śassanian kingdom was yet to come into existence. There was, therefore, no power to challenge the supremacy of the Western Kshatrapas in their dominion.

Dāmajada I had two sons Jīva-dāman and Satya-dāman. Of these the former was the elder and succeeded his father as a Mahākshatrapa in *c.* 175 A.D. Jīva-dāman had not much

[1] On his own coins this name appears in the Scythian form Damaghsada ; later it was Indianised by his descendants as Dāmajada.

administrative experience before his accession[1] and he was relatively young when he ascended the throne. He had further the misfortune of having an ambitious and experienced uncle in Rudra-siṁha. For a few months after his accession Rudra-siṁha continued to profess loyalty to him and accepted the subordinate position of a Kshatrapa in his administration. He was, however, all along conspiring to make a bid for the throne. In his plans he received material assistance from the Ābhīras,[2] whose leaders were at this time serving as generals in the Kshatrapa armies. With their assistance he dethroned his nephew Jīva-dāman[3] and became Mahākshatrapa himself. The dethroned nephew was not allowed to function even as a Kshatrapa, and he and his younger brother Satya-dāman probably went into exile.

Rudra-siṁha I, however, did not enjoy an undisputed possession of his ill-gotten throne for a long time. Īśvara-datta, another Ābhīra general who has carved a principality for himself in Nasik, deposed him and became Mahākshatrapa himself in 188 A.D. Rudra-siṁha I submitted to the inevitable and consented to rule as the feudatory of the conqueror in the capacity of a Kshatrapa. He utilised his position to undermine the power and the influence of Īśvara-datta and managed to oust him in about two years.[4] The year 191 A.D. saw him ruling again as

---

[1] Coins issued by him as Kshatrapa during his father's rule have not been found, hence this conjecture.

[2] In the Gunda inscription, dated 181 A.D., the Ābhīra general Rudra-bhūti is referring to Rudra-siṁha as a Kshatrapa, ignoring altogether the existence of Jīva-dāman, who was then still a Mahākshatrapa. General Rudra-bhāti must have been one of the partisans of Rudra-siṁha. See *EI.* XVI, 233.

[3] Dr. D. R Bhandarkar's view that Jīva-dāman was not a Mahākshatrapa before 181 A.D. is untenable. See *JNSI. I*, 18-20.

[4] Rapson places the Ābhīra intervention under Iśvara-datta in 236-238 A.D., during which time no coins were issued by the Western Kshatrapas. Since the Ābhīras are known to be serving as generals under the Western Kshatrapas in *c.* 180, it is more probable that the degradation of Rudra-siṁha I during 178-180 A.D. was due to their *coup* under Īśvara-datta, as suggested by Dr. D. R. Bhandarkar (*ASI*, 1913-4,

Mahākshatrapa, which he continued to do down to *c.* 197 A.D.

The struggle for the throne between the uncle and the nephew and the revolution at the capital which put the Ābhīras in power for a couple of years could not but affect the fortunes of the Western Kshatrapas. The contemporary Sātavāhana king Yajñaśrī Sātakarṇi was an able and ambitious ruler and managed to reconquer northern Konkan from the Kshatrapas.[1] The Mālavas also began to show signs of restiveness in the Udaipur-Ajmer tract.

Rudra-siṁha I was succeeded by his dethroned nephew Jīva-dāman as Mahākshatrapa in 197 A.D. (For his coins see Pl. II, Nos. 3-4). Whether a reconciliation was effected between the uncle and the nephew, or whether the nephew defeated the uncle and ascended the throne, is not definitely known. The former alternative seems more likely ; for we find Rudra-siṁha's son Rudra-sena working under Jīva-dāman as a Kshatrapa towards the end of his reign.[2] Like Humayun in later days, Jīva-dāman did not have a long reign after his second accession, for we find his nephew Rudra-sena I ruling as Mahākshatrapa in 200 A.D.

2. RUDRA-SENA
(200 A.D. to 222 A.D.)

Rudra-sena I enjoyed a fairly long reign of 22 years, which was not disturbed by any internecine wars. He had two brothers, Saṅgha-dāman and Dāma-sena, and two sons, Pṛithivi-

pp. 227-45). Rapson attributes this degradation of Rudra-siṁha to the reassertion of his power by his nephew Jīva-dāman. But in the absence of any coins issued by Jīva-dāman as Mahākshatrapa during the period 178-180 A.D. the theory seems quite unconvincing.

[1]Coins and inscriptions of this ruler are found in this province. The former are in imitation of the Kshatrapa coinage and attest to the expansion of the Sātavāhana power at the cost of Western Kshatrapas.

[2]Jīva-dāman's younger brother Satya-dāman also ruled as a Kshatrapa under him just after his second accession. The features of Satya-dāman on his solitary coin show that he was a man of about 45 when he became a Kshatrapa and this could be only in *c.* 198 A.D. For the

sena and Dāmajada. Circumstances were thus quite favourable for a prolonged and bitter struggle for the throne. But growing wiser by the war of succession in the preceding generation, which had led to the diminution of the kingdom, it seems that the Western Kshatrapas decided that usually the crown should pass from the reigning sovereign to his younger brothers in succession and not to his eldest son. We thus find Rudra-sena being succeeded by his younger brothers Saṅgha-dāman and Dāma-sena in succession. In the next generation we find three sons of Dāma-sena ruling one after another. A generation later Viśva-sena was succeeded by his brother Bhartṛi-dāman. This arrangement seems to have been preferred, because it ensured the presence of experienced rulers on the throne and removed the temptation to rebel from the path of the brothers of the reigning sovereign. It, however, made it more or less impossible for the eldest son of the ruling king to succeed him as the supreme ruler of the state. He was, however, offered the position and status of a Kshatrapa under his ruling uncles. Thus we find both Pṛithivi-sena and Dāmajada II ruling as Kshatrapas in successions under their uncles Saṅgha-dāman and Dāma-sena.

During the reign of Rudra-sena I, Malwa, Gujarat, Kathiawar[1] and Western Rajputana continued to be under the sway of the Western Kshatrapas. It is not known with certainty whether Sindh still continued to be under their rule. Northern Konkan had been lost in the previous decade to the Sātavāhanas. A little later the Ābhīras carved out a principality for themselves in that province. In the beginning they must have professed themselves to be the feudatories of the Sātavāhanas ; later they became independent. They were ruling in northern

---

contrary view that Satya-dāman may have been the elder brother, who ruled for a short time as a Kshatrapa under his father, see Rapson, *Catalogue*, pp. cxxviii-cxxix.

[1]Several inscriptions of Rudra-sena I are found in Kathiawar.

Konkan and Mahārāshṭra throughout the 3rd century A.D.[1] Very little, however, is known either of the names of the rulers of this dynasty or of their achievements.

Ujjayinī, as before, was the capital of the Western Kshatrapas, and they continued to enjoy the prestige of a great power in spite of the turmoils of the preceding generation. They were by this time not only completely Hinduised but were also well known as patrons of Sanskrit learning and Hindu religion. It is, therefore, no wonder that rulers of far-off provinces should have sought the hands of their princesses. Vīrapurusha-datta, the Ikshvāku king of Andhra country (*c.* 240 to 265), had married a Śaka princess, Rudradhara-bhaṭārikā by name, who is described as the daughter of a king of Ujjayinī[2]. She was perhaps a daughter of Rudra-sena I whose marriage took place after the death of her father or she may have been his grand-daughter. Śaka Moda, whose sister is recorded to have made a donation of a sculpture of the foot-prints of the Buddha at Amarāvati, was probably a member of the entourage that accompanied the princess to her new home. A sister of Rudra-sena named Prabhudāmā is known from a seal found at Vaiśāli.[3] The seal describes her as a Mahādevī, Chief Queen, but does not give her husband's name. It is not unlikely that he may have been either a hitherto unknown Hindu ruler of eastern India, who had married a Scythian princess, or a Hinduised Kushān chief, ruling over a small principality in Magadha, which had survived the collapse of the Kushān empire.[4]

[1]The Purāṇas state that 10 Ābhīra rulers will rule for 67 years after the fall of the Sātavāhanas. The information about the duration of their rule seems to be incorrect ; for an Ābhīra ruler is known to have sent an embassy to congratulate the Sassanian emperor Narseh on his success in the war for the throne in 293 A.D.

[2]*EI. XX*, 19.

[3]*ASI.* 1913-14, p. 136.

[4]*EI. XX*, 37. Sculptures of two warriors in Scythian dress may also be due to the same circumstances.

3. SANGHA-DĀMAN AND DĀMA-SENA.

(222 to 238 A.D.)

Rudra-sena I had two sons, Pṛithivī-sena and Dāmajada. The former was ruling as a Kshatrapa under him towards the end of his reign, but the crown passed to his younger brother Saṅgha-dāman according to the convention about succession referred to above. Though not more than 40 at his accession, Saṅgha-dāman ruled only for about a year and half ; for we find his younger brother Dāma-sena ruling as Mahākshatrapa in 223 A.D.

It is not impossible that Saṅgha-dāman may have met with a natural premature death. It is, however, more likely that he may have died in battle, while fighting against the Mālavas of Ajmer-Udaipur tract, who made a successful bid for independence at about this time. A Mālava chief, (Sri ?) Soma by name, is known to have performed an important sacrifice at Nāndsā in Udaipur State to celebrate the liberation of his country.[1] An inscription of this ruler, dated in 226 A.D., has been recently discovered, announcing how freedom and prosperity had returned to the country of the Mālavas by that time, and how the fame of his exploits had filled the wide space between the earth and the heaven. The enemies of the Mālavas are not mentioned in the record, but they must have been obviously none others than the Western Kshatrapas, as western Rajputana is known to have been under their rule ever since the days of Rudra-dāman I. The war for freedom of the Mālavas, which was over before 226 A.D., may have lasted for three or four years and Saṅgha-dāman may have lost his life in it in 223 A.D.

Along with the Ajmer-Udaipur tract, Sindh also must have

[1]This information is supplied by the Nāndsā Yūpa inscriptions, which will be soon published by the writer in the *Epigraphia Indica*. The Mālava country, which was liberated, comprised portions of the states of Udaipur, Jaipur, Tonk and the British district of Ajmer.

slipped away from the hands of the Western Kshatrapas soon after this time : they could not have effectively controlled it after the loss of the above territory. We, however, do not know who succeeded the Western Kshatrapas in Sindh and who was ruling there till 284 A.D. when the province passed under the sway of the Sassanians. Very probably some local Scythian chiefs were ruling there during this period.

During the reign of Dāma-sena, the kingdom of the Western Kshatrapas thus became confined to Malwa, Gujarat and Kathiawar. Ujjayini still continued to be the capital.

During the first ten years of the reign of Dāma-sena, Pṛithivī-sena and Dāmajada II, sons of his deceased eldest brother Rudra-sena I, ruled under him as Kshatrapas. During the last four years of his reign, however, his own son Vīra-dāman was raised to that status. He seems to have pre-deceased his father, for his younger brother Yaśo-dāman succeeded his father, and ruled as Mahākshatrapa in 238 A.D.[1]

4. Yaśo-dāman I, Vijaya-sena, Dāmajada III and Rudra-sena II.

(238 A.D. to 279 A.D.)

Yaśo-dāman was only about 40 at his accession, but he governed the kingdom only for two years. In 240 A.D. he was succeeded by his younger brother Vijaya-sena, who ruled as Mahākshatrapa from 240 to 250 A.D. He had ruled for a year as a Kshatrapa during the short reign of his elder brother.

The premature deaths of the two brothers, Vīra-dāman and Yaśo-dāman, in the short space of two years appear to indicate some trouble in the body politic, but its nature cannot at present be ascertained. The succession to the throne was according to

[1]There is a gap of two years in the Mahākshatrapa coinage during 236-38 A.D. and Rapson places Iśvara-datta's usurpation during this interval ; Rapson, *Catalogue*, pp. cxxiii-cxxvii.

the accepted convention and there was at this time no outside power, strong enough to create trouble in the Śaka kingdom. Vijaya-sena had, however, a peaceful and prosperous reign, for his coins are found in large numbers throughout Gujarat and Kathiawar.

Vijaya-sena was succeeded by his youngest brother Dāmajada III in 250 A.D. Being the youngest of four brothers, he naturally had a short reign of five years, and was succeeded in 255 A.D. by Rudra-sena II, who was the son of his eldest brother Vīra-dāman. Rudra-sena II had a long reign of 22 years, but very few of its political incidents are definitely known.

We have seen already how a junior prince of the royal family was usually associated with the reigning king with the status of the Kshatrapa since the beginning of this dynasty. During the period 239 to 275 A.D. no prince, however, is found to be associated in this capacity with the reigning Mahākshatrapa. A change, therefore, seems to have been effected in the system of administration and the office of the crown prince (Kshatrapa) seems to have been abolished for reasons which are not known at present. It was, however, revived by Rudra-sena II towards the end of his reign, for his son Viśva-siṁha is known to have functioned as a Kshatrapa for a short time before his father's death.

Our sources of information are silent about the history of the Western Kshatrapas during the period *c.* 230 to 275 A.D. But it seems fairly certain that their kingdom suffered further contraction during the latter part of this period. The copper coinage of the Western Kshatrapas, which was current only in Malwa up to *c.* 240 A.D., suddenly comes to an end after that year. This would, to some extent, support the theory that the Śakas lost Malwa soon after that date. Vindhyaśakti, the founder of the Vākāṭaka kingdom, ruled for about 20 years from *c.* 255 to 275 A.D. He was a contemporary of Rudra-sena II and seems to have annexed a part of eastern Malwa. An upstart

Śaka chief named Śrīdhara-varman was ruling as an independent king at Sanchi (near Bhopal) probably from *c.* 266 A.D.[1] With the loss of Malwa the capital of the kingdom must have been shifted from Ujjayinī in Malwa to Girinagara (Junagadh), in Kathiawar.

The view that the Kshatrapas had annexed Mahārāshṭra during the latter half of the 3rd century, when the Sātavāhana power had collapsed,[2] is untenable. The epigraphical and Purāṇic evidence shows that the Ābhīras rose to power in Mahārāshṭra during the 3rd century and there is no evidence to show that the Kshatrapas defeated them in *c.* 250 A.D. and annexed their kingdom. The discovery of the hoard of Kshatrapa coins near Karhad (in Satara district), in which the rulers in the latter half of the 3rd century are represented, can be easily explained otherwise. Karhad was a famous holy place. Its Brāhmaṇas were noted for learning and they were welcomed in distant royal courts. The Kshatrapa hoard found near that town may have been brought with him by a Brāhmana emigrant of the town, returning to it in panic when a revolution broke out in the Kshatrapa kingdom in *c.* 304 A.D. which will be described in due course.

5. Viśva-simha and Bhartṛi-dāman.

(*c.* 279 A.D. to *c.* 304 A.D.)

Rudra-sena II seems to have had no younger brothers; hence he was succeeded by his eldest son Viśva-siṁha in *c.* 279 A.D. He had, however, a short reign of about 3 years only, for we find his brother Bhartṛi-dāman ruling as Mahākshatrapa

[1] This is the date according to Mr. R. D. Banerji (*EI.* XVI, 232). Mr. N. G. Majumdar places him forty years later (*JASB.* NS. XIX, 343).

[2] *JBBRAS.* VII, 16-17; BG. I, 48-49

in 282 A.D. He had governed as a Kshatrapa for about four years before his accession.

The reign of Bhartṛi-dāman most probably extended up to 304 A.D. and his son Viśva-sena was functioning under him as Kshatrapa from 294 onwards. The coins of Bhartṛi-dāman as Mahākshatrapa and of Viśva-sena as Kshatrapa are found in large numbers ; we may therefore assume that they succeeded in retrieving the fortunes of their family to a large extent.

In 284 A.D. the Sassanian emperor Varahran II conquered Seistan and Sindh and appointed his brother Varahran III as the governor of the new province with the title *Śakān Shāh.* This event did not directly affect the fortunes of the Western Kshatrapas, for most probably they had already lost control over Sindh a few decades earlier. The local Śaka chiefs in Sindh and Seistan had to transfer their allegiance to the Sassanian emperor after this conquest.[1]

The conquest of Sindh by Varahran II brought the Western Kshatrapas into closer contact with the Sassanians, and Bhartṛi-dāman naturally felt it desirable to cultivate friendly relations with the new neighbours. He did not take part[2] in the war of succession that ensued between Varahran III and Narseh, but when the latter came out successful, he sent ambassadors to congratulate him and to intimate his recognition of the new

[1]There is no sufficient evidence to show that the eastern conquests of any Sassanian emperor in the 3rd century A.D. had extended to the Punjab or Gujarat and Kathiawar. Only one solitary coin has been found in the Punjab showing some Sassanian influence, and it cannot support the theory of Sassanian conquest of that province. The rulers of Avantī and Kathiawar are no doubt mentioned as recognising the title of Narseh, but they are expressly described as independent princes in the Paikuli inscription.

[2]The Paikuli inscription mentions the king of Avantī as siding with Varahran III in the war of succession ; but at this time Avantī or Ujjayini did not form part of the dominians of the Western Kshatrapas. Some local ruler of Avantī, possibly a Śaka, may have joined the side of the Varahran III.

regime. The even tenor of the reign of Bhartṛi-dāman was not affected by any events in contemporary Sassanian history.

6. The Rise of a New Śaka House.

Rudra-simha II and Yaśo-dāman II.

(*c*. 304 to *c*. 345 A.D.)

Some events, however, occurred towards the end of the reign of Bhartṛi-dāman, which put an end to the house of Chashṭana, ruling over Gujarat and Kathiawar for more than 175 years. We find that the successor of Bhartṛi-dāman was not his son Viśva-sena, who had functioned as Kshatrapa under him for about ten years, but one Rudra-siṁha II, who is described as the son of Svāmī Jīva-dāman, a person mentioned without any royal titles like *rajān* or Kshatrapa. The relationship of Rudra-siṁha II with Bhartṛi-dāman is unknown ; he seems to have been an upstart or at most a member of a collateral Śaka branch. His accession in 304 A.D. was not a peaceful one. It was attended by a severe struggle, which rendered life and property unsafe at the capital, inducing people to bury their valuables and flee away for safety.[1] Rudra-siṁha II, however, succeeded in getting an effective control over the kingdom in less than a year and ruled over it down to 316 A.D., when he was succeeded by his son Yaśo-dāman II, who ruled certainly down to 332 A.D. and perhaps for a few years more.

Both Rudra-siṁha II and Yaśo-dāman II, however, did never assume the higher title of the Mahākshatrapa and after 332 A.D., there is a break in the Kshatrapa coinage for 16 years, during which period no ruler is known to have issued coins either as a Kshatrapa or as a Mahākshatrapa. When the curtain rises in 348 A.D. we find a new chief, Rudra-sena III, on the

[1] A hoard of 520 coins buried towards the end of the reign of Bhartṛi-dāman was found at Junagadh. *Num. Supp.* XLVII, 97.

throne ruling as Mahākshatrapa. It is, however, certain that his father Rudra-dāman II had also ruled as Mahākshatrapa for a few months or years before that date, though no coins of his have been so far discovered.

The circumstances which compelled Rudra-siṁha II and Yaśo-dāman II to be content with the lower title of the Kshatrapa and caused the total cessation of the Kshatrapa coinage during 332 to 348 A.D. are not yet sufficiently known. One view is that the Sassanian intervention was responsible for this gradual decline and total eclipse of the power of the Western Kshatrapas.[1] This view does not seem to be correct. The Sassanian emperor Narseh, who was ruling from 293 to 303 A.D. was signally defeated by the Roman emperor Galerius. Narseh had to cede extensive provinces to the conqueror in order to recover his family which had fallen into the hands of the enemy. Narseh therefore was not in a position to bring about the downfall of Bhartṛi-dāman. His successor, Hormuzd II, had a short reign of seven years (303 to 310 A.D.) and is not known to have undertaken any expeditions to the east. The next ruler, Shapur II, was a baby of less than one year at the time of his accession in 310 A.D. When he grew into manhood, he was involved in Roman wars during 337-8 A.D. Sassanian intervention therefore does not seem to have been responsible for the decline and eclipse of the power of the Western Kshatrapas during 304 to 348 A.D. It may be pointed out that no Sassanian coins of this period are found in Gujarat and Kathiawar ; nor does the coinage of Rudra-siṁha II and Yośo-dāman II show any Sassanian influence.

It seems more probable that the conquests of the Vākāṭaka emperor Pravara-sena I were responsible for the decline of the Kshatrapa power during the early decades of the 4th century A.D. There is, however, no direct evidence to show that Pravara-

[1] *PHAI*[4]. p. 428.

sena I had reduced the Western Kshatrapas to his vassalage. He, however, is the only Vākāṭaka ruler to assume the title of *Samrāṭ*, emperor, and is known to have performed as many as four horse-sacrifices (*aśvamedhas*) to celebrate his different conquests. His father Vindhyaśakti had ousted the Kshatrapas from a part of Malwa ; he may therefore well have tried to extend his sphere of influence in the west by supporting the claims of the upstart Rudra-siṁha II and by giving him help to oust Bhartṛi-dāman or his son Viśva-siṁha or both, who were the legitimate claimants to the throne. Imperialism generally tries to extend its sphere of influence in this manner. One can hardly believe that Rudra-siṁha II and Yaśo-dāman II had voluntarily remained content with the lower title of Kshatrapa, which at this time denoted a feudatory status. No other neighbouring power was in a position to impose its sovereignty upon the Kshatrapa rulers. The theory that Rudra-siṁha II and Yaśo-dāman II had become Vākāṭaka feudatories for some time gets some further support from the discovery of the hoard of Kshatrapa coins at Chhindwara in C.P., in which Rudra-siṁha II and Yaśo-dāman II happen to be the latest kings to be represented.[1] It is not unlikely that both these rulers were sending occasional tributes to Pravara-sena I which was responsible for the entry of the Kshatrapa coins in the Vākāṭaka dominions. The tribute ceased to come with the deaths of Pravara-sena I and Yaśo-dāman II, when the Vākāṭakas lost their overlordship ; and so later Kshatrapa coins are not to be seen in the hoard. It must, however, be clearly understood that Pravara-sena's overlordship over the Kshatrapas is only a theory, no doubt more probable than any other, but still lacking conclusive proof.

What was the cause of the total stoppage of the Kshatrapa coinage during 332 to 348 A.D. ? When we note how there are

---

[1] *Num. Supp.* XLVII, 97.

hardly any gaps of more than two or three years in the dates of the Kshatrapa coinage from 178 to 332 A.D., we cannot but suspect some serious political disturbance during this period. The usual view that the Kshatrapa power was in complete abeyance during this period does not seem to be correct. Neither the Vākāṭakas nor the Sassanians were at this time in a position to effect a total eclipse of the Kshatrapa power. The Vākāṭaka king Rudra-sena I, who succeeded the emperor Pravara-sena in *c.* 335, was relatively a weak ruler and could not have undertaken any expedition against the Kshatrapas. The Sassanian emperor Shapur II was engaged in Roman wars during 337-8 A.D. It seems that there was a struggle for the Kshatrapa throne which was responsible for part of this gap. It is not unlikely that future discoveries will narrow it down, showing that Yaśo-dāman II ruled for a few years after 332 and Rudra-dāman II for a few years before 348 A.D. The intervening period may have been spent in a bitter struggle for the throne during which neither claimant found it possible to issue any coinage. We must remember in this connection that Mahākshatrapa Rudra-dāman II, whose son Rudra-sena III was ruling as Mahākshatrapa in 348 A.D., is not known to be related to Yaśo-dāman II, who was ruling as a Kshatrapa down to 332 A.D. Possibly he was a rival claimant from a collateral branch and could substantiate his claim only by a successful appeal to arms. A bitter struggle for the throne was therefore inevitable. It is this internecine struggle rather than a foreign conquest which seems to be responsible for part of the gap of 16 years. Future discoveries alone can, however, finally solve the riddle.

RUDRA-DĀMAN II AND HIS SUCCESSORS.

(*c.* 345 A.D. to *c.* 395 A.D.)

Rudra-dāman II, who supplanted Yaśo-dāman II, was very probably a scion of the house of Chashṭana, which had been ousted by Rudra-siṁha II in 304 A.D. probably with the assistance of the Vākāṭaka emperor Pravara-sena I. The weakening of the Vākāṭaka power at the end of the reign of that emperor in c. 335 A.D. enabled Rudra-dāman II to oust the son of his nominee and become Mahākshatrapa himself. How long Rudra-dāman II ruled we do not know, for no coins of his have been found so far. We may assume that he may have ruled at least for two or three years before 348 A.D., when his son Rudra-sena III was ruling as Mahākshatrapa. The sway of Rudra-dāman II extended over Kathiawar and northern Gujarat.

Rudra-sena III had a long reign of more than 30 years (c. 348 to c. 380 A.D.). It was, however, not a peaceful one. A great political upheaval once more occurred soon after 351 A.D., which rendered life and property unsafe throughout his kingdom. We find people burying hoards for safety both in the heart of the kingdom as well as in its outlying cities.[1] The disturbance lasted for 13 years, from c. 351 to c. 364 A.D., during which Rudra-sena III could issue no coins whatsoever. He, however, regained his position in 364 A.D. and we find him issuing coins regularly down to 378 A.D.

The cause of this sudden eclipse of the power of Rudra-sena III is not definitely known at present. It could not have been an invasion by the Vākāṭakas ; for they were too weak to think of any such venture at this time. Dr. K. P. Jayaswal has suggested that it may have been an attack on the Kshatrapa power by Samudra-gupta. This view also does not seem to be convincing. The Kākas and Sanakānikas of eastern Mālava are known to have been the western neighbours of Samudra-gupta. It is not likely that he had invaded the Kshatrapa dominion which lay further to the west in Gujarat and Kathiawar. It is important to note that the Allahabad eulogy of Samudra-gupta,

---

[1] *JBBRAS*. 1899, pp. 203-09 for the Uparkot hoard and *ASI*. 1913-14, pp. 227-45 for the Sarvanta hoard.

which gives an exhaustive account of his conquests, does not mention any smashing defeat inflicted on the Śakas of Western India. Shapur II, the contemporary Sassanian emperor, is known to have led an expedition to the east in 356-7 A.D. Can it be that after conquering the Kidāra king of the Punjab in 357 A.D. he turned to Kathiawar from his base in Sindh and totally eclipsed the power of Rudra-sena III for some time? Had Sassanian coins been found in Kathiawar, this conjecture might have appeared probable; as it is, there is nothing to support it. The view that Śarva Bhaṭṭāraka, who started the so-called Valabhī coinage, may have temporarily overpowered Rudra-sena III is also not free from difficulties.[1] It must, therefore, be admitted that the cause of the eclipse of the power of Rudra-sena during 351 to 364 is still unknown. Nor do we know how he re-established it in *c.* 365 A.D.

378 A.D. is the last known date of Rudra-sena III. He may have ruled for a year or two more and we may place his death in *c.* 380.

The history of the Western Kshatrapas subsequent to the death of Rudra-sena III is again shrouded in mystery. He was succeeded by Siṁha-sena who was his sister's son, and not his own. The succession therefore may not have been a peaceful one. We find Siṁha-sena ruling as Mahākshatrapa in 382 A.D., but within the next six years or so not only his own reign but that of his son Rudra-sena IV came to an end, for in 388 A.D., or soon after we find Rudra-siṁha III on the throne ruling as Mahākshatrapa. The relationship of this ruler to his predecessor Rudra-sena IV is not known. It is not unlikely that his father Satya-siṁha may have been a brother of Rudra-sena III; he may, therefore, have felt that he was a better claimant to the throne than Rudra-sena IV, who derived his title from a sister of Rudra-sena III.

---

[1] *JNSI.* VI, 19-23.

Rudra-siṁha III, however, could not rule the kingdom for a long time. In less than 10 years from 388 A.D. he was completely defeated by Chandra-gupta II, who annexed Gujarat and Kathiawar to the Gupta empire and put an end to the Śaka rule. An account of this conquest will be given in Chapter VIII.

CHAPTER IV

EASTERN DECCAN

1. Andhra

During the age of the Later Śātavāhanas the heart of the Andhra country, corresponding to the districts round the mouths of the Kistna and the Godāvarī, appears to have had its headquarters at Dhānyakaṭaka. The city has been identified by some scholars with Bezwada, while others, with greater plausibility, have suggested its location in the present Amaravati-Dharanikota area of the Kistna District.[1] The extinction of Śātavāhana rule in the above region is usually placed towards the end of the first quarter of the third century A.D. Local feudatory families had no doubt been gaining strength as a result of the weakness of their Later Śātavāhana overlords and must have contributed largely to the latter's downfall. But the Ikshvākus of the Kistna-Guntur region possibly struck the strongest blow to the suzerain power.

The Ikshvākus.

The earliest known Ikshvāku king Vāsishṭhīputra Śāntamūla (Chāntamūla) I flourished about the second quarter of the third century, that is to say, immediately after the fall of the Śātavāhanas in the country round Dhānyakaṭaka. The assumption of independence by a Muslim ruler of medieval India was

[1] The Amarāvati inscription of Ikshvāku Vīrapurusha-datta (*SIE.*, 1937-38, No. 529) refers to the installation of two *Dhammachakras* at the eastern entrance of the *Mahāvihāra* at Dhaṃñakaḍa (Dhānyakaṭa). An Amarāvati pillar inscription of Keta II, dated A.D. 1182, mentions Śrī-Dhānyakaṭaka with its temple of Śiva Amaresvara and the lofty *Chaitya* of Lord Buddha (*EI.*, VI, 146).

characterised by the issue of his own coins and by an order to insert in the *Khuṭbah* (sermon delivered after divine service on Friday) his own name instead of his overlord's. The independent status newly acquired by Indian ruling families of the early centuries of the Christian era was likewise signalised usually by the celebration of the Aśvamedha. It is, therefore, interesting to note that Śāntamūla I was the performer of a horse-sacrifice.

We know little about the predecessors of Śāntamūla I. It is not impossible that the Ikshvākus of the Andhra-desa actually represented a branch of the celebrated Ikshvāku dynasty of Ayodhyā which migrated to the Deccan and settled there. The Ikshvākus of the Far South appear to have had their capital at Vijayapurī situated in the valley of the Nagarjunikonda hills[1]. No record of Śāntamūla's time has so far been discovered. Details of the political career of this king as well as the extent of his kingdom are, therefore, unknown. Śāntamūla I was a staunch Brahmanist and performed not only the Aśvamedha but also the Vājapeya and other Vedic sacrifices. Like the Kadambas and the Chālukyas of later times, he is described as "favoured by Mahāsena (Skanda-Kārttikeya)". Śāntamūla I had at least two sisters, the first of whom was married to a feudatory chief who had the style *Mahāsenāpati Mahātalavara* and belonged to the Pukīya family. The king's daughter Aṭavī-Śāntiśrī was married to an official styled *Mahāsenāpati Mahādaṇḍanāyaka* and reported to have belonged to the noble family of the Dhanakas. The word *Pukīya* has been connected by some scholars with the Pungi district covering parts of southern Guntur and the adjoining region. The Hiraṇyaka family, related to the Ikshvākus, has been similarly connected with the Hiraṇyarāshṭra which must have included the northern and western parts of the Nellore District and the adjacent area.

[1]The Ikshvākus were probably the Śrīparvatīya Andhras of the Purāṇas. Śrīparvata was the ancient name of the Nallamlaur Range.

Śāntamūla I was succeeded by his son Māṭharīputra Vīrapurusha-datta (third quarter of the third century) who ruled at least up to his twentieth regnal year. One of his queens was Rudradharabhaṭṭārikā who is described as the daughter of the Mahārāja of Ujjain.[1] It is not impossible that Rudradharabhaṭṭārikā was related to Rudra-sena II (*c.* 254-74 A.D.) or Rudra-sena I (*c.* 199-220 A.D.) the Śaka rulers of Western India. Vīrapurusha-datta gave his daughter in marriage to the Mahārāja of Vanavāsa which has been identified with modern Banavāsi in the North Kanara District of the Bombay Presidency. The son-in-law of the Ikshvāku king seems to have been no other than a ruler of the Chuṭu family supposed to have been a branch of the Śātavāhana dynasty settled in the ancient Kuntala country. Matrimonial alliances with the royal houses of Ujjain and Banavāsi no doubt strengthened the position of the Ikshvākus during the reign of Vīrapurusha-datta, although the credit for contracting these relations might belong actually to the king's father Mahārāja Śāntamūla I.

Records belonging to the reign of Vīrapurusha-datta have been discovered at the Buddhist sites of Amaravati, Jaggayapeta and Nagarjunikonda.[2] The latest date supplied by the epigraphs is the king's twentieth regnal year. The inscriptions are, however, not official documents, but records of private donations in favour of several Buddhist establishments. Most of the Nagarjunikonda epigraphs record the benefactions of some female members of the Ikshvāku family to the Great Monastery lying near the capital city of Vijayapurī. These ladies were apparently Buddhists in faith. It is, however, unknown whether king Vīrapurusha-datta himself and his son were actually

---

[1]It is interesting to note that three of Vīrapurusha-datta's queens were daughters of his paternal aunts. Such alliances were evidently familiar in this region even in the early period. Cf. *Baudhāyana Dharma-sūtra*, I.II. 1-4.

[2]*EI.* XX, 1 ff; XXI, 60 ff.

Buddhists. But attention in this connection may be drawn to the fact that, unlike Śāntamūla I, neither of these rulers has been described as the performer of any Brahmanical sacrifices or as favoured by the god Mahāsena. It is, therefore, not improbable that the immediate successors of Śāntamūla I were Buddhists and not staunch Brahmanists like their ancestor.

Māṭharīputra Vīrapurusha-datta was succeeded by his son Vāśisṭhīputra Ehuvula[1] Śāntamūla II who ruled at least up to his eleventh regnal year. The independent rule of the Ikshvākus in the heart of the Andhra country appears to have ended about the close of the third century A.D. This is suggested by the Mayidavolu charter recording an order of the Pallava crown-prince Śivaskanda-varman of Kāñchī to the provincial governor of the Andhrāpātha residing at Dhānyakaṭaka. Though there is difference of opinion amongst scholars as regards the date of Śivaskanda-varman[2] and his father during whose reign the grant was issued, it seems quite reasonable to ascribe the overthrow of the Ikshvākus and the Pallava occupation of the Kistna-Guntur region to about the end of the third century A.D. It is, however, uncertain whether Ehuvula Śāntamūla was himself ousted by the Pallavas.[3]

There is evidence to show that the Ikshvāku dynasty lingered long as a local power. A record of the Kekaya family of northern Mysore belonging to the fifth century A.D. refers to matrimonial relations between the Kekaya kings and the

[1] Of the two forms, Ehuvula, and Ehuvala, the former is to be preferred. Cf the name Haṁguṇavula-Devana, *Suc.Sāt.* p. 391.

[2] Some scholars would like to assign him to the middle of the third century A.D. For an examination of the question and for reasons why he should be ascribed to the first half of the fourth century, see *Suc. Sāt.* pp. 161-68.

[3] Mahārāja Ruḷupurusha-datta, mentioned in an inscription at Gurzala in the Guntur District (*EI.* XXVI, 123 ff), may have been the successor of Ehuvula Śāntamūla II. The palaeography of the record as well as the name-ending *datta* seems to connect him with the royal family of the Ikshvākus, specially with Vīrapurusha-datta.

royal sages of the Ikshvāku dynasty. These Ikshvākus are almost certainly to be identified with the descendants of Śāntamūla I. In this connection it is interesting to recall the epic instance of a matrimonial alliance between the Ikshvākus of Ayodhyā and the Kekayas of Girivraja and Nandigrāma in the Punjab. Vague reminiscences of the southern Ikshvākus may probably be traced in the late Kannada poem entitled *Dharmāmṛita* by Nayasena.

The Bṛihatphalāyanas.

There was an old kingdom covering the present Bandar (Masulipatam) *tāluk* of the Kistna District and the adjoining region with its capital at a city called Pithuṇḍa (=Pṛithūda ?) lying not very far from Masulipatam.[1] According to the Hathigumpha inscription, king Khāravela of Kaliṅga, who may be assigned to the second half of the first century B.C., devastated the royal city of Pithuṇḍa. About the middle of the second century A.D. the Greek geographer Ptolemy mentions "the metropolis of Pitundra" which is located in the Masulipatam area. There is hardly any doubt that the inscription of Khāravela and the Geography of Ptolemy refer to the same royal city. Towards the end of the third century A.D., a king named Jayavarman is known to have been ruling over the above region very probably with his capital at the city of Pithuṇḍa.[2] King Jaya-varman belonged to the Bṛihatphalāyana *gotra* ; but no other king of his line is as yet known.

---

[1]According to Ptolemy's *Geography* (VII, i, § 79, 93), Pitundra= Pithuṇḍa was in the land of the people called Maisōloi. The name of this country is given as Maisōlia which is apparently identical with the first part of the name of Masulipatam. See *infra*.

[2]Some scholars believe that Kudūra, the place whence the Kondamudi grant was issued, was the capital of the Bṛihatphalāyana kings. See Dubreuil, *AHD.*, pp. 84-85. For a criticism of this view, cf. *Suc. Sāt.* pp. 41-49.

A copperplate charter dated in the tenth regnal year of Jaya-varman who is described as a devotee of Maheśvara (Śiva) was discovered at Kondamudi in the Tenali taluk of the Kistna district.[1] It was issued from the victorious camp of Kudūra to the governor of the Kudūra *āhāra* (district) in regard to a grant of land in favour of a number of Brāhmaṇas. Kudūra, which appears to have been the headquarters of the district of that name, has been identified with modern Guduru near Masulipatam. Some scholars locate it at Koduru on the sea not far from Ghantasala which is the same as Kaṇṭakaśaila or Kaṇṭakaśaula of old records and as Kantakassulos of the Greeks.

Unfortunately the relations of the Bṛihatphalāyanas of Pithuṇḍa with the neighbouring kingdom of the Ikshvākus and with the Pallavas of Kāñchī cannot be determined in the present state of our knowledge. It appears that the earlier kings of Pithuṇḍa accepted the suzerainty of the Later Śātavāhanas and, later, possibly also of the Ikshvākus. On the eve of the Pallava occupation of the Andhrāpatha, Jaya-varman Bṛihatphalāyana seems to have ruled for some time as an independent king. The sudden rise of the Bṛihatphalāyanas may have been at the expense of the Ikshvākus. But very soon both the dynasties appear to have been subdued by the Pallavas of Kāñchī. It is, however, impossible to be definite on this point as materials for the history of the Masulipatam region during the early centuries of the Christian era are scanty. With the rise of the Śālaṅkāyanas of Veṅgī, some of the territories originally enjoyed by the Bṛihatphalāyanas seem to have passed to them.

The Ānandas.

Epigraphic evidence points to the existence of a royal family ruling in the Guntur district about the second half of the fourth

---

[1] *EI.* VI, 315.

century A.D. and parts of the fifth.[1] Only three kings of this dynasty are known from inscriptions. An epigraph in the Kapoteśvara temple at Chezarla to the west of Guntur speaks of Satsabhāmalla who was the daughter's son of king Kandara belonging to the *gotra* (lineage) of a great sage named Ānanda. In the Gorantla copperplate grant of Attivarman, the king is described as "sprung from the family of king Kandara", while the family itself is said to have "arisen from the lineage of the great sage Ānanda". The Mattepad grant of Dāmodara-varman was issued from Kandarapura (a city very probably founded by Kandara) and the king is represented as having belonged to the Ānanda *gotra*. The three kings, Kandara, Atti-varman and Dāmodara-varman should therefore be assigned to the same family which may be called the Ānanda dynasty of the Guntur region.[2] It should, however, be noticed that the name of Ānanda is not found in the list of *gotrarshis* in the Purāṇas and other early works. Apparently the dynasty could not boast of its relations with any acknowledged *gotrarshi* of old.

Of the three kings of the Ānanda family, kandara who seems to have founded the city of Kandarapura is evidently

---

[1]There is difference of opinion amongst scholars as regards the chronology of the Ānanda kings. Gopalachari assigns them to the sixth and seventh centuries A.D He believes that the Chezarla inscription palaeographically resembles the records of the Pallava king Mahendra-varman I (c.600-30 A.D.). See *EHAC.*, p.185. Rama Rao (*JAHC.* I,11) places the Ānandas in the period 375-500 A.D.

[2]Some recent writers prefer the dynastic name Ānandagotra to Ananda, but apparently they forget the fact that the word *gotra* means family and that kings of the Śālaṅkāyana *gotra* represent themselves in their official records simply as Śālaṅkāyana. Attention in this connection may also be drawn to such dynastic names as Ikshvāku which is after an illustrious early member of the family. Expressions like "the Bṛihatphalāyana *gotra* kings", "the Ānanda *gotra* kings", etc., can therefore hardly be entertained. *Cf.* V. S. Ramachandramurty, *JAHRS.* XI, 43 ff ; Rama Rao, *op. cit.* Gopalachari is inclined to style the family as "Kandara" (*op. cit.* p. 185). Apparently however king Kandara himself cannot be described as belonging to "the Kandara family". Of course Kandara's descendants may be designated by that style.

the earliest. There is, however, difference of opinion amongst scholars as regards the relative chronological position between Atti-varman and Dāmodara-varman. It is interesting to note that Dāmodara-varman is described in his own record as *hiraṇyagarbha-odbhav-odbhava*, i.e., one whose father was a performer of the *mahādāna* (great gift) ceremony known as the Hiraṇyagarbha. Atti-varman's record, on the other hand, represents him as a *hiraṇyagarbha-prasava*, i.e., performer of the Hiraṇyagarbha. Dāmodara-varman may have, therefore, been actually a son of Atti-varman. According to some scholars, however, the former was not a successor but a predecessor of the latter.[1]

Kandara, like *Kandhara*, *Kandhāra*, *Kanhara*, *Kanhāra* and *Kannara*, is a Prākṛitic corruption of the Sanskrit name *Kṛishṇa* influenced by words like *Skandha* (Prākṛit *Kandhara*). The Prākṛitic names of Kandara and Atti-varman and especially the fact that the names of a large number of Brāhmaṇa donees of the Mattepad grant of Dāmodara-varman are given in their Prākṛit forms would suggest the ascription of these kings to a period not much later than the middle of the fourth century A.D. when Prākṛit was ousted by Sanskrit from the field of South Indian epigraphy.

The Chezarla inscription[2] represents king Kandara as lord of the Kṛishṇaveṇṇā (i.e., Kistna), of the hill called Trikūṭa and the city called Kandarapura and of two *janapadas* or provinces. It has been suggested that the Trikūṭaparvata of the Chezarla record is the same as the Trikūṭamalaya mentioned in a Vishṇukuṇḍin inscription and is no other than present

[1]Gopalachari believes that Dāmodara-varman flourished about a century before Atti-varman (*op. cit.* p. 194), Rama Rao places Kandara and his grandson in 375-400 A.D., Dāmodara-varman in 435-460 A.D. and Atti-varman in 480-500 A.D.

[2]*SII*, VI, No. 594. For a different interpretation of this record. see Rama Rao, *op. cit.* p. 5, cf. *Suc. Sāt.* p. 396 ff.

Kotappakonda near Kāvūr.[1] Of the two provinces under Kandara's rule one seems to have been the district round Kandarapura which has not been satisfactorily identified.[2] The banner of king Kandara is said to have borne the representation of a *golāṅgula* (a species of monkey). As the banner and crest of a royal family are sometimes found to be the same, it is not impossible that the defaced seals of the Gorantla and Mattepad grants actually bear the figure of a *golāṅgula*. Prince Satsabhāmalla was the daughter's son of Kandara and probably belonged to a viceregal line. Kandara appears to have been called Pṛithivīyuvarāt and is possibly also credited with victory in some battles at Dhānyakaṭaka. This seems to suggest that about the middle of the 4th century Kandara and his feudatories drove out the Pallavas from Dhānyakaṭaka which is known to have been the early Pallava headquarters in the Andhrāpatha.

It appears from the Gorantla Inscription[3] that Attivarman and possibly also his predecessors were devotees of Śiva. The locality called Vakeśvara where the temple of the family deity once stood has, however, not been identified. We have possibly to look to Chezarla which is famous for the temple of Kapoteśvara. In that case, Kandarapura, capital of the Ānanda kings, was probably not very far from Chezarla.

Dāmodara-varman was certainly a Buddhist.[4] The Kapoteśvara temple at Chezarla has been supposed by scholars to have been a structural *Chaitya* Hall, originally Buddhist, but

---

[1]Krishna Rao, *EDA*. p. 430.

[2]Rama Rao identifies Kandarapura with Kanteṛu in the Guntur *tāluk* (*op. cit* p. 12). Somasekhara Sarma believes that the village of Chēbrōlu in the Bapatla taluk of the Guntur Dist., which is famous for the temple of Skanda, might have been known after that god as Skandapura, Kandapura and K a n d a r a p u r a. He further identifies Chēbrōlu, called Chēmbrōlu or Tāmbrapura in local inscriptions, with Tāmbrāpa of the Early Pallava charters. See *J. Mad. Un*. XII, 154.

[3]*IA*. IX, 102 fl.

[4]*Cf*. Mattepad Grant, *EI*. XVIII, 327 ff.

later converted to Hindu usage.[1] It is usually ascribed to the fourth century A.D. which date probably connects it with the kings of the Ānanda dynasty.

The end of the Ānandas is wrapped in obscurity. They were possibly subdued by the Śālaṅkāyanas, though both the dynasties appear to have been originally responsible for overpowering the Pallavas in the heart of the Andhra country. It is also possible to suggest that the decline of the Ānandas was brought about by their constant struggle with the Pallavas.[2]

The Śālaṅkāyanas.

According to Ptolemy's Geography[3], assigned by scholars to the middle of the second century A.D., a people called the Salakênoi lived to the north of the Maiselôi who apparently belonged to the Masulipatam region. The word Salakênoi appears to be a Greek corruption of the Indian name Śālaṅkāyana.[4] It is again not improbable that Benagouron, the premier city of the Salakênoi according to Ptolemy, is a copyist's mistake for Bengauron, i.e. Veṅgapura=Veṅgīpura which is known to have been the capital of the Śālaṅkāyana Mahārājas. All the Śālaṅkāyana charters, so far discovered, were issued from Veṅgī or Veṅgīpura and a Śālaṅkāyana king is actually mentioned in the Allahabad pillar inscription of Samudra-gupta as *Vaiṅgeyaka*, indicating no doubt "the lord of Veṅgī." The city of Veṅgī has been located at the site of the modern village of Peddavegi near Ellore in the Godāvarī district.

Some of the Śālaṅkāyana charters mention the names of the reigning monarchs without any reference to their predecessors. The position of these rulers in the genealogy is there-

---

[1] *Cf.* Coomaraswamy, *HIIA*. p. 77.

[2] *Cf.* Ramachandramurty, *JAHRS*. XI, 43-50 ; *cf.* also Sircar, *Ibid.* pp. 129-130.

[3] VII, i, 79.

[4] *PHAI*[4]. p. 419 n.

fore difficult to determine. They are Deva-varman of the Ellore grant,[1] Nandi-varman of the Kanterū grant (No. 1)[2] and Skanda-varman of the Kanterū grant (No. 2)[3]. The Kollair grant[4] is, however, issued by a king named Nandi-varman who is called the eldest son of king Chaṇḍa-varman, while, in the Peddavegi grant[5], apparently the same ruler is represented as Nandi-varman II who is not only called the eldest son of Chaṇḍa-varman but also the grandson of Nandi-varman I and the great-grandson of Hasti-varman. We do not know if Nandi-varman of the Kanterū grant (No. 1) has to be identified with Nandi-varman II of the Kollair and Peddavegi grants. But the identification is not improbable in view of the facts that all the three epigraphs belong to the same epoch according to the evidence of palaeography and that unlike the other members of the family the reigning monarch is described as a *parama-bhāgavata*, i.e., devotee of Lord Vishṇu, in all the grants. The exact relation of Deva-varman of the Ellore grant and Skanda-varman of the Kanterū grant (No. 2) with any of the other four kings cannot be determined in the present state of our knowledge. The Ellore grant is, however, written in Prākṛit, while all other records of the family are couched in Sanskrit. It is therefore evident that Deva-varman ruled earlier than both Nandi-varman II and Skanda-varman, as Prākṛit was ousted by Sanskrit from the epigraphy of the Lower Deccan about the middle of the fourth century A.D. In case it is conjectured that there was no break in the succession from Hasti-varman to Nandi-varman II it has to be assumed that Deva-varman ruled earlier than Hasti-varman[6] and Skanda-varman after Nandi-

[1] *EI.* IX, 56 ff.
[2] *JAHRS.* V, 21.
[3] *Ibid.*
[4] *IA.* V, 176.
[5] *JAHRS.* I, 92.
[6] Some scholars believe that Deva-varman was a successor, possibly a son, of Hasti-varman ; cf. *Suc. Sāt.* p. 73 n.

varman II. It must, however, be admitted that palaeography does not suggest a long interval of time between the rule of Deva-varman and that of Nandi-varman II and Skanda-varman.[1]

Besides the evidence of palaeography, there is an interesting reference that helps us in determining the epoch to which the Śālaṅkāyana kings, known from inscriptions, belonged. Hardly any doubt can be entertained as to the identity of Śālaṅkayana Hasti-varman, great-grandfather of Nandi-varman II of the Peddavegi grant, with the king Hasti-varman of Veṅgī who was defeated by Samudra-gupta according to the Allahabad pillar inscription. The southern expedition of Samudra-gupta is usually ascribed to the middle of the fourth century A.D. to which epoch Śālaṅkāyana Hasti-varman has also to be assigned.

Lord Chitraratha-svāmin was the family deity of the Śālaṅkāyana Mahārājas. It is interesting to note that in 1902 a mound was shown by the villagers to Hultzsch on his visit to Peddavegi as the site of the ancient temple of Chitraratha-svāmin.[2] The word *chitraratha* means the sun ; the family deity of the Śālaṅkāyanas may therefore have been the sun-god. But the personal faith of individual Śālaṅkāyana monarchs is known to have been in some cases Śaivism and in others Vaishṇavism.

The seals attached to the Śālaṅkāyana charters bear the figure of a bull which seems to have been the crest of this family of rulers. The word *śālaṅkāyana* indicates Nandin, the bull of Śiva. It is therefore not improbable that the crest of the Śālaṅkāyana kings was connected with the name of their family. *Śālaṅkāyana* has been rightly taken to be the name of the *gotra* to which the family belonged, although the kings are

---

[1]For the supposed existence of a prince named Buddha-varman in the Śālaṅkāyana dynasty, cf. Sircar, *IHQ*. 1933, p. 208 ff ; *Suc. Sāt.* pp. 63-68. Skanda-varman is usually supposed to have been a younger brother of Nandi-varman. II.

[2]*EI.* IX, 51.

simply called *Śālaṅkāyana* instead of the usual epigraphic style *Śālaṅkāyana-sagotra*.

The Ellore grant of the *parama-māheśvara* Mahārāja Deva-varman was issued in the thirteenth year of the king's reign. Deva-varman is described in the grant as a performer of the Aśvamedha sacrifice. This possibly suggests that he established the greatness of his family after having defeated some enemies who might have been no other than the Pallava conquerors of the Andhrāpatha.

The known dates of Nandi-varman II (first half of the fifth century) are his seventh and tenth regnal years. He, therefore, ruled at least for more than nine years.

The end of the Śālaṅkāyanas, like that of the other royal families of the region, is shrouded in darkness. It is, however, very probable that towards the close of the fifth century A.D. they were overpowered by the Vishṇukuṇḍins whose history will be treated in the next volume.

2. KALIṄGA

After the downfall of the Chedi or Chaidya dynasty of Kaliṅga, to which the great Khāravela belonged, the Kaliṅga country (roughly speaking, the coastal land between the Mahanadi and the Godavari) was split up into a number of petty principalities. This state of things is indicated by the Allahabad pillar inscription of Samudra-gupta which refers to the Gupta emperor's victory over some South Indian kings in the fourth century A.D. The Dakshiṇāpatha contemporaries of Samudra-gupta, who are usually assigned to the Kaliṅga region, are Svāmi-datta of Koṭṭūra, Mahendragiri of Pishṭapura, Damana of Eraṇḍapala and Kubera of Devarāshṭra.[1] Koṭṭūra is identified with Kothoor near the Mahendragiri in the Ganjam district

[1]These are fully dealt with in Chapter VII.

and Eraṇḍapalla is believed by some scholars to have been situated near Chicacole in the same district. Little, however, is known about these states. But there is evidence of the continued existence of the kingdoms of Pishṭapura and Devarāshṭra which are to be identified respectively with the modern state of Pithapuram in the Godavari district and the Yellamanchili *tāluk* of the Vizagapatam district. Some kings of these kingdoms are known from their copper-plate grants palaeographically assigned by scholars to about the fifth century A.D. Other records of the same period disclose the name of the royal city of Siṁhapura which is not mentioned in the Allahabad pillar inscription and probably flourished after the middle of the fourth century. Siṁhapura, identified with Singupuram near Chicacole, is supposed to have been the capital of a Kaliṅga kingdom as late as the twelfth century.[1]

The Pitṛibhaktas

A Mahārāja, named Chaṇḍavarman, is known from the Komarti grant[2] issued from victorious Siṁhapura in the king's sixth year of reign. The record describes Chaṇḍavarman as a *Kaliṅgādhipati* (lord of Kaliṅga), and the seal bears the word *Pitṛibhakta* (devoted to father). All the peculiarities of the above charter are present in the Tiritthana copper-plate grant[3] of the fourth regnal year of a king of the same name who seems to be no other than Chaṇḍavarman of the Komarti record. As, however, the script of the second charter is somewhat different, the existence of two kings named Chaṇḍavarman in the family of the rulers of Siṁhapura has been suggested. Another charter issued from Siṁhapura (here given in the Prākṛit from Sīhapura)

[1] R. C. Majumdar, Outline of the History of Kalinga in *DUS*. Vol. II. No. II, 1 ff.

[2] *EI*. IV, 142 ff.

[3] *ASI*. 1934-35, p. 64.

is the Bṛihatproshṭha grant[1] dated in the thirtieth regnal year of Mahārāja Umavarman, lord of Kaliṅga. The Dhavalapeta grant[2] and the Tekkali charter[3] of the year 9, issued by a king of the same name respectively from Sunagara and Vardhamānapura (modern Vadama in the Palakonda *tāluk* of the Vizagapatam district), probably belong to Mahārāja Umavarman of Siṁhapura, known from the Bṛihatproshṭha record. Sunagara and Vardhamānapura were probably secondary capitals or temporary residences of the king. That Umavarman and Chaṇḍavarman belonged to the same family is indicated by the word *Pitṛibhakta* said to be found on the seal of the Tekkali charter. The proximity of the reigns of these two rulers is not only suggested by palaeography, but is further supported by another fact. It is interesting to note that the Tiritthana grant of Chaṇḍavarman refers to a certain Rudradatta, son of Māṭrivara who seems to be the same as Māṭṛivara, son of Haridatta, mentioned in the Bṛihatproshṭha record of Umavarman. If this suggestion is to be accepted, Umavarman may probably be regarded as a near ancestor (possibly the father) of Chaṇḍavarman. Some scholars however take Māṭṛivara of the Bṛihatproshṭha inscription to be the grandson of his name-sake of the Tiritthana plates, and Mahārāja Umavarman as the son of king Chaṇḍavarman.

Another king associated with the above rulers seems to be Mahārāja Nanda-Prabhañjanavarman of the Chicacole grant,[4] which not only belongs to the same epoch, but bears on the seal the word *Pitṛibhakta* as on the seals of some of the charters of Umavarman and Chaṇḍavarman. The king is also described as 'lord of the entire Kaliṅga'. His charter was issued from the *Vāsaka* (the kings residence or camp) at the victorious Sārapallikā. The word *Pitṛibhakta* found on the seals of Umavarman

[1] *EI.* XII, 4 ff.
[2] *JAHRS.* X, 143-44.
[3] *Ibid.* VI, 53 ff.
[4] *IA.* XIII, 48 ff.

Chaṇḍavarman and Nanda-Prabhañjanavarman probably suggests that all of them belonged to the same family and that the word was used as a dynastic designation. It is, however, tempting to suggest that the name Nanda-Prabhañjanavarman actually indicates Prabhanjanavarman of the Nanda family. One may point out in this connection that a king of the Nanda dynasty of Pāṭaliputra is associated with Kaliṅga in the Hathigumpha inscription of Khāravela and that a Nanda or Nandodbhava family is known to have ruled in the Jeypore-Nandapur region of Orissa, at least from the ninth century A.D.[1]

The Māṭharas

Almost contemporaneously with the Pitṛibhaktas of Siṁhapura in central Kaliṅga ruled the royal family of the Māṭharas who had originally their capital at Pishṭapura. The Ragolu grant[2] of Mahārāja Vāśishṭhīputra Śaktivarman which records a gift of land near Chicacole and describes the king as the lord of Kaliṅga and the ornament of the Māṭhara dynasty, was issued in the regnal year 13 from the city of Pishṭapura. The Māṭharas of south Kaliṅga thus appear to have conquered the heart of the kingdom of the Pitṛibhaktas in central Kaliṅga by the time of this monarch. It is interesting to note that the Sakunaka grant[3] of the regnal year 28 of Mahārāja Ananta-Śaktivarman, who is also called the lord of Kaliṅga and 'ornament of the Māṭhara family', was issued from Siṁhapura which was the capital of the Pitṛibhaktas. That Ananta-Śaktivarman was either identical with Śaktivarman of the Ragolu plates or, as is more probable, his immediate successor (possibly a son), seems to be indicated by the fact that apparently the same high official called *deśākshapaṭalādhikṛita*

[1] *Suc. Sāt.* p. 77 n.
[2] *EI.* XII, 1 ff.
[3] *ASI. op. cit.* p. 65.

talavara Arjunadatta in the Sakunaka grant of Ananta-Śaktivarman is mentioned in the Ragolu plates of Śaktivarman with a humbler title as *amātya* Arjunadatta. The *amātya* seems to have been raised to higher offices during the later part of his life. According to some scholars, the name Ananta-Śaktivarman really indicates king Śaktivarman who was the son of Anantavarman, while others suggest that Ananta-Śaktivarman was a uccessor of Śaktivarman with the possibility of a king named nantavarman intervening between them.

The Vāsishṭhas

Another 'lord of Kaliṅga' who had his *adhishṭhāna* (capital) at Pishṭapura was the *Paramamāheśvara* Anantavarman who issued the Srungavarapukota[1] and Siripuram grants,[2] palaeographically assigned to the second half of the fifth or the beginning of the sixth century. King Anantavarman was the son of Mahārāja Prabhañjanavarman and the grandson of Mahārāja Guṇavarman. The Srungavarapukota charter, issued from Pishṭapura, describes Guṇavarman as the lord of Devarāshṭra and Prabhañjanavarman as the moon in the Vāsishṭha family. In the Siripuram grant, issued from Devapura which was apparently the capital of Devarāshṭra in the Vizagapatam district, Guṇavarman is mentioned as the moon in the Vāsishṭha family but not as the lord of Devarāshṭra. The above facts may suggest that these kings of the Vāsishṭha family were originally rulers of central Kaliṅga, but that they later conquered South Kaliṅga from the Māṭharas and transferred their headquarters to Pishṭapura. It is, however, uncertain whether the Vāsishṭhas were related to the family of the rulers of Siṁhapura represented by Umavarman, Chaṇḍavarman and Nanda-Prabhañjanavarman. But it is tempting to suggest the identification of the Vāsishṭha

[1] *EI.* XXIII, 56 ff.
[2] *EI.* XXIV, 47 ff.

king Prabhañjanavarman with Nanda-Prabhañjanavarman. If this suggestion is accepted, we may possibly regard the king as born of a girl of the Nanda family.[1] But the identification must be regarded as tentative as the seal of Anantavarman's records does not bear the word *Pitṛibhakta* like those of the charters of Umavarman, Chaṇḍavarman and Nanda-Prabhañjanavarman. The Vāsisṭhas as well as the Māṭharas of Kaliṅga appear to have been matrimonially related to many royal families represented by kings who had the metronymics Vāsishṭhīputra and Māṭharīputra.

Other Dynasties

A king named Viśākhavarman is known to have issued the Koroshanda grant[2] in his seventh regnal year from victorious Śrīpura which is identified with modern Siripuram in the Vizagapatam District. He does not call himself the lord of Kaliṅga and his relations with other kings of the same region and period cannot be determined with any amount of certainty.

The history of Kaliṅga about the fifth century A.D. seems to have been marked by the struggle between the royal houses of Pishṭapura and Siṁhapura for the supreme authority over Kaliṅga. The regular use of the title *Kaliṅgādhipati* by most of the rulers no doubt points to the political ideal of the period which may or may not have been realised in practice. The epithet *Sakala-Kalīṅgādhipati* (lord of the entire Kaliṅga country) applied to Nanda-Prabhañjanavarman probably shows that some of the *Kaliṅgādhipatis* ruled only over parts of the country. When the kings of central and southern Kaliṅga were struggling for supremacy, a new royal line, that of the Gaṅgas of Kaliṅganagara (often identified with Mukhaliṅgam in the Ganjam Dis-

[1] Cf. Sircar, *JIH.* XV, 270; R. C. Majumdar, *HBR.* I, 190.
[2] *EI.* XXI, 23 ff.

trict), was established in the northern part of the country. Kings of the Gaṅga dynasty used an era of their own which is supposed by some scholars to have started from about 496 A.D. The Jirjingi grant[1] (year 39=*c.* 535 A.D.) of Indravarman is possibly the earliest record dated in the Gaṅga era. It was the Gaṅgas who subdued the rulers of central Kaliṅga in the sixth century, while the rulers of South Kaliṅga were supplanted by the Chālukyas in the beginning of the seventh century. We do not know what relations the early rulers of Pishṭapura and the Chālukya conquerors of that kingdom had with king Pṛithivī-Mahārāja of the Tandivada[2] plates (issued in the year 46 from Pishṭapura and palaeographically assigned to the beginning of the seventh century), who was the son of Vikramendra and grandson of Mahārāja Raṇadurjaya.

Besides the 'lords of Kaliṅga', there is reference to an unnamed 'lord of Chikura' in an inscription[3] found at Sarabhavaram lying about 20 miles from Rajahmundry. He was probably a feudatory of the kings of Pishṭapura. Another inscription[4] has been discovered at Podagarh in the Jeypore Agency (Vizagapatam District) belonging to the twelfth year of the son of king Bhavadatta of the Nala dynasty. It is not known whether these Nalas were related to the mighty Nalas of Nandivardhana in Berar who subdued the Vākāṭakas and were themselves overthrown by the Chālukyas of Badami in the second half of the sixth century.

Another dynasty of rulers holding sway over parts of the Ganjam and Puri Districts in northern Kaliṅga was that of the Śailodbhavas who had their capital in Koṅgoda in the Ganjam District. According to the Khurda[5] grant and the Ganjam plates

---

1 *Sel. Ins.* I, p. 458 ff.
2 *JOR.* IX, 188 ff.
3 *EI.* XIII, 304.
4 *SIE.* 1921-22, p. 95 ; *EI.* XIX, 101.
5 *JASB.* LXXII, Part I, 284 ff.

(dated 619 A.D.),[1] *Mahārāja Mahāsāmanta* Sainyabhīta-Mādhavarāja II, who was a feudatory of king Śaśāṅka of Gauḍa, was the son of Ayaśobhīta and grandson of Sainyabhīta-Mādhavarāja I.[2] Sainyabhīta-Mādhavarāja II appears to be no other than Sainyabhīta II-Mādhava-varman who issued the Buguda, Puri, and Cuttack Museum grants.[3] The Buguda record, like the Parikud charter[4] of the son of Sainyabhīta-Mādhava-varman II, refers to some members of this family *viz.*, Pulindasena, who was famous amongst the peoples of Kaliṅga, Śailodbhava, Raṇabhīta and his son Sainyabhīta I, and Ayaśobhīta and his son Sainyabhīta II, the exact relation between the last two groups and between them and their predecessors not being stated. The Śailodbhava feudatory of Śaśāṅka seems to have ruled for some time after the death of his overlord when probably he issued the Khurda grant as an independent 'lord of Kaliṅga', although it is uncertain whether his son Ayaśobhīta II-Madhyamarāja performed the Vājapeya and Aśvamadha sacrifices before or after 643 A.D. when Harsha, after subduing the Gauḍas, made an attempt to recover Koṅgoda, the recently lost dependency of Gauḍa. As Sainyabhīta-Mādhava-varman II seems to have flourished about *c.* 610 to 630 A.D., his great-grandfather Raṇa-

[1] *EI.* VI, 143 ff.

[2] He is called Mādhavarāja in the Ganjam grant and Sainyabhīta in the Khurda plates.

[3] *EI.* III, 43 ff; Bhandarkar's List, No. 1674; *EI.* XXIV, 149. The Puri grant calls the king also Śrīnivāsa. Some scholars assign Sainyabhīta II-Mādhava-varman of the Buguda and Parikud grants (which are considered late on grounds of palaeography) long after the issue of the Khurda and Ganjam records; cf. *JAHRS.* X, 1 ff. But the striking resemblance in the Śailodbhava genealogy furnished by both sets of the records can hardly be explained away. The passage *tasy-āpi vaṁśe* (*i.e.*, [born] in his family) in regard to the relation between Sainyabhīta I and his successor Ayaśobhita in the second set of the charters probably suggests that Ayaśobhīta, a member of the Śailodbhava family, was the adopted son of Sainyabhīta I. The palaeographical problem seems to be solved by the Cuttack Museum grant which is written in a script similar to that of the Ganjam grant, but gives the genealogy as in the Buguda charter.

[4] *EI.* XI, 284 ff.

bhīta may have founded the Śailodbhava dynasty of Koṅgoda in the first half of the sixth century. The names of Śailodbhava (possibly an eponym) and Pulindasena do not appear to be historical. The title *Mahāsāmanta*, sometimes applied to the names of the predecessors of Sainyabhīta-Mādhavarāja II, probably suggests that Koṅgoda acknowledged the suzerainty of Gauḍa even before Śaśāṅka's time (*c.* 600 to 625 A.D.). It is, however, also not unlikely that the Śailodbhavas were originally feudatories of the Māṇa Kings, whose original principality lay somewhere in the hilly region between the Midnapore and Gaya Districts, but who gradually extended their sway over nearly the whole of modern Orissa by the latter part of the sixth century A.D.[1]

3. KOSALA (DAKSHIṆA-KOSALA) AND MEKALA

Dakshiṇa-Kosala (literally, South Kosala) comprising roughly the present Raipur, Bilaspur and Sambalpur districts of the Central Provinces and Orissa was one of the earliest Aryan settlements in the Deccan. The name of the country suggests its colonisation by the princes of the Ikshvāku dynasty of Ayodhyā, capital of the Kosala (Uttara-Kosala, Mahā-Kosala[2]) *janapada*, in the Fyzabad region of the United

---

[1]Cf. *JRASBL.* XI, 4-5. King Śambhuyaśas of the Mudgala or Maudgalya family, known from the Soro (579 A.D.) and Patiakella (602 A.D.) grants (*EI.* XXIII, 197 ; X, 285), ruled over Dakhiṇa-Tosalī (territory round Dhauli in the Puri and Cuttack Districts) and Uttara-Tosalī (the Soro region in the Balasore District) as a feudatory of kings of the Māṇa family. The foundation of the Māṇa and Mudgala houses may probably be placed long before the date of Śambhuyaśas. The Soro area in Uttara-Tosalī forming part of the Oḍra *vishaya* soon passed from the Mudgalas into the hands of Soma-datta and Bhānu-datta who held sway over Utkala (north-eastern Balasore and the adjoining region) and sometimes also over Daṇḍabhukti (area round Danton in the Midnapore District) under Śaśāṅka of Gauḍa. The Māṇas were probably responsible for the name of Manbhum.

[2]South Kosala is sometimes wrongly represented as Mahā-Kosala by modern writers ; cf. *IC.* VIII, 57. The name is also spelt Kośala, and the capital city is sometimes called Kośalā ; cf. Mekala and Mekalā.

Provinces. The early history of South Kosala is wrapped in obscurity. According to traditions recorded by the Chinese pilgrims who visited India, the celebrated Mahāyānist teacher Nāgārjuna lived for some time at a Buddhist monastery near the capital of Śouth Kosala which was then under the rule of a king of the Sātavāhana dynasty. The Sātavāhana contemporary of Nāgārjuna, who is said to have flourished in the second century A.D., is called *tri-samudrādhipati* in the *Harsha-charita* and may be identified with the *Dakshiṇāpathapati* Gautamīputra Śātakarṇi (*c.* 106 to 130 A.D.), called *tri-samudra-toya-pīta-vāhana* in a Nasik inscription.[1] It must however be admitted that the elaborate list of countries over which Gautamīputra Śātakarṇi is stated in the Nasik record to have held direct sway does not contain the name of Kosala. A king named Mahendra ruled over the South Kosala country about the middle of the fourth century A.D. when the Gupta emperor Samudra-gupta led his victorious campaigns against the kingdoms of the Dakshiṇāpatha. The influence of Gupta coin-types on the coinage of Dakshiṇa-Kosala[2] as well as the use of the Gupta era in this land probably suggests that the kings of South Kosala became subordinate allies of Samudra-gupta and his immediate successors. The Arang (Raipur district, C.P.) plates[3] of *Mahārāja* Bhīmasena II were issued from Suvarṇa-nadī (the river Son) in the year 282 of the Gupta era, corresponding to 601 A.D. The record mentions *Mahārāja* Sūra, his son *Mahārāja* Dayita I, his son *Mahārāja* Vibhīshaṇa, his son *Mahārāja* Bhīmsena I, his son *Mahārāja* Dayitavarman II, and his son *Mahārāja* Bhīmasena II. Allowing, as is usual, a quarter of a century for each generation, king Sūra, the founder of this line of kings, may be assigned to the second half of the fifth

---

[1]Cf. *PHAI*[4]. p. 391 n.

[2]The silver coins of Prasannamātra bear the figure of Garuḍa together with the discus and conch symbols.

[3]Hiralal, *DL*, p. 100, No. 127.

century A.D. when the Imperial Gupta dynasty began to decline. Sūra's family seems to have ruled in the northern part of Dakshiṇa-Kosala.

The Śarabhapurīyas

Contemporaneously with the family of Śūra was ruling a line of kings who had their capital at the city of Śarabhapura. The city has not been satisfactorily identified, different scholars locating it at Sambalpur, Sarangarh, Sarpagarh and other places.[1] But as the charters issued from Śarabhapura have been found about the Raipur District, C.P., the royal city appears to have been situated not far from modern Sirpur (ancient Śrīpura which became the later capital of the Śarabhapurīyas) in the same district.

The city of Śarabhapura was apparently founded by a king named Śarabha who seems also to have been the founder of the dynasty of the Śarabhapura rulers. King Śarabha is actually known to have been the father of *Mahārāja* Narendra who issued the Pipardula grant[2] from Śarabhapura in the third year of his reign. This Śarabha may further be identified with Sarabharāja, maternal grandfather of Goparāja, who was a vassal of Bhānugupta of the Imperial Gupta dynasty and died at Eran in 510 A.D.[3] If this identification is to be accepted, both the kings Śarabha and Narendra would probably be placed about the latter part of the fifth century when the hold of the Guptas on their subordinate allies began to weaken. The emblem of the Śarabhapura kings was the Gaja-Lakshmī which is engraved on the seals attached to their copper-plate charters.

A later king who ruled at Śarabhapura was Jayarāja (often called Mahā-Jayarāja), son of Prasanna, known from his own

---

[1] *IHQ*. XIX, 144 n.
[2] *Ibid*. p. 139 ff.
[3] *CII*. III, 91.

Arang grant[1] as well as from his seals attached to some of the charters of his brother's son Sudevarāja (sometimes called Mahā-Sudevarāja). King Sudeva, who was the son of Mānamātra and grandson of Prasanna, issued his Khariar, Arang, Sarangarh and Raipur grants[2] from Śarabhapura, the latest of the charters being dated in the regnal year 10. The fuller form of the name of Prasanna was Prasannamātra as is known from his silver coins, only a few of which have so far been discovered and published[3]. We do not know if king Prasannamātra was the immediate successor of *Mahārāja* Narendra, but apparently the interval between the reign-periods of the two rulers was not long.

King Prasannamātra had at least two sons, *viz.* Jayarāja and Mānamātra, the first of whom ruled for more than four years. It is as yet uncertain whether Mānamātra was an older or younger brother of king Jayarāja and whether he ruled at all as a king of Śarabhapura. He is no doubt usually identified with king Mānāṅka, "the ornament of the Rāshṭrakūṭas", who is known from the Uṇḍikavāṭikā grant[4] of his great-grandson Abhimanyu residing at Mānapura (supposed to be the modern Manpur near Bandhogarh in the Rewah State). Mānāṅka was the father of Devarāja (identified by some scholars with Sudevarāja of Śarabhapura), grandfather of Bhavishya and great-grandfather of Abhimanyu. These kings apparently had the dynastic name Rāshṭrakūṭa which points to the fact that the progenitor of the family was a *Rāshṭrakūṭa* (governor of a *rāshṭra* or province) under some king. The facts that the

---

[1]*CII.* III, 193 ff.

[2]*EI.* IX, 172 ff; *MKSP.* II, 39-40 ; *EI.* IX, 283 ff ; *CII.* III, 197 f.

[3]Two of Prasannamātra's coins were discoverd by the Maha-Kosala Historical Society; cf. *MKSP.* II, p. 24 of the Appendix. Two other coins are known to be in the possession of Mr. S. K. Saraswati of the Calcutta University. One of these is in a very satisfactory state of preservation and the legend *śrī-prasannamātra* in box-headed characters is perfectly clear.

[4]*EI.* VIII, 165 f; Dubreuil, *AHD.*, p. 77.

Śarabhapura kings never refer to themselves as belonging to the Rāshṭrakūṭa dynasty, that the territories over which the two ruling families held sway are not identical, and that unlike the Śarabhapura charters the Uṇḍikavāṭikā grant with its seal containing the figure of a lion is not written in the box-headed script, render the identification of the Rāshṭrakūṭa king Mānāṅka with Mānamātra of Śarabhapura highly improbable.[1]

Two sons of Mānamātra certainly became kings, the eldest of them probably being Sudeva who ruled at least for about ten years. *Mahārāja* Pravararāja, probably a younger son of Mānamātra, is known from the Thakurdiya grant[2] issued from Śrīpura (modern Sirpur) in the third year of his reign. King Pravara seems to have been the founder of the new capital where he transferred his headquarters from the old city of Śarabhapura, the capital of his predecessors. He probably flourished about the middle of the sixth century in the latter half of which the Pāṇḍuvaṁśī kings, originally rulers of the land towards the west and north-west of Dakshiṇa-Kosala, became lords of South Kosala. The rule of the Śarabhapurīyas was probably terminated by the Pāṇḍuvaṁśi ruler Tīvara who issued his charters from

[1]The identification of Mānāṅka of the Uṇḍikavāṭikā grant with Mānāṅka, father of Devarāja and grandfather of Avidheya who issued the Pandarangapalli grant discovered near Kolhapur, is very probable. Although the Pandarangapalli charter does not refer to the Rāshṭrakūṭa lineage of the kings, the script and the seal of the two records are remarkably similar. Mānāṅka seems to be described in this inscription as the conqueror of Vidarbha (modern Berar region) and Aśmaka (district round Bodhan, ancient Paudanya, in the Hyderabad State according to Raychaudhuri). He is probably also said to have been the chastiser (*Praśāsitā*) of the Kuntalas, referring no doubt to the Kadambas of Banavāsī. It is probable that these Rāshṭrakūṭas ruled somewhere in the southern part of the Bombay Presidency. Mirashi locates them about the Satara District; cf. *ABORI*. XXV, 36 ff. His suggestions that Mānāṅka and his successors were the 'lords of Kuntala' referred to in the *Kuntaleśvaradautya* and the Vākāṭaka grants and that Devarāja may be identified with Devarāja of the Gomin dynasty who issued the Siroda grant from Chandrapura (Chandor near Goa) are unconvincing. For some unwarranted suggestions about the 'empire' of these Rāshṭrakūṭas; see *ASM*. 1929, p. 197 ff.

[2]*EI*. XXII. 15.

Śrīpura. Tīvara may have occupied the kingdom of the Śarabhapurīyas either in the reign of king Pravara or in that of one of his immediate successors.[1]

The Pāṇḍuvaṁśīs

There is difference of opinion as regards the date of king Tīvara (often called Tīvaradeva and Mahāśiva-Tīvararāja) of the Pāṇḍuvaṁśa.[2] Some scholars assign his records to the eighth century A.D. The theory seems to have been influenced by the fact that the box-headed script employed in Tīvara's copper-plate grants resembles that used in the charters of Vākāṭaka Pravara-sena II who was ascribed by early writers to the same century. It is now well known that Vākāṭaka Pravara-sena II was the daughter's son of Chandra-gupta II (376-414 A.D.) and that he must have flourished in the fifth century A.D. The Pāṇḍuvaṁśī king Ṭīvara may likewise be placed about the fifth or sixth century.[3] The ascription of this ruler to about the middle of the sixth century is suggested by his probable contemporaneity with the Vishṇukuṇḍin king Mādhavavarman I (*c.* 535 to 585 A.D.) and the Maukhari prince Sūryavarman (553 A.D.). According to the Ipur and Polamuru grants, Mādhavavarman I, who flourished more than a generation earlier than the Eastern Chālukya king Jayasiṁha I (*c.* 633-63 A.D.), claims to have captured Trivaranagara, *i.e.* the capital city of king Trivara (Tīvara). The Sirpur inscription of Bālārjuna,

[1]See *infra*, p. 90. Mirashi suggests the dates *c.* 515-30 for Pravara and *c.* 530-50 for Tīvara the conqueror of Kosala.

[2]The family is called the Pāṇḍuvaṁśa or Pāṇḍavavaṁśa in earlier records; but in later records it is referred to as 'the family of the Moon' (*Chandrānvaya*, *Śaśadharānvaya*, *Somavaṁśa*). It is however better to call these kings Pāṇḍuvaṁśī to avoid a confusion with the later Somavaṁśis of Kosala.

[3]*Suc. Sāt.* pp. 129, 400; *IHQ*.XIX, 143 f. His identification with Trivara mentioned in the Kondedda grant of Śailodbhava Dharmarāja-Mānabhīta, grandson of Mādhavavarman II, is improbabb.

who was a grandson (actually, brother's grandson) of Tīvara, refers to the king's maternal grandfather Sūryavarman, a ruler (*nṛipa*) belonging to the dynasty of the Varmans who became great owing to their suzerainty over Magadha.[1] As these Varmans appear to be no other than the Maukharis, Sūryavarman, contemporary of Tīvara, is probably identical with Maukhari Iśānavarman's son of that name who, according to the Haraha inscription of 553 A.D., was possibly ruling over part of eastern U.P. as his father's viceroy. King Tīvara of the Pāṇḍuvaṁśa thus appears to have flourished about the middle of sixth century (*c.* 565-80 A.D.).

Tīvara, who issued his Rajim and Baloda grants[2] respectively in his seventh and ninth regnal years, was the son of king Nanna (called Nannadeva, Nannarājādhirāja and Nanneśvara), grandson of king Indrabala and great-grandson of king Udayana. If Tīvara ruled about the middle of the sixth century, the accession of his great-grandfather Udayana can hardly be assigned to a period later than the close of the fifth century. A rock inscription[3] at Kalanjar in the Banda district of U.P. mentions king Udayana of the Pāṇḍava family. His identification with his Śabara namesake defeated by a general of Pallava Nandivarman (*c.* 717-79 A.D.) is based on the supposed late date of the Pāṇḍuvaṁśis.[4] The Sirpur inscription[5] of Bālārjuna speaks of Indrabala as the son of Udayana. According to a record[6] of Nanna's time, originally discovered at Bhandak in the Chanda District of C.P., Indrabala appears to have had at least four sons. The eldest of them, Nanna, succeeded his father and is said to have 'conquered the earth'. The same record mentions the fourth brother of Nanna as Bhavadeva (also as Raṇakeśarin and Chintādurga) who restored a decayed

---

[1] *PHAI*[4]. p. 512 n; *IHQ*. XIX, 278 n; *EI*, XI, 190 ff.
[2] *CII*. III, 294; *EI*. VII. 104 ff. [3] *EI*. IV, 257 n.
[4] The fact that Sabara Udayana was defeated at Nelveli (Tinnevelly) points to his southern origin.
[5] *IA*. XVIII, 179 f. [6] *JRAS*. 1905, p. 624 ff.

temple founded by an ancient king of the Bhandak region named Sūryaghosha. The earliest record of the Pāṇḍuvaṁśīs in South Kosala seems to be the Kharod (Bilaspur District) inscription[1] of Iśānadeva, another brother of Nanna. It therefore seems that the Pāṇḍuvaṁśīs originally ruled over wide regions of Central India and that they invaded Dakshiṇa-Kosala during the rule of Nanna. But Tīvara is called *Kosalādhipati* (lord of Kosala) on his seal and *Prāpta-sakala-Kosalādhipatya* (one who obtained the sovereignty of the entire Kosala country) in his charters. It is thus possible that the occupation of the country was completed by this king.

King Bālārjuna (sometimes called Mahāśivagupta Balarjuna or Śivagupta Bālārjuna) who, according to the Sirpur inscription, 'conquered the earth' with the help of his brother Raṇakeśarin, was the son of Harshagupta and Vāsaṭā (daughter of Suryavarman of the Varman dynasty of Magadha), and grandson of Chandragupta, a brother of Tīvara. It is uncertain whether Chandragupta was an older or younger brother of Tīvara, but he seems to have ruled as a king. His identification with a prince of the same name mentioned in the Sanjan grant as defeated by Rāshṭrakūṭa Govinda III (*c.* 794-814 A.D.) cannot be accepted if his brother Tīvara is to be placed about the middle of the sixth century. Bālārjuna, grandson of Chandragupta, may be assigned to the first half of the seventh century. He himself or one of his immediate successors may have been defeated by Chālukya Pulakeśin II who led an expedition against Kosala some time before 634 A.D.[2] Little is known about the end of the dynasty and its relations with the later Somavaṁśīs of Kosala who flourished about the tenth, eleventh and twelfth centuries A.D.

---

[1]Hiralal, *DL.* p. 113 ff, No. 149.

[2]A Sirpur inscription refers to Sivanandin, son and governor of Nityānanda who has been identified with Bālārjuna; cf. Bhandarkar's List, p. 396 n.

We are equally ignorant of the relation of this family with the Pāṇḍuvaṁśīs of Mekala, the region round the modern Amarakantaka hills. A copper-plate charter,[1] recently found at a village, called Bamhani, in the Sohagpur *tahsīl* of the Rewa State in Baghelkhand, gives the names of four members of this family, viz., Jayabala, his son Vatsarāja, his son *Mahārāja* Nāgabala, and his son *Mahārāja* Bharata or Bharatabala (*alias* Indra). The last two kings are not only styled *Mahārāja* but also bear the epithets *Parama-māheśvara*, *Parama-brahmaṇya* and *Parama-guru-devatādhidaivata-viśesha*. Queen Lokaprakāśā, wife of the fourth king Bharatabala, is supposed to have been described as a princess of Kosalā and as one having a divine origin. It has been suggested that she belonged to the family of the Pāṇḍuvaṁśīs of Kosala ; but it is improbable in view of the late date of the Pāṇḍuvaṁśī occupation of that country. The palaeography of the Bamhani record seems to indicate that the Pāṇḍuvaṁśīs of Mekala, named above, ruled in the fifth century A.D., and this agrees fairly well with what has been said above regarding the origin and early history of the Pāṇḍuvaṁśīs in Central India. It may be surmised that while Jayabala and Vatsarāja were mere feudatories, either of the Guptas or of the Vākāṭakas, Nāgabala established an independent principality in Mekala in the second half of the fifth century A.D., and was more or less a contemporary of Udayana, the founder of the other branch of the family.

The Vākāṭaka king Narendra-sena (second half of the fifth century), who re-established the fortunes of his family, claims to have the kings of Kosalā, Mekalā and Mālava as his subordinate allies, and apparently the Pāṇḍuvaṁśīs were ruling in Mekala about this time. It has been suggested that there is a veiled reference to Narendra-sena in the Bamhani grant, indicating that Bharatabala recognised him as his overlord ; but this is extremely doubtful.

[1] *Bhārata-Kaumudī*, p. 215 ff.

CHAPTER V

THE VĀKĀṬAKAS

1. The Deccan at *c*. 250 a.d.

The history of Berar and Central Provinces during the first half of the 3rd century a.d. is still shrouded in considerable mystery. These territories constituted the kernel of the Vākāṭaka kingdom, but we do not know who was ruling over them before the rise of that dynasty. When the Sātavāhana empire collapsed by *c*. 225 a.d., we know how the Ikshvākus, the Chutu-Sātakarṇis and Ābhīras succeeded in carving out small principalities in its outlying provinces like central Andhra-deśa, southern Karṇātaka and western Mahārāshṭra ; but what happened in the central territories of that empire is not known. Probably local officers developed into small independent kings, each seeking to extend his kingdom at the cost of others.

Circumstances were thus favourable for the establishment of a new empire in the Deccan, when the Vākāṭakas rose to power in the latter half of the 3rd century a.d. The rulers of none of the kingdoms mentioned in the last paragraph had shown the capacity to extend their dominions or spheres of influence beyond their small principalities, and found a Deccan-wide empire. The achievements of the Western Kshatrapas under Rudra-dāman I, had no doubt shown that they once possessed the grit and leadership necessary for this purpose. But their power was on the decline by the middle of the 3rd century ; the Mālavas had inflicted a smashing defeat upon them (*ante*, p. 34) and wrested several districts from their dominion. The Śakas therefore could no longer aspire to control the politics or the destinies of the Deccan. The Yaudheyas, the

Arjunāyanas, the Nāgas and the Mālavas had reasserted their independence recently, but in ancient times it was almost impossible for a trans-Vindhyan power to establish a stable empire in the Deccan. By *c.* 250 A.D. the political situation therefore was fairly favourable for a spirited and ambitious chieftain to found a new empire, which might recall the glories of the defunct Sātavāhana power. The first two rulers of the Vākāṭaka family eventually succeeded in achieving this goal.

2. Vākāṭak Chronology

Before however proceeding to narrate the Vākāṭaka history, we shall have to say a few words about its chronology, which is not yet definitely settled. The theory that the Chedi era, starting in 248-9 A.D., marks the establishment of the Vākāṭaka[1] power would have given us a fixed starting point, but it is altogether untenable. It is but reasonable to expect that the Vākāṭakas would have used this era at least in their own official documents, if they had started it themselves. As it is, not a single Vākāṭaka copper-plate is dated in this era ; everyone of them refers to the regnal year of the grantor.[2] The theory that the Vākāṭakas founded the Chedi era to mark the foundation of their power is thus untenable and it cannot be argued that they

[1]Jayaswal, *History of India* 150 A.D.-350 A.D., pp. 108-11; Pai in *JIH.* XIV, 184 ff.

[2]It is no doubt argued by Pai and Jayaswal that a seal of the emperor Pravara-sena I found at Bhita is dated in the 37th year of the Chedi era (*Ibid.*). The seal bears only the title *Mahārājādhiraja* and has no complete proper name, the letters *raka* alone being preserved. It also bears no date, as is usually the case with seals.

Jayaswal argues that we have got a coin of Rudra-sena I dated in the year 100 of the Chedi era. The coin in question bears no date, and was issued at Kauśāmbi about 400 years before the birth of this ruler. Similarly what Jayaswal holds to be a coin of Pravara-sena, dated in the year 76 of the Chedi era is really an undated coin issued by king Virasena of Mathura. *JNSI.* V, 130-4.

rose to power in 248-9 A.D., because that is the starting point of the Chedi era.

We can determine the main outline of the Vākāṭaka chronology only with the help of the known date of Prabhāvatī-guptā, the queen of the Vākāṭaka king Rudra-sena II, who was a daughter of the Gupta emperor Chandra-gupta II (*c.* 375-414 A.D.). Prabhāvatī-guptā was widowed early in her life and her surviving son could assume the reins of the administration only in *c.* 410 A.D. Her husband Rudra-sena II, therefore, probably died in *c.* 390 A.D. He had a short reign of about five years. But his father Pṛithvī-sheṇa had a fairly long and prosperous reign and we may place it between *c.* 360 A.D. and 385 A.D. An expression[1] used in connection with this ruler in several Vākāṭaka charters shows that the family was ruling prosperously for about a hundred years before his accession in *c.* 360 A.D. We can, therefore, place the reign of the founder of the family Vindhyaśakti between *c.* 255 and 275. His son Pravara-sena I, who assumed the imperial title as a result of extensive conquests, had a long reign. The Purāṇas say that it lasted for 60 years and we may well accept that statement, for inscriptions show that he was succeeded not by a son, but by a grandson. The rule of Pravara-sena I, therefore, may be placed between *c.* 275 and 335 A.D. and that of his grandson Rudra-sena I between *c.* 335 and 360 A.D. We have shown already how the next ruler Pṛithvi-sheṇa I is known to have been ruling from *c.* 360 to 385 A.D. The known synchronism of Rudra-sena II with Chandra-gupta II, along with other fairly reliable evidence referred to above, thus enables us to determine the approximate date of Vindhyaśakti, the founder of the dynasty, as *c.* 255-275. The discovery of new epigraphs may necessitate some adjustment in the chronology suggested above, but it will not be considerable.

---

[1] समुदितस्यवर्षशतमभिवर्धमानकोषदण्डसाधनसन्तानपुत्रपौत्रिण: *EI.* III, 261.

3. The Home of the Vākāṭakas

Like the Śuṅga, the Kāṇva and the Sātāvahana rulers of the earlier period, the Vākāṭakas were Brāhmaṇas, their *gotra* being Vishṇuvṛiddha. Their original home is not yet definitely known. One view is that the family hailed from Bijnaur-Bagāṭ, a village in Bundelkhand.[1] It is quite possible that a family coming from the village Bagāṭ or Vakāṭ may have been known as Vākāṭaka, but the connection of early Vākāṭakas with this territory is not yet definitely proved. The Kureha inscription does not refer to the Vākāṭakas,[2] as has been contended, nor do the Purāṇas refer to any connection of the early rulers of this dynasty with the Kilakilā river of the Punna State,[3] as has been maintained. A third century inscription from Amarāvatī in Andhra country refers to a Vākāṭaka pilgrim, who had come to visit the local *stūpa* ; this may suggest that the village Vākāṭa, to which he belonged, was rather to the south than to the north of the Vindhyas. We must await further discoveries to settle satisfactorily the question of the home of the Vākāṭakas.

4. Vindhyaśakti. *c.* 255—275 A.D.

Whatever may have been the original home of the Vākāṭakas, there is clear evidence to show that the sphere of their early activity was neither in Bundelkhand nor in Andhra country, but in Western C.P. The Purāṇas mention Vindhyaśakti, the founder of the dynasty, as a ruler of Vidiśā (modern Bhilsa near Bhopal), and Purikā, which is mentioned as its early capital, is connected with Vidarbha (modern Berar) and Aśmaka by ancient geographers.[4] We may, therefore, well

[1] *HIJ*. pp. 66-68.

[2] Its reading is *Vaṅkatrika* and not *Vākāṭaka*; see *HIJ*. Pl. V.

[3] The Purāṇas state that Vindhyaśakti came after Kilakila kings and not from Kilakila country. *DKA*. p. 48.

[4] The Purikā province is coupled with Dāśārṇa in *Brihatsaṁhita*, XIV, 10, and mentioned along with Vidarbha and Aśmaka in the *Mārkaṇḍeya Purāṇa*. CVII, 48.

presume that the nucleus of the original Vākāṭaka principality lay in Western C.P. or Berar.

Vindhyaśakti is probably not the personal name but the title (*biruda*) of the founder of the dynasty, and he may have probably got it because he had succeeded in incorporating in his original patrimony the territories on the outskirts of the Vindhya range. What induced Vindhyaśakti to make a bid for founding an independent kingdom, we do not know. It was probably personal ambition, not untinged with a desire to establish a Brāhmaṇa state which may encourage the old orthodox Vedic religion.

Vindhyasakti has been described as 'the founder of the family' in the Purāṇas and as its banner '*Vaṁśaketu*' in one official inscription.[1] It is thus clear that it was he who secured for the family a definite status among the contemporary rulers. How he succeeded in doing this, and what were the main incidents of his career is still a mystery ; it can be solved only by new discoveries. We may, however, well presume that the ancestors of Vindhyaśakti were probably local officers in Berar under the defunct Sātavāhana empire, and that they continued to administer the territories under their charge even when that power disappeared. The patrimony, which Vindhyaśakti inherited, probably comprised of a district or two in Berar or Western C. P. ; his achievement consisted in extending its limits across the Vindhya range, so as to include a portion of Malwa. This may perhaps explain why the Purāṇas mention Vindhyaśakti among the kings of Vidiśā in eastern Malwa.

The districts annexed by Vindhyaśakti were mostly a kind of no man's land at that time, and the expansion of the patrimony was probably achieved more by diplomacy than by force. Vindhyaśakti, however, assumed no regal titles and probably received no formal coronation. His achievements were soon

[1] *Hyd. Ar. S.* No. 14.

eclipsed by the glorious exploits of his illustrious son. His name, therefore, was omitted from the family genealogy when it was first compiled for the copper-plate charters about 125 years after his death.

5. Emperor Pravara-sena I

(*c.* 275 to *c.* 335 A.D.)

Vindhyaśakti was succeeded by his son Pravara-sena I. He is the only ruler of the dynasty to assume the title of *Samrāṭ* or emperor, and we may therefore well presume that it was he who succeeded in extending the Vākāṭaka hegemony over the greater part of the Deccan. How he succeeded in doing this is however not yet known ; the Purāṇas and inscriptions grow eloquent in referring to his four Horse-sacrifices but not in describing the specific exploits that justified their performance.

The career of the emperor Pravara-sena I has at present to be reconstructed with the help of very meagre data. His grandson, Rudra-sena I, who succeeded him, was ruling over the greater part of C.P. One of his sons Sarva-sena, who founded a branch line, is known to be ruling over southern Berar and north-western portions of the Nizam's dominion.[1] The Purāṇas state that he had two other sons, who were assigned separate principalities, presumably outside these areas. The empire of Pravara-sena I was thus fairly extensive at the time of his death and it is a pity that we should not be able to fix its boundaries definitely.

The development of the small patrimony of Pravara-sena in western C. P. into this empire probably took place stage by stage. He is known to have performed four Horse-sacrifices,

[1]The Basim plates of this ruler give a village in the Nanded district of Hyderabad state. There are several Vākāṭaka records at Ajanta.

and they probably marked the termination of four successful campaigns.

One of them may have been directed towards the east and resulted in the annexation of the eastern and north-eastern districts of C. P. right up to Jubbulpore and Balaghat. In course of time, one of the princes was put in charge of this territory.

A second campaign may have been directed towards the south and it resulted in the annexation of southern Berar and the north-western part of the Nizam's dominions. Epigraphs definitely show that its north-western portion was under the Vākāṭaka rule, and was being ruled by Sarva-sena, another son of Pravara-sena, who eventually founded a branch line in that territory. It is, however, not unlikely that it may have extended further to the south. A tradition recorded in *Śrīśailasthala-māhātmya* states that a daughter of king Chandra-gupta, named Chandrāvatī, daily used to offer a garland of jasmine flowers to god Mallikārjuna of Śrīśaila, situated in the Karnool district on the Kṛishnā.[1] The daughter of Chandra-gupta, here referred to, may have been Prabhāvatī-guptā, Chandrāvatī being possibly her pre-marriage name. This tradition would suggest the inclusion of Śrīśaila in the Vākāṭaka kingdom, showing thereby that it extended over a considerable part of the Nizam's dominions even in the time of Pravara-sena I, since none of his successors has been credited with any important military expedition in this direction.

The history of Andhradeśa, Southern Kośala and Baghelkhand is still imperfectly known during the reign of Pravara-sena I. The Ikshvākus of Andhradeśa had ceased to reign by *c.* 290 A.D. and the Śālaṅkāyanas came on the scene about 40 years later. The Naḷas of Chhattisgarh and Bastar state rose to power still later. Whether Pravara-sena took advantage of the

[1] *SIE.* 1914-15. p. 91

absence of a strong power in this region and brought it under his control, we do not definitely know. But there is nothing improbable in his having done so and appointed a third son to rule over the area. It is important to note in this connection that petty rulers in Baghelkhand like Vyāghrarāja of Ganj continued to acknowledge Vākāṭaka sovereignty even during the reign of Pṛithvī-sheṇa I[1] (360-385 A.D.), who is never credited with the conquest of this area. It is therefore very probable that Pravara-sena may have extended his sphere of influence over a considerable portion of Baghelkhand and Chhattisgarh.

The Śaka rulers of Gujarat and Kathiawar were the north-western neighbours of Pravara-sena. We have already shown how it is very probable that Pravara-sena succeeded in extending his suzerainty over them during the first quarter of the 4th century (*ante*, pp. 58-59). It must, however, be clearly stated that Pravara-sena's overlordship both over eastern Deccan, as well as Malwa, Gujarat and Kathiawar is still a theory, very probable no doubt, but lacking definite and conclusive proof.

The achievements of Pravara-sena I were thus indeed remarkable and they fully justified his assumption of the title of *samrāṭ* or emperor. From the position of the king of a petty kingdom in western C.P. he rose to be the ruler of a big empire comprising northern Mahārāshṭra, Berar, Central Provinces (to the south of the Narmadā) and a considerable part of Hyderabad state, which were all under the direct administration of the emperor or his sons. His sphere of influence extended over southern Kośala, Baghelkhand, Malwa, Gujarat and Kathiawar. A large part of the Deccan and some territories adjacent to it were thus included in his empire, and he could well adopt the title of emperor, which was not subsequently claimed by any of his descendants.

Dr. Jayaswal has, however, argued that Pravara-sena was

---

[1] *EI*. XVII, 13.

the lord paramount practically of the whole of India,[1] but this view is altogether untenable. The theory that this ruler controlled South India through one of his sons, who founded the Pallava dynasty, is yet a mere hypothesis, with no evidence whatsoever to support it ! The conquest of U.P. by Pravara-sena is based upon the attribution of the Mathurā coins of Vīrasena to the Vākāṭaka emperor. This attribution is altogether untenable.[2] It is further interesting to note that these so-called coins of Pravara-sena are never found in the heart of the Vākāṭaka kingdom, but only near Mathura. If Pravara-sena had really issued them, one cannot explain why they should be conspicuous by their absence in the home provinces of his dominions. There is no evidence whatsoever to support the view that Pravara-sena had at any time conquered the Punjab and driven out the Kushāṇas into Afghanistan. There is nothing to indicate that the Kushāṇas welcomed the Sassanian sovereignty as a means of protecting themselves against the attacks of Pravara-sena; as a matter of fact it was imposed upon them as early as *c.* 250 A. D., when Pravara-sena was probably yet to be born.

There is, therefore, no evidence whatsoever to show that Pravara-sena ever exercised any control either over South India or over the United Provinces or the Punjab. Nevertheless, his achievement in becoming the lord paramount of nearly the whole of the Deccan was fairly dazzling, well justifying his claim to the title of *samrāṭ*, which he formally assumed at the end of a Vājapeya sacrifice, specially celebrated for the purpose. Pravara-sena was an orthodox Hindu and in addition to the Vājapeya, he performed a number of other Vedic sacrifices like Bṛihaspatisava, Aśvamedha, Agnishṭoma, Āptoryāma, Ukthya, Shoḍaśin and Atirātra. Of these he performed Aśvamedha four

[1] *HIJ.* pp. 82-94.
[2] *JNSI.* *V*, 130-4. The legend clearly reads *Vīrasena* and not *Pravara-sena*; cf. Pl. II. 1.

times, probably at the conclusion of four different military campaigns.

Pravara-sena had four sons. These were appointed as viceroys over different provinces of the rapidly extending empire and they became independent after the death of the father, thereby considerably weakening the power of the Central Government. Of the four sons Gautamīputra[1] was the eldest. He, however, predeceased his father. Sarva-sena was probably the second son; he became the founder of a branch of the dynasty at Basim in southern Berar, which continued to flourish almost contemporaneously with the main Vākāṭaka house down to *c.* 525 A.D. The names of the third and fourth sons of Pravara-sena are not known; very probably they were ruling as viceroys in the eastern territories of the empire.

6. Rudra-sena I

(*c.* 335 A. D. to *c.* 360 A. D.)

Pravara-sena was succeeded by his grandson Rudra-sena, the son of Gautamīputra, in *c.* 335 A. D. His reign is shrouded in considerable mystery and has given rise to a number of controversies. The Vākāṭaka genealogy usually mentions his maternal grandfather, king Bhava-nāga of the Bhāraśiva dynasty ruling at Padmāvatī near Gwalior.[2] It is clear that he must have been of considerable help to his young grandson at some critical juncture.[3] What its nature was is, however, not yet definitely known. Rudra-sena had three uncles, who had

[1]The view that Gautamīputra Śiva-magha of the Bhita seal was the third son of Pravara-sena and the founder of the Magha dynasty is untenable. Śiva-māgha had at least three predecessors; see *ante* Chap. II, p. 44.

[2]For the identity of this Bhava-nāga, see *JNSI.* V, 21-7, and *ante* pp. 38-39.

[3]As a general rule, maternal grandfathers are mentioned in royal genealogies only when they happen to have rendered conspicuous help to their daughter's sons.

established separate kingdoms, carved out of the parent empire They were all relatively more experienced than the heir to the imperial throne. It is possible that some or all of them may have tried to oust him, and his maternal grandfather, king Bhava-nāga, may have saved the situation by intervening on behalf of his grandson. The family of only one uncle of Rudra-sena continued to rule. It is not unlikely that the other two uncles may have perished in the struggle or may have been dispossessed of their territories by quondam local rulers.[1]

It has, however, been argued with considerable force that the danger which threatened and eventually destroyed Rudra-sena proceeded not from his uncles but from the Guptas. If Rudra-sena could not continue to be a *Samrāṭ* or emperor like his grandfather, it was because the Guptas managed to rise to the imperial status. Before they could succeed in doing this, they had to humble down the power of the Vākāṭakas, whose emperor Pravara-sena I had for a while overwhelmed the founder of their dynasty, Chandra-gupta I, and reduced him and his son Samudra-gupta to the feudatory status. Eventually, however, Samudra-gupta inflicted a smashing defeat upon Rudra-sena I, the successor of Pravara-sena, in a sanguinary battle fought at Kauśāmbī in which the Vākāṭaka king lost his life on the battlefield in *c.* 345 A.D. The Vākāṭakas then sank into the position of mere feudatories of the great Gupta empire.[2]

It is not possible to examine this theory here in all its details.[3] Suffice it to say that we have really no evidence to show that the power of Chandra-gupta I had ever been overthrown by Pravara-sena I or that Samudra-gupta was at any

---

[1]The last alternative would appear as the more probable one, if we assume that they were viceroys over northern Andhradeśa and southern Kośala. These territories were being governed by a number of independent kings at the time of Samudra-gupta's invasion.

[2]*ABORI*. IV, 30-40; Jayaswal, *HIJ*. pp. 80-2.

[3]See Altekar in *IC*. IX, 99-106 for a detailed refutation of this view.

time a feudatory of the Vākāṭakas and wreaked his vengeance upon them by killing their king Rudra-sena on the battlefield of Kauśāmbī. The king Chaṇḍasena of *Kaumudīmahotsava*, who is stated to have been driven out from Pāṭaliputra, cannot be identified with the Gupta emperor Chandra-gupta I.[1] The tiger type of the coins of Samudra-gupta describes him as a *rājā*, not because he was then a simple feudatory, but because the flan of the coins could not accommodate at the particular place a longer word like *Rājādhirāja* or *Mahārājādhirāja*. It is true that Rudradeva is one of the nine kings forcibly uprooted by Samudra-gupta, but he cannot be identified with Rudra-sena, the Vākāṭaka king. Rudradeva of the Allahabad inscription was a ruler in northern India, Rudra-sena of the Vākāṭakas was a king of the Deccan. We must further remember that the Allahabad pillar inscription is a *praśasti* of Samudra-gupta, which seeks to give a full and glorious picture of his different achievements. In order to heighten the effect on the mind of the reader, the full imperial titles of the Kushāṇa kings, who had probably offered a mere nominal submission, are given in the record. Is it then likely that the most sensational achievement of Samudra-gupta, which enabled him to regain the imperial status for his family, would have been summarily dismissed by mentioning the mere name of the Vākāṭaka emperor, Rudra-sena, along with those of half a dozen non-entities? If Rudradeva defeated by Samudra-gupta had belonged to the Vākāṭaka dynasty, which had thwarted the imperial plans of Chandra-gupta I and Samudra-gupta, the Allahabad record would have grown very eloquent in referring to this most glorious achievement of the Gupta emperor; it would have described it in several verses or in a string of long compounds, and would certainly not have dismissed it merely in four letters. Rudradeva overthrown by Samudra-gupta was a third rate

[1] *Ibid.*

chieftain of a petty state in the Gangetic valley, and not the Vākāṭaka king Rudra-sena. It may further be pointed out that if Rudra-sena had died at the hands of Samudra-gupta in the battle of Kauśāmbī, it is extremely unlikely that his son Pṛithvīsheṇa would ever have selected, as the bride for his heir-apparent, Prabhāvatī-guptā, who was a grand-daughter of the enemy who had been instrumental in shortening his father's life.

It is thus clear that Samudra-gupta did not overthrow Rudra-sena I. The conquests of Samudra-gupta did not materially affect the Vākāṭaka interests. Even in his southern campaign Samudra-gupta did not come into any direct conflict with Rudra-sena. During the reign of Pravara-sena I, the Vākāṭakas probably exercised a kind of overlordship over southern Kośala and the eastern Deccan, the kings in which were defeated and reinstated by Samudra-gupta in the course of his southern expedition. But this venture was undertaken by Samudra-gupta by *c.* 360 A.D., and a decade or two before that date the local kings of these provinces had disowned Vākāṭaka supremacy and asserted independence, taking advantage of the weakness of the imperial power during the rule of the inexperienced and weak Rudra-sena. Nor can we identify king Vyāgharāja of the Great Forest, who transferred his allegiance to Samudra-gupta, with Vyāgharāja, king of Ganj, who was a Vākāṭaka feudatory. The former was a king in the Deccan, ruling to the *south* of the Vindhyas, while the latter was a king in Baghelkhand, ruling to the *north* of that mountain range.

It is true that the title emperor (*samrāṭ*) which was assumed by Pravara-sena I, is not known to be used by Rudra-sena I. But that was in no way a consequence of the assumption of the imperial title *Mahārājādhirāja* by his contemporary Samudra-gupta. According to the sacred texts it is the proper performance of the Vājapeya sacrifice which entitles a king to the title of *Samrāṭ*.[1] Rudra-sena I had not, like Pravara-sena, performed this sacrifice and, therefore, could not assume that title. It must be further remembered that the title *Mahārāja*, which he had assumed, did not at this time indicate any subordinate position in the Deccan, as it did in the Punjab. It was used even by independent rulers like the Ikshvāku king Śāntamūla and the Vishṇukuṇḍin king Mādhava-varman, who had performed several Horse-Sacrifices. The same was the case with great Pulakeśin II, who had defeated Harsha, the lord paramount of northern India. The officers who drafted the Vākāṭaka plates during the regency of Prabhāvatī-guptā, were bred up in the Deccan tradition in this respect and do not appear to have distinguished very much between the titles *Mahārāja* and *Mahārājādhirāja*. It is definitely known that Chandra-gupta I and Samudra-gupta had both assumed the higher title *Mahārājādhirāja*, but the Poona plates of Prabhāvatī-guptā describe Chandra-gupta I as a simple *Mahārāja*. In the Riṭhapur plates, not only Chandra-gupta I, but also his illustrious son Samudra-gupta, is called as mere *Mahārāja*, the title *Mahārājādhirāja* being given only to Prabhāvatī's father Chandra-gupta II.

When the stereotyped text of the Vākāṭaka plates was fixed by Pravara-sena II on attaining majority, he was still under the spell of the Gupta influence. He may have naturally felt a disinclination to claim for his ancestors a title which was claimed for themselves for more than half a century by the members of the family of his quondam guide and protector Chandra-gupta II. He decided to designate his namesake Pravara-sena I by the title of *Samrāṭ*, because he was entitled to it by the performance of a Vājapeya sacrifice. He saw no objection in describing all the succeeding rulers, including

[1] Cf. राजा व राजसूयेन इष्ट्वा भवति सम्राट् वाजपेयेन; अवरं हि राज्यं पर साम्राज्यम् । *Śatabatha Br.* V, 1. 1. 13.

himself, as Mahārājas, because that title still indicated the independent status in the Deccan.

Rudra-sena ruled for about 25 years down to *c.* 360. The division of the empire into four parts that followed his accession and the opposition, open or covert, which his uncles were offering to him, weakened the Vākāṭaka power and influence for some time. He was himself young and inexperienced and could smooth down the situation only with the help of his maternal grandfather Bhava-nāga. The quarrels at the capital enabled the feudatories of outlying provinces to become independent. They also prevented Rudra-sena from sending help to Yaśo-varman II, the Vākāṭaka protege on the Kshatrapa throne, who was soon ousted by Rudra-dāman II, who immediately assumed the title of *Mahākshatrapa*, indicative of independent status. Rudra-sena had to reconcile himself with these developments. With the help of his meternal grandfather Bhava-nāga, he however soon managed to get an effective control over the rest of his kingdom. Its south-western part had however to be allowed to remain in the hands of his uncle Sarva-sena, whose descendants continued to rule in southern Berar and north-western Hyderabad till the end of the 5th century. Nothing is heard of the remaining two uncles of Rudra-sena; probably he overthrew them with the help of his maternal grandfather.

Rudra-sena was thus eventually able to control the situation and once more establish the prestige of the Vākāṭaka power. It is interesting to note that Samudra-gupta did not attack the Vākāṭakas, either during his Deccan expedition or when he penetrated into Central India and occupied the Saugor district of C. P.[1] He probably felt that the Vākāṭakas would be useful

[1] If we assume, as is very probable, that Samudra-gupta reached Eran *via* Padmāvatī and Jhansi, or *via* Kauśāmbī, Chitrakūṭa and Jhansi, rather than *via* Katni and Jubblepore, the necessity of his conflict with the Vākāṭakas can be eliminated. The last mentioned route is the most difficult of the three.

allies and may have thought it prudent not to provoke an unnecessary conflict with them. The Vākāṭaka records assert that their treasury, army and prestige were continuously on the increase for a hundred years at the time of the accession of Pṛithvī-sheṇa I, the son and successor of Rudra-sena I.[1] We may, therefore, confidently conclude that no catastrophe like the defeat and death of the king on the battlefield had overtaken the Vākāṭakas by the middle of the 4th century A. D. Rudra-sena continued to rule down to *c.* 360 A. D. and was successful in restoring, to a great extent, the prestige and power of his house, that had suffered considerably owing to the division of the empire that had been unwisely assented to by his grandfather.[2]

7. Pṛithvī-sheṇa I

(*c.*360 A.D. to *c.* 385 A.D.)

Rudra-sena was succeeded by his son Pṛithvī-sheṇa I in *c.* 360 A.D. He may be presumed to have had a reign of about 25 years, for in the Vākāṭaka records he is often described as a patriarch, surrounded by sons and grandsons.

The contemporary of Pṛithvī-sheṇa in the Basim branch was Vindhya-sena, the son of Sarva-sena. The relation between the two houses had become fairly cordial by this time. The Basim branch probably recognised a nominal overlordship of the main family, while enjoying full internal autonomy.[3] It was at one time held that it was Pṛithvī-sheṇa I, who had annexed Kuntala or southern Mahārāshṭra to the Vākāṭaka

---

[1]See *ante*, p. 95, n 1.

[2]The view that the Lankey Bull type of coins are the coins of Rudra-sena is untenable; see Chap. XV.

[3]The kings are seen making land-grants without the sanction of the rulers of the main house; *EI.* XXVI, 137 ff. Their relations with the rulers of the main branch were probably similar to those of the branches of the Chālukya and Rāshṭrakūṭa families in Gujarat and Andhradeśa with the rulers of the main houses.

empire. The revised readings of the Ajanta inscription in cave XVI however show[1] that it was king Vindhya-sena of the Basim branch who was mainly responsible for this annexation. It is however very probable that he received material assistance in this venture from Pṛithvī-sheṇa ; otherwise it would be difficult to explain how the rulers of the main branch should have been described as *Kuntaleśes* or lords of Kuntala in some literary works.

The identity of the Kuntala king defeated by the Vākāṭakas cannot yet be satisfactorily determined. It is usual to assume that he was a Kadamba ruler, most probably king Kaṅga-varman, who was ruling over Kuntala or northern Karṇāṭaka at this time. It is also possible, but not probable, that he may have been an ancestor of the Rāshṭrakūṭa king Avidheya, who was ruling in Sholapur district at the beginning of the sixth century A.D. The point, however, cannot be satisfactorily settled at present. As a result of the conquest of Kuntala, southern Mahārāshṭra was incorporated in the Vākāṭaka kingdom.

The power of the Western Kshatrapas was at this time again eclipsed between 351 and 364 A.D. The Kshatrapa debacle does not, however, seem to be the result of any effort made by the Vākāṭakas to reassert their overlordship over Gujarat and Kathiawar. As observed already,[2] its cause is still unknown.

Two records found in Baghelkhand show[3] that a local king, named Vyāghrarāja recognised the overlordship of Pṛithvī-sheṇa. It is very likely that this Pṛithvī-sheṇa is Pṛithvī-sheṇa I and not Pṛithvī-sheṇa II. The records would thus show that Baghel-

[1] *Hyd. Ar. S.* No. 14.

[2] See Chap. III, *ante*, pp. 61-62.

[3] Ganj inscription, *CII.* III, No. 54; Nachne-ki-Talai inscription, *EI.* XVII, 12.

[4] If we assume that Vyāghrarāja of these records is the Uchchakalpa ruler of that name, then his overlord will be Pṛithvī-sheṇa II. This, however, is very improbable. All the territories between the Jamuna and the Narmadā were under Gupta overlordship in *c.* 465 A. D. Even the

khand was under the Vākāṭaka sphere of influence during the reign of Pṛithvī-sheṇa I.

The conquest of Kuntala had increased the prestige of the Vākāṭakas, and the Gupta emperor Chandra-gupta II, who was contemplating the overthrow of the Western Kshatrapas at this time, felt that it would facilitate his task if he could secure a helpful ally on his southern flank, while his armies were operating in Malwa and Gujarat. He, therefore, proposed a matrimonial alliance to Pṛithvī-sheṇa by offering his daughter Prabhāvatī-guptā in marriage to the Vākāṭaka crown prince Rudra-sena. The offer was accepted by Pṛithvī-sheṇa and the marriage was celebrated with great pomp, probably at Pāṭaliputra, in *c.* 380 A.D.[1]

Pṛithvī-sheṇa died about five years after the marriage in *c.* 385.

8. Rudra-sena II

(*c.* 385 to *c.* 390 A.D.)

Rudra-sena II ascended the throne in *c.* 385 A.D. He was under considerable influence of his illustrious father-in-law Chandra-gupta II, for we find him giving up his ancestral religion, Śaivism and becoming a Vaishṇava like the latter.

The Vākāṭaka kingdom was in a prosperous condition at

Parivrājakas, who were the western neighbours of the Uchchakalpas and thus nearer to the Vākāṭaka capital, were acknowledging the Gupta sovereignty. It is therefore very improbable that Pṛithvī-sheṇa could have exercised his overlordship over the Uchchakalpa king Vyāghrarāja in *c.* 465 A.D.

[1]A literary tradition states that Pravara-sena II, the youngest son of this union, was spending his early youth in the pursuits of pleasure in *c.* 410 A.D., as his maternal grandfather Chandra-gupta II could be relied upon to look after his administration. Cf. *Pibatu madhusugandhīnyānanāni priyāṇām | Mayi vinihitabhāraḥ kuntalānāmadhīśaḥ ||* At the time of the death of Chandra-gupta II in *c.* 414 A.D., his grandson would be about 25; his birth, therefore, may be placed in *c.* 390 A.D. He was at least the second if not the third or fourth child of his parents, and so their marriage may be placed in c. 380 A.D.

this time. Its treasury was full and its armies had secured victories in the south in recent times. The new king was a young and energetic man, and we may well presume that he may have heartily welcomed the plan of his father-in-law to attack the Kshatrapas and even offered a willing co-operation to the military project, anticipating that a portion of the Kshatrapa kingdom would naturally fall to his own share. Unfortunately however, before the plans could materialise Rudra-sena died suddenly in *c*. 390 A.D. at the premature age of about 30 after a short reign of five years. This unexpected calamity must have come as a great shock to both the royal families and it may have postponed the contemplated invasion of Gujarat by a few years.

9. Regency of Prabhāvatī-guptā

(*c*. 390 to *c*. 410 A.D.)

Soon after the bereavement, Chandra-gupta must have paid a visit of condolence to his daughter Prabhāvatī-guptā. She was only about 25 at this time and had two sons, Divākara-sena and Dāmodara-sena,[1] the former being about 5 years in age and the latter about 2. Chandra-gupta advised his daughter to assume the reins of administration as regent for the minor king Divākara-sena, promising all help, military and administrative. She decided to follow the advice and began to rule as regent.

[1]Dāmodara-sena later assumed the coronation name of Pravara-sena at the time of his accession. The expression *Mahārāja-Dāmodara-sena-Pravara-sena-jananī* used of Prabhāvatī-guptā in the Riṭhapur plates does not show that she had then two sons living, Dāmodara-sena and Pravara-sena. Had such been the case, the order of the two names in the compound would suggest that Dāmodara-sena was the elder one and the ruling king. The plates however were issued in the 19th regnal year of Pravara-sena and not of Dāmodara-sena. It is, therefore, clear that Dāmodara-sena is identical with Pravara-sena, the latter being his coronation (*abhisheka*) title.

It is not unlikely that besides these two sons, Prabhāvatī-guptā may have had a daughter or two, whose names are not mentioned in the records handed down to us.

She carried on the administration ably for a period of about twenty years with the valuable assistance of the officers that had been deputed by her father from Pāṭaliputra.[1]

In the Basim branch Vindhyaśakti II was the contemporary of Prabhāvatī-guptā at the time of her bereavement. He does not seem to have offered any opposition to the administration of the regency. Being the eldest agnatic male in the Vākāṭaka family, he may have felt naturally disappointed that he should not have been made regent for the minor king. But as Prabhāvatī-guptā had the solid backing of her mighty father, Vindhyaśakti had to bow down to the inevitable. The relations between the main Vākāṭaka house and its Basim branch were fairly peaceful throughout the regency.

It was during the regency of Prabhāvatī-guptā that the Gupta conquest of Gujarat and Kathiawar was accomplished, and we may well presume that the dowager queen afforded all possible assistance to her illustrious father. There is, however, no direct evidence to support this conjecture.

Chandra-gupta II not only helped the regency administration by sending experts, but seems to have also taken active interest in the training of his young grandsons. There is a literary tradition to the effect that the poem *Setubandha* was composed by king Pravara-sena of Kuntala soon after his accession and was later revised by Kālidāsa. It is not unlikely that this great poet may have been one of the tutors appointed by Chandra-gupta to educate the Vākāṭaka princes.[2]

---

[1]The Poona plates of Prabhāvatī-guptā, which use the eastern Gupta script and begin with the Gupta genealogy, instead of the Vākāṭaka one, make it fairly clear that they were drafted by a Gupta officer, imported from Pāṭalīputra.

[2]Rāmagiri-svāmin of Pamtek was highly revered by the Vākāṭakas and Prabhāvatī-guptā made her last grant in his presence. Is it not likely that Kālidāsa too may have visited Ramtek several times in the company of his wards and their mother, and that it may have been during one of these visits that the idea occurred to him make this hill the place of the exile cf his Yaksha in the *Meghadūta* ?

Prabhāvatī-guptā was destined to suffer one more tragic bereavement. Divākara-sena, her eldest son and the minor king, died soon after the 13th year of her regency.[1] This must have been a great blow to the dowager queen, for she must have been then looking eagerly to the day when she would be relieved of the onerous duties of administration. Dāmodara-sena, her younger son, was installed on the throne, and Prabhāvatī-guptā continued to be the regent for another five or six years. Eventually the regency terminated in *c.* 410 A.D., when Dāmodara-sena took up the reins of administration, assuming the coronation name of Pravara-sena II.

Prabhāvatī-guptā continued to live for a long time after the termination of her regency. We find her making a grant in the 19th year of her son Pravara-sena's reign. Four years later the son is seen making a grant for the spiritual welfare both of himself and his mother in *this* and after life.[2] Prabhāvatī-guptā, therefore, seems to have lived for about 25 years in her son's reign and died at the ripe age of about 75.

10. PRAVARA-SENA II (*c.* 410—*c.* 440 A.D.).

At his accession in *c.* 410 A.D., Pravara-sena was a youth of about 20. A literary tradition records that he spent the first few years of his reign in the pursuits of the pleasures of youth.[3] When, however, his illustrious grandfather died in 414 A.D., he must have assumed the full control of the administration. He may not have felt that the affairs of his government would be as safe in the hands of his maternal uncle Kumāra-gupta I as in those of his grandfather.

Nearly a dozen copper plates of Pravara-sena II have been discovered so far ; neither they nor any later Vākāṭaka records

---

[1]He was the reigning king when Prabhāvatī-guptā issued her Poona plates in the 13th year of her regency.

[2]*EI.* XXII, 170 ff.

[3]See *ante*, p. 111, n. 1.

refer to any military exploits, of the new king. It is, therefore, clear that he had no military or territorial ambitions and was satisfied with the patrimony he had inherited. He was a man of literary tastes and composed a Prākṛit poem, named *Setubandha*, describing the exploits of Rāma in the capture of Laṅkā. Rāmasvāmin of Ramtek was highly revered by his family, and it was but natural that Pravara-sena, who was a Vaishṇava, should have turned to the exploits of Rāma, an incarnation of Vishṇu, for the theme of his poem.

Purikā situated somewhere in Berar or Western C.P., was the earliest Vākāṭaka capital, as mentioned in the Purāṇas. Later on it was shifted to Nandi-vardhana, which is most probably Nagardhan (also spelt as Nandardhan) near Ramtek, about 13 miles north of Nagpur.[1] Pravara-sena, however, decided to found a new capital, to be named after him as Pravarapura. This city has not yet been satisfactorily identified. It has been suggested that it may be Pavanār in Wardha district, having a strong fort overlooking a river.[2] If excavations or explorations lead to the discovery of any Vākāṭaka antiquities at this place, the theory may become generally acceptable. Headquarters were shifted to the new capital sometime after the 18th year of Pravara-sena's reign (*c.* 430 A.D.).

The evidence supplied by the place-names in the numerous charters of Pravara-sena makes it clear that the districts of Amraoti, Wardha, Betul, Chhindwara, Nagpur, Bhandara and Balaghat were under the administration of the main branch of the Vākāṭaka dynasty. The same was probably the case with the remaining portions of C.P. and Khandesh. Southern Berar, north-western Hyderabad and southern Mahārāshṭra were under the administration of the rulers of the Basim branch of the Vākāṭaka family. Curiously enough, the Basim contem-

[1]This city is also identified with Nandpur, 34 miles north of Nagpur (*JASB*. NS. XXIX, 159).

[2]*Ibid.*

porary of Pravara-sena II was a ruler bearing the same name, who was also Pravara-sena II of his own branch.

In *c.* 430 A.D., Pravara-sena married his crown prince Narendra-sena to Ajitabhaṭṭārikā, a daughter of a king of Kuntala. The identification of the family of this princess is not yet satisfactorily settled, but very probably she was a daughter of the Kadamba king Kākustha-verman, who is known to have married his daughters in Gupta and other royal families. Among the 'other' royal houses selected by him, the Vākāṭaka family may have been naturally included, for its prestige at this time was second only to that of the Guptas. This marriage may have put an end to the ill-feeling created between the two families by the Vākāṭaka conquest of southern Mahārāshṭra.

The 27th year is the last regnal year of Pravara-sena II known so far.[1] We may, therefore, assume that he ruled for about 30 years and died in *c.* 440 A.D.

11. Narendra-sena

(*c.* 440 to *c.* 460 A.D.).

Pravara-sena was succeeded by his son Narendra-sena in *c.* 440 A.D. The Vākāṭaka rocords observe that he had to regain the fortunes of his family, and that the sterling qualities which he had inherited stood him in good stead in this connection. What the great calamity was from which the Vākāṭakas suffered during the reign of the new king could not, however, be satisfactorily determined for a long time. The few known facts of history seemed to be presenting almost an insoluble puzzle. Majority of scholars were inclined to assume that there was a long war of succession after the death of Pravara-sena II, and that Narendra-sena could eventually get the throne only after defeating a rival brother and his son, who were believed to be

[1] *EI.* XXIII, 81

mentioned in the fragmentary inscription of Cave XVI at Ajanta.[1] There were considerable difficulties in establishing this theory also, but it seemed that the known facts of history could be best explained by it.

It has, however, been proved now[2] that the rulers mentioned in the Ajanta record do not belong to the main branch of the Vākāṭaka family and that the minor king and his son Deva-sena need not be sandwiched between Narendra-sena and Pṛithvī-sheṇa II. They in fact belong to the Basim branch, which had separated from the main stock, not at the death of Pravara-sena II in *c.* 440, but at the death of Pravara-sena I nearly a century earlier.[3] There is no evidence to show that either Deva-sena or his father contested the throne of the main branch, and the war of succession, therefore, was not the cause of the misfortunes from which Narendra-sena suffered.

The debacle, which temporarily overwhelmed the Vākāṭaka family in the reign of Narendra-sena, was the invasion of its dominions by the Naḷa king Bhavadatta-varman, ruling in Bastar state. A grant of this king shows that he had succeeded in penetrating deep into the Vākāṭaka dominion and occupied Nandi-vardhana, its erstwhile capital.[4] The precise time of this record is not known, but its palaeography suggests that it would belong to the middle of the 5th century A.D., which was just the time when Narendra-sena was in the whirlpool of difficulties. The victory of Bhavadatta-varman was a decisive one. We find him granting a village in Yeotmal district, situated in the very heart of the Vākāṭaka dominions. It is clear that Bhavadatta-varman succeeded, not only in defeating Narendra-sena but also in effectively occupying a part of his kingdom. After this great achievement we find the conqueror repairing to holy Prayāga,

[1] *ABORI.* V, 33 ff; *HIJ.* pp. 100 ff.
[2] *Hyd. Ar. S.* No. 14.
[3] *EI.* XXVI, 141-2.
[4] *EI.* XIX, 102.

apparently as a thanksgiving pilgrimage. The victory of Bhavadatta-varman may be placed in *c.* 445 A.D.

The Naḷas, however, were not in a position to occupy the Vākāṭaka districts for a long time. Soon after the death of Bhavadatta-varman, Narendra-sena succeeded in driving them out. His victory was a decisive one, for he not only reoccupied all his territory, but carried the war into the enemy's country, and captured and devastated that capital. Arthapati, the immediate successor of Bhavadatta-varman, was probably killed in the war and was succeeded by his brother Skanda-varman, who retrieved the fortunes of his family and repopulated the capital.[1]

It is very porbable that Narendra-sena received substantial help from the Kadamba relations of his queen in regaining his kingdom. Otherwise we cannot explain why Pṛithvī-sheṇa II, the son of Narendra-sena, should have mentioned his maternal grandfather in the genealogy of his family. It does not seem that Kumāra-gupta I helped his grand-nephew in the hour of his calamity. By *c.* 450 A.D., when Narendra-sena was in the thickest trouble, Kumāra-gupta himself was tottering on his throne owing to the rising of the Pushyamitras and the invasion of the Hūṇas. He could, therefore, have ill afforded to send any help, even if he were anxious to do so.

Narendra-sena is described as the overlord of Mālava in his son's record. Did he snatch it from the Guptas by siding with their enemies, the Pushyamitras ? This does not seem probable. His hands were too full with the Naḷa invasion and he would certainly have been very reluctant to incur the enmity of his Gupta relations by making a common cause with their enemies. It appears that when the prospects of the Gupta emperor of re-establishing his authority in the distant provinces of his empire seemed very remote in *c.* 455, the local feudatory in Mālava may have for some time transferred his allegiance to the

[1] *EI.* XXI, 153; XXVI, 52.

Vākāṭaka king Narendra-sena, in the hope that he may assist him in maintaining his own position in the troubled times. We should not forget in this connection that the prestige of the Vākāṭakas had increased at this time by their overthrow of the Naḷa power. Mālava, however, did not long remain under the Vākāṭaka sphere of influence, for it came back under the Gupta overlordship during the reign of Skanda-gupta.

The overlordship over Mekala and Kośala has also been ascribed to Narendra-sena by his son. There is nothing improbable in this claim. He had smashed the power of the Naḷas ruling in Chattisgarh and Bastar state, and it is quite likely that he may have annexed a part of the territories, which bordered upon or were included in their kingdom. The Parivrājakas and the Uchchakalpas however did not become Vākāṭaka feudatories.

The termination of Narendra-sena's reign may be placed *c.* 460 A.D. He was a fairly efficient ruler, for he not only retrieved the fortunes of his family, but eventually extended the boundaries of its kingdom by annexing a large part of the Naḷa kingdom. His relations with the kings of the Basim branch were fairly cordial.

12. Pṛithvī-sheṇa II.

(*c.* 460—*c.* 480 A.D.)

Definite dates about the limits of the reign of Pṛithvī-sheṇa are not known, but we may place it between *c.* 460 and *c.* 480 A.D. with fair confidence. His contemporary in the Basim branch was Deva-sena, who was more devoted to pleasures than to the pursuits of war. The relations between the two rulers were, therefore, cordial.

Pṛithvī-sheṇa like his father, had not a smooth reign. His Balaghat plates tell us that he had to rescue the fortunes of his family twice, but do not enlighten us about the enemies whom he had to overcome. It is probable that the first of these occasions was the expulsion of the Naḷa invaders, in which he may have taken an active part during the reign of his father; in *c.* 450 he was a youth of about 20. The second occasion was probably an invasion of the Vākāṭaka kingdom by the Traikūṭaka king Dahra-sena ruling in southern Gujarat during *c.* 445-475 A.D. This ruler is known to have performed a Horse-sacrifice, and the expansion of power suggested by it was probably at the cost of the Vākāṭakas, who were his eastern neighbours. Pṛithvī-sheṇa only regained his lost districts but was unable to smash the Traikūṭaka power; for it continued to prosper and expand during the reign of Vyāghra-sena, the successor of Dahra-sena.

No son of king Pṛithvī-sheṇa is known to have succeeded him. After his death we find the leadership of the Vākāṭaka family passing to king Hari-sheṇa of the Basim branch, who is described in the Ajanta inscription as the conqueror of Kuntala, Avantī, Lāṭa, Kośala, Kaliṅga, and Andhra countries. He could have made these conquests only by first securing the effective possession of the territories and resources of the kingdom of the main Vākāṭaka branch. We shall proceed to describe his career, but it will be convenient to preface it by a connected, though brief, history of the earlier rulers of the Basim branch.

13. Basim Branch of the Vākāṭakas.

Sarva-sena, a younger son of the emperor Pravara-sena I, founded the Basim branch in *c.* 330 A.D.[1] Since Pravara-sena had a long reign of 60 years, we may well presume that the reign of his son Sarva-sena, was probably a short one, terminating by *c.* 350 A.D. No events of his reign are known, but it is not unlikely that he and his brothers may have tried to thwart the accession of their young nephew, Rudra-sena II.[2] Vindhya-sena,

---

[1] *EI.* XXVI, 137 ff; *Hyd. Ar. S.* No. 14.
[2] *Ante*, p. 103.

the son and successor of Sarva-sena, had a long reign of about fifty years.[1] He was an able and ambitious ruler and annexed Kuntala (southern Mahārāshṭra) to his patrimony. It is very probable that he may have received some help in this undertaking from Pṛithvī-sheṇa I, the ruler of the main Vākāṭaka branch. Vindhya-sena ruled over a fairly extensive kingdom including southern Berar, northern Hyderabad, and the districts of Nagar, Nasik, Poona and Satara. His descendants continued to rule over most of this territory, probably professing a kind of nominal allegiance to the rulers of the parent stock.

Vindhyasakti II was succeeded by his son Pravara-sena II who had a short reign of about 15 years[2] (*c.* 400 to *c.* 415 A.D.). Curiously enough, for about five years from *c.* 410 to *c.* 415 A.D. the rulers of both the main Vākāṭaka line and its Basim branch bore the same name.

The name of the minor son of 8 years, who succeeded Pravara-sena at Basim in *c.* 415, has not been preserved in the fragmentary Ajanta record. We possess no information about the manner in which the administration was carried on during his minority. It is not unlikely that Pravara-sena II of the main branch may have acted as the regent ; this may have resulted in the amalgamation of the governments of the two lines for about ten years or so.[3] Pravara-sena handed over the administration to his Basim cousin when he attained majority. He may be presumed to have continued to rule down to *c.* 455. He is praised in the Ajanta record for being a good ruler ; welfare of his subjects, rather than warfare with his neighbours seems to have been his chief concern. It is, however, likely

---

[1]His Basim plates were issued in his 37th regnal year.

[2]His father had ruled for about 50 years and he was succeeded by a son who was a minor of 8 years at his accession. Hence the reign of Pravara sena II was very probably a short one.

[3]This will explain how Pravara-sena II of the main line became known in literary tradition as the ruler of Kuṇtala, though it was the Basim branch which had conquered the province and was ruling over it.

that he may have sent military aid to Narendra-sena, when he was trying to oust the Naḷa conqueror. The invasion of the Naḷas did not cause any appreciable disturbance in the kingdom of the Basim branch, but its ruler may have apprehended that his turn might come next and may therefore have offered help out of enlightened self-interest.

The 'nameless' king was succeeded by his son Deva-sena in *c.* 455 ; he may be presumed to have continued to rule down to *c.* 475 A.D. He was a pleasure-loving ruler, but had the wisdom to entrust the administration to the care of an efficient minister named Hastibhoja, who was both able and popular.

Deva-sena was succeeded in *c.* 475 A.D. by his son Hari-sheṇa, who continued to rule down to *c.* 510 A.D. Hari-sheṇa was the most powerful ruler of the Basim branch. Soon after his accession, Pṛithvī-sheṇa II of the main Vākāṭaka family died. He either left behind no son, or what is equally probable, the one who succeeded him was overthrown by Hari-sheṇa. Whatever may have been the real case, there is no doubt that the Basim ruler soon managed to get effective possession of the entire dominion of the main line.

He was, however, not satisfied with this achievement, for his Ajanta-record claims that he conquered or extended his sphere of influence over Gujarat, Mālava, southern Kośala, Andhra and Kuntala provinces.[1] There is nothing improbable in the claim put forward. The Traikūṭaka ruler Dhara-sena died in *c.* 495 A.D. No successor of his is known and Hari-sheṇa may well have managed to get control over his kingdom at least for a short time. The conquest of Mālava attributed to him was quite possible at the end of the 5th century, when it had slipped out of the hands of the Guptas after the death of Budha-gupta. Hari-sheṇa may have succeeded in compelling the Varman family ruling in that province to transfer its allegiance

---

[1] *Hyd. Ar. S.* No. 14, p. 11.

to him, but probably for a short time only. South Kośala was under the rule of the Naḷas, who being afraid of the rising power of Hari-sheṇa, may have thought it prudent to acknowledge his suzerainty, lest their kingdom should once more suffer from a hostile invasion. Vikramendra, the contemporary Vishṇukuṇḍin king in Andhra country, had married his son Mādhava-varman I to a Vākāṭaka princess, who was probably a grand-daughter of king Hari-sheṇa. His court poet, therefore, could have felt no objection in including him among his master's feudatories.

The mother of Pṛithvī-sheṇa II (of the main house) was a Kuntala (Kadamba) princess, and if it is true that Hari-sheṇa had superseded her son, it is not unlikely that the latter may have invoked the help of the Kadambas to regain his throne. This would have naturally caused a clash between Hari-sheṇa and the Kuntala power, which may have been glorified into a victory by the court poet of Hari-sheṇa. The Kadamba records do not disclose that kings Mṛigeśa and Ravi-varman, who were the contemporaries of Hari-sheṇa, had ever suffered any serious defeat at the hands of any enemy. The defeat of the Kuntala king by Hari-sheṇa, therefore, probably refers only to some frontier skirmishes between the Kadambas and the Vākāṭakas, in which the latter may have come out successful.[1]

At the death of Hari-sheṇa in *c.* 510 A.D. the Vākāṭaka kingdom was at the zenith of its power and prestige. Practically the whole of Hyderabad state, Bombay, Mahārāshṭra, Berar, and most of C.P. were under its direct administration, and northern Konkan, Gujarat, Mālava, Chattisgarh and Andhra province were under its sphere of influence. The extent of the Vākāṭaka empire at this time was thus even greater than what it was

[1]Mahamahopadhyaya V. V. Mirashi suggests that the Kuntala kings referred to in the Vākāṭaka records may have belonged to the Rāshṭrakūṭa family mentioned in the Pandurangapalli plates. *ABORI.* XXV, 36-50.

during the reign of *Samrāṭ* Pravara-sena I. In fact, no contemporary kingdom was so extensive and powerful. Hari-sheṇa must have been an able ruler, a skilful administrator, and a renowned general to render this achievement possible.

14. The Fall of the Vākāṭakas.

The Vākāṭaka empire, which was thus at the zenith of its glory at about 510 A.D., disappeared within less than forty years. By *c.* 550 A.D. the Chālukyas occupied the greater part of it. How this decline and disappearance of the Vākāṭaka power took place is, however, still a mystery ; for the records of the Chālukyas, who succeeded them as the overlords of the Deccan, do not disclose any conflict between them and the Vākāṭakas.

It has been argued that the immediate cause of the disappearance of the Vākāṭaka power was the rise of a Rāshṭrakūṭa empire, which ruled over the whole of Deccan during the 6th century A.D.[1] It has, however, to be observed that there is no evidence to prove that such a Rāshṭrakūṭa empire ever existed, anywhere except in the poetic imagination of the 10th century court poets of the later Chālukyas.[2] The Chālukya records of the 6th century A.D., which describe in detail even the minor exploits of the earlier members of the dynasty, are silent about their ever having overthrown any mighty Rāshṭrakūṭa empire, that stood between them and the overlordship of the Deccan. Nor is there any evidence to show that the king Mānāṅka of Chattisgarh was a Rāshṭrakūṭa or that his grandsons Jayarāja, Bhavishya and Avidheya were ruling as members of a powerful Rāshṭrakūṭa federation in Kośala, Berar and southern Mahārāshṭra, and thereby dominating the whole of the Deccan. They were mere local feudatories. None of them was even known

[1] *MAR.* 1929, pp. 197 ff.

[2] For a detailed refutation of this theory, see Altekar in *ABORI.* XXIV, 149 ff.

as a Rāshṭrakūṭa. It is only in the reign of Abhimanyu, a son of Bhavishya, that his family is described as a Rāshṭrakūṭa family ; that may have been probably due to his having recently won that office.

We cannot thus attribute the decline of the Vākāṭaka power to the sudden emergence of a Rāshṭrakūṭa empire at the beginning of the 6th century. Its real causes are, however, still unknown.

No successor of Hari-sheṇa is so far known to us. We may, however, assume that on his death he was succeeded by a son of his, who may be presumed to have ruled down to *c.* 530 A.D. The Vishṇukuṇḍin king Mādhava-varman I (*c.* 525 to *c.* 570 A.D.) had married a Vākāṭaka princess ; she may have been a daughter of this ruler.

In the reign of this king, the disintegration of the empire started apace. Chattisgarh slipped from the Vākāṭaka control and passed under the rule of Tivaradeva, a Somavaṁśī Pāṇḍava king, who was ruling also over Chanda district.[1] In Mālava and Northern C. P. Yaśodharman of Mandsore suddenly rose to power and assumed imperial titles by *c.* 525 A.D. He proudly claims that the territories conquered neither by the Hūṇas nor by the Guptas recognised his overlordship. These most probably were the northern districts of the Vākāṭaka dominions. The power of Yaśodharman did not last long, but the loss of these districts must have lowered the prestige of the Vākāṭakas. They were unable to re-establish their authority in them, for soon after the disappearance of Yaśodharman, we find the Kaḷachuris rising to power in this area. In southern Mahārāshṭra the Rāshṭrakūṭa king, named Avidheya, set up an independent principality. It also did not flourish long, but it is important to note that it was wiped out not by the Vākāṭakas

[1] *EI.* XXII, 15-23. Dr. D. R. Bhandarkar however places this ruler in the 8th century (*List*, p 396). See *ante*, pp. 89-90.

but by the Kadambas. In the east the Naḷas once more became powerful and repudiated the Vākāṭaka overlordship.

The Vākāṭaka empire thus disappeared by *c.* 540, because the Kadambas of Karṇāṭaka, the Kaḷachuris of Noṛthern Mahārāshṭra and the Naḷas of Bastar state managed to absorb most of its territories during the weak rule of the successor (or successors) of Hari-sheṇa. None of these powers however succeeded in building up an empire embracing the whole of the Deccan. Quite unexpectedly there arose a new ruling house in Karṇāṭaka, that of the Chālukyas, which soon managed to defeat every one of these powers and annex its territory. How this happened will be narrated in the next volume.

CHAPTER VI

THE RISE OF THE GUPTAS

Gupta families or clans existed in India from very early times. The names of officials ending in Gupta are found in the records of the Sātavāhanas, and even a queen of Gupta family (*Gupta-vaṁśoditā*) is referred to in an old Brāhmī inscription. The well-known Bharhut Pillar inscription of the Śuṅga period also refers to the son of Rājan Visadeva as *Gotiputa*, indicating thereby that his queen was a *Gauptī* (*i.e.*, belonging to the Gupta clan). The same surname, *Gotiputa*, occurs in many other ancient records.[1] These instances show the importance and antiquity of the Gupta family or clan. Whether there was one parent clan from which all others branched or there were different families, without any connection, who adopted this name at different times, cannot be determined with any degree of certainty. But the latter seems more probable in view of the widespread of the name all over North India and the Deccan.

We possess very little information regarding the early history of the Gupta family that was destined to raise the name to an imperial dignity. Practically all that is *definitely* known is contained in the conventional genealogical account given in several Gupta records. According to this Samudra-gupta was "the son of the son's son of the *Mahārāja*, the illustrious (*Śrī*) Gupta; the son's son of the *Mahārāja*, the illustrious (*Śrī*) Ghaṭotkacha; the son of the *Mahārājādhirāja*, the illustrious

[1]For the inscriptions referred to, cf. Lüder's List, Nos. 1105, 1125, 11, 687, 92a, 94, 96, 156, 194, 271, 442, 663, 680-2, 1088. In No. 681 the Gotiputra is said to be of the Kauṇḍinya *gotra*.

(*Śrī*) Chandra-gupta, and the daughter's son of Lichchhavi (*Lichchhavi-dauhitra*) begotten on the *Mahādevī* Kumāradevī".

This brief account not only gives the names of the first three kings of the dynasty, but indirectly also supplies very valuable information about them. In the first place, the contrast between the titles *Mahārāja* of the first two kings and the *Mahārāj-ādhirāja* of the third (and his successors) cannot but be regarded as deliberate, indicating a difference in rank and status. There can be little doubt, therefore, that Chandra-gupta was a more powerful king than his father and grandfather. The latter are generally regarded as feudatories, for it has been held that "in the early Gupta and subsequent periods the title *Mahārāja* was applied only to feudatories, not to independent sovereigns". This view can, however, hardly be accepted as correct.[1] Further, even assuming that they were feudatories, we cannot say who was the paramount sovereign to whom they might have owed allegiance. We must, therefore, leave undecided the question whether the first two Gupta kings were really independent rulers or feudatory chieftains.

The epithet *Lichchhavi-dauhitra* (daughter's son of the Lichchhavi) applied to Samudra-gupta in the Gupta records down to the latest period seems to suggest that the marriage of Chandra-gupta I with the Lichchhavi (princess) Kumāradevī was an event of considerable importance. V. A. Smith expressed the view that Kumāradevī brought to her husband as her dowry valuable influence, which in the course of a few years secured to him a paramount position in Magadha and the neighbouring countries.[2] He even went so far as to suggest that 'the Lichchhavis were masters of Pāṭaliputra and Chandra-gupta, by means of his matrimonial alliance, succeeded to the power pre-

[1]The examples of the Lichchhavis (Nepal), the Maghas, the Bhāra-śivas and the Vākāṭakas are sufficient to prove that the title *Mahārāja* does not necessarily indicate a feudatory rank.

[2]*EHI*[3]. 279.

viously held by his wife's relatives. On the other hand Allan thinks that "the pride of the Guptas in their Lichchhavi blood was probably due rather to the ancient lineage of the Lichchhavis than to any material advantages gained by this alliance."[1] It is to be remembered, however, that the *Mānava-dharmaśāstra* (X. 20, 22) regards the Lichchhavis as descendants of *Vrātya Kshatriya*, and Vrātyas are defined as those who, not fulfilling their sacred duties, were excluded from the *Sāvitrī*. As purity, in the orthodox sense, counted far more than the antiquity of a family in ancient times, it may be doubted whether the Guptas laid so much stress on their Lichchhavi descent merely for the sake of social prestige. It appears more probable, therefore, that the marriage alliance of Chandra-gupta I was highly important from a political rather than social point of view.

This view gains considerable strength if we carefully weigh the evidence of a class of coins (Pl. II, 7), which have "on the obverse the figures and names of Chandra-gupta and Kumāradevī, and on the reverse a goddess seated on a lion, along with the legend *Lichchhavayaḥ* (the Lichchhavis)." Mr. Allan's contention that these were struck by Samudra-gupta to commemorate the marriage of his parents is hardly convincing. The view, held by the old numismatists, that these coins were issued by Chandra-gupta jointly with the Lichchhavis and their princess Kumāradevī, who was his consort, has been very ably defended by Dr. Aiyangar and Dr. Altekar.[2] Altekar has rightly deduced from these coins "that Kumāradevī was a queen by her own right, and the proud Lichchhavis, to whose stock she belonged, must have been anxious to retain their individuality in the new imperial state." Indeed, it is difficult to offer any other reasonable explanation for the occurrence of the name '*Lichchhavayaḥ*' on these coins. The use of the tribal name in plural number seems to imply that a vestige of

[1]CGD, p. xix.
[2]Num. Suppl. XLVIII, 105 ff; *JIH*. VI, Suppl. 10 ff.

the old republican constitution still persisted among the Lichchhavis, but the position of Kumāradevī indicates something like a hereditary monarchical constitution in actual practice. In any case, on the basis of the available evidence, we may reasonably assume that the marriage of Chandra-gupta and Kumāradevī led to the amalgamation of the Gupta principality with the Lichchhavi state, and the epithet *Lichchhavi-dauhitra* was deliberately given to Samudra-gupta to emphasise his right of succession to the dual monarchy.

So far we are on tolerably sure grounds. But the location of the two states is a matter of considerable difficulty. Both the Gupta and the Lichchhavi kingdoms have been located by different scholars in Magadha, with Pāṭaliputra as capital, but these views are not supported by any positive evidence. Some light is thrown on this question by I-tsing. This Chinese pilgrim, who travelled in India during the period 671-695 A.D., refers to a king Śrī-Gupta (Chi-li-ki-to) as having built a temple for the Chinese priests and granted twenty-four villages as an endowment for its maintenance. This temple, known as the "Temple of China", was situated close to a sanctuary called Mi-li-kia-si-kia-po-no which was about forty *Yojanaṣ* to the east of Nālandā, following the course of the Ganges. Allan proposed to identify this king Śrī-Gupta, with Gupta the founder of the Gupta dynasty.[1] Unfortunately, this identification is by no means certain. For I-tsing places Śrī-Gupta about 'five hundred years before his time', whereas the founder of the Gupta dynasty cannot be placed more than four hundred years before he wrote. Allan does not take this as a serious objection against the proposed identification in view of the "lapse of time and the fact that the Chinese pilgrim gives the statement on the authority of a tradition handed down from ancient times by old men." While there is a great deal of force in this

[1]*CGD*, p. xv.

argument, the chronological difficulty cannot be altogether ignored, and the identification of I-tsing's Śrī-Gupta with the founder of the Gupta dynasty, although highly probable, cannot be regarded as absolutely certain. We may, however, accept it as a provisional hypothesis and regard the original kingdom of Gupta as having comprised a portion of Bengal.[1]

As regards the Lichchhavis, they are known to have been settled in Vaiśālī (modern Basarh in Muzaffarpur district) in the time of Gautama Buddha, and, though conquered by Ajātaśatru, they continued as an important clan, as shown by references in Kauṭilya's *Arthaśāstra* and *Manu-Smṛiti*. The Lichchhavis founded a kingdom in Nepal probably as early as the first or second century A.D. Whether they still continued to occupy Vaiśālī and the neighbouring region is not definitely known, but it is not unlikely, for reference to Nepāla in Samudra-gupta's inscription proves that it was different from the Lichchhavi kingdom which he had inherited from his mother. On the whole, as in the case of the Guptas, although nothing is definitely known, the Lichchhavi kingdom of Kumāradevī may be provisionally located in North Bihar with Vaiśālī as its centre.

It is very likely that the Guptas and Lichchhavis ruled over two contiguous states which were amalgamated by the marriage of Chandra-gupta and Kumāradevī. In view of what has been said above, we may regard a portion of North and West Bengal as forming a part of the Gupta territory, and North Bihar as that of the Lichhchhavis. We do not know how far the former extended towards the west and the latter towards the south, but it seems probable that a considerable part of Bihar and Northern and Western Bengal was included in the joint kingdom. Beyond this it is impossible to say anything more even with a tolerable degree of plausibility.

---

[1] *HBR*, pp. 69-70.

A strict and literal interpretation of the expression 'five hundred years', in the passage of I-tsing, would go to establish the rule of a king Śrī-Gupta (or Gupta with honorific Śrī, as is the case with the founder of the Gupta family) in Bengal in the last quarter of the second century A.D. Even if such a king really existed, we do not know his relationship, if any, with his namesake who flourished about a century later. A daughter of Chandra-gupta II, married to a Vākāṭaka prince, is said to have belonged to *Dhāraṇa-gotra* which must consequently have been the *gotra* of the Gupta family. It has been suggested from this that they may have been related to queen Dhāriṇī, the chief consort of Agnimitra.[1] But this is highly problematical. On the whole it is impossible, at the present state of our knowledge, to say anything about the antecedents of the royal family founded by *Mahārāja* Gupta. Reference may be made in this connection to two seals, one with the legend *Gutasya* (in mixed Sanskrit and Prākṛit) and the other with the Sanskrit legend "*Srīguptasya*".[2] Both of these, or at least the latter, might belong to the founder of the Gupta family, but this is by no means certain.

The third king Chandra-gupta I is undoubtedly the first powerful king of the family who extended its power and prestige to a considerable extent. But beyond his marriage with the Lichchhavi princess, and the assumption of the title *Mahārājādhirāja*, we hardly possess any definite information about him. It is generally assumed that he founded a new era, dating from his coronation, which took place on December 20, 318 A.D., or February 26, 320 A.D. according to different calculations of the exact epoch of the Gupta Era. But there is nothing to prove definitely that it was he who founded this era. It merely rests on the belief that he was a very powerful king and his two predecessors were too insignificant to found an era. Both these

[1] *PHAI.*[4] 443 fn.

[2] *JRAS*, 1901, p. 99; 1905, p. 814.

assumptions are highly probable but lack convincing proof. At the same time we should not lose sight of the possibility that the era commemorates the accession of Samudra-gupta who is definitely known to have established a vast empire. This theory finds support in the two copper-plate grants of Samudra-gupta found at Nālandā and Gayā and dated respectively in the years 5 and 9. The genuineness of these two plates is certainly not above suspicion, but it is difficult to assert positively that at least the first of these is a forged one.[1] If, therefore, we believe that it was issued in year 5 of Samudra-gupta, it would be more reasonable to regard the Gupta era as commemorating the year of Samudra-gupta's accession, rather than that of his father. In any case we should not forget that the almost unanimously accepted view that Chandra-gupta I founded the Gupta era is at best a reasonable and probable hypothesis, but by no means an established fact.

It is difficult to form an exact idea of the extent of the Gupta kingdom under Chandra-gupta I. It almost certainly included the greater part of Bihar and also very probably a portion of U. P. and Bengal. But any attempt to define it more precisely is beset with difficulties. (See Appendix).

The foregoing discussion would make it clear that we possess very little definite information regarding the origin and early history of the Guptas. It would be idle to speculate further on this subject until more facts come to light. It has been suggested that Chandra-gupta I liberated "the people of Magadha from the thraldom of the hated Scythian foreigner." The history of the Kushāṇas has been dealt with in a preceding chapter, and there is not a particle of positive evidnce to support the view that Chandra-gupta I "simply drove out the Scythians and gave independence to the province of Magadha

---

[1] *IC.* XI, 225.

after three centuries of subjection and foreign oppression".[1] Such speculations are useless,[2] and for the present we may sum up the position somewhat as follows:—

Towards the close of the third and the beginning of the fourth century A.D. there was no paramount political power in Northern India, and it presented the spectacle which usually follows the disintegration of an empire. The whole country was divided into a number of independent states both monarchical and non-monarchical. Two of these in Eastern India, *viz.*, the Lichchhavi state and the principality founded by Gupta, were united by a marriage alliance, and Chandra-gupta, grandson of Gupta and son of Ghaṭotkacha, ruled over a powerful kingdom which probably included not not only the modern province of Bihar but also parts of U. P. and Bengal. He signalised his increased power and prestige by changing the title *Mahārāja* used by his father and grandfather for the higher imperial title *Mahārājādhirāja*, and probably also by founding an era.

It is a pity that nothing is known of the heroic deeds by which Chandra-gupta paved the way for the future greatness of his kingdom. But one of his last acts, which perhaps contributed more than anything else in this direction, was the selection of his son Samudra-gupta as his successor, who built on the foundation, so well laid by him, a noble structure that has immortalised his family.

---

[1]*AIG*, pp. 3, 5.

[2]Jayaswal's reconstruction (*ABORI.* XII, 50; *JBORS.* XIX, 113) of the origin and early history of the Guptas, on the basis of the drama *Kaumudī-mahotsava*, though supported by some (*JBORS.* XXI, 77; XXII, 275), has been justly rejected by most other scholars (*Aiyangar Comm. Vol.* pp. 359-362; *IC.* IX, 100; *IHQ.* XIV, 582; *Thomas Comm. Vol.* p. 115; *JAHRS.* VI, 139). Still more illusory is a recent attempt (*JBRS.* XXX,) to write the Gupta history in detail with the help of a passage in *Bhavishyottra-Purāṇa*, which is a palpable modern forgery (*IHQ.* XX, 345). It is impossible to take all these views seriously and notice them in a sober historical work.

APPENDIX

The extent of the kingdom of Chandra-gupta I

The idea that Chandra-gupta's dominions comprised Sāketa (Oudh), Prayāga (Allahabad) and Magadha (South Bihar) is widely accepted. It rests upon a Purāṇic verse which is restored as follows by Pargiter :

Anu-Gaṅgā Prayāgaṁ cha Sāketam Magadhāṁs tathā |
Etān janapadān sarvān bhoksyante Gupta-vaṁśajāḥ ||

He translates it as follows:—"*Kings* born of the Gupta race will enjoy all these territories, namely, along the Ganges, Prayāga, Sāketa and the Magadhas." The expression *anu-Gaṅgā* (along the Ganges) is somewhat vague, and may be connected with the next word to mean all the territories along the Ganges, from its mouth to Prayāga. Some have taken it as a qualifying epithet to the three other place-names, but then Sāketa can hardly be regarded as a territory along the Ganges. But this is not all. Some Purāṇic texts substitute '*Gupta*' '*Guhya*' '*Sapta*' or '*Maṇidhānyājāḥ*' for '*Gupta-vaṁśajah*' of the above passage. The corresponding prose passage in *Vishṇu* is "*Anu-Gaṅgā Prayāgam Māgadhā Guptāś-cha bhokshyanti*" *i.e.*, the territory along the Ganges (up to) Prayāga will be enjoyed by the people of Magadha and the Guptas.[1] This considerably modifies the extent of the Gupta kingdom.

These discrepancies render it a difficult task to reconstrue from the Purāṇic passage the extent of territory ruled over by the Guptas. But many scholars go even further and identify the territories, as enunciated in Pargiter's emended text, as those of Chandra-gupta I. It should be remembered that the passage in the Purāṇa is followed by a description of other kingdoms, and at least two individual rulers are mentioned. In the particular passage the Guptas, in plural number are

[1]*DKA*, p. 53 fn. 8.

described as the rulers. It is *prima facie* unreasonable, therefore, to think that the author of the passage had specifically the kingdom of Chandra-gupta I in view. Even taking the extended territory of the emended text of Pargiter, it may describe equally well the territory of Chandra-gupta I or that of Samudra-gupta at a certain stage of his victorious career. Some have even taken it as the Gupta dominions in the period of decline after Skanda-gupta. In any case, considering the various difficulties of interpretation and uncertainties in the texts, it is hardly justified to assign too great an importance to the Purāṇic passage, and far less to rely upon it in deducing the extent of territory ruled over by Chandra-gupta I.

CHAPTER VII

THE FOUNDATION OF THE GUPTA EMPIRE

With the accession of Samudra-gupta our knowlede of the political history becomes fuller and more precise. This is due to a large number of records, engraved on stone and copper during the reigns of this monarch and his successors, which have been found all over Northern India from Bengal to Kathiawar. It has become possible with their help to reconstruct the chronology and the main outline of the history of the Guptas with a tolerable degree of certainty.

Of Samudra-gupta himself we possess two records on stone and two on copper (Nos. 1-4).[1] The first two bear no dates, but the others are dated respectively in years 5 and 9. The genuineness of these two dated copper-plate charters has been doubted by many, but so far at least as the first of them is concerned, grounds for this opinion, as stated above, are certainly very inadequate.

The inscriptions engraved on the Aśoka Pillar at Allahabad (No. 3) is by far the most important record not only of Samudra-gupta, but also of the whole Gupta series. It describes the political condition of India and the achievements and personality of Samudra-gupta with such fullness of details as is not to be found in the record of any other king of Northern India, with the single exception of Aśoka. It forms our principal, and

---

[1]The figures within brackets refer to the serial number in the List of Gupta inscriptions given in the Bibliography at the end of the volume.

almost the only, source of information about the history fo Samudra-gupta and as such requires careful study.

This long royal *praśasti* (eulogy) of 33 lines was composed by Harisheṇa, who held various important offices in the state. Although Fleet held that the record was incised after the death of Samudra-gupta, there are no adequate grounds against the natural assumption that it was set up during the life-time of the great emperor.

2. Samudra-gupta's accession.

The fourth verse of this inscription refers to a memorable scene in the court of Chandra-gupta I. We are told that, in the presence of a full assembly in the open *Durbar*, the king embraced his son Samudra-gupta, and overcome with emotion, with the hairs of his body standing erect, said, with tears in his eyes : "Thou art worthy, rule this whole world". The poet adds that while this declaration caused the joy (*lit.* made them heave a sigh of relief) of the courtiers (*sabhya*), it caused heart-burning among others of equal birth, who looked with sad faces at Samudra-gupta, the fortunate winner of the prize.

It is generally assumed that the above verse refers to the selection of Samudra-gupta as heir-apparent by Chandra-gupta. But literally interpreted, the passage would rather imply that Chandra-gupta I formally renounced the throne and anointed his son as king. It may, no doubt, be argued that the poet's dramatic account was a bit exaggerated, and the words put in the mouth of the king were to refer to future events. But the emotion of the king, so vividly described, suits more with his abdication and final leave-taking than merely a formal announcement of his successor. On the other hand, the attitude of the king and the tense atmosphere prevailing in the Court might have been due to special circumstances which invested the selection of the heir-apparent with an extraordinary interest. The possibility of this is hinted at by the opposite reactions of the royal announcement on the courtiers and 'others of equal birth'. It clearly implies that other princes of the royal blood had coveted the throne and these contending claims for succession were exciting the public, and perhaps even disturbing the political life. In order to put a stop to all dangers for the present and future, the king, perhaps in the presence of all, nominated Samudra-gupta as his successor. But the view that Chandra-gupta I abdicated the throne in favour of his son Samudra-gupta is also not unlikely and is probably hinted at even in Ins. No. 4.

The fact that the court-official Harisheṇa referred to this incident, with clear emphasis on the displeasure of rival princes, although it happened long ago, may not unreasonably be taken to imply that it contains allusions to an historical event attended by important consequences. It has accordingly been suggested that Samudra-gupta's brothers rebelled against him, and put Kācha, the eldest, on the throne.[1] This ruler is known to us only from coins which bear such a close resemblance to those of Samudra-gupta, that almost all numismatists have identified the two. Allan even suggests that "Kācha was the original name of the emperor and that he took the name Samudra-gupta in allusion to his conquests.". This is, however, by no means certain, and we shall have occasion to discuss another probable identification. But even if Kācha be not identical with Samudra-gupta there is nothing to support the view that he headed a rebellion against the latter. It is perhaps possible to detect some reference to the political disturbance at the beginning of the reign of Samudra-gupta in the fragmentary verses (5 and 6) which describe how some were attracted to him by his extraordinary deeds of valour, and others submitted after

---

1. *ABORI*. IX, 83. V. A. Smith also formerly held the view that Kācha was in all probability the brother and predecessor of Samudra-gupta (*JRAS*. 1893, p. 87).

being afflicted by his prowess. But the precise implications of these vague statements are unknown at present.

3. SAMUDRA-GUPTA'S CONQUESTS

The Allahabad inscription gives a very detailed account of the conquests of Samudra-gupta. It not only refers in a general way to the emperor's skill in a hundred battles which left scars of wounds all over his body, but mentions specifically the enemies with whom he fought.

The seventh verse refers to important military achievements of Samudra-gupta, but we are unable to understand the full implication, as part of the verse is lost. Mention is first made of his complete victory over two rulers named Achyuta and Nāgasena, and a third, belonging to the family of the Kotas. This is followed by a statement that he took his pleasure at the city called Pushpa. The *lacuna*, caused by the peeling off of the surface of the stone in this part of the record, leaves us in the drak about the connection between these events, but the construction of the sentence makes it very likely that Samudra-gupta's victory over the kings, at least the third one, is closely connected with his visit to the city called Pushpa. In other words, it was probably the victory over one, or all of them, that enabled him to take possession of the city.

Both Achyuta and Nāgasena are named later in the record along with other kings as having been exterminated by Samudra-gupta. Whether this result was achieved by the campaign we are discussing, or by others at a later date, connot be definitely decided, but the former appears more probable, in view of the use of the word *unmūlya* (to uproot) about them. Achyuta probably ruled in Ahichchhatra (near Bareilly) and Nāgasena probably belonged to the Nāga royal family of Padmāvatī (Padam Pawaya, 25 miles north-east of Narwar, in Gwalior State). As to the Kotas, coins bearing the name have been found in E. Punjab and Delhi, and they probably ruled in the Upper Gangetic valley. In view of the location of these kingdoms, it may be held that the city which Samudra-gupta took possession of after his great victory, was Kānyakubja, which was called Pushpapura in ancient times.

Pushpapura was, however, also a well-known name of Pāṭaliputra, which is generally supposed to have been the capital of Samudra-gupta, and it is just possible that the poet refers to the triumphal entry of Samudra-gupta into his own capital after his brilliant military campaign. But it has been held by some that Achyuta, Nāgasena and other kings attacked him in Pāṭaliputra, and the new king had to fight in his own capital against a confederacy of kings that challenged his accession.[1] Others have held that the Kotas were at that time ruling over Pāṭaliputra and it was by defeating them that Samudra-gupta seized the city.[2] But there is no positive evidence in support of any of these views. Pushpapura may denote Pāṭaliputra, but then we can hardly be definite about its connection with Samudra-gupta's victory over the three kings named above.

After this account of the first military campaign of Samudra-gupta follows a long list of kings, states and peoples who were conquered by him and acknowledged his suzerainty. These are clearly divided into four categories, and the relation of each with Samudra-gupta is described in different terms.

The first category includes twelve states of Dakshiṇāpatha (Deccan and South India) with the names of their rulers who were defeated and captured, and then liberated.

The second category contains the names of nine rulers of Āryāvarta (Northern India) who were violently exterminated. Here we must presume that their kingdoms were annexed to the dominions of Samudra-gupta.

---

[1] *JIH.* VI, Suppl., pp. 24, 27, 37.
[2] *JBORS.* XIX, 113, 119.

To the third category belong the rulers of five kingdoms, expressly referred to as frontier chiefs, and nine tribal states, who "paid taxes, obeyed orders and performed obeisance in person to the great emperor."

Before describing the fourth category which requires a more detailed treatment on account of difficulties in interpretation we may try to form an estimate of the empire of Samudra-gupta on the basis of his relation with the states described so far. It is obvious that the dominions, directly ruled over by Samudra-gupta, included, in addition to the ancestral territories inherited by him, those of the rulers included in the second category. This is proved not only by the word 'exterminated' used in respect of these kings, but also by the fact that they are named without their kingdoms, unlike the South Indian rulers in category I. Evidently these states are not named as they no longer existed as separate units. But howsoever that may be explained, the omission of their names renders it difficult to localise the nine kings whose dominions were incorporated in the Gupta Empire[1]. Of them Gaṇapati-nāga was probably the Nāga king of Mathura,[2] and Chandra-varman may be identified with the king of that name whose record has been found at Susunia in Bankura district, Bengal. Two others, Achyuta and Nāgasena, have been discussed above. The dominions of the remaining five *viz.* Rudradeva, Matila, Nāgadatta, Nandin

[1] Identifications of kings and states mentioned in the Allahabad Ins. have been discussed in detail by V.A. smith (*JRAS*. 1897, pp. 87 ff), Dr. D.R. Bhandarkar (*IHQ*. I, 251 ff.) and Dr. H·C.Raychaudhuri (*PHAI*[4]. pp. 449 ff). The views in the text, unless otherwise stated, are based on their writings, to which reference may be made for the grounds on which the proposed identifications are made and also for other probable identifications. Cf. also *JIH*. VI, Suppl., p. 27 for some new suggestions which are, however, very problematical.

[2] Bhandarkar locates Gaṇapati-nāga's kingdom in Vidiśā. Although Bhandarkar does not mention it, the existence of a Nāga House of Mathurā, like that of Vīdśā, is attested to by the Purāṇas. Dr. Altekar found hundreds of Gaṇapati's coins in Mathurā, while only a few coins have been found at Vidśā. It is, therefore, more likely that he ruled in Mathurā.

and Bala-varman cannot be located at present. The identification of the four states would show that Samudra-gupta's dominions included the greater part, if not the whole, of U. P., a portion of Central India, and at least the south-western part of Bengal.

The states in the third category also supply indirect testimony to the extent of the territories which were directly under the rule of Samudra-gupta. As the five kingdoms in this category are specifically referred to as frontier-states, it may be safely presumed that they bordered on the dominions directly under the sway of the great emperor. Three of these, *viz.* Samataṭa, Kāmarūpa and Nepāla, are well known, corresponding respectively to South-east Bengal, Upper Assam and Nepal. The fourth Ḍavāka, was probably situated in Nowgong district in Assam.[1] The fifth, Kartṛipura, has been identified with Kartarpur in Jalandhar District, and according to some it even comprised the territory of the Katuria Raj of Kumaon, Garhwal and Rohilkhand. Some have, however, identified it with Kahror, between Multan and Lohni.[2]

Among the tribes whose states were also presumably on or near the frontier, the Mālavas, Arjunāyanas, Yaudheyas and Madrakas form the first group. The Mālavas settled in various localities in Western India after having migrated from the Punjab where they had fought with Alexander on the banks of the lower Ravi. At the time of Samudra-gupta they probably occupied Mewar, Tonk and adjoining regions of S.E. Rajputana. The Yadheyas inhabited the territory still known as Johiyabar, along both banks of the Sutlej on the border of the Bahawalpur state, but their dominions at one time extended almost up to Kangra in the north, Shaharanpur in the east and Bharatpur in the south. The Madrakas occupied the territory between the

---

[1]Barua, *Early History of Kāmarūpa*, p. 42. There is a place still called Doboka in the valley of the Kapili and the Jamuna rivers in Nowgong district (*Journ. Assam Res. Society*, I, 14-15, 124; V, 14-57).

[2]*JRAS*. 1898, pp. 198-99; *JIH*. XIV, 30.

Ravi and the Chenab, bound modern Sialkot, which represents their ancient capital city Sākala. The territory of the Arjunāyanas cannot be located with certainty, but if the group Mālava-Arjunāyana-Yaudheya-Madraka has been named in the record in geographical order, as is generally believed, the country of the Arjunāyanas may be placed between Bharatpur and Eastern Rājputāna somewhere near Jaipur.

The location of the other group of five tribes viz. the Ābhīras, Prārjunas, Sanakānīkas, Kākas and Kharaparikas is somewhat uncertain. The Ābhīras had their main settlement in W. Rājputāna which is called Abiria in the Periplus, and we have record of Ābhīra chiefs both in this part as well as in Mahārāshṭra. But they had another settlement in Central India, which was called after them Ahirwara, between Bhilsa and Jhansi. This was probably the state referred to in the Allahabad record.

As regards the Sanakānīkas, a feudatory chief of this tribe recorded his gift on a Vaishṇava cave temple at Udayagiri, a well-known hill about two miles to the north-west of Bhilsa, during the reign of Chandra-gupta II (Ins. No. 6). It may be therefore, surmised that the Sanakānīkas lived in the neighbourhood of Bhilsa, but it would be too much to presume that they held the province of Vidiśā.[1]

Kākapur, a village about 20 miles north of Bhilsa, has been identified as the ancient seat of the Kākas,[2] while the Kharaparikas have been located in the Damoh district in C. P. But these identifications cannot be regarded as certain.

According to the identifications proposed above this second group of tribes ruled over territories to the north and east of Bhilsa. If the tribes in this group have also been named in geographical order, the Prārjunas, about whom nothing is

[1]This view of Dr. Bhandarkar is inconsistent with his identification of Gaṇapati-nāga as a king of Vidiśā.
[2]*JBORS*. XVIII, 212-3.

known, may, be located to the north of Bhilsa, and in any case they probably did not live very far from this city.

It may be noted in passing that the Sanakānīka feudatory chief of Chandra-gupta II, as well as his father and grandfather, bore the title Mahārāja, indicating that the Sanakānīkas, and probably other tribes in this group, were not tribal republics, as is generally supposed, but were ruled by hereditary chiefs.

If we now consider the position of those states in the third category whose identification is more or less certain, and regard them all as situated on the frontier, we may form a fairly accurate idea of the extent of the territory under the direct rule of Samudra-gupta. In the east it included the whole of Bengal, excepting its south-eastern part. Its northern boundary ran along the foothill of the Himālayas. In the west it extended up to the Punjab and probably included its eastern districts, between Lahore and Karnal. From the last named town the boundary followed the Jumna river up to its junction with the Chambal, and thence along an imaginary line passing by the west of Narwar almost due south to Eran. Ins. No. 4 definitely proves that Eran, in Saugor district, C. P., about 50 miles to the N. N. E. of Bhilsa, was included in the dominions of Samudra-gupta.

The southern boundary ran from Eran to Jubbulpore and thence along the Vindhya range. This may be inferred from the statement in the Allahabad inscription that Samudra-gupta made all the Āṭavikarājas *i. e.*, kings of the forest countries to become his servants. In two inscriptions in Baghelkhand, dated in the years 199 and 209 of the Gupta era, king Hastin is said to have ruled over Ḍabhāla together with the eighteen forest kingdoms (*aṭavīrājya*). These were therefore contiguous to Ḍabhāla which denoted the territory round Jubbulpore. The eighteen forest kingdoms may thus be taken to have denoted the hilly tracts, full of dense forest, that extended further towards the east, across the whole of Chota Nagpur.

The conquest of these hilly states undoubtedly facilitated the campaign of Samudra-gupta against the twelve kings of Dakshiṇāpatha mentioned in category I. These are Mahendra of Kosala, Vyāghrarāja of Mahākāntāra, Maṇṭarāja of Kaurāḷa (Kerala), Mahendragiri[1] of Pishṭapura, Svāmidatta of Koṭṭura, Damana of Eraṇḍapalla, Vishṇugopa of Kāñchī, Nīlarāja of Avamukta, Hasti-varman of Veṅgī, Ugrasena of Pālakka, Kuvera of Devarāshṭra and Dhanañjaya of Kusthalapura. Among these Vishṇugopa must have been a king of the well-known Pallava dynasty,[2] and Hasti-varman was almost certainly the king of the Sālaṅkāyana dynasty whose record has been found at Peddavegi. The remaining kings are not known from any other source, but we are better informed about the location of the kingdoms named. Of these Kosala undoubtedly denotes Dakshiṇa-kośala (South Kośala) comprising the districts of Bilaspur, Raipur and Sambalpur. Pishṭapura is modern Pithapuram in the Godavari district, and Kāñchī is Conjeeveram in the Chingleput district, Madras. The name Veṅgī, the capital city of the kingdom of that name, is still preserved in Vegi or Peddavegi, 7 miles north of Ellore between the Kṛishṇā and the Godāvarī rivers. Names of Eraṇḍapallī and Devarāshṭra occur also in the records of Kaliṅga kings, and these were probably situated in Vizagapatam district. Pālakka has been identified with Paḷakkada, the capital of a Pallava viceroyalty, and was probably situated in the Nellore district.[3] Keraḷa, Koṭṭura, Avamukta and Kusthalapura cannot be located with

[1]Fleet took the name of the king to be simply 'Mahendra', connecting '*giri*' with the place-name Koṭṭura that followed. But Dr. Bhandarkar seems to be right in the view that Mahendragiri was the name of the king of Pishṭapura (*IHQ*. I, 252; *Aiyangar Comm. Vol.* p. 155; *IC*. II, 761-62). This view is also supported by actual instances of personal names ending in '*giri*' (*IC*. III, 230).

[2]According to Dubreuil, the name of this king occurs in Vayalur Ins. (*AHD*., p. 61), but Prof. Nilkanta Sastri doubts it. (Cf. Ch. XII).

[3]Prof. Nilkanta Sastri regards Ugrasena as a feudatory of Vishṇugopa (Ch. XII).

certainty.[1] Vyāghrarāja of Mahākāntāra has been identified with the Vākāṭaka feudatory prince Vyāghra whose inscriptions have been found at Nach-ne-ki-talai and Ganj in Central India, while some hold that he was also the ruler of the Uchchakalpa dynasty in Bundelkhand mentioned in Ins. Nos. 60-66. The principal objection against this identification is that Vyāghrarāja is included among the rulers of Dakshiṇāpatha, while it would place his kingdom north of the Vindhyas, and in a region included in Aṭavirājya which is separately mentioned in the same record. These are not insuperable objections, but certainly very weighty arguments against the proposed identification. It has accordingly been suggested that Vyāghrarāja ruled in Jeypore forest (in Orissa) which is referred to as Mahā-vana, a synonym of Mahā-kāntāra, in an old inscription.[2]

Leaving aside this doubtful point it seems to be clear that in course of his southern campaign Samudra-gupta passed through the eastern and southern part of the Central Provinces to Orissa, and then proceeded along the eastern coast[3] up to the Pallava kingdom of which Kāñchī was the capital. Doubts have been expressed as to his actually proceeding so far south, and it has been suggested that he fought with a confederacy of these southern princes somewhere further to the north.[4] This, how-

[1]Mr. R. Sathianathaier proposes to identify, among others, Mahākāntāra with Kanker and Bastar, Kerala with Cherla (Nagpur Taluk, E. Godavari district), Koṭṭura with Koṭṭura near Tuni (E. Godavari district), Eraṇḍapalla with Erraguntapalle in the Chentalapudi taluk of the West Godavari district, and Devarāshṭra with the place of that name in the Khanapur Sub-division of the Satara district. He thus maintains, against the generally accepted view, that Samudra-gupta did not pass through Orissa, Ganjam and Vizagapatam, but first emerged on the east coast at Pishṭapura (Pithapuram) and that he also conquered Western Deccan. *Studies in the Ancient History of Toṇḍamaṇḍalam*, pp. 13-19).

[2]*JAHRS.* I, 228.

[3]But cf. fn. 1 above.

[4]J. Dubreuil is of opinion (*op. cit.* pp. 60-61) that Samudra-gupta, who advanced up to the river Krishna, was opposed by a confederacy of the kings of the E. Deccan, and being repulsed, abandoned the conquests he had made in the coast of Orissa and returned home. This is pure imagination and directly contradicted by the explicit statements in the Allahabad Ins. cf. also N. Sastri's views in Ch. XII.

ever, is a gratuitous assumption, which seems to be belied by the detailed mention of the kings defeated by him.

Having thus discussed the first three categories of states mentioned in the Allahabad Pillar Inscription we may now proceed to a consideration of the fourth.

The fourth category consists of afew independent or semi-independent principalities. Unfortunately the interpretation of the passage describing these has proved very difficult, both as regards the names of the states as well as the different kinds of homage performed by them. As regards the former, we have, in addition to Siṁhala and other islands, a compound word *Daivaputra-Shāhi-Shāhānushāhi-Śaka-Muruṇḍa*. The first three are well-known titles borne by the Kushān kings, and may refer to one of them. It has been urged, however, that they denote, not a single Kushān king, but three of the smaller states into which the Kushān empire was divided, the ruler of each of them appropriating one of the titles for himself. Although supported by great authorities, this view seems hardly justified by available evidence, and the probability rather is that reference is made here to a Kushān ruler exercising sway over Kabul and a part of the Punjab, and possibly other territories further to the west[1].

Of the two remaining words of the compound, Śaka is a well-known tribal name, and we have positive evidence that the Śaka (Western) Kshatrapas were ruling in W. India, and other persons of that nationality were ruling in and about Sāñchī.[2] As regards Muruṇḍa, some regard it as the name of a powerful foreign tribe, ruling in the Upper Ganges valley,[3] while others

[1]*CGD*. pp. xxvi-ii; *PHAI*. 4, p. 460; *AIG*. p. 24: Cf. *supra*. Ch. I.

[2]*EI*. XVI, 230; *JASB* N.S. XIX, 537.

[3]*CGD*. p. xxix. According to the Chinese authority, the capital of Meou-lun (a word equated with Muruṇḍa) was 7000 *li* from the mouth of th Great River, which was undoubtedly the Ganges. Allan is, therefore, hardly, correct when he says that the Chinese description of the capital seems to suggest Pāṭaliputra.

hold that "Muruṇḍa is not the name of a tribe, but a Śaka word meaning *lord*, which was used as a title by the Śakas, and after them by the Kushāṇas", and that Śaka-Muruṇḍa denotes the Western Satraps.[1]

We may hold, therefore, that the fourth category includes the Śaka and Kushāṇa princes of the west together with the peoples of Siṁhala and other islands, and for the present it is impossible to be more precise.

The words denoting different kinds of homage performed by these states are:—1. *Ātma-nivedena*; 2. *Kanyopāyana-dāna*; and 3. *Garutmad-aṅka-sva-vishaya-bhukti-śāsana-yāchana.*

The first means literally, offering oneself as sacrifice, and probably means personal attendance. The second means 'presenting unmarried daughters and giving them in marriage', but it is not easy to distinguish between the two. For it would be unreasonable to think that rulers who enjoyed at least some degree of autonomy would present their daughters for any other purpose than marriage.

The third compound presents some difficulty. It has been urged that it means a two-fold request asking for charters (*śāsana-yāchana*) (*i*) for the use of the Gupta coin bearing Garuḍa symbol (*Garutmad-aṅka*) and (*ii*) for the Government of their own territories (*sva-vishya-bhukti*)[2]. On the other hand '*Garutmad-aṅka*' has been translated as 'bearing the Garuḍa seal' and regarded as a qualifying epithet of *Śāsana*, the whole compound being taken to mean the soliciting of imperial charters, confirming them in the enjoyment of their territories, bearing the Garuḍa seal.[3]

[1] *EI.* XIV, 292-3; *JBORS.* XXIII, 449. Jayaswal took Śaka-Muruṇḍa to denote the smaller Śaka rulers like the Shalada, Shaka, and the Gaḍahara chiefs as well as the Western Satraps' (*JBORS.* XVIII, 210).

[2] *JBORS.* XVIII, 207; XIX, 145.

[3] *CGD.* p. xxv. It has been suggested that the different forms of homage or submission apply respectively to the different groups of states included in the category (*JBORS.* XIX, 145). But this is very unlikely (*JBORS.* XXIII, 447-48).

We have discussed this category at some length, for an accurate idea of the nature and extent of the Gupta empire, specially its relation with the outlying Śaka and Kushāṇa principalities, depends upon a proper identification of the states named and correct interpretation of the forms of homage paid by them. In spite of difference of views, 'attendance in person' and 'asking for imperial charters for the enjoyment of territories', the two forms of homage, about which there is no difference of opinion, would certainly imply that the Śaka and Kushāṇa rulers of West and North-West India acknowledged the suzerainty of Samudra-gupta. But whether this represents the actual state of things, or is a mere boastful rhetoric on the part of the panegyrist, it is difficult to say. The inclusion of even distant Siṁhala (Ceylon) and all other islands in this category raises great doubts about this interpretation, and we shall hardly be justified in taking the words of the court-poet in their literal sense without corroborative evidence.

So far as Ceylon is concerned, we have fortunately an independent evidence of its political relation with Samudra-gupta. According to a Chinese text, Meghavarṇa, king of Ceylon, sent two monks to Bodh-Gaya to visit the sacred spots, but they were put to great inconvenience for want of suitable accommodation. To remove this difficulty for future pilgrims to the holy place, Meghavarṇa decided to found a monastery there. He accordingly sent a mission to Samudra-gupta with rich presents and asked for permission to build a monastery and a rest-house for Ceylonese pilgrims. Samudra-gupta readily granted the permission, and the Ceylonese king built a splendid monastery to the north of the Bodhi tree.[1] By the time of Hiuen Tsang it had developed into a magnificent establishment, with

[1] *JA.* 1900, pp. 316 ff., 401 ff.; *I.A.* 1902, p. 194. The date of Meghavarṇa is uncertain. Geiger *Mahāvaṁsa* Eng. Transl., p. xxxix) places him between 352-379 A.D., but according to Mr. Parnavitana (cf. Ch. XIII, he ruled from 304 to 332, A.D.

more than 1,000 priests, and the pilgrim has described the rich decorations and massive grandeur of the buildings. Referring to the old history of its foundation Hiuen Tsang says that the Ceylonese king 'gave in tribute to the king of India all the jewels of his country'. It is likely that Samudra-gupta's courtier also regarded the rich present as tribute, and construed the Ceylonese king's prayer for permission to build a monastery into an 'application for charter confirming him in the enjoyment of his territories', one of the forms of homage paid by the category of states into which Siṁhala is included. There may be similar basis for the inclusion of the other states in this category, the offer of a daughter's hand being very common among neighbourly kings. In view of the great name and fame of Samudra-gupta, the neighbouring Śaka and Kushāṇa rulers might have thought it politic to cultivate friendly relations with him and strengthen them by personal visit or matrimonial alliance. This might have been easily twisted into *ātma-nivedana* and *kanyopāyana-dāna*, the two other forms of homage referred to above. It may be easily admitted that the weaker states of the fourth category, situated just outside the limits of the mighty empire, maintained diplomatic relations with Samudra-gupta and deliberately sought to win his favour and goodwill by various measures which, however derogatory to a sense of royal pride and position of equality, did not theoretically infringe their independent status. But it is difficult to believe, without more positive evidence, that these rulers in any way openly acknowledge the suzerainty of the Gupta Emperor, or enjoyed their kingdoms merely as fiefs on the basis of charters granted by Samudra-gupta. Such evidence is, however, not altogether wanting. The discovery of Kushāṇa type of coins with the names of Samudra and Chandra may be taken to indicate the suzerainty of Samudra-gupta over the Kushāṇas.[1]

[1]For these coins, cf. *JARS.* 1893, p. 145. See also Ch. I.

The inclusion of 'all islands' in addition to Siṁhala, in this category, is worthy of note. Although none is specifically named, it very likely refers, in a general way, to the Hindu colonies in Malay Peninsula, Java, Sumatra and other islands in Indian archipelago. As will be shown in a separate chapter, the Hindus had established colonies and kingdoms in these regions during or before the Gupta period, and the influence of Gupta culture is deeply imprinted on most of them. That there was a constant and intimate intercourse between India and these colonies is proved by Fa-hien's narrative, and it is only natural that the Hindu colonists in these far-off regions would maintain contact with the most powerful empire in their motherland. Many of them must even have originally migrated from the different regions which constituted that empire. The reference to homage paid by dwellers of all islands need not, therefore, be treated as mere rhetoric, but may be based on actual relationship with some of them, the exact nature of which, however, cannot be ascertained.

As in the case of the fourth category, there is some element of doubt in respect of Samudra-gupta's exact relationship with the rulers mentioned in the first. All that is said in the record is that he acquired glory by the favour shown in capturing and then liberating the kings. The natural conclusion, of course, is that these vanquished rulers were re-instated on their throne as feudatory kings, and whatever might have been the actual terms imposed upon each of them in respect of payment of tribute or other services, they at least had to acknowledge the suzerainty of the Gupta emperor and owe allegiance to him. But there is no specific mention of the exact status of these kings after their restoration to the throne.

The above discussion enables us to describe the nature and extent of the empire of Samudra-gupta with an accuracy and fulness of details which are rare in ancient Indian history. It comprised nearly the whole of Northern India, with the exclusion of Kashmir, Western Punjab, Western Rājputāna, Sindh and Gujarat, together with the highlands of Chattisgarh and Orissa and a long stretch of territory along the eastern coast extending as far south as Chingleput and probably even further. Of these vast territories, a considerable portion of Northern India, more accurately defined above, was directly administered by the emperor through his own officials. This was surrounded on all sides except the south by an almost continuous line of tributary states, five kingdoms on the north and east, and nine tribal states on the west mentioned above. The twelve conquered kingdoms in the south also probably occupied similar status. Beyond these tributary states, lay the Śaka and Kushāṇa principalities on the west and north-west, and Ceylon and other islands in the south and south-east, whose rulers were within the sphere of influence of the empire and, even if not actually subordinate, maintained a submissive and respectful attitude towards their powerful neighbour and endeavoured by all means to win his grace and favour. Thus was "the (whole) world bound", as the courtly author puts it, "by means of the amplitude of the vigour of the arm" of Samudra-gupta.

The organisation of the conquered territories reflects great credit upon the statesmanship of Samudra-gupta. The Allahabad inscription clearly demonstrates that he was inspired by the vision of an all-India empire. But he did not attempt the almost impossible task of bringing the whole country under his direct rule. At the same time he established a strong central authority, sufficiently powerful to check the disruptive tendencies of smaller states and their mutual dissensions which had proved to be India's ruin in the past. By a ruthless campaign he extinguished the numerous petty states contiguous to his own dominions and carved out a big empire. But he was not intoxicated by his success. He did not follow the Kauṭiliyan policy of establishing one imperial sway over all and try to annex the frontier kingdoms like East Bengal, Assam and Nepal which were hard to conquer and still harder to retain, as the Muslim and British rulers of India were to realise at a later date. Towards the distant tribal states on the western frontier he adopted the same policy, specially perhaps as they were buffer-states against the foreign rulers like Śakas and Kushāṇas. By retaining these frontier states as faithful tributaries, he added to the defensive strength of the infant empire. The rulers of the states in South India were made to feel the weight of the new power, but were conciliated by a wise and liberal policy. Solid and lasting foundations were thus laid for a great imperial fabric on which the successors of Samudragupta were to build in future.

The vast empire was undoubtedly the fruit of numerous military campaigns extending over many years which testify to his prowess and military skill of a very high order. It is not necessary to suppose that he had to fight with every ruler or state mentioned in the Allahabad inscription, for many might have submitted without opposition. It is known from the coins and inscriptions that Samudra-gupta performed an *Aśvamedha* sacrifice, and no historical Indian ruler, either before or after him, had greater justification for this time-honoured ceremony and age-old unique method of establishing universal supermacy. But it may justly be doubted whether he scrupulously followed the prescribed method of letting loose the sacrificial horse and these extensive conquests were undertaken merely as the necessary prelude to the great ceremony. For it is significant that the Allahabad inscription which describes these conquests in detail does not refer at all to the *Aśvamedha* sacrifice. The probability rather is that the *Aśvamedha* sacrifice was thought of towards the close of his reign as a fitting symbol to signalise the wonderful results achieved by arduous military campaigns of a long life. The statement that Samudra-gupta restored the *Aśvamedha* sacrifice, which had long been in abeyance, cannot be regarded as correct, for we have many known instances of this ceremony extending over the whole period between Pushyamitra and the rise of the Guptas.

Although the author of the *praśasti* refers to 'hundred battles' in which Samudra-gupta was engaged, he does not mention the number or sequence of these campaigns. All that we can reasonably assume is that the campaigns against Achyuta, Nāgasena and the Kotas were probably the earliest in the reign. Although the campaign in South India is mentioned next, it is difficult to believe that Samudra-gupta would have undertaken an expedition so far away from his kingdom, without bringing under his sway (or finally settling the affairs of) the numerous states in his immediate neighbourhood. It is not, therefore, safe to rely on this order of enumeration in forming an idea of the military campaigns of Samudra-gupta.

We can certainly regard him as a hero of hundred battles —in a figurative rather than a literal sense—but no details of these are vouchsafed to us.

4. Personality of Samudra-gupta

Brilliant as a general and as a statesman, Samudra-gupta possessed many qualifications which are more suited to a life of peaceful pursuits. It is unreasonable to accept all that Harisheṇa says of his royal patron's qualities of head and heart at its face value,[1] but, even making due allowance for exaggerations in royal *praśastis*, no doubt is left of the striking personality of Samudra-gupta, and it would be quite in the fitness of things, if, as it seems likely, he assumed the proud

[1]Dr. R. K. Mookerji has made a detailed analysis of the 'many-sided genius and character of Samudra-gupta' on the basis of his inscriptions and coin-legends (*IC.* IX, 77). But we shall hardly be justified in accepting the expressions occurring in them at their face-value.

title of Vikramāditya[1], presumably in imitation of that king of legendary fame.

Harisheṇa lays special emphasis upon Samudra-gupta's learning and wisdom, sharp and polished intellect, and above all his poetical and musical talents. It is specifically stated that he 'established his title of king of poets by various poetical compositions that were fit to be the means of subsistence of learned people'. There are also other references to his poetic works and poetic style. Evidently he was the author of some poems which unfortunately have not survived even in quotations. We are more fortunate in possessing a unique evidence of his skill in music in the shape of a class of gold coins which portray the emperor as playing on a lyre.

The references to Vasubandhu in Buddhist works throw light on the literary patronage of a Gupta king whose identity cannot be established with certainty. It is said by the rhetorician Vāmana that the son of Chandra-gupta, known as Chandra-prakāśa, was a great patron of letters, and appointed the famous Buddhist scholar Vasubandhu as his minister. If Vasubandhu flourished in the fourth century A.D. and died soon after the middle of that century, as is generally held, we have to take Chandra-gupta as Chandra-gupta I and regard Chandra-prakāśa as another name of Samudra-gupta.[2] Vāmana's reference to his patronage of letters would be quite in keeping with what Harisheṇa says of the great Gupta emperor.

---

[1]This is inferred from the title "*Srī Vikramaḥ*" recently found on one of his coins (*JNSI.* V, 136). Some scholars, however, do not accept the view.

[2]The whole question has been fully discussued by V. A. Smith in *EHI.*[3] pp. 328 ff. Takakusu held that Vasubandhu lived from about 420 to 500 A.D. (*JRAS.* 1905, pp. 43 ff). Against this M. Peri maintained (*SEFEO.* XI, 339 ff.) that Vasubandhu lived in the fourtn century A.D. and died soon after the middle of the century. This view is generally accepted. Takakusu opposed it and reaffirmed his old view (*Indian Studies in honour of C. R. Lanman*, pp. 79 ff). For other views cf V.A. Smith, *op. cit.*

Harisheṇa also refers to Samudra-gupta's charity and kindness, even to conquered kings. 'He re-established many royal families, fallen and deprived of sovereignty, and his officers were always employed in restoring the wealth of the various kings conquered by him. He was a great patron of learning and by his liberal munificence removed the eternal discord between good poetry and plenty'. His devotion to religious duties and sacred scriptures is referred to, and he is said to be the giver of many hundreds of thousands of cows, evidently as gift to Brāhmaṇas.

The rich variety of gold coins issued by Samudra-gupta not only indicate the power, wealth and grandeur of his empire, but also give us some idea of his appearance and a fair insight into his personal qualities.

The coins of Samudra-gupta show no less than six different types, five of which are distinctly characteristic of his life and reign. Three of them represent him in his military aspect. In one he stands fully dressed, with a bow on the

---

In addition to the passage of Vāmana referred to above in the text we have reference to Vasubandhu's relation with the Guptas in Paramārtha's biogaraphy of that Buddhist scholar, which may be summed up as follows:—

King Vikramāditya of Ayodhyā became a patron of Buddhism on account of Vasubandhu's success in religious activity. He sent his crown price Bālāditya to Vasubandhu to learn Buddhism, and the queen too, became one of his disciples. When he came to the throne king Bālāditya in conjunction with his queen-mother invited Vasubadhu (who had gone to his native place, Peshawar) to Ayodhyā and favoured him with special patronage (*JRAS*. 1905, pp. 33 ff).

It is generally accepted that Vikramāditya and Bālāditya refer to two Gupta emperors, but it is not possible to identify them so long as the date of Vasubandhu is not definitely fixed.

An interesting side-issue arises out of the statement in Paramārtha's biography of Vasubandhu that the city of Ayodhyā was the residence of both the kings Vikramāditya and Bālāditya. It has been inferred from this that the Imperial Guptas had a secondary capital at Ayodhyā, for which, however, there is no other evidence.

An inscription found at Sarnath mentions a royal dynasty in which there was more than one king name Bālāditya (*CII*. III, 284). It is not altogether impossible that Vasubandhu's patron belonged to this or a similar local dynasty of Ayodhyā.

left and an arrow on the right hand, with the legend "having conquered the earth, the invincible one wins heaven by good deeds". In another, he hold a battle-axe with the legend, "wielding the axe of Kṛitānta (the god of death), the unconquered conqueror of unconquered kings is victorious." In the third the king, wearing turban and waist-cloth, is trampling on a tiger which falls backwards as he shoots it, with bow in right hand and the left hand drawing its string back behind left ear. The legend refers to the king as 'having the prowess of a tiger'. There can be hardly any doubt that these figures of the king are drawn from real life, and the same thing is true of the fourth type in which the king, wearing waist-cloth, is seated cross-legged on a couch, playing on a *vīṇā* (lute or lyre) which lies on his knees. The legend on this type of coins simply gives his name without any reference to his martial exploits. The fifth type of coins (Pl. III, 1) commemorates the *Aśvamedha* sacrifices. It shows, on one side, a spirited horse standing before a sacrificial post, and on the other the figure of the queen-empress. The legend on this type reads : "The king of kings, having conquered the earth, wins heaven, being the performer of Aśvamedha." These five types of coins thus symbolise the warlike and peaceful pursuits of the king, and form a suitable and illustrative commentary on his prowess and military glory as well as his versatile genius, so ably described in the Allahabad inscription. It is interesting to note also how the legend corresponds to the particular aspect of the king figured on each type of coins, and give expression to the bravery and heroism of the king as well as his great military genius. The personal appearance of the king, so far as we can judge from his figure on the coins,[1] is also fully in keeping with ideal we otherwise form of

[1]For a detailed description of the coins, cf. *CGD*. pp. 1-23, cvii-cxii. pll. I-V. For some corrections of the legends on Aśvamedha coins of *JASB* NS., X, 255; XI, 477.

him. Of tall stature and good physique, his body is marked by strong muscular arms and a fully developed chest.

The artistic execution of the gold coins of Samudra-gupta gives us a foretaste of the wonderful progress of art which was to mark the Gupta period as the Classic Age in India. The emperor Samudra-gupta, such as we know him even from the scanty materials at our disposal, was a visible embodiment of the physical and intellectual vigour of the coming age which was largely his own creation. As we study his coins and inscriptions we seem to visualise a king of robust and powerful build, whose physical vigour, matched by his intellectual and cultural attainments, heralded a new era in which Āryāvarta regained new political consciousness and national soildarity after five centuries of political disintegration and foreign domination, and reached the high-water mark of moral, intellectual, cultural and material prosperity which marked it as the Golden Age of India to which untold generations of the future were to look back for guidance and inspiration.

Samudra-gupta must have had a fairly long reign. He died some time before 380 A.D., the earliest known date for the reign of his son Chandra-gupta II, and probably before 376 A.D. It is difficult to determine, even approximately, the year of his accession. It depends largely on the solution of the question, —who founded the Gupta era. If, as is generally assumed, the Gupta era dates from the accession of Chandra-gupta I, who married Kumāradevī shortly afterwards, Samudra-gupta probably did not come to the throne till about 350 A.D. For we can hardly believe that Samudra-gupta gave evidence of his prowess and ability and was selected by his father as the fittest prince to succeed him before he attained the age of twenty-five to thirty years.[1] To hold that Samudra-gupta ascended the

[1] There is a certain amount of loose thinking about the date of Samudra-gupta. Thus Allan places the accession of Chandra-gupta I in 320 A.D. and holds that he married Kumāradevī after conquering

throne about 335 A.D., or even somewhat earlier, certainly implies that Chandra-gupta I married Kumāradevī long before he became a king or that he established the era long after he had ascended the throne.

But, as already pointed out above, there is no positive evidence to support the theory that the Gupta era was founded by Chandra-gupta I or dates from the first year of his reign, and it is equally likely that the era dated from the accession of Samudra-gupta, the greatest of the Gupta emperors. This would be regarded as almost certain if the Nālandā charter of the 5th year be regarded as a genuine grant of Samudra-gupta, or even a late copy of genuine grant.

There is one serious objection against this view. As Kumāra-gupta I, the grandson of Samudra-gupta, was on the throne in the year 136 of the Gupta era, it would give a total duration of 136 years to three generations which is far above the average. The objection applies almost equally to the current view that Samudra-gupta ascended the throne in 325 or 335 A.D. If the Nālandā grant prove to be genuine we have to accept it as a fact that three generations of Gupta rulers reigned for at least 131 years, and there can be hardly any objection to the addition of five years to this total by regarding Samudra-gupta as the founder of the era. It may be pointed out that although a period of 136 years for three generations of kings is undoubtedly very high, it cannot be regarded as impossible, for we know that three generations of Western

---

Vaiśāli (*CGD*. pp. xix-xx). Yet he places the accession of Samudra-gupta in 335 (*CGD*. p. xxxii) when Samudra-gupta could not have been more than 13 or 14 years old. It is difficult to suppose that a boy of 14 would be selected by the father as the fittest among rival princes. Dr. H.C. Raychaudhuri also holds that Chandra-gupta I ascended the throne in 320 and strengthened his position by a matrimonial alliance with the Lichchhavis (*PHAI*.[4] p. 445), yet he does not rule out the possibility that Samudra-gupta might have ascended the throne in 325 A.D. (*Ibid*. p. 446).

Chālukya kings from Vikramāditya V to Someśvara III ruled for 118 years.

It would thus follow that while there is much to support the view that Samudra-gupta ascended the throne in 320 A.D. or *c.* 350 A.D. there is little justification for the date 325-335 A.D. usually assigned to his accession.

CHAPTER VIII

THE EXPANSION OF THE GUPTA EMPIRE.

Rāma-gupta

Until about twenty years ago it was unanimously held that the great emperor Samudra-gupta was succeeded by his son Chandra-gupta II. Since then, the recovery of a few passages of a lost dramatic work, *Devī-Chandra-gupta* by Viśākhadatta, has thrown altogether new light on this question.[1]

By piecing together the scattered evidences contained in this drama and supplementing them by isolated references contained in the *Harsha-charita*, Sanjan and Cambay copper-plates, and the *Kāvyamīmāṁsā*, some scholars have reconstructed the story somewhat as follows:—

Samudra-gupta was succeeded by his son Rāma-gupta whose wife was Dhruvadevī. In course of a war with the Śaka king he was closely besieged and placed in such a difficult position that, in order to assure the safety of his people,[2] he agreed to surrender his queen to the Śaka king. His younger brother Chandra-gupta protested against this act of dishonour, and offered to go to the enemy's camp in the disguise of queen Dhruvadevī in order to kill the hated Śaka king. The stratagem succeeded, and Chandra-gupta saved the empire and its honour.

[1]The question has been discussed by a large number of scholars among whom the following deserve special mention : S. Lèvi (*JA*. CCIII, pp. 201 ff); R. Sarasvati (*IA*. LII, pp. 181 ff); A. S. Altekar (*JBORS*. XIV, 223 ff; XV, 134 ff); R. D. Banerji (*AIG*. pp. 26 ff); Dr. D. R. Bhandarkar (*Malaviya Comm. Vol.* pp. 189 ff); K. P. Jayaswal (*JBORS*. XVIII, 17 ff); Winternitz (*Aiyangar Comm. Vol.* pp. 359 ff); Sten Konow (*JBORS*. XXIII, 444); V. V. Mirashi (*IHQ*. X, 48; *IA*. LXII, 201); N. Das Gupta (*IC*. IV. 216); V. Raghavan (*Benares Hindu University Magazine*, II, 23-54, 307); H. C. Raychaudhuri (*PHAI*.[4] p. 465.

[2]"*Prakṛitīnām=āśvāsanāya*". Some take it to mean for satisfying the Councillors".

The incident must have raised him in the estimation of his subjects as well as of queen Dhruvadevī, and the character and reputation of Rāma-gupta must have suffered a corresponding decline. There was an estrangement between the two brothers, and Chandra gupta, presumably afraid of his elder brother's design on his own life, pretended madness. Ultimately, by some means which is not known, Chandra-gupta succeeded in killing his elder brother and not only seized his kingdom but also married his widow.

The patience, industry and ingenuity of a number of scholars have thus laid bare a fairly complete picture of a momentous but hitherto unknown episode in the history of the imperial Guptas. We have now to decide whether the picture represents actual facts or is based merely on the imagination of dramatists and story-tellers.

While the issue is an important one, the judgment is not an easy process. On the one hand we have the two historical names—Chandra-gupta (II) and Dhruvadevī—as the hero and heroine of a drama whose author, even if not a contemporary of them, as some contend, probably flourished not long afterwards;[1] and the essential parts of their story, on which the drama was based, are corroborated by two authoritative sources like Bāṇa's *Harsha-charita* (7th century A.D.) and Rāshṭrakūta copper-plates (9th-10th century A.D.) originating from two distant parts of India. On the other hand it has been pointed out that the version of the story given by Bāṇa and his commentators differs from that known to the author of the *Kāvya-mīmāṁsā*, and that details not fouud in the earlier accounts are added in the days of Amoghavarsha and Govinda IV.

[1] S. Lèvi places Viśākhadatta some time between the Gupta dynasty and Harsha. Jayaswal, Sten Konow and N. Das Gupta regard him as a contemporary of Chandra-gupta II. Winternitz, who originally held the same view, gave it up on the discovery of *Devī-Chandra-gupta*. and assigned its author to the sixth century A.D. (cf. *B. C. Law Volume*. p. 50).

Further, the story in itself, even apart from such supernatural elements as *Vetāla-sādhanā* (goblin-worship), is not only unusual, almost bordering on the romantic and incredible, but is also *prima facie* so much opposed to our knowledge of facts and belief in practices of the period, that nothing but the strongest evidence should induce us to place any credence in it.

We have, for instance, a pretty large number of coins and inscriptions of the Gupta period, but they contain no reference to a king Rāma-gupta, who must be presumed, according to the story, to have ruled over the Gupta empire after the death of Samudra-gupta. Again, while the murder of a brother for the sake of kingdom is by no means unusual, the marriage of his brother's widow by the rebel and the regicide clashes with our cherished notions about morality and social custom prevalent in those times.

These objections are not unanswerable. It has been pointed out that neither Śāstric injunctions nor social practices prohibited a marriage between a widow and the younger brother of her husband. But we should remember that the Sangali and Cambay plates definitely condemn the act and even describe it as illicit intercourse. As regards the other point, it has been argued that as the official records give the genealogy, and not the succession of kings, the omission of the name of Rāma-gupta need cause no surprise. The absence of coins is a more serious objection. But some have explained it away by assuming a very short rule of the king, while others have attributed to him the gold coins bearing the name Kācha, already referred to above. Dr. Bhandarkar holds that the name Rāma-gupta, which occurs only once in the passages quoted from the *Devī-Chandra-gupta*, is a misreading of Kācha-gupta, the real name of the king, while Jayaswal regarded Kācha and Rāma as two different names of the same king.

These arguments in support of the story are no doubt plausible, but certainly not convincing. There are, however, other objections besides the two mentioned above. It is difficult, for instance, to believe that the inheritor of the mighty empire of Samudra-gupta could be so decisively defeated by a Śaka king that he had no means of saving his army or kingdom save by consenting to an act, which would be regarded as the most ignominious by any king in any age or country, not to speak of the mighty emperor of the golden age of India who had the blood of Samudra-gupta running in his veins. A story preserved in the *Mujmalū-t-Tawārikh* has been seized upon as a suitable explanation of this enigma. It has been suggested that the king and his retinue were besieged in a hill-fort, and his army having been defeated by the Śaka king he was at the complete mercy of the latter. But even such a situation can hardly condone the utter infamy and disgrace involved in the proposed means of escape from it. It should be remembered that we can not explain it merely as a caprice of a monarch, who might be imbecile or insane, for we are asked to believe that his action had the full approval of the people, even if it was not instigated by them. The code of honour in the golden age of India must be assumed to have been very different from the later and more degenerate days, when, in similar peril women, preferring death to dishonour, are known to have thrown themselves in blazing fire, and men rushed out and fought till they avenged the insult with the last drop of their blood.

These considerations stand in the way of accepting as historical the strange episode of Rāma-gupta, until at least the existence of this king is established on unimpeachable grounds. While the story cannot be dismissed off-hand, as altogether a figment of imagination, we must not rush to the other extreme of accepting, *in toto*, plots of drama and popular tales as reliable facts. In other words, we must suspend our judgment upon the historical character of Rāma-gupta, his fight with the Śakas, and the strange event which deprived him of his throne, life and the natural affection and fidelity of his wife.

In view of this, it would hardly serve any useful purpose to discuss at length whether the Śaka opponent of Rāma-gupta was the Śaka Satrap of Western India or a Kushāṇa king of the Punjab, and whether the battle took place in the Himālayas, or a place called Alipura (in the Punjab), or Nalinapura (near Jelalabad).

These problems cannot be solved until further evidence is available, nor is their solution very material for the broad and general historical question that concerns us for the present. We may therefore proceed to discuss the reign of Chandra-gupta II without any further reference to the episode of Rāma-gupta.

2. Chandra-gupta II.

When Samudra-gupta died, probably in ripe old age, he left many sons and grandsons behind him. Whether Chandra-gupta II was his eldest son is not definitely known. In the conventional Gupta genealogy, as recorded in royal grants and seals, the expression *tatparigṛihīta* (accepted by him *i.e.* Samudra-gupta) is applied to Chandra-gupta II, whereas the corresponding expression applied to the kings succeeding him is *tat-pādānudhyāta* (meditating on or favoured by the feet of). This has been taken to indicate that Samudra-gupta chose him as his successor out of his many sons. The acceptance of this view would cut at the very root of the theory that Rāma-gupta succeeded Samudra-gupta. But the two phrases indicating the relationship of two successive kings may be taken as merely conventional expressions of good-will and respect without implying anything more about special selection or immediate succession. We should not, therefore, definitely infer, without any corroborative evidence, that Chandra-gupta II "was chosen out of many sons by his father as the best fitted to succeed him", though this is by no means unlikely.

Chandra-gupta had a second name Deva and is referred

to as Deva-gupta, Deva-rāja or Deva-śri. His mother's name is Dattadevī and we know the names of two of his queens Dhruvadevī (or Dhruvasvāminī) and Kuveranāgā. He is styled Parama-Bhāgavata and was evidently a staunch devotee of the Vaishṇava faith.

Six records (Nos. 5-10) of the time of Chandra-gupta II are known so far. The earliest, found at Mathura (No. 5), is dated in the year 61 of the Gupta era, corresponding to A.D. 380. The inscription also contains his regnal year. Unfortunately this part of the stone is damaged, and the regnal year cannot be read with absolute certainty. Some have read it as '*prathame*' (first), and others '*pañchame*' (fifth). The latter reading seems more probable, and accordingly Chandra-gupta's accession would fall in A.D. 376-7. The inscription proves that on this date Mathura formed an integral part of the Gupta empire. It thus stretched beyond the Jumna river which has been provisionally accepted above as the western boundary of the territory directly administered by Samudra-gupta. Whether it indicates further conquests of Chandra-gupta II or whether Mathura had already formed an integral part of the kingdom ruled over by his father, it is difficult to say. In any case it may be taken to prove that the empire did not probably suffer any diminution, towards the west, after the death of Samudra-gupta.

There are clear indications that Chandra-gupta II emulated his father's military career and went out in a campaign of conquest. A cave in Udayagiri hill, about two miles to the north-west of Bhilsa, was dedicated to Sambhu by Vīrasena, a 'minister of peace and war' of Chandra-gupta II. It is stated in the short inscription (No. 10), recording this gift, that the minister was an inhabitant of Pāṭaliputra, and had accompanied his royal master to Udayagiri while the latter was 'seeking to conquer the whole world'. This undoubtedly refers to a military campaign undertaken by Chandra-gupta II towards the south-western part of the empire.

The great success achieved by the Gupta emperor is indirectly attested by coins. It is a significant fact that the long series of coins testifying to the almost unbroken rule of the Western Kshatrapas for more than three hundred years comes to an end between A.D. 388 and 397 and is replaced by coins of similar design issued by Chandra-gupta II. This leaves no doubt that Chandra-gupta II extinguished the power of the Western Kshatrapas and annexed their dominions. This was undoubtedly the main result of the military campaign which he had undertaken 'to conquer the world', as his minister so characteristically describes it.

In addition to the record of the minister Vīrasena, we have another (No. 6) in the same locality referring to the gift of a Sanakānīka Mahārāja, a feudatory of Chandra-gupta II, in the year 82 (=A.D. 401-2). Another inscription (No. 8.) dated 93 (=A.D. 412-13), records some donations to the great Buddhist Vihāra at Sanchi by Amrakārddava, who was an official of Chandra-gupta II, and 'acquired banners of victory and fame in many battles'.

The presence of a feudatory, a minister and a military officer of Chandra-gupta II in the same locality in Eastern Malwa may not unreasonably be connected with the protracted military campaign of Chandra-gupta II which may thus be placed during the early years of the fifth century A.D., though it might have commenced even earlier. The coins issued by Chandra-gupta II in imitation of those of the Western Kshatrapas bear dates in Gupta era of which only the first symbol denoting 90 is clearly legible. These coins must therefore have been issued between A.D. 409 and 415 (when Chandragupta had ceased to reign). Everything thus indicates that Chandra-gupta's military campaign was planned, and the conquest of the Śaka dominions completed, during the closing decade of the fourth and the first decade of the fifth century A.D.

By this brilliant conquest the Gupta emperor not only

put an end to the domination of the foreigners, who occupied the soil of India for the longest period, but added the rich provinces of Kathiawar and N. Gujarat to the empire which now extended from the Bay of Bengal to the Arabian Sea. The Gupta empire now controlled a large part of the Indian commerce with the western world and was brought into closer contact with the western civilisation. Chandra-gupta's exploits naturally recalled those of king Vikramāditya of Ujjain who is described in Indian legends as having expelled the first Śaka conquerors of India more than four hundred years before. It is presumably in imitation of this legendary hero that Chandra-gupta, like his father, assumed the title Vikramāditya which gradually came to be regarded as a title of distinction by mighty rulers of India famed for their military exploits. It is also not unlikely that the literary references to Chandra-gupta's wars with the Śaka chief, reviewed in the last section, contain an echo of this great victory.

The claims for Chandra-gupta's almost equally brilliant military campaign in the north-west rest on less solid grounds. A record (No. 67) engraved on the iron pillar which now stands near Kutb Minar at Delhi refers to a king called Chandra, 'who defeated a confederacy of hostile chiefs in Vaṅga, and having crossed in warfare the seven mouths of the river Sindhu, conquered the Vāhlikas.' As Vāhlika denotes Bactria, we have to presume that this king, who crossed the Punjab rivers and carried his victorious arms beyond the Hindu Kush mountains, was also in a position to fight, with equal success, against a powerful enemy in Bengal. Even if, as some hold, Vāhlika is located in the Beas valley bordering on Kashmir, the military exploits of king Chandra must be regarded as remarkable.

It is, however, difficult to regard as certain the proposed identification of king Chandra with Chandra-gupta II.[1] It is

[1]For the different views on the identification of Chandra and the

undoubtly more probable than the proposed identification of Chandra with Chandra-gupta I or Chandra-varman, but in the absence of any corroborative evidence we cannot definitely credit Chandra-gupta II with these brilliant military exploits simply on the basis of the record on the iron pillar at Delhi. The Kushāṇa type of coins, with the name Chandra, however, indicates his supremacy in the N. W. Frontier Province.

No political event of the reign of Chandra-gupta II, except his conquest of the Śaka territory, is known with certainty.[1] But some of his matrimonial alliances might have some political significance. He married Kuberanāgā, a daughter of the Nāga family, and the issue of this marriage, his daughter Prabhāvatī, was married to the Vākāṭaka king Rudra-sena II. The Nāgas, as noted above, were a powerful ruling clan and a marriage alliance with them might have been of great use to Chandra-gupta in consolidating the newly established imperial position of the Guptas. As regards the Vākāṭaka king, it has been rightly pointed out by V. A. Smith[2] that the geographical position of his kingdom was such that "he could be of much service or disservice to the northern invader of the dominions of the Śaka satraps of Gujarat and Surāshṭra." The assistance which Chandra-gupta II possibly derived from the Vākāṭakas and his influence over that kingdom have already been discussed above (Ch. V). It is not, therefore, an unreasonable assumption that these matrimonial alliances were deliberately made with a political motive. If we remember how marriage of Chandra-gupta I with à Lichchhavi princess had enable the

---

tion of Vāhlika cf. *JRASBL*. IX, 179. In addition to the references contained therein cf. *EI*. XIV, 367: *JAHRS*. X, 86; *JIH*. XVI, 13.

[1] Mr. J. Ratnakar describes (*IHQ*. III. 719) a stone horse found at a village named Nagawa in the south-east corner of Benares. The short record on it is read by him as Chandraṁgu (whom he identifies with Chandra-gupta II). But the published fascimile does not support the reading, and we cannot, therefore, credit Chandra-gupta II with the performance of an Aśvamedha sacrifice.

[2] *JARS*. 1914, p. 324.

Guptas to rise to a position of supremacy, and Samudra-gupta regarded the offer of a daughter as a normal feature of his feudatories' relationship with himself, we may well believe that 'the matrimonial alliance played no insignificant part in the foreign policy of the Guptas'.[1] An inscription of the Kadamba ruler Kākustha-varman of Kuntala (Kanarese country in the Bombay Presidency) tells us that his daughters were married to the Gupta and other kings. It has been suggested that Chandra-gupta II arranged a marriage between his son and the daughter of Kākustha-varman, the most powerful ruler of the family.[2] Although we cannot be sure whether the alliance was arranged by Chandra-gupta II or his successor, it also proves the traditional policy of the Guptas to form matrimonial alliances with the most powerful and distinguished royal families in different parts of India.

Chandra-gupta II introduced a currency in silver and copper. His gold coins, like those of his father, reflect the pomp, power and grandeur of the empire, and to some extent also his striking personality. Some of his coin-types resemble those of his father, but the difference is significant. Thus in one type the king is represented as slaying a lion (Pl. III, 2) instead of a tigers, as on his father's coin. The legends on these coins refer to him as *Siṁha-vikrama* (having the prowess of a lion) and '*Narendra-chandra*' or best of kings, unconquered in the world. The substitution of lion for tigers probably represent his conquest of Gujarat where lions are available. The Couch-type of coins resemble the lyre-type of his father, but instead

---

[1] *PHAI.*[4] p. 466.

[2] *JBORS.* XII, 462. It may be noted in this connection that certain mediaeval chiefs of the Kanarese country claimed descent from Chandra-gupta, and according to some literary traditions Vikramāditya sent the poet Kālidāsa as an ambassador to a Kuntala king. The value of these, and their connection with Chandra-gupta II are, however, uncertain (cf. *PHAI*[4] p. 475, fn. 2) cf. Chs. V, XII.

of a *vīṇā* or lyre he holds a flower in uplifted right hand and the legend '*rūpākṛiti*' probably emphasises his intellectual and physical eminence, or his artistic sense. In a new type of coin introduced by Chandra-gupta II the king is represented as standing with left hand on sword-hilt, while a dwarf-attendant holds a parasol over his head. Here the umbrella is no doubt the insignia of universal sovereignty. In another new type the king rides on a fully caparisoned horse and holds a bow or a sword. This type, which was used extensively, and the lion-slayer type, with its numerous varieties, probably reflect the personal habits of the king, but the couch-type shows that, like his father, his martial spirits were not incompatible with an artistic and intellectual temperament. It is perhaps not without significance that in his coins, the figure of a throned goddess derived from foreign coinage, was finally replaced by the purely Indian a type of a goddess.

As noted above, Chandra-gupta II assumed the title Vikramāditya, which, along with Vikrama and Vikramāṅka, occurs in his coin legends. It is held by many scholars that he is the original of the legendary king Vikramāditya who is said to have defeated the Śakas, ruled at Ujjayinī' and founded an era (Vikrama Saṁvat) in 58 B.C. Chandra-gupta II defeated the Śaka Satraps and his association with Ujjayinī, is rendered probable by his long stay in Malwa in connection with his fight against them. Without entering into the debatable question whether there was a king Vikramāditya in 58 B.C., it may be regarded as probable that one cycle of the legends concerning him refers to Chandra-gupta II, and in this category we may include the presence of the famous poet Kālidāsa in his court. It should be remembered, however, that the title Vikramāditya was also assumed, probably by Samudra-gupta, and certainly by at least two successors of Chandra-gupta II *viz.*, Skanda-gupta and Pūru-gupta (or Budha-gupta). It is, therefore, equally likely that the cycle of legends, referred to above, reflects the gupta age as a whole rather than the reign of an individual Gupta king.

Reference may be made to some feudatories of Chandra-gupta II. One of them is Mahārāja Trikamala, known from an inscription, dated year 64, engraved on the image of a Bodhisatva at Gaya.[1] Another feudatory was Svāmidāsa, ruler of Valkha, probably situated somewhere in Central India, who issued a land-grant in the year 67.[2] Mahārāja Śri Viśvāmitra-Svāmī, whose name occurs on a seal found at Besnagar, was also probably a feudatory chief of Chandra-gupta II.[3]

The last known date of Chandra-gupta II is 93 (=412-3 A.D.), and he could not have ruled much longer, as his son was on the throne in 96 (=415-16 A.D.). He thus enjoyed a fairly long reign of more than thirty-six years. His reign saw the consolidation of the Gupta empire, and if we may credit the stories about Vikramāditya as applicable to him, it also witnessed an outburst of intellectual activity which has made the Gupta age, the classical age or the golden age of India.

An idea of the peace and prosperity prevailing in the vast empire may be had from the account of the Chinese pilgrim Fa-hien who travelled through Chandra-gupta's wide dominions for more than six years. Unfortunately Fa-hien does not give any account of the political condition of India,—he does not even mention the name of the great Gupta emperor. Still Fa-hien's book is of great value in forming an estimate of the culture and civilasation in the Gupta age to which reference will be made later. The art and literature of the period will also be dealt with in separate chapters. It is only necessary to emphasise here that the conquests of Samudra-gupta and Chandra-gupta II brought about that imperial peace and prosperity to which we mainly owe the flourishing state of

[1] *ASI.* 1922-3, p. 169.
[2] *EI.* XV, 289. But this is doubtful, cf. *ABORI.* XXV, 159.
[3] *ASI.* 1914-15, p. 81.

art, literature and the other aspects of civilisation which distinguished the age.

3. Kumāra-gupta I.

On the death of Chandra-gupta II, his son Kumāra-gupta, born of queen Dhruvadevī, ascended the throne about 414 A.D. and enjoyed a long reign of more than forty years. No less than thirteen records of his reign (Nos. 12-24) have come to light, the largest number that we possess of any Gupta ruler. Although they do not throw much light on the events of his reign, they convey in a general way that he maintained intact the vast empire that he had inherited from his father. This conclusion is also supported by the finds of numerous coins of his in Western India, as far as Ahmadabad and Bhaunagar. The coins further prove that Kumāra-gupta, like his grandfather, performed an Aśvamedha sacrifice. A large hoard of Kumāra-gupta's coins, found at Satara in Bombay, has been taken by some as a possible indication of Gupta influence in the South-Western Deccan[1], though obviously we cannot draw any definite conclusion from this or the find of 13 coins of his at Ellichpur.

Kumāra-gupta issued several new types of gold coins, one of which depicts Kārtikeya riding on his peacock on the reverse, and the king feeding a peacock on the obverse. He extended the silver coinage and introduced it for the first time in the central provinces of the empire where the peacock was substituted for Garuḍa on the reverse of the coins. It appears from the legends on his coins that he assumed the title Mahendrāditya, and he is referred to as Śrī-Mahendra, Mahendra-siṁha, Aśvamedha-Mahendra etc.

The inscriptions have preserved the names of some of his feudatories and governors. Ghaṭotkacha-gupta, a member of

[1] *PHAI.*[4] pp. 475 (fn. 2), 480.

the royal family, and probably a son or brother of the emperor, was ruling in E. Malwa with jurisdiction over Tumbavana about 50 miles to the north-west of Eran (Ins. No. 17). He was probably the governor of Airikiṇa (Eran) known to be a Gupta province (*pradeśa*) in the time of Samudra-gupta (Ins. No. 4). Further west, Bandhuvarman, probably also a feudatory chief, was ruling at Daśapura, Mandasor in Western Malwa (Ins. No. 52). The emperor's younger brother Govinda-gupta was also probably a governor in this region.[1] Another governer, Chirātadatta, was ruling over Puṇḍravardhana or N. Bengal (Ins. Nos. 20-21). These records may be taken to indicate progress in the development of administrative machinery during the reign of Kumāra-gupta I, but as the absence of similar documents for the earlier period may be purely accidental, we may not regard it as a special characteristic of his reign.

Whether the *Aśvamedha* sacrifice of Kumāra-gupta implies any new conquests on his part we cannot say. But towards the close of his reign the kingdom was certainly disturbed by wars, the exact nature of which it is difficult to determine. The passage in the Bhitari Stoṇe Pillar Inscription (No. 30), which is our sole authority for this notable event, is unfortunately not free from difficulties. According to the reading generally accepted, the adversary of the Gupta emperor was the king of the Pushyamitras, but according to a proposed emendation of the text,[2] the hostile chiefs are simply referred to as enemies. If we adopt the reading 'Pushyamitras', it is not easy to locate the tribe. They are referred to in the *Vishṇu*

[1]The cases of Bandhu-varman and Govinda-gupta have beeṇ discussed in detail under the reign of Skanda-gupta.

[2]Fleet read the crucial expression as *Pushyamitrāṁś=cha*", but noted that the second syllable of the name is damaged (*CII.* III, 54, 55, fn. 2). Mr. H. R. Divekar proposes to read the whole thing as '*Yudhyamitrāṁś=cha*' (*ABORI.* I, 99 ff).

Purāṇa and probably lived in the valley of the Narmadā or near the source of that river. But this is by no means certain.[1]

But whoever might have been the adversary (or adversaries), he was very powerful and his progress must have constituted a grave menace to the empire.[2] The inscription expressly states that the enemies 'had great resources in men and money', and in course of his fight with them 'to restore the fallen fortunes of his family', Skanda-gupta passed a whole night on bare earth. Inspite of possible poetic fancies and exaggerations, the statement leaves the impression that the Gupta emperor had met with serious reverses and was threatened with utter ruin, when Kumāra-gupta's son Skanda-gupta turned the scale in his favour by inflicting a crushing defeat upon the enemy. The poet tells us that this heroic achievement of Skanda-gupta was sung in every region 'by happy men, even down to the children'. The sense of relief echoed in these laudatory songs may be regarded as a proper measure of the apprehended calamity. It is significant that in four successive verses, the poet refers no less than three times to the 'ruined fortunes of the Gupta family', and there restoration by Skanda-gupta. This emphasises the serious nature of the crisis that was averted by Skanda-gupta, but its exact nature still remains unknown.

4. SKANDA-GUPTA.

The aged emperor Kumāra-gupta I died in the year 136 (=A.D. 455-6) before Skanda-gupta returned from his victorious campaign. Indications are not wanting that there were some

---

[1] *IA.* XVIII, 228. For other views cf. *CDG.* xlv-xlvi.

[2] Dr. H. C. Raychaudhuri infers from the title *Vyāghra-parākrama*' that Kumāra-gupta probably-invaded the tiger-infested forest territory beyond the Narmadā, and the imperial troops met with disaster, which was retrieved by Skanda-gupta (*PHAI.*[4] p. 480). But neither the assumption of the title nor the find of coins in the Satara district would justify such an inference.

troubles over the succession, and the brother and other sons of Kumāra-gupta probably set up rival claims for the throne.[1] But the evidence is so vague and uncertain that no definite conclusions are possible.

According to the royal seals Pūru-gupta was the son of Kumāra-gupta I and his chief queen (*Mahādevī*) Anantadevī. Curiously enough the royal seals ignore Skanda-gupta, and while the genealogical portion, even in the inscription of Skanda-gupta (No. 30), refers to the chief queens, who were mothers of his three predecessors, it is silent about his own mother. This undoubtedly raises a suspicion that his mother did not occupy the status of a *Mahādevī*, though we cannot be quite sure on this point.[2] It has been suggested that his mother's name was Devakī, but this view rests merely on an analogy which the poet had drawn between his visit to his widowed mother after his victory and that of Kṛishṇa to Devakī.[3] This analogy might have been due to similarity of

---

[1]Arguments in support of this hypothesis are given in *JASB*. NS., XVII, 253 ff. They have been criticised in detail in *PHAI.*[4] pp 481 ff. The criticism misses the real points of many of the arguments. Thus regarding the omission of the name of Skanda-gupta's mother in the Bhitari pillar Ins., it is merely observed that 'the names of the mothers of kings are sometimes omitted' and 'there was no rule prohibiting the mention of ordinary queens in inscriptions'. These remarks show a lack of appreciation of the main argument, *viz.*, "that the omission of the Mahādevī of Kumāra-gupta I, the mother of the reigning king, *in striking contrast to the mention of the other Mahādevīs of earlier kings in the same record*, cannot but be looked upon as significant". It is true that almost all the facts, on which the hypothesis is based, may be explained away in a different manner. If they were not, then the view would not be a mere hypothesis but a definite fact. But nothing has been said to indicate that the proposed view is not a probable and a reasonable inference from the facts before us.

[2]The analogy of the Banskhera and Madhuban plates does not, as has been suggested (*PHAI.*[4] p. 483), take away the force of the argument. For here Rājya-vardhana's mother is mentioned and as Harshavardhana is said to be his *anuja*, the separate mention of his mother is rendered unnecessary.

[3]Sewell. *Hist. Ins. of South. India*, p. 349; *PHAI.*[4] p. 480.

circumstances[1] rather than similarity of names, and here, again no definite conclusion is possible.

The same uncertainty prevails regarding the early events of Skanda-gupta's reign. Apart from the war of succession, if there were any, there are references in the Junagadh inscription (No. 26) to a struggle with hostile kings including those against the Mlechchhas. This presumably refers to a series of engagements at the very beginning of his reign, though unfortunately no details are preserved. The war with the Mlechchhas probably refers to his fight with the Hūṇas which is specifically referred to in the Bhitari Pillar Inscription. But whether the Mlechchhas are the same as Hūṇas, or were a different tribe, both the records claim that Skanda-gupta completely defeated these enemies.[2] The verse describing the conflict with the Hūṇas, though mutilated, leaves no doubt that it was a severe one. The Hūṇas who appear now for the first time in Indian history were destined to play an important rôle which will be discussed later. For the present, it will suffice to state that they lived in Central Asia on the western border of China as far back as the second century B.C. In course of their migrations to the west one branch (or race) of them, known as the Ephthalites or White Huns, occupied the Oxus valley and conquered Gandhāra. They destroyed this kingdom and set up a king who was cruel and vindictive and practised the most barbarous atrocities. According to the Chinese pilgrim Sung-yun, this took plack two generations before his time (520 A.D.). It is evident, therefore, that not long after his accession to the throne Skanda-gupta found his

---

[1] *JASB*. NS., XVII, 254.

[2] Allan finds an echo of Skanda-gupta's victory over the Hūṇas in a story of king Vikramāditya preseived in Somadeva's *Kathāsaritsāgara*. According to it Vikramāditya, son of Mahendrāditya, king of Ujjain, having succeeded to the throne on his father's abdication, utterly defeated the Mlechchhas who were overrunning the earth (*CGD*. p. xlix. fn. 1).

empire menaced by the onrush of these barbarians who had crossed the Indus, carrying devastation and destruction all around. Where Skanda-gupta met them we cannot say, but the statement in his inscriptions that he thoroughly defeated them seems to be borne out by the fact that we have no evidence of the Hun depredations east of Gandhāra till the close of the fifth or the biginning of the sixth century A.D.[1]

If we remember that the cruel devastations of the Huns had spread from the Danube to the Indus, that their leader Āttila, who died in 453 A.D., was 'able to send equal defiance to the courts of Ravenna and Constantinople', and that thirty years later they overwhelmed Persia and killed its king, we can well realise the value of the great victory of Skanda-gupta over them. All over the vast empire the people must have heaved a sigh of relief at the great deliverance. This heroic achievement that saved his kingdom from the scourge of a cruel barbaric invasion justified the assumption of the title of Vikramāditya by Skanda-gupta which we find on his coins along with Kramāditya.[2] The continual stress of wars during the reign is also reflected in the coinage. The gold coins of Skanda-gupta are comparatively few and belong mostly to the

[1]According to a Buddhist text '*Chandragarbha-pariprichchhā*', King Mahendrasena, who was born in the country of Kauśāmbī, had a valiant son. After he had passed the age of twelve Mahendra's kingdom was invaded by three foreign powers in concert—Yavanas, Palhikas and Sakunas who took possession of Gandhāra and countries to the north of the Ganges. The young son of Mahendrasena led his father's army of two hundred thousand men against the enemy whose soldiers numbered three hundred thousand. The prince, however, broke the enemy's army and won the battle. On his return his father crowned him king saying "henceforth rule the kingdom", and himself retired to religious life. For twelve years after this, the new king fought these foreign enemies and ultimately captured and executed the three kings. It has been suggested that this story gives an account of the fight between Skanda-gupta and the Hūṇas (*IHI*. p. 36). But no great reliance can be placed on the details of such stories.

[2]According to Ārya-Mañjuśrī-Mūlakalpa, Skanda-gupta was also called Deva-rāja. This, as well as the title of Vikramāditya, was borne by his grandfather Chandra-gupta II.

archer-type. This as well as a depreciation in the purity of gold was possibly due to the financial drain caused by the war. His silver coinage was, however, very extensive and presents a variety of types.

One type of Skanda-gupta's gold coins is of more than usual interest. In it the king is represented standing with a bow in one hand and an arrow in the other; in front of him is the Garuḍa standard; beyond it, on the right side, stands a female figure facing the king and holding a lotus in her left, and an uncertain object, probably a fillet, in her right hand. She was formerly identified as the queen of Skanda-gupta, but Allan regards her as Lakshmī, the goddess of sovereignty. Allan rightly associates this picture with the statement in the Junagadh Inscription that the goddess of sovereignty 'of her own accord selected him as her husband, having in succession discarded all other princes'. It is possible to interpret this coin as a memorial to the fact that Skanda-gupta did not owe the throne to the right of succession but to his own prowess and valour.

Skanda-gupta is said to have appointed governors of different provinces (*lit.* all provinces), almost immediately after his accession. Special reference may be made to the appointment of Parṇadatta as governor of Surāshṭra. The restoration of the ancient embankment of the great lake or water-reservoir on the Girnar hill, which had burst in the very first year of Skanda-gupta's reign, was a great achievement that redounds to the credit of the governor Parṇadatta and his son Chakrapālita, the local Magistrate. They saved the country from a great disaster and the poet, echoing the voice of the grateful peoples, lauded up to the skies the virtues and merits of both the father and the son, in a composition which is expressly stated to be the 'Book on the repair of Sudarśana Lake' (*Sudarśanataṭāka-saṁskāra-grantha-rachanā*) (Ins. No. 26).

More than usual interest attaches to another governor of

Skanda-gupta. An inscription found at Mandasor[1] records some constructions by Dattabhaṭa, Commander-in-chief of the forces of king Prabhākara, in the Mālava Samvat 524 (=467-68 A.D.), The inscription mentions emperor Chandra-gupta II and his son Govinda-gupta, and we are told that Dattabhaṭa's father Vāyurakshita was the general (*senādhipa*) of Govinda-gupta. The date of the record places it during or immediately after the reign of Skanda-gupta and presumably Prabhākara was his governor. But it raises several interesting problems. First, as to the position of Govinda-gupta. He is also known to us from a clap-seal at Vaisālī which records the name of *Mahādevī* Śrī Dhruvasvāminī, wife of the *Mahārājādhirāja* Śrī Chandra-gupta, mother of the *Mahārāja* Śrī Govinda-gupta'. It has been suggested that Govinda-gupta was the governor of Vāiśālī during his father's reign.[2] In that case it is not very likely that he was alive in the year 467-68 A.D., far less that he held any important position in that year. How are we then to explain the reference to him as a great ruler in the Mandasor record does not even mention the name of the emperor Skanda-gupta ? Dr. Bhandarkar has pointed out that 'as Indra is represented as being suspicious of Govinda-gupta's power, the latter seems to have been a supreme ruler'. This would mean that he had rebelled, either against his brother Kumāra-gupta or the latter's son Skanda-gupta, a presumption that lends colour to the theory of internal troubles during the closing years of Kumāra-gupta I or the early part of his son's reign. Viewed in this light, the omission of all references to Skanda-gupta in the Mandasor Inscription of 467-8 A.D. becomes significant. This date is the last-known date of Skanda-gupta and it is just possible that troubles broke out again immediately

---

[1]Bhandarkar's List No. 7. The inscription was noticed in *ASI*, 1922-23, p. 187 but has not yet been edited.

[2]*CGD*. p. xl.

after his death,—but all these must remain a pure conjecture for the present.

We must also consider in this connection another feudatory line ruling in W. Malwa with its capital Daśapura, modern Mandasor, in which place and its neighbourhood four records (Nos. 49-52) of this family have been discovered. The first two rulers of this family, Jaya-varman and his son Siṁha-varman, seem to be independent rulers in the latter half of the fourth century A.D. Nara-varman, the son of Siṁha-varman, was ruling in 404 A.D., and Viśva-varman, the son of Nara-varman, in 423 A.D. Although these dates fall within the reigns of Chandra-gupta II and Kumāra-gupta I, there is nothing in the records of the two rulers of Mandasor to show that they acknowledged the supremacy of the Guptas. The records sing their glories as if they were independent kings, and make no reference to the Guptas. It is interesting to note also that all the records of this family are dated in the Mālava era and not in the Gupta era.

Only the last record of Mandasor (No. 52) connected with this family explicitly refers to Kumāra-gupta as the overlord. It is a long record composed in beautiful verses. After referring to Kumāra-gupta as the ruler of the earth, it mentions king Viśva-varman and his son Bandhu-varman. While this Bandhu-varman was ruling over Daśapura a temple of the Sun-god was built by the guild of silk-cloth weavers in the Mālava year 493 (=436 A.D.) In course of time, under other kings, part of this temple fell into disrepair and so in the year 529 (=472 A.D.) the same guild repaired the temple.[1]

The main object of the inscription was thus to record the repair of the temple in 472 A.D., and it must have been composed in or shortly after that date. Under ordinary rules of

[1] For the long and protracted controversy over the interpretation of this record, and particularly the date when the temple was repaired and the record set up, cf the references given under Ins. No. 52.

construction, Kumāra-gupta should be understood to have been the overlord at the time the record was set up *i.e.*, in 472 A.D. but most of the scholars have taken the reference to Kumāra-gupta in connection with the original consturction of the temple. In other words, they hold that in 436 A.D., when the temple was built, Bandhu-varman was the governor of Daśapura, and Kumāra-gupta was his overlord. According to this view, the Gupta suzerainty was established over Mandasor in or before 436 A.D. In that case it becomes significant that the record does not name either the Gupta overlord or the local governor of Mandasor in 472 A.D. *i.e.*, at the time when it was actually set up. On the other hand, it vaguely refers to other kings (the plural number denoting at least three) ruling between 436 and 472 A.D. Whether these refer to the local rulers or Gupta overlords we cannot say, but it gives the impression of some trouble or confusion prevailing in the region between A.D 436 and 472. The importance of this will appear in the discussion of the history of the Guptas after Skanda-gupta. But whether Bandhu-varman was really a feudatory of Kumāra-gupta or not, it may be reasonably held that Western Malwa had probably already been a feudatory state under Skanda-gupta, as it undoubtedly was in 472.

It is necessary to discuss in this connection the claims put forward by the Vākāṭaka king Narendra-sena that his 'commands were obeyed by the lords of Kosalā, Mekalā and Mālava'.[2] It is undoubtedly tempting to connect Narendra-sena's invasion with the early struggles of Skanda-gupta's reign or the troubled state in Malwa between 436 and 472 A.D. as disclosed by the Maṇdasor inscription, discussed above, but it is difficult to come

[1]This is the view of Pannalal (*Hindustan Review*, 1928, p. 31) and Mr. Diskalkar (*JBBRAS*. NS., II, 176) who naturally take this Kumāra-gupta to be Kumāra-gupta II.

[2]*EI*. IX, 271. For the history of Narendra-sena cf. *ante* Ch. V.

to any definite conclusion until the date of Narendra-sena is more definitely known.

On the whole, so far as the available evidence goes, we may reasonably hold that in spite of the Hūṇa invasion and other troubles, probably at the beginning of his reign, Skanda-gupta maintained till the last his hold over the vast empire that now literally stretched from the Bay of Bengal to the Arabian Sea, and comprised practically the whole of Northern India to the east of the Punjab and Rājputāna. The poet who referred in the year A.D. 460-1 (Ins. No. 27) to the tranquil reign of Skanda-gupta, the lord of hundred kings, was not probably guilty of serious exaggeration. When this great Gupta emperor died about 467 A.D., little did he or anyone else dream that the mightly empire which he left in peace and security would crumble away almost before the eyes of the existing generation.

CHAPTER IX

THE IMPERIAL CRISIS

1. Internal Troubles.

It is impossible, at the present state of our knowledge, to give a definite outline of the history of the Imperial Guptas after the death of Skanda Gupta. We know the names of a number of kings, and in some cases also their relation to each other and definite dates. But their are kings whose date or relationship to other kings is not known with certainly, and naturally views differ widely about their place in the line of succession. Without discussing these differences in detail[1] we may offer below a provisional reconstruction of the Gupta history as appears to be the most reasonable.

A number of royal seals (Nos. 34, 35, 41 and 44) discovered at Nālandā and Bhitari enable us to draw the following genealogy of the successors of Kumāra-gupta I all of whom are also known from their coins.

Kumāra-gupta = Anantadevī
Skanda-gupta   Pūru-gupta = Chandradevī
Budha-gupta   Narasiṁha-gupta = Mitradevī
Kumāra-gupta (II or III)
Vishṇu-gupta

The last known date of Skanda gupta is 148 (=467-8 A.D.) and the next known date is 154 (=473-4 A.D.), found in a record of a Gupta king Kumāra-gupta. It does not seem to be very

[1] Cf. *IC.* X, 172-3.

likely that this Kumāra-gupta is identical with the son of Narasiṁha-gupta bearing the same name. It is more reasonable to regard him as a different king, and he was possibly the son and successor, either of Skanda-gupta, or of Pūru-gupta.

Pūru-gupta might have contested the throne after the death of his father Kumāra-gupta I, and in that case we may presume that he was defeated by his brother Skanda-gupta. It is very likely, however, that he seized the throne after the death of Skanda-gupta. In this case, and if Kumāra-gupta II, of 473 A.D. be regarded as a successor of Skanda-gupta, it was evidently by dispossessing him that Pūru-gupta could come to the throne. But it is also not unlikely that Kumara-gupta II was a son of Pūru-gupta and succeeded him after his death.

In any case the reigns of Pūru-gupta and Kumāra-gupta II were short, and must have comprised a period of less than ten years between 467 and 477 A.D.

Whatever we might think of the alternative views put forward above, it is extremely likely that the years immediately following the death of Skanda-gupta were full of troubles, both internal and external. Reference has already been made to Ghaṭotkacha-gupta, a member of the imperial family, who was Governor of Malwa in 116 (=435-6 A.D.). He, as well as Prakāśāditya, otherwise unknown, issued gold coins which have been assigned to this period. The case of Prabhākara, ruler of Malwa in 467-8 A.D., is also very suspicious as noted above. The claim of the Vākāṭaka king Narendrā-sena to have exercised supremacy in Mālava, Kosalā, and Mekalā probably also belongs to this period. Due significance should also be attached to the reference in the Mandasor Inscription of 472-3 A.D. to the reigns of many kings between 436 and 472 A.D. and its silence about the contemporary local ruler and also of the emperor (according to the current interpretation), in contrast to the meticulous care with which they are mentioned in regard to a past event. Though vague and indefinite, the cumulative effect of all these circumstances seems to point to a considerable decline in the power of the imperial Guptas, a conclusion strengthened by the lack of epigraphic or other evidence of a positive nature that the emperors Pūru-gupta and Kumāra-gupta II maintained intact the mighty empire inherited by them. Excepting the royal seals, only one short record of Kumāra-gupta II (No. 33) has been found at Benares. This negative evidence of inscriptions is confirmed by the positive evidence of their coins which offer a striking contrast to those of their predecessors. They all belong to only one type and many of them are of very rude execution and debased metal. It has been doubted whether the coins, very few in number, usually attributed to Pūru-gupta really belong to him.[1] The coins no doubt show that Kumāra-gupta II assumed the title Kramāditya, and Pūru-gupta (if the coins really belong to him), that of Śrī-Vikrama (or Vikramāditya), but these are probably more indicative of pride and prestige than real power.

With the accession of Budha-gupta we are on a somewhat firmer ground in respect of the history of the empire. Six of his records (Nos. 36-41) have come to light, and these prove beyond doubt that he ruled over extensive dominions stretching from Malwa to Bengal. We have no positive evidence that the Gupta empire under him extended further west and included Kathiawar Peninsula as it did in the days of Skanda-gupta. But a careful consideration of the records of the Maitraka dynasty of Valabhī seems to indicate that the Gupta supremacy over that region continued during the reign of Budha-gupta.

The Maitraka dynasty which ruled over Kathiawar Peninsula with Valabhī as its capital from 500 to 770 A.D. has

---

[1]Mr. S. K. Saraswati thinks that the gold coins attributed by Allan to 'Pūru-gupta' belong really to Budha-gupta (*IC.* I, 691-92). I have come to the same conclusion on a close examination of a cast of the coin. But the question cannot be finally decided till clear specimens of this type of coins are available.

left numerous records. We learn from them that the founder of the dynasty was *Senāpati* Bhaṭārka and his son was *Senāpati* Dharasena. The latter's younger brother was Mahārāja Droṇasiṁha "whose installation in the royalty by besprinkling was performed by the paramount master in person, the sole lord of the circumference of the territory of the whole earth." It is evident from this that Bhaṭārka, a general of the emperor, grew to be an important chief of Surāshṭra, and was in position to bequeath his power to his son. But as they both bore the title 'general', it is evident they did not assume the rôle of independent kings. It was not till the time of Droṇasiṁha that the paramount ruler formally invested him with the position of a feudatory ruler. This conclusion is borne out by an inscription of Droṇasiṁha himself dated 183 (=502 A.D.).[1] This official record begins with the phrase "*Parama-bhaṭṭārakapādānudhyāta*", and shows clearly that Droṇasiṃha still recognised the suzerainty of the emperor. There is hardly any doubt that the imperial power can only refer to the Guptas.[2] It is, therefore, obvious that although the Maitrakas were gradually growing powerful, and the Gupta authority was declining, still the Gupta emperor was acknowledged as the suzerain in 502 A.D. Droṇasiṁa undoubtedly occupied a higher status than that occupied by Parṇadatta, the governor of Surāshṭra in 138 (=457-8 A.D.), but the province was not lost to the empire during the reign of Budha-gupta.

In the Sarnath Inscription (No. 36), which is not an official record, the poet describes Budha-gupta as having ruled the earth (*pṛithivīṁ praśāsati*). Two of his governors of Northern Bengal, Brahmadatta (482 A.D.) and Jayadatta, record their allegiance to him. (Ins. Nos. 38, 40) in the same phrases as were used before, but it is interesting to note that both of them are styled *Uparika-Mahārāja*, instead of simply *Uparika*, as in the

[1] *EI*. XVI, 18.
[2] This point has been fully discussed in *IC*. V. 409-10.

days of Kumāra-gupta I. Another governor, Suraśmichandra, also called *Mahārājā*, was ruling over the extensive territory between the Kālindī (Jumna) and Narmada rivers, and under him, Mātṛivishṇu, also a *Mahārāja*, was governing the district (*Vishaya*) round Eran in 484 A.D. (No. 39).

To the east of the territory under Suraśmichandra lay the feudatory state ruled over by the Parivrājaka Mahārājas, so-called because they were descended from the kingly ascetic (*nṛipa-parivrājaka*) Suśarman. Six copper-plate grants of this dynasty have come to light (Nos. 53-58). They belong to two kings, Hastin (156-198 *i.e.*, from 475 to 517 A.D.) and Saṁkshobha (199-209 *i.e.*, from 518 to 528 A.D.), and begin with the date followed by the phrase '*Gupta-nṛipa-rājya-bhuktau*' *i.e.*, in the enjoyment of sovereignty by the Gupta kings. Although no individual Gupta emperor is named, there cannot be any doubt that the Parivrājaka Mahārāja Hastin was a feudatory of Budha-gupta.

Contiguous to the Parivrājaka kingdom lay another, with Uchchakalpa as the capital. A stone pillar at Bhumara, about 9 miles to the north-west of Uchahara in Nagod (Bundelkhand) marks the boundary between these two kingdoms (Ins. No. 59).[1] We have seven copper-plate grants of this dynasty (Nos. 60-66) which mention two kings, Jayanātha (years 174, 177) and his son Sarvanātha (191-214), and four ancestors of the former. There is, however, no reference to the Gupta sovereignty, as in the grants of the Parivrājaka Mahārājas. There is also some doubt about the era to which the dates of these records should be referred, some taking it to be the Kalachuri, and others, the Gupta era.[2] The absence of any reference to the Gupta sovereignty in all their grants, in marked contrast to those of

---

[1]This is, however, denied by some who infer from the record on the pillar that the Uchchakalpas were subordinates of the Parivrājakas (*IHQ*. XXI, 137).

[2]This point is fully discussed in *EI*. XXIII, 173.

the Parivrājakas, markes it likely that they did not acknowledge the supremacy of the Guptas. But as the territory of the Parivrājakas lay beyond them to the south, it is just possible that the Uchchakalpa rules owed allegiance to the Guptas.

Leaving aside the doubtful case of the Uchchakalpa state, Budha-gupta may be regarded as having exercised sway over nearly the whole of the Gupta empire as left by Skanda-gupta. It is obvious, however, that the power and prestige of the Gupta empire was visibly on the decline. The fact that the feudatory Maitrakas and the Parivrājakas refer only in vague general terms to the paramount Gupta emperor is perhaps not without significance. It is also to be noted that the governors of Bengal and Malwa are called *Mahārāja*, and in the first case we definitely know it to be an innovation introduced since the time of Kumāra-gupta I. These tell their own tale. The coins of Budha-gupta support this inference. His gold coins, if they exist at all, are very rare. He issued silver coins current only in the central provinces of the Gupta empire, and discontinued the type current in Gujarat and Kathiawar. In addition to a general decline of power, they prove his hold over the central, but considerably loss of authority in western, parts of the empire.

As noted above, some of the coins of Budha-gupta are dated 175 (494-5). On some of his coins, however, it is possible to read the date as 180 with or without a numeral in the unit's place.[1] We may, therefore, hold that Budha-gupta died about 500 A.D. or shortly after it.[2]

The death of Budha-gupta seems to have been followed by a disputed succession. We possess an inscription of Vainya-gupta dated 506 A.D. (No. 45) and one of Bhānu-gupta dated

---

[1] *IA.* XVIII, 227. But the reading of the symbol for 80 is very uncertain (*IA.* XIV, 68).

[2] C. V. Vaidya refers to a passage in *Skanda-Purāṇa* according to which Budha-gupta was ruling in 499 A.D. (*POC.* VII, 576).

510-11 A.D. (No. 47), found respectively in E. Bengal and Malwa. The copper-plate grant of Vainya-gupta shows that Samataṭa, which was an autonomous feudatory state in the days of Samudra-gupta, had lost that status and formed part of the dominions directly held by the Guptas. The probably took place long before the reign of Vainya-gupta. Although Vainya-gupta is styled merely *Mahārāja* in his grant, he is given the full imperial titles in the Nālandā Seal (No. 46), and he also issued gold coins of the type used by the Gupta emperors after Skanda-gupta. There is, therefore, hardly any doubt that he belonged to the imperial family, and it is not unlikely that he was the son and successor of Budha-gupta, though of this we have no positive evidence.

Bhānu-gupta is known from a single inscription (No. 47) at Eran dated 191 (=510-11 A.D.). Neither his coins nor any royal seal mentioning him have as yet come to light. The inscription records how a feudatory chief named Goparāja accompanied 'the mighty king, the glorious Bhānu-gupta, the bravest man on the earth', and fought a famous battle. Goparāja died in this battle and his wife accompanied him on to the funeral pyre. The small pillar, now worshipped as a Śivaliṅga, on which the record is engraved may thus be regarded as a memorial *Satī* Stone Pillar.

It appears from the description that Bhānu-gupta was the suzerain or the Gupta emperor in 510 A.D. Whether he succeeded Vainya-gupta, or the two ruled at the same time respectively over the western and eastern parts of the empire, it is difficult to determine. The latter view seems more probable and this internal dissension perhaps paved the way for the downfall of the empire.

The famous battle in which Bhānu-gupta and Goparāja were engaged at Eran was probably fought against Toramāṇa. For at a date, which cannot be long removed from 510-11 A.D. we find Toramāṇa as the overlord of Eran. Two records found at this place unmistakably indicate this transfer of sovereignty. The earlier one (No. 39) dated 165 (=484-5 A.D.) records some pious construction by *Mahārāja* Mātṛivishṇu and his younger brother Dhanyavishṇu during the reign of Budha-gupta. The later one (No. 68) records the construction of a temple by Dhanyavishṇu, after the death of his brother Mātṛivishṇu, 'in the first year while the *Mahārājādhirāja*, the glorious Toramāṇa of great fame, is ruling the earth'. It is evident, therefore, that some time after 484-5 A.D., but within one generation of that, Toramāṇa, who had already conquered the Punjab and part of Rajputana, also made himself master of E. Malwa. The battle fought by Bhānu-gupta might have been *either* the unsuccessful resistance offered to Toramāṇa, or a campaign for putting an end to Toramāṇa's occupation of Malwa. In the former case Toramāṇa's conquest of Malwa must have taken place in or after 510 A.D., and in the latter case, some time before that date. Unfortunately, the Eran inscription of Goparāja is silent about the result of the battle.

Bhānu-gupta, in spite of the high encomiums paid to his bravery in the Eran Ins., remains a shadowy figure, and we do not know what his position in the Gupta imperial family, or what part he played in the dark days of the Gupta empire. It is not unlikely that he had freed Eran from the yoke of Toramāṇa, for the Gupta sovereignty was acknowledged by the Parivrājaka Mahārājas, who ruled in the adjoining province from 510 to at least 528 A.D. But it is somewhat strange that if he had really achieved such a great victory it should not have been expressly stated in the record while referring to him.

In any case, for reasons just stated, we may hold that the Gupta suzerainty in this region was soon re-established and continued till at least 528 A.D. (Ins. No. 58). Fifteen years later, the suzerainty of a Gupta emperor was acknowledged in N. Bengal (Ins. No. 48). It is obvious, therefore, that the

Guptas still ruled over the old empire from Bengal at least to Central India or E. Malwa. The phrase *Parama-bhaṭṭāraka-pādānudhyāta*' occurs in the records of the Valabhī ruler Dhruva-sena I who ruled till at least 545 A.D. All these indicate that the Gupta empire continued, at least in name, down to about the middle of the sixth century A.D.

The genealogy given at the beginning of this chapter shows that Budha-gupta's brother Narasiṁha-gupta occupied the imperial throne, and was followed by his son and grandson. The reigns of these three emperors may thus be placed between 500 and 550 A.D. This half-century saw the decline and downfall of the Gupta empire.

We do not know whether Narasiṁha-gupta was the immediate successor of his brother Budha-gupta. In that case we must presume a struggle for succession among two or possibly three rival claimants and a partition, however temporary, of the Gupta empire,—Vainya-gupta ruling in Bengal, Bhānu-gupta in Malwa, and Narasiṁha-gupta probably in Magadha. But it is also possible that Narasiṁha-gupta ascended the throne after Bhānu-gupta.

Narasiṁha-gupta issued gold coins of a single type which show that he assumed the title Bāladitya. It is possible that he is the king Balāditya who is mentioned by Hiuen Tsang as a great patron of Buddhism, and the builder of a great *saṅghārāma* at Nālandā. Hiuen Tsang also describes in a long story how he fought with, and defeated the terrible Hūṇa chief Mihirakula.

An inscription found at Nālandā,[1] and belonging to about the middle of the eighth century A.D., also refers to 'Bālāditya, the great king of irresistible valour' who, 'after having vanquished all the foes and enjoyed the entire earth, erected a great and extraordinary temple at Nālandā'. We need hardly

---

[1] *EI.* XX, 43.

doubt his identification with Bālāditya mentioned by Hiuen Tsang. Two independent sources thus confirm the tradition of a great ruler called Bālāditya, noted alike for his prowess and construction of a famous sanctuary at Nālandā. His identification with the Gupta emperor Narasiṁha-gupta cannot be regarded as certain, but seems to be very plausible. As, in that case, the chief event of his reign is his fight with the Hūṇa chief Mihirakula, it would be convenient, before proceeding further, to describe at length the Hūṇa invasion of India and the political convulsion caused thereby.

2. The Hūṇa Invasion.[1]

The Huns, a band of nomad savages, lived originally in the neighbourhood of China. Advancing towards the west, they divided into two main streams, of which one was directed towards the Volga and the other to the Oxus. The activities of the former find prominent mention in the annals of the Roman empire and need not be referred to here. The other band, originally subject to the Joan-Joan tribe, became powerful in the Oxus valley towards the middle of the fifth century. From the name of their ruler's family they came to be known as Ye-tha, Hephthalites or Ephthalites, and the Greek accounts refer to them also as White Huns.

From the Oxus valley these Huns came down upon both

[1]The general account of the Hūṇas is based on the following authorities—

1. Chavannes—*Documents sur les Toukiue Occidentaux*, pp. 223 ff.
2. Sir Aurel Stein—White Huns and Kindred tribes in the history of the Indian North-western frontier; *IA.* 1905, pp. 73 ff.

For the Hūṇa activities in India reference may be made to the following, though many of the statements contained in these articles require modification or are palpably wrong : *IA*, XV, 245 ff ; 346 ff ; *IHQ*. III, 1. ff ; *NIA*. IV, 36. For Hūṇa coins cf. *JASB*. LXIII. Part I, pp. 191 ff. For the antiquity of the Hūṇas and their activity in Iran cf. *Bhandarkar Comm. Vol.* pp. 65 ff.

Persia and India. Skanda-gupta; as already noted above, inflicted a crushing defeat upon them some time between 455 and 467 A.D., and saved his empire from their ravages. Persia was at first less successful. The Huns proved to be her most redoubtable enemy, and in 484 A.D. their king Akhschounwar defeated and killed Firoz, the Sassanian ruler of Persia. This success raised the power of the Huns to its greatest height, and towards the close of the fifth century A.D. they ruled over a vast empire with their principal capital at Balkh. But when the Western Turks became powerful in the middle of the sixth century A.D. the Sassanian king Anushirwan of Persia made an alliance with them against the Huns. The allied power dafeated the Huns and killed their king some time between 563 and 567 A.D. After this the Oxus became the boundary between the Turks and the Persians and the latter conquered most of the Hun possessions to the south of that river.

Very little is definitely known of the activities of the Huns in India proper, and in view of the prevailing misconceptions on the subject, it requires a somewhat detailed treatment.

Beyond a general reference in a few inscriptions to the defeat inflicted upon the Huns, contemporary Indian records do not throw any light upon their activities. Two kings, Toramāṇa and Mihirakula, known from coins and inscriptions, are regarded as Huns, perhaps correctly, but there is no conclusive evidence as to their nationality.

After the defeat inflicted upon the Huns by Skanda-gupta, the earliest information regarding their relation with India is supplied by the account of Sung-Yun, one of the ambassadors sent by the Empress of the Northern Wei dynasty in China in 518 A.D. Passing through Udyāna, Sung-Yun reached Gandhāra in 520 A D., and gives the following account of the country.

"This is the country which the Ye-thas destroyed and afterwards set up a *tegin*[1] (prince or member of the royal family) to be king over the country ; since which events two generations have passed. The disposition of this king (or dynasty) was cruel and vindictive, and he practised the most barbarous atrocities. He did not believe the law of Buddha, but loved to worship demons. . . . Entirely self-reliant on his own strength, he had entered on a war with the country of Ki-pin (Kashmir), disputing the boundaries of their kingdom, and his troops had been already engaged in it for three years. The king has 700 war-elephants. . . . The king continually abode with his troops on the frontier and never returned to his kingdom..." Somewhat later in date in the account given by Cosmas, surnamed Indicopleustes (Indian navigator),[2] an Alexandrine Greek, in his *Christian Topography*, which was probably begun in 535 but not put in its final form till 547 A.D. In one place he says : "Higher up in India, that is farther to the north, are the White Huns. The one called Gollas when going to war takes with him, it is said, no fewer than two thousand elephants and a great force of cavalry. He is the lord of India, and oppressing the people, forces them to pay tribute." After narrating some stories about him the same wrirer remarks : "The river Phison separates all the countries of India from the country of the Huns." Fortunately the author clearly says, elsewhere, that the Phison is the same as the river Indus. The date to which this account refers cannot be exactly determined but may be placed between 525 and 535 A.D.

As regards Indian records we have first the Eran insciption (No. 68), referred to above, dated in the first year of *Mahārājādhirāja* Toramāṇa. Next, there is an inscription at Gwalior, dated in the 15th regnal year of Mihirakula (No. 69). The

[1] Beal, *Records*, I, pp. xv ff; xcix ff. Beal misunderstood the word, but the correct meaning was first pointed out by Marquart, cf. Chavannes, *op. cit.*

[2] Tr. in English, by J. W. McCrindle (London, 1897), cf. pp. 366, 371-2.

name of his father is mentioned, but only the first two letters 'Tora' can be read, the rest being utterly lost. It has been restored as Toramāṇa. There is another inscription found at Kura (Salt Range, the Punjab) referring to *Rājādhirāja Mahārāja* Toramāṅa-Shāhi-Jaū (bla), whom some scholars identify with the king mentioned in the Eran Inscription, but others regard as quite different.[1] None of these inscriptions calls these kings Huns or contains any reference to that people.

We find an interesting account of Toramāṇa in a Jaina work, *Kuvalayamālā*, composed in 700 Śaka (=778 A.D.).[2] Toramāṇa (written as Torarāya in one manuscript), we are told, enjoyed the sovereignty of the word, or rather of Uttarāpatha. He lived at Pavvaiyā on the bank of the Chandrabhāgā (Chenab river). His *guru* was Hari-gupta, who himself was a scion of the Gupta family and lived there.

Hiuen Tsang gives a long account of Mihirakula in connection with the old city of Sākala, which was his capital. "Some centuries ago," we are told, "Mihirakula established his authority in this town and ruled over India. He subdued all the neighbouring provinces without exception." At first he took some interest in Buddhism and ordered that a Buddhist priest should meet him. The priests sent to him one who had been a servant in the king's household. Feeling deeply insulted at this he "issued an edict to destroy all the priests through the five Indies, to overthrow the law of Buddha, and leave nothing remaining."

The subsequent defeat of Mihirakula by Bālāditya, as told by Hiuen Tsang, will be referred to later. But the most important point to be noted is that Hiuen Tsang places this defeat "some centuries ago" *i.e.*, several hundred years before

---

[1] Bühler held that they were different (*E.I.* I, 239), but Sten Konow, following Cunningham and V. A. Smith (*JASB.* LXIII, 186), holds that they were identical (*IHQ.* XII, 531).

[2] *JBORS.* XIV. 28 ff.

c. 633 A.D., when he visited Sākala. This is hardly compatible with the view that the incident referred to by him took place about 530 A.D. As Watters has pointed out, other Chinese authorities also seem to place Mihirakula long before that date. This naturally casts grave doubts on the credibility of Hiuen Tsang's story about Mihirakula.

Both Toramāṇa and Mihirakula are referred to in *Rājc-taraṅgiṇī*, but their history, as recorded therein, can hardly be reconciled with that of the two Hūṇa chiefs.

Stray reference to the Huṇas occurs in Indian literature A *Sūtra-vṛitti* in the *Chāndra Vyākaraṇa* gives the sentence *Ajayad-gupta* (? or *Japto*) *Hūṇān* as an illustration of the use of the imperfect to express an event which occurred within the life-time of the author.[1] This probably refers to the victory of Skanda-gupta over the Hūṇas. Again, the Jaina author Somadeva (10th cent.) refers to a tradition that a Hūṇa king conquered Chitrakūṭa.[2] Reference here is probably to Mihirakula.

In the Mandasor inscription of Yaśodharman reference is made both to Mihirakula and to the Hūṇas, but in a manner which far from connecting the two, might even suggest a definite distinction between them. Similarly, we have the coins of Toramāṇa and Mihirakula, and also those bearing the name Tora. Although some of them are barbarous imitations of the Sassanid kings, there is nothing to indicate them definitely as Hūṇa.

In these circumstances it might appear as somewhat sur-

[1]Belvalkar, *Systems of Sanskrit Grammar*, p. 58. The emendation of the original *Jato* or *Japto* into Gupta is not, however, accepted by all. Kielhorn read the word as *Jarto* and took it as the name of a people and its ruler (*NGGW*. 1903, p. 305). Hoernle identified the people with the Jāṭhs and regarded it as a reference to the defeat of the Hūṇas by Yaśodharman (*JRAS*. 1909, p. 114). Jayaswal takes it as a reference to Skanda-gupta and relies upon this passage as an evidence that the Guptas were Jāṭhs (*JBORS*. XIX, 115-16). It is difficult to take these conclusions seriously.

[2]*Bhandarkar Commemoration Volume*. p. 216.

prising that scholars have almost unanimously regarded the Hūṇas as having played a decisive part in bringing about the fall of the Gupta empire. This belief rests solely upon the identification of Toramāṇa and Mihirakula (also called Mihiragul) as Hūṇa leaders. Although this view is generally assumed, there is no definite evidence in support of it, and we cannot altogether rule out the possibility that Toramāṇa was a Kushāṇa chief, and being allied to the Hūṇas, was mistaken as such in India, specially because he led the Hūṇa hordes.[1]

King Gollas, mentioned by Cosmas, has been identified with Mihiragul or Mihirakula This identification is based on the similarity of Gollas with the name-ending Gul, but chiefly rests on the assumption that Mihirakula was a Hūṇa chief. It must be noted, however, that whereas the chief seat of Hūṇa power, according to both Sung-Yun[2] and Cosmas, was to the west of the Indus, Mihirakula's capital, according to Hiuen Tsang was at Sākala (Sialkot) and that of Toramāṇa, according to the Jaina book, on the river Chenab.

We may now go back a little and take a comprehensive view of the Hūṇa activities in India. We may trace two distinct waves of this foreign invasion. The first may be dated about 460 A.D. or somewhat earlier, when Skanda-gupta defeated the Hūṇas but they were able to retain possession of Gandhāra

---

[1]Sir Aurel Stein (*op. cit*) and Jayaswal (*JBORS*. XVIII, 203) held that Toramāṇa was a Kushāṇa. Fleet also held the same view (*IA*. XV, 245). Sten Konow holds that Toramāṇa was, in all probability, a Hūṇa, as has usually been assumed, and not a Kashāṇa. (*IHQ*. XII, 532).

[2]Sung-Yun described the vast extent of the Hun empire and noted its boundaries. It extended from Khotan in the east to Persia on the west. Beal's identification (p. xci) of the northern and southern boundaries with Mālava (or Valabhī) and Tīrabhukti is absolutety unfounded. Chavannes describes the extent of the Hūṇa empire in 500 A.D. It included Tokharistan, Kabulistan and Zabulistan, but no part of India proper. Chavannes adds that according to Chinese history (presumably the account of Sung-Yun) the only Indian countries under the Huns were Gandhāra and Chitral (*op. cit.* pp. 224-5). Evidently he disregarded Beal's fanciful identifications.

and set up a new ruling chief, perhaps a member of the royal family. One or two generations passed before the Hūṇas were on the move again. The leader of this second movement was Toramāṇa, but we cannot say whether be represented the Huṇa principality of Gandhāra or was ruler of a separate state in the Punjab. Proceeding from his base at Gandhāra or the Punjab he carried his victorious arms as far as Malwa. His success was, however, short-lived, due probably to the defeat inflicted upon him bo Bhānu-gupta in 510 A.D.

For the time being the Hūṇa advance was checked, but Mihirakula revived the ambitious project of his father. He, too, had some success at first, as we know that his suzerainty was acknowledged in Gwalior in the 15th year of his reign (*c.* 530 A.D.). Besides, according to Hiuen Tsang he subdued the whole of India and Cosmas also describes the Hūṇa chief at this time as the lord of India. But the Hūṇas were not destined to enjoy success for long, and Mihirakula, too, soon met his doom in the hands of two Indian rulers Yaśodharman and Narasiṁha-gupta.

In his Mandasor Inscription (No. 70) Yaśodharman claims that "respect was paid to his feet by even the (famous) king Mihirakula". Mihirakula was evidently defeated, but his kingdom or power was not destroyed. With the fall of Yaśodharman, which probably took place not long after, he again came to the forefront.

The Gupta king who then occupied the imperial throne was probably Narasiṁha-gupta Bālāditya. He was temporarily everwhelmed by the victorious raids of Yaśodharman (to be referred to later), and Mihirakula evidently took advantage of this imperial crisis to extend his power. Narasiṁha-gupta, far from playing the traditional rôle of his family of checking the Hūṇa aggression was, according to Hiuen Tsang, forced to the humiliating position of paying tribute to Mihirakula. After mentioning Mihirakula's great power and persecution of Buddhism, already narrated above, Hiuen Tsang tells a long story how finally Bālāditya triumphed over his rival. This may be summed up as follows :—

"Bālāditya-rāja, king of Magadha, profoundly honoured the law of Buddha. When he heard of the cruel persecution and atrocities of Mihirakula, he strictly guarded the frontiers of his kingdom and refused to pay tribute. When Mihirakula invaded his dominions, Bālāditya took refuge with his army in an island. Mihirakula left the main part of his army in charge of his younger brother, embarked on boats, and landed, with a part of his troops on the island. He was, however, ambushed by the troops of Bālāditya in a narrow pass and was taken prisoner. Bālāditya resolved to kill Mihirakula but released him on the intercession of his mother. Mihirakula found on his return that his brother had gone back and occupied the throne. He, therefore, sought and obtained an asylum in Kashmir. Then he stirred up a rebellion there, killed the king and placed himself on the throne of Kashmir. He next killed the king of Gandhāra, exterminated the royal family, destroyed the *stūpas* and *saṅghārāmas*, plundered the wealth of the country and returned. But within a year he died."

Apart from the fact that the general account of Hiuen Tsang is liable to suspicion, on the ground of his placing Mihirakula several centuries ago, it is difficult to believe many of the details in this story.

It has already been noted above, that Kashmir probably and Gandhāra certainly was already a part of the Hūṇa empire in India, and Hiuen Tsang was evidently wrong in describing them as new conquests by Mihirakula. The long account of the defeat and discomfiture of Mihirakula in the hands of Bālāditya, and particularly the manner in which it was achieved, undoubtedly contains a great deal of exaggeration. But in spite of all these we may, in the absence of a better or more satisfactory hypothesis, provisionally regard Bālāditya as 'having defeated Mihirakula and saved the Gupta empire from the Hūṇa depredations. That would explain why, as noted above, his name and fame as a great hero survived even two centuries later. The defeat of Mihirakula[1] appears to have finally crushed the Hūṇa political supremacy in India. For although the existence of a Hūṇa community, and even of small Hūṇa principalities, is known in later periods, the Hūṇas no longer appear as a great power or even as a disturbing element in Indian history.

[1]The way in which Yaśodharman refers to Mihirakula, particularly that his head was never before bent to anybody, is hardly compatible with the view that the latter had already suffered defeat in the hands of Bālāditya. I have therefore accepted the statement of Hiuen Tsang that Mihirakula's power was finally broken by Bālāditya, and consequently Yaśodharman's victory must have preceded it. This view was held up Heras (*IHQ*. III, 1). It is not, however, unlikely as Hoernle suggested (*JASB*. LVIII, Part I, p. 96) that Yaśodharman, as a feudatory chief, helped Narasiṁha-gupta in his expedition against Mihirakula, and later asserted independence and carried on victorious raids even against his suzerain. In later and more prosperous days his earlier successful operations against Mihirakula might have been easily construed as an independent victory.

CHAPTER X

THE DISINTEGRATION OF THE GUPTA EMPIRE

About the time of the inroads of Toramāṇa and Mihirakula, and largely as a direct consequence of them, we notice a steady progress of the forces of disintegration within the empire itself. Feudal chiefs and high officials gradually assumed great power and authority and finally set up as independent kings. The dwindling resources of the empire are shown by the poor and scanty coinage of a single type. The inscriptions of different chiefs such as the Maukharis and Later Guptas refer to battles in all directions, and although we cannot always locate them, they unerringly indicate a period of unrest and excitement. Taking advantage of this situation Harisheṇa, the Vākāṭaka ruler, invaded Malwa. According to the Vākāṭaka records he conquered or extended his political authority over Mālava, Gujrat and other countries (see *ante* Ch. V). Although the exact date of Harisheṇa is not known, he flourished towards the close of the fifth and the beginning of the sixth century A.D. It is probable, therefore, that it was during the trouble and confusion following the invasion of Toramāṇa that he invaded the distracted province of Mālava and obtained some success. But his triumph was short-lived. Soon an ambitious and enterprising hero appeared on the scene. This was Yaśodharman, who not only established independent authority in Mālava but was soon in a position to hurl open defiance against the emperor.

Little is known of Yaśodharman's origin save that he had probably some connection with the family to which belonged the long line of rulers ending with Bandhu-varman who governed Mālava or a part of it, as a feudatory chief under Kumāra-gupta I with Daśapura (Mandasor) as his capital.

But nearly a century intervened between Bandhu-varman and Yaśodharman, and we do not know anything about the history or activities of this family during this period. Suddenly, some time about 530 A.D. Yaśodharman appears as a meteor in the political horizon, carries his victorious arms far and wide, and sets up a big empire. Like a meteor again, he suddenly vanishes, and his empire perishes with him.

All that we know of the achievement of Yaśodharman by way of military conquests is derived mainly from an inscription (No. 70) engraved in duplicate on two stone pillars at Mandasor. It is a *praśasti* of the type of Samudra-gupta's Allahabad Pillar Inscription, but unlike the latter it does not specify the countries conquered by Yaśodharman. Instead we find only a somewhat vague and boastful assertion that "spurning (the confinement of) the boundaries of his own house", he conquered 'those countries which were not enjoyed (even) by the Gupta Lords and which the command of the chiefs of the Hūṇas failed to penetrate', and, further, that to his feet bow down chiefs "from the neighbourhood of the river Lauhitya up to the mountain Mahendra, and from Himālaya up to the Western Ocean". The only specific reference to any conquest is that over Mihirakula, referred to above.

Such a general and conventional description of universal conquest (*digvijaya*), so familiar to us in Sanskrit poetry and royal *praśastis*, cannot of course be taken at its face value, and we shall hardly be justified in regarding Yaśodharman, on the basis of this record alone, as the sole monarch of Northern India. At the same time such a claim, publicly made, must have some basis in fact, and we need hardly doubt that Yaśodharman was a great conqueror. It seems also to be quite clear that his arms were mainly directed against, and his conquests were mostly accomplished at the cost of, the Hūṇas and the Guptas, though probably some other powers also had to feel the weight of his power.

The fact that the region round Mandasor formed the centre of Yaśodharman's empire and the principal seat of his authority makes it probable that he first rose to power and distinction by freeing the country from the Hūṇa yoke. He probably completed the task which Bhānu-gupta failed to accomplish or only partially succeeded in doing. It was probably in course of this struggle with the Hūṇas that he came into conflict with Mihirakula and defeated him. By this great victory he must have risen to power and distinction, and then he made a bold bid for the imperial power. The gupta emperor, Narasiṁha-gupta, was unable to check his growing power, and for some time Yaśodharman seemed to have carried everything before him. But in spite of his brilliant military success he failed to achieve any permanent result. This is demonstrated by the fact that in 543 A.D. a Gupta emperor, and not Yaśodharman, was invoked as suzerain in a land-grant in N. Bengal.[1] As we have noted above, the Parivrājaka rulers acknowledged Gupta suzerainty as late as 528 A.D. Yaśodharman's short-lived triumph may, therefore, be reasonably placed during the interval between these dates. This is confirmed by the only other inscription (No. 71) that we possess of the time of Yaśodharman, also found at Mandasor, dated in 533-4 A.D.

How Yaśodharman's power came to an end still remains a mystery. It may be due to his natural death, or the assertion of centrifugal forces in the empire which he had himself brought into being. His dazzling success probably led others, such as the Maukharis or the Later Guptas, to imitate his example, and there was perhaps a general uprising among the feudatories of the Gupta empire. The bond that had hitherto knit together, however loosely, the vast dominions from the Bay of Bengal to the Arabian Sea was cut by the cruel sword, not of the Hūṇa chiefs, but of the ambitious Yaśodharman, and he

---

[1]This point will be further discussed in the next chapter.

was probably the first victim to perish in the resulting chaos and conflagration.

Shortly after the great coup of Yaśodharman, and perhaps as an inevitable consequence thereof, several powerful feudal principalities were established in the very heart of the Gupta empire. The most powerful of them were the Maukharis and the Later Guptas. The history of both these dynasties will be treated in greater detail in the next volume, and here we shall only briefly notice their activity during the first half of the sixth century A.D.

The Maukharis[1] were a very ancient family, but did not come into prominence as a political power till the sixth century A.D. Two branches of this family ruled as feudatory chiefs under the Guptas, one in Bihar and the other in U.P. Of the first we know only the names of three kings from three inscriptions engraved on the Barabar and Nagarjuni Hills, about 15 miles to the north-east of Gaya. These were Yajñavarman, who probably founded this family, his son Śārdūlavarman, and his grandson Anantavarman. We hardly know anything about them.

The other branch of the Maukharis ultimately became more powerful. The founder of this family, Harivarman, was succeeded by his son Ādityavarman, and the latter by his son Īśvaravarman. All these three bear the title *Mahārāja* and nothing definite is known about them. But Īśānavarman, the son of Īśvaravarman, assumed tho title *Mahārājāhirāja*, and we know from his record[2] that he defeated the Gauḍas, the Andhras and the Śūlikas. The Gauḍas, whom he is said to have forced to take shelter towards the sea-shore, were undoubtedly the people of Western Bengal. The Andhras probably refer to the Vishṇukuṇḍins of Eastern Deccan ; but the Śūlikas cannot be identified with certainty. It would thus appear that Īśāna-

[1]For the Maukhari inscriptions cf. *CII.* III, Nos. 47-51.

[2]*EI.* XIV, 111.

varman was the first Maukhari chief to set up an independent kingdom. He was undoubtedly a powerful king, for he not only assumed the title *Mahārājādhirāja*, but also issued coins in his own name. These coins very closely resemble those of Toramāṇa, and as the Maukharis are expressly mentioned in a Later Gupta record as having defeated the Hūṇas, that great achievement might also be probably set to his credit. One of his known dates is 611 *Saṁvat* or 554 A.D., and there is thus no doubt that his rise to power and greatness synchronises with the downfall of the Gupta empire.

The Later Guptas were also at first feudatories of the Imperial Guptas. As Kumāra-gupta, the fourth king of this family, dafeated Īśānavarman, the fourth Maukhari king, we may hold that the Later Guptas rose into prominence about the same time as the Maukharis. We know very little of the three predecessors of Kumāra-gupta *viz.*, Kṛishṇā-gupta, Harsha-gupta and Jīvita-gupta. Reference is made in the Aphsad Inscription,[1] a late seventh century record of the family, to the military campaigns of Jīvita-gupta both in the Himalayan region and on the sea-shore ; but as no earlier record of the family is available, we cannot say whether these campaigns were undertaken by him as a feudatory on behalf of the Imperial Guptas, or as an independent king on his own behalf. The same uncertainty prevails, to a certain extent, in regard to the defeat inflicted by the next king Kumāra-gupta upon Īśānavarman. But whether Kumāra-gupta fought with Īśānavarman on behalf of his imperial master, or on his own behalf for the spoils of the empire, his success must have paved the way to the fortunes of his own family. When we remember that there is no reference in any record to a Gupta emperor after 543 A.D., we may well believe that from the time of Kumāra-gupta, if not before, the Later Guptas had, to all

[1] *CII.* III, 200.

intents and purposes, assumed an independent position. That the success attained by Kumāra-gupta was both great and permanent is proved by the fact, recorded in the Aphsad inscription, that he had advanced up to Prayāga where he died, and that his son Dāmodara-gupta again defeated the Maukharis though he himself probably died or was seriously wounded in the battle.[1]

The subsequent history of the Later Guptas does not concern us here. But we have to discuss two questions of great importance concerning them which have a bearing on the history of the Imperial Guptas. In the first place, the name-ending Gupta of all the kings, save one, raises the question whether this family was in any way related to the Imperial Guptas. The contemporaneity, the similar name-ending, and the possession of a part of the Gupta empire no doubt raise a strong presumption in favour of this view. But on the other hand, considering the usual tendency of the court-writers to exaggerate the importance of the royal families even to the extent of giving them pedigrees reaching not only to epic heroes but also to the sun and the moon, it must be regarded as very surprising that no allusion should have been made in their inscriptions to any connection with the Imperial Guptas if there were even any remote basis for it. In the Aphsad Ins., for example, Kṛishṇa-gupta, the first king, is simply said to belong to a good family (*sad-vaṁśaḥ*), and one wonders whether the author of this long *praśasti* would have omitted to refer to the Gupta lineage if there were even any tradition to that effect current in his time. This evidence, though negative in

[1]Fleet's translation of the passage, conveying the idea that the king expired in the fight, is generally accepted. Mr. K. C. Chattopadhyaya, however, argues that the passage does not refer to Dāmodara-gupta's death, but only speaks of his *swoon* and of his subsequent awakening, *i.e.*, regaining consciousness. (*D. R. Bhandarkar Volume*, pp. 181 ff). He has also pointed out that the insciption refers to the victory and not defeat of Dāmodara-gupta, as supposed by Dr. Basak (*HNI.* p. 123).

character, at least raises great doubts about any connection whatsoever between the Imperial Guptas and the Later Guptas. In the absence of any positive corroborative evidence, it is difficult to accept the view that the Later Guptas were related by blood to the Imperial Guptas, although they inherited the family-title and part of their territories.[1]

Far more difficult is the question of the original home of the Later Guptas. Ādityasena, the first king of the family of whom wẹ possess contemporary records, undoubtedly ruled in Magadha towards the close of the seventh century A.D., and so did all his successors. But although all their inscriptions, so far discovered, have been found in Magadha, doubts have been entertained whether originally they were rulers of this province.

It has been suggested by some that the Later Guptas were rulers of Mālava till Ādityasena founded a kingdom in Magadha. The main argument in favour of this view seems to be that as the Imperial Guptas certainly ruled in Magadha up to 530 A.D. and the Maukharis held sway over it in the latter half of the sixth century A.D., the early rulers of the Later Gupta family could not rule in that province, and as Mahāsena-gupta is said to be king of Mālava in the Harsha-Charita, all his predecessors, too, presumably ruled in that province.[2]

This view is based on the assumption that Kṛishṇa-gupta, Ha sha-gupta and Jīvita-gupta all ruled as independent sovereigns from the latter part of the fifth century A.D. Of this there is no evidence whatsoever. They might have been provincial governors or other high officials who, as we have seen above, assumed the titles of *Mahārāja*, and their military campaigns described in Aphsad Inscription might have been undertaken on behalf of the Imperial Guptas. There are at least two important considerations which militate against the view that

[1] *IC*. VIII, 38.
[2] *JBORS*. XIX, 402.

they were originally rulers of Mālava. In the first place, it is incompatible with the history of Yaśodharman whose centre of authority was Mālava. Secondly Jīvita-gupta, of the Later Gupta family, who flourished about the same time, is said to have fought on the sea-shore which indicates the eastern region of the Gupta empire.

The probability, therefore, is that the Later Guptas had not founded any distinct kingdom until after the overthrow of the Gupta empire, and then they fought with the Maukharis and other powers for a share of the spoil. They probably retained as much of it as they could and may be regarded as the residuary legatee of the Gupta empire. Magadha[1] and Northern Bengal, which were the last strongholds of the Gupta emperors, were probably seized by them. They also probably had claims to other parts of the empire including Malwa, of which they might have got possession even somewhat earlier, after the downfall of the short-lived empire of Yaśodharman. Later, when Śaśāṅka established an independent kingdom in Gauḍa, the Later Guptas were confined to Mālava. Although this view cannot be spported in all details by positive evidence, it reconciles all that we know about the Later Guptas and is not contrary to any known fact. But a detailed discussion of this topic takes us beyond the period under review and must be reserved for the next volume.

The Maukharis and the Later Guptas were not the only powers that came into prominence by the decline of the Gupta Empire. Vaṅga (South and East Bengal) also finally shook off the suzerainty of the Guptas, and at least from the second

[1]Even if we assume that two Maukhari kings were in possession of the village of Vāruṇikā (Shahabad district) in the latter half of the sixth century A.D. it does not necessarily follow that the Later Guptas could not hold sway in any part of Magadha. Mahāsena-gupta must have been in possession of at least a part of Magadha before he could reach the Lauhitya (Brahmaputra) river. Portion of Magadha might have frequently changed hands in the long struggle between the Maukharis and the Later Guptas.

quarter of the sixth century A.D., if not before, ranked as an independent kingdom.[1]

Reference has already been made above to Vainya-gupta ruling over this region in 506 A.D. His status and position in the Imperial Gupta family are unknown. A copper-plate (No. 45) found at Gunaighar, 18 miles to the north-west of Comilla in E. Bengal, records a grant of land in that neighbourhood to a Buddhist monk by *Mahārāja* Vainya-gupta, who madiates on the feet of Mahādeva, in the current year 188 (=506 A.D.). The grant was made at the instance of his vassal *Mahārāja* Rudradatta, and another vassal-chief, *Mahārāja* Vijayasena, who held several high offices, was its *dūtaka*. Although Vainya-gupta is styled *Mahārāja*, he had more than one vassal-chief under him bearing the same title, and there is no doubt that he held a fairly high position, even though he was not the suzerain ruler at that time. That he certainly occupied this position, either then or later, is indicated by his gold coins and the Nālandā Seal referred to above. Whether in that capacity he ruled over the whole empire or merely a portion of Bengal, if not the whole of it, cannot be determined, but the latter view seems more probable. In other words, it is just possible that he proclaimed himself the rightful emperor, but his actual authority was confined to Bengal or a part thereof. If this were the case, we may trace from this time the existence of an independent kingdom in Bengal. But, in any case, not long after his death, Vaṅga rises into importance as an independent kingdom under local rulers who assumed the title *Mahārājādhirāja*. The first of them, Gopachandra, had a vassal-chief *Mahārāja* Vijayasena ruling over Vardhamāna-*bhukti*, *i.e.* Burdwan division in W. Bengal. It is probable that this Vijayasena is identical with the chief of the same name who served as *dūtaka* in the Grant of Vainya-gupta. In that case

[1]For detailed discussion of this topic cf *HBR*. pp. 51 ff.

we may consider it as highly probable, that Gopachandra succeeded to the dominions of Vainya-gupta, not long after 506-7 A.D. that these extended from Burdwan to Comilla. But be that as it may, Gopachandra and two other kings, Dharmāditya and Samāchāradeva, must be regarded as independent kings, as they all assumed the title *Mahārājādhirāja.* Samāchāradeva also issued gold coins resembling those of the last Gupta emperor and assumed the title Narendrāditya. The records of these kings refer to two important provinces, Vardhamāna-*bhukti* and Navyāvakāśikā (or Suvarṇavīthi) as being ruled by their governors. It may thus be held that they ruled over South Bengal and at least a portion of Eastern and Western Bengal during the second and third quarters of the sixth century A.D.

It has been stated above that Iśānavarman defeated the Gauḍas and forced them to take shelter in the sea-shore. It is not unlikely that this refers to a conflict with Gopachandra or one of his successors. For Gauḍa denoted in a vague way both Western and Northern Bengal, and Gopachandra's dominions certainly included territories in Western Bengal. It is worthy of note that no record of the two successors of Gopachandra has been found in Western Bengal. It is not impossible, therefore, that Iśānavarman succeeded in driving these kings from Western Bengal, and as they were forced to fall back on the marshy and deltaic lands of Southern Bengal, the Maukhari king could fittingly describe them as *samudrāśraya* (sheltered by the sea). It may be recalled that Jīvita-gupta of the Later Gupta family is also said to have fought against enemies who lived on the sea-shore. Here, too, the reference might be to the people of Lower Bengal who had declared independence of the Gupta empire. The probability is not altogther excluded that the military campaigns of Īśānavarman and Jīvita-gupta were undertaken, jointly or severally, on behalf of the Gupta emperor, their nominal overlord. But in view of the very meagre data that we possess, these conclusions are very uncertain. If the Gauḍa-enemy of Īśānavarman were different from Gopachandra or his successor, we have to presume that the people of West Bengal, too, were asserting their authority and had come to be recognised as an important political entity. But we have no definite information of its political status at this period.

CHAPTER XI

THE FALL OF THE GUPTA EMPIRE

We are now in a position to resume the history of Narasimha-gupta Bālāditya (See p. 193) and to view his reign in a true perspective. He had ascended the throne at a time when internal dissensions and foreign invasion (under Harisheṇa and Toramāṇa) had still further weakend the power and prestige of the empire which had already been considerably diminished even in the reign of Budha-gupta. The Gupta empire now resembled the Mughal empire after the death of Aurangzeb. The imperial authority was acknowledged in name, but already some provincial satraps and feudatory chiefs behaved almost like independent rulers. It was not long before Yaśodharman openly took up arms against the Gupta emperor and began his victorious raids. But although we may credit Yaśodharman with a number of successful military campaigns, it is difficult to believe that he could cansolidate his conquests and establish a big empire. It is interesting to note in this connection how epigraphic evidence clearly indicates that his conquests did not bring about any political change either in the eastern or in the western extremities of the area over which he is said to have carried his victorious arms. No less than fourteen Valabhī Grants ranging in date between 525 and 545 A.D. have been discovered so far. They all refer to *Mahārāja* Dhruvasena and are drawn up in the normal style reflecting no political change of any importance. In N. Bengal, as we shall see, a grant dated 543 A.D. definitely refers to the Gupta emperor. These may not be regarded as conclusive evidences, but certainly favour the supposition that Yaśodharman's campaigns were of the nature of military raids and marked no important change in the political map of Northern India.

But although Narasiṁha-gupta had survived the onslaught of Yaśodharman, the prestige and authority of the Gupta empire received a shattering blow. Taking advantage of the situation, Mihirakula, whose power was curbed but broken by Yaśodharman, began his depredations into the very heart of the empire, and if we may believe Hiuen Tsang, the Gupta emperor was even forced to pay tribute to Hūṇa chief. But when his oppression and cruelties exceeded all bounds, the proud descendant of Skanda-gupta made a final effort to rid the country of this cruel scourge. How he achieved complate success has already been described.

Narasiṁha-gupta's victory over Mihirakula must have enhanced the imperial prestige and given it an added lease of life. He was followed on the throne by his son and grandson, Kumāra-gupta III and Vishṇu-gupta, whose reigns may by placed between 535 and 550 A.D.

The hoard of gold coins found at Kalighat, as far as they can be traced now, consisted, according to Allan, "mainly of coins of Narasiṁha-gupta, Kumāra-gupta II and coins identical in type to the preceding bearing the name Vishṇu under the king's arm." These coins can now be reasonably attributed to the three successive kings Narasiṁha-gupta, Kumāra-gupta III and Vishṇu-gupta, known from the royal seals. It appears from the coins that they assumed, respectively, the titles Bālāditya, Kramāditya and Chandrāditya. It is, however, just possible that some of the coins bearing the name of Kumāra-gupta might really belong to Kumāra-gupta II. Some of these coins are of very rude workmanship and base metal, and this debasement of coins, which commenced from the end of Narasiṁha-gupta's reign, continued right through to the end. The rebellion of Yasodharman and the invasion of the Huṇas might well account for this. But the very fact that gold coins were still being issued by the emperors shows that the great imperial fabric had not finally collapsed even in Vishṇu-gupta's time.

The same inference may be derived from a study of the only epigraphical record of the period that we possess. It is the latest of the five copper-plates found at Damodarpur in N. Bengal (No. 48). The record, which closely resembles in contents and phraseology the other four plates (Nos. 20, 21, 38, 40) belonging to the reigns of Kumāra-gupta I and Budha-gupta, is dated in the year 224 (=543 A.D.) and refers to the Gupta emperor in the usual style. Unfortunately the first part of the name of the emperor cannot be read with certainty, though the name-ending Gupta is quite clear. Dr. Basak, who edited the record, read the name doubtfully as Bhānu-gupta, but according to Y.R. Gupte and H. Krishna Sastri the name is probably Kumāra.[1] If this latter view be accepted, it would support the genealogical and chronological scheme adopted by us, and we might refer the record to the reign of Kumāra-gupta III. The attribution to Bhānu-gupta is less likely as the date of the record is now known to be 224, and not 214 as Dr. Basak thought, and there is an interval of 33 years between this and the only other (No. 47) known record of Bhānu-gupta.

But whosoever may be the king who issued the record, it proves the continued existence of the Gupta empire, at least in eastern parts, even after the triumphant progress of Yaśo-dharman to the banks of the Lauhitya river. A comparison of it with the fourth Damodarpur Copper-plate (No. 40) issued in the reign of Budha-gupta shows what little impression the raid of Yaśodharman produced on the Gupta administrative machinery in N. Bengal, a province which the great conqueror almost certainly must have passed on his way, if he had really proceeded as far as the Brahmaputra river. Although the two

[1] *JIH.* IV, Part III, pp. 118-9; *EI.*, XVII, 193, fn. 1.

records are separated by an interval of nearly half a century, we find the same administrative machinery at work in the district, the same method and procedure followed in the transactions for sale of lands, and what is most interesting, probably one of the members of the district court (or Board) *viz. Nagara-śreshṭhin* Ribhupāla continued in service throughout this long period. There does not appear to have been any violent break in the history or tradition of the imperial Gupta rule in Eastern India.

One significant change has, however, to be noticed. The Uparika-Mahārāja who was governing Puṇḍravardhana-*bhukti* in 543 A.D. is called "*Rāja-putra-Deva-bhaṭṭāraka*". The most reasonable interpretation seems to be that Deva, the son of the emperor, was then the governor of N. Bengal. This evidently gave an added importance to the province which is indicated by the addition of '*hastyaśva-jana*' before that word '*bhoga*' following the governor's name. During the century preceding this record, N. Bengal was governed by Chirāta-datta, Brahma-datta and Jaya-datta, probably all belonging to the same Datta family. The reason why an imperial prince replaced this family is not known to us. But the fact is not without significance. Usually, at the time of the decline of an empire, the provincial governors become almost like independent hereditary rulers. Here the process is entirely reversed. This unerringly indicates the strong hold of the Gupta emperors in this region.

Hiuen Tsang described Bālāditya as king of Magadha, and it is doubtful if after Yaśodharman's *coup d' etat*, any territory further west acknowledged the suzerainty of the empire. As noted above, immediately to the north-west of Magadha, the Maukharis were coming into prominence, and although it is very likely that they joined Bālāditya in the crusade against the Hūṇas, as suggested above, they soon set up an independent kingdom. Further west, in Mālava, the Later Guptas had probably established virtual independence after the death of Yaśodharman. Southern, and a part of Western and Eastern, Bengal had already formed an independent kingdom. The rule of the last two emperors was, therefore, confined to Magadha and N. Bengal.[1] How and when the imperial Gupta family came to lose this last stronghold of their power still remains unknown. But the growing power of the Maukharis and the Later Guptas, and to a certain extent the rise of Gauḍa and Vaṅga (Bengal) as political powers, must have been the most important factors that brought about the final collapse of the imperial Guptas. A copper-plate Grant found at Amauna[2] in the Gaya District was issued by *Kumārāmātya-Mahārāja* Nandana in 232 (=551-52 A.D.) without any reference to the Gupta Emperor. This probably indicates the virtual end of the Gupta empire before that date.

In spite of the many uncertain factors in the history of the period, the above review will make it clear that the Hūṇa invasion cannot be regarded as the chief cause of the downfall of the empire. It no doubt operated as an important contributory factor, but the internal dissensions in the imperial family, the ambitious enterprise of Yaśodharman and the assertion of independence by feudal vassals and provincial governors were mainly instrumental in bringing about its collapse.[3] The Hūṇa menace was great, but that barbarous horde was kept in check throughout the fifth century A.D., and although later they caused damages and devastations on a large scale, they never counted as a lasting factor in Indian politics. But for the short period of Mihirakula's success after Yaśodharman's death, they never played even any important

[1]A mission was sent by the Chinese emperor in A.D. 539 to the Court of Magadha, and Paramārtha accompanied this mission to China where he spent the rest of his life. The Court of Magadha evidently refers to the Gupta Emperor, and proves the existence of this kingdom in 539 A.D.

[2]*EI.* X, 50.

[3]Cf. *PHAI.*[4] App. D, p. 531.

political rôle save in the border regions of Kashmir and Afghanistan. The decline and downfall of the Gupta empire was brought about by the same causes which operated in the case of the Maurya empire in the older and the Mughal empire in later days.

CHAPTER XII

SOUTH INDIA.

The three centuries and a half of South Indian history, forming the subject of this Chapter, are full of unsettled questions. The fitful evidence, alike of literature and epigraphy, admits of diverse interpretations; consequently there is no consensus of opinion among the scholars who have written of this period. However, no attempt will be made here to review rival theories ; our aim will be rather to state the evidence concisely and offer the minimum of comment calculated to set forth our view of the most probable course of the events of the period.

1. The close of the Śangam age.

The later phases of Śangam poetry in Tamil may well be taken to fall within our period, and the celebrated Chola monarch Karikāla and his contemporary who ruled in Kāñchī, Toṇḍaimān Iḷam Tiraiyan (Iḷandiraiyan), may well be placed about its commencement or a little earlier. The two kings are extolled in two poems by one poet, Uruttiraṅgaṇṇanār, a Brāhmin of Kaḍiyalūr. To a somewhat later period belonged Nannan of Kaṇkānam and the minor chieftains famed for their patronage of the arts and for that reason counted along with some earlier names as Kaḍai-yelu-vallalkaḷ, the Seven Patrons of the last Śangam. Later than this generation was that dominated by the Pāṇḍyan ruler, Neḍuñjeliyan. This may be inferred from the facts that Nakkirar who celebrates him in the Neḍu-nal-vādai mentions Karikāla in one of his poems[1] and

[1] *Aham*, 141.

that non of the poets of the age of Karikāla makes any reference to Neḍuñjeliyan though they know of lesser Pāṇḍyan names. This Pāṇḍya was also a great patron of learning, but there is evidence that even after him the patronge of Śangam Tamil literature was continued for a time by Nalliyakkōḍan, Kumaṇan[1] and others, though not on the same scale as before. The several generations of Chēra princes who were contemporary with all these monarchs and chieftains complete the picture of the political map of the Tamil country in this period.

No connected account of political history is possible in the absence of a settled chronology and of genealogies of the ruling dynasties. All our knowledge comes from disconnected poems of various poets preserved in schematic anthologies put together long after the time of original composition ; the occasion of the poem and the name of its author rest on colophons added to the poems by their editors, and we have no means of controlling the tradition preserved in these colophons. We have indicated above the relative chronology of the most important land-marks in our period.[2] Within the broad framework of this relative chronology some outstanding facts may be briefly noticed, and the social life of the age may be sketched with greater confidence in the light of contemporary literature. Karikāla and Kōccengaṇān are two most prominent rulers of the Chola kingdom and the names of both have been decked by posterity in rainbow hues of legned. The son of Ilañjētchenni, who was distinguished for the beauty of his numerous war-chariots, Karikāla was deprived of his birth-right by his enemies and confined in a prison for some years. He effected his escape by overpowering the prison guards, and made himself king. In a great battle at Veṇṇi[3] now called Kōyil Veṇṇi, fifteen miles to

[1] *Sirupān.*, *Puram.* 158.

[2] *The Chronology of the Early Tamils* by K. N. Sivaraja Pillai (Madra 1932) is of no value owing to its grave defects of method.

[3] *Aham*, 55, 246; *Puram*, 66; and *Porunar-āṛṛuppaḍai*, 11. 146.8.

the east of Tanjore, he inflicted a defeat on the Pāṇḍya and the Chēra who appear to have lent their support to Karikāla's domestic enemies, along with eleven minor chieftains who shared the defeat with them; the Chēra king Perum Śēral Ādan, who received a wound on his back in the course of the battle, expiated the dishonour by starving himself to death on the field. Veṇṇi was thus the turning point in Karikāla's career; the victory seated him firmly on his ancestral throne and secured for him the hegemony of the Tamil state system for the rest of his life. Another engagement at Vāhaipparandalai[1] and expeditions against the Aruvālar[2] in the lower valley of the Peṇṇar, and the Oḷiyar, probably a predatory tribe of Nāga extraction, who were tamed by Karikāla into a settled life, are among the other known events of this great king's reign. A certain Ādimandi is the subject of many poems; one of them by Paraṇar[3] states that her husband Āṭṭan Atti was being drowned in the mouth of the Kaveri and that he was rescued from the sea by another woman Marudi. The *Śilappadikāram* says that Ādimandi was Karikāla's daughter. Karikāla was a follower of the Vedic religion, a patron of Brāhmins and poets, and a promoter of art, industry and trade. He made his mark as an impartial judge. He was also a good liver who spent a fair amount of time in feasts, drinking and the company of women. In later ages the achievements of Karikāla were magnified into a conquest of practically the whole of India; but the most celebrated among his legendary achievements is the construction of the floodbanks of the Kaveri with the aid of prisoners from Ceylon (Ceylonese story) and with that of several subordinate kings among whom was Triṇētra Pallava who lost his

[1]*Aham*, 125.
[2]*Paṭṭinappālai*, 11. 274-5.
[3]*Aham*, 222.

third eye for refusing to carry out the emperor's behest (Telugu-Choḍa inscriptions).

Toṇḍaimān Iḷandiraiyan who ruled in Kāñchīpuram must have been a younger contemporary of Karikāla who reached eminence after the death of the great Chola monarch ; for not only does he not figure among the enemies of Karikāla, but he is clearly said to have commanded the raspect of the three crowned kings of the Tamil land.[1] He was doubtless an independent ruler, and there is no support for the views often put forward that he was a grandson of Karikāla or a viceroy appointed to rule Kāñchī after Karikāla's conquest of that city. Iḷandiraiyan is said to have been born in the line of Vishṇu in the family given by the waves of the sea (*tirai*) and thence called Tiraiyan ; the family had also the name of Toṇḍaiyar and were noted for their prowess in war and success in the storming of enemy fortresses. Iḷandiraiyan's sceptre shunned evil and scrupulously followed the path of *Dharma.* The name Toṇḍai then applied both to the ruling dynasty and the country, exactly like Chola, Chēra and Pāṇḍya ; but *toṇḍai* is also the name of a creeper (*Capparis horrida*), and to this fact must be traced the name Pallava (sprout) of the rulers of Toṇḍaimaṇḍalam in later times, and the legend recorded by the commentator Naccinārkkiniyar that the child born a liaison between a Chola prince and a Nāga maiden was floated on the sea with a twig of the *toṇḍai* tied to him for identification in accordance with the prior understanding between the lovers—a case of euhemerism accounting at once for the names Tiraiyan and Toṇḍaiyar. What the relation was, if any, between the Tiraiyar.—Toṇḍaiyar and the Pallavas, and what the interval was between the two lines of the rulers of Kāñchī, can hardly be determined at present.

---

[1]Pērāśiriya, however, in his comment on *Tol. Maṛapu,* 83 counts this ruler as a princeling not of full regal rank. We follow the words in the text of the poem here as elsewhere.

Iḷandiraiyan thus stands alone as we know nothing of his predecessors or successors of the Toṇḍaiyar line from any source. He is counted among the poets of the Śangam age like many another prince and patron of poets in that period.

Of a later generation than Karikāla and Iḷandiraiyan was Neḍuñjeliyan, the Pāṇḍyan king who is always distinguished from his namesakes by the attribute Talaiyālaganāttucceru-venra, *i.e.*, victorious in the battle of Talaiyālagānam. Among the predecessors of this ruler, was Mudukuḍumi Peruvaludi, a fierce warrior as well as the performer of many sacrifices; who is styled Paramēśvara in the Vēḷvikuḍi grant of the eighth century A.D. which renewed his original grant of the village of Veḷvikuḍi (sacrifice settlement). Neḍuñjeliyan himself was called to the throne as a youth. Tempted by his tender age and their own cupidity, his two neighbours, the Chola and the Chēra entered into a combination with five minor chieftains and planned an invasion of the Paṇḍyan kingdom. Neḍuñ-jeliyan, however, rose equal to the occasion, and simple poem of great force and beauty attests the youthful king's heroic resolve to hold his own at all costs.[1] His enemies took the offensive greatly underrating his strength and ability, and hoping for an easy partition of his territory among themselves. Neḍuñjeliyan had to commence the fight almost at the gates of Madura; but he soon threw the enemies out of his kingdom and pursued them across the frontier into the Tanjore district. The decisive engagement took place at Talai-yālangānam, which probably is now represented by the village with an identical name Talai-ālam-kāḍu, eight miles to the north-west of Tiru-vālūr. Chēy,[2] the Chēra king of the Elephant-look, was captured alive[3] in literal fulfilment of the vow taken by Neḍuñjeliyan on the eve of the campaign. After his brilliant success in

[1] *Puram*, 72.
[2] *Tirukkuṛal*, 355 comm.
[3] *Puṛam*, 17.

defending his kingdom against foreign aggression, Neḍuñjeliyan was engaged in successful wars against the Kongu chieftain Adigan, and another petty ruler nearer home, Evvi of Nīḍūr, from whom he wrested the two districts called Milali and Muttūru and annexed them to his own kingdom. The battle of Talai-yālangānam was a turning point in Pāṇḍyan history and was long cherished with pride by Neḍuñjeliyan's successors; a brief but vivid allusion to it occurs in a Pāṇḍyan charter of the tenth century—the Śinnamanūr plates of Rājasiṁha II. Neḍuñjeliyan was a follower of the Vedic religion and performed sacifices. Himself a poet of no mean order, he patronised many poets like Māngudi Marudan, Nakkīrar and his father, and Kallādanār; their poems contain many traces of an intimate admiration for the king and his qualities and achievements.

The Chola monarch Seṅgaṇān (Red-eye) defeated his Chēra contemporary Kaṇaikkāl Irumporai in the battle of Kalumalam near Karuvūr in the Kongu country and took him prisoner. The victor finds a place in the hymns of the Śaiva devotees Sambandar and Sundaramurtti, a well as of the Vaisṇava Tirumangai Āḷvār, and in the legendary genealogy of the Cholas of the Vijayālaya line. Śeṅgaṇān was believed to have worshipped Vishṇu in Tirunaraiyūr, and constructed seventy beautiful temples enshrining the eight-armed Īśa (Śiva).

The Chēras have been mentioned more than once in the preceding paragraphs. We hear generally little of them besides their names, which are too cumbrous to be included in a general account like this. Students of Tamil literature have discussed at great length, but with inconclusive results, two questions of Chēra history—the location of the Chēra capital Vañji, and the rule of succession in the royal line. Some would locate Vañji in Karūr in the Western confines of the modern Trichinopoly district, while others identify it with Tiruvañjaikkaḷam on the west coast in the Cochin State.

Whether the succession in the Chēra royal line went from father to son or followed the matriarchal rule of inheritance by sister's sons (marumakkaḷ-tāyam) has also been debated at undue length ; and discussion has centred round dubious and cryptic expressions in the colophons to the extant portions of the anthology known as 'the Ten Tens' (*Padiṟṟuppattu*). The only positive evidence on the matter points to succession in the male line.[1]

Two facts of Chēra history deserve to be mentioned here. One is the victory of Imaiyavaramban Neḍuñjeral Ādan against the Yavanas of 'graceless harsh speech', who were made prisoners and subjected to ill-treatment, their hands being tied behind and oil being poured on their heads ; besides they were relieved of many precious utensils and a good quantity of diamonds. These Yavanas were either Greeks or the Arab intermediaries who took a prominent share in the trade between India and the West. The other fact is the overthrow of the Kaḍambu located in a delta near the sea—another achievement attributed to the same ruler. One of his successors is said to have decapitated Nannan whose capital city had the round-blossomed Kaḍambu near its portal. This recurring warfare in which the Chēras seem to glory in the seizure and destruction of the Kadamba tree as their trophy deserves to be noted ; it may well be that Nannan's line and their 'guardian tree' (*kāval maram*) of the Kaḍambu anticipate in the West the Kadambas of Vanavāsī celebrated in inscriptions of a slightly later age, very much in the same manner as Iḷandiraiyan and the line of Toṇḍaiyar in Kāñchī anticipate the Pallavas in the east. But to conclude from this that the Pallavas and Kadambas were indigenous lines of rulers of South Indian origin may not be correct ; for the probability remains of incoming dynasties of northern origin adopting prevalent local traditions and

[1]*Padiṟṟuppattu*, 74.

assimilating them, thus winning for themselves a larger claim to the affections of the local population.[1]

In striking contrast to the obscurity of the political history of the period, is the vivid picture of the social and cultural conditions that stands out from the numerous poems of the age. The most prominent feature of its culture is its composite quality. It is the unmistakable result of the blend of two originally distinct cultures, best described as Tamilian and Aryan, though it is by no means easy, without much preliminary study that must engage scholars for some years to come, to isolate the elements of the Pre-Aryan Tamil culture that have entered into the amalgam. Everything has already been thoroughly overlaid with the Aryan influences which act sometimes as no more than a superficial yeneer thinly disguising the original traits, but more often pervades through and through transforming practices and institutions beyond recognition. There are at present no traces of any literary work in the Tamil language, however ancient, which does not betray Sanskrit influence to some extent. Yet we may be quite certain that the bulk of the population, like the bulk of the words employed in the literature of the time, were of pre-Aryan Tamilian origin ; only the spirit animating both has been thoroughly Aryanized. And this great cultural transformation was apparently effected in a very peaceful manner ; the literature bears no sign of opposition to the inflow of the new influences or conflict with them ; on the contrary there is abundant evidence that they were everywhere welcomed and embraced with alacrity. The same process was continued, as we know, in Ceylon and in the eastern colonies farther afield.

The vision of the poets of our age was not limited to the

[1]The 'Kadambas' have sometimes been spoken of as pirates and the Chēra victories as great naval achievements. There is no talk of Kadambas in this context but only of the Kaḍambu tree in our sources. A unique naval achievement against an unnamed island occurs however in Nos. 45 and 46 of *Padiṟṟuppattu*.

confines of the Tamil country ; the whole of India from the Himalayas to Cape Comorin is often referred to especially in connection with the conquests of different heroes. The Hindu colonies in the east across the seas and the regular trade that was carried on by them and other countries with South India are also mentioned. Urban life was fairly developed in a few centres, particularly the capital cities of Kāñchī, Uraiyūr, Madura and Vañji; these cities were well fortified, were surrounded by deep moats, and their streets were broad and *bazaars* crowded. In the chief sea-port towns like Māmallapuram, Puhār and Koṛkai the same features of urban life were reproduced with the addition of the residences of foreign merchants from many lands and the activities of busy customs officials and those engaged in loading and unloading vessels in the harbour.[1] The row of boats, that had returned after disposing of cargoes of white salt in exchange for paddy and were lying in harbour, are compared, by the author of *Paṭṭinappālai*,[2] to a number of war horses tethered in a row. In the extensive *bazaar* of Puhār were many grand and spacious mansions, raised on platforms reached by high ladders; these were naturally centres of art, culture and fashion.[3] In all parts of the town there were flags of various kinds and shapes flying in the air. Some were flags that were worshipped by many as a high divinity and the entrances to their precincts were decorated with flowers. Others were white flags raised on frames supported by posts, below which were made offerings of rice and sugar to precious boxes of merchandise. Yet others were flags that announced the challenge of great and renowned teachers who had mastered many sciences and proclaimed their readiness to hold a public debate with other scholars. There were also flags waving on the masts of ships heaving in the port of Puhār like huge elephants chafing

[1] *Maduraikkāñji*, ll. 536-44.

[2] ll. 29-32.

[3] ll. 142-80

at their posts. Yet others, flying over shops where fish and flesh were being sliced and fried and whose thresholds were strewn with fresh sand and flowers, announced the sale of high-class liquor to their numberless customers. Drink was a very common luxury among high and low; imported wines figured prominently in royal banquets, while lesser folk had to be content with country toddy and other varieties of drinks, among which *tōppi* prepared from fermented paddy is spoken of very highly.[1] Courtesans skilled in music were another attraction of the city life, but the poets point out how their wily love cannot be compared with the deep devotion of the wedded wife.

Our poets give us beautiful pictures of other aspects of life also. The rural landscape, studded with coconut and mango trees, and characterised by the different agricultural activities, is often described in rich colours. The interesting features of the life of hunters with their paraphernalia of dogs, nets and traps are also referred to. We get a vivid account of the life of the fishing folk of Puhār—how they caught and cooked fish on the shore, how they spent their leisure time in fierce duels, how they worshipped their traditional deities and how they spent their nights is music and love-making. The pure and homely atmosphere of an *Agrahāra* village, where even the parrots in the unpretentious dwellings of the pious and learned Brahmins could recite the Vedic hymns, is also reproduced with equal success. And finally the poets do not fail to describe in glowing colours the warm and rich hospitality they often received from their royal patrons—how they spent their time pleasantly in the palace listening to exquisite music, drinking delicious wines and eating to their hearts' content rich dishes, vegetarian and non-vegetarian, 'till the edges of their teeth became blunt like the plough-shares after ploughing dry lands.' The kings used to supervise personally the reception of their minstrel

[1] *Perumbāṇ-ārruppaḍai*, I, 142.

guests, and they had very good reasons to do so; for they were apprehensive that they would be pilloried in their songs by disappointed and irate bards.

2. The Early Pallavas.

The Sātavāhana empire tottered to its fall towards the close of the second century A.D. or the beginning of the third. Heirs to the great Mauryas in the Deccan, the Sātavāhanas must have come into possession of all the country that had formed part of Aśoka's empire; certainly Vanavāsī in the West, and probably also Toṇḍaimaṇḍalam in the east thus came under Sātavāhana rule for a time. The families of Nannan in the West and Tiraiyar in the East are, as we have seen, mentioned in Tamil works that are best placed in the period or the withdrawal of Sātavāhana power from the South. They may well represent the natural power of the Tamil state system to extend into the region vacated by the rulers of the Deccan, or possibly of the Tamil states in these regions to emerge into independence after a period of subordination to northern rule. However that may be, it was not long before rulers of northern origin and affiliation once more took possession of these lands and ruled them for several generations, the Chūṭus and the Kadambas in the West, and the Pallavas in the East.

Epigraphy affords clear evidence that these three lines of rulers, like the Ikshvākus and Bṛihatphalāyanas in the Telugu country, continue the Sātavāhana tradition in administration, and *prima facie* they are all instances of powerful local officials setting up independent rule with the weakening and disappearance of the central power to which they had been subject earlier. Everywhere the charters of the new dynasties retain the language, the script and the official titles of the Sātavāhanas; later the language changes into Sanskrit and the script develops new forms, and a further stage in the development occurs when the inscriptions become bi-lingual, partly Sanskrit and partly local idiom, Telugu Tamil or Kanarese. The last stage was not reached within the limits of our period.

The origin of the Pallavas has been much debated; some would postulate for them a Parthian (Pahlava) origin, and suppose that, like Suviśākha, the Pallava minister (*amātya*) of Rudra-dāman in Surāshṭra, the founder of the Pallava dynasty might have been a Sātavāhana official of foreign extraction; this is a hypothesis which can neither be confirmed nor contradicted in the present state of the evidence, but strictly speaking it is unnecessary when the question is viewed in a wider background. For there is good reason to think that the Pallavas and the Kadambas, and even the Chūṭus before them to some extent, sought to adopt local traditions for their own use to incorporate them in their charters. Thus Sātakarṇi of the Chūṭu-kula, ruler of Vanavāsī worships and endows at the shrine of the god of Malavalli;[1] on the same pillar which bears this brief record, we find immediately after it a longer inscription of a Kadamba king, described as *Vaijayantī-dhamma-mahārāja*, and also, like Sātakarṇi, worshipper of the god of Malavalli. A little later the Kadamba line began to declare their devotion to Svāmi Mahāsena, whom Tamil tradition regarded as dwelling in the Kaḍambu tree. In the same manner, Pallavas, as the name of dynasty of Kāñchīpuram, must be taken to be the Prākṛit-Sanskrit rendering of Toṇḍai, the Tamil name of the land and its rules. Curiously enough, poet Oṭṭakkūttan who wrote in the twelfth century A.D. seems vaguely to recall these early attempts at mutual adaptation between the North and the South when, referring to the tree sacred to the local deity (*sthala-vṛiksha*), the mango, he calls it Chūta-pallava.[2]

---

[1] *EC.* VII, Sk. 263.
[2] *Takka Yāgapparani*, v. 625.

The eastren and south-eastern section of the Sātavāhana empire fell to the Ikshvākus, the Bṛihatphalāyanas and the Pallavas. The History of the first two of these houses has been dealt with in Chapter IV, and we shall therefore trace here that of the last mentioned one.

The early history of the Pallavas of Kāñchī is to be traced from three copper-plate grants, in the Prākṛit language, two issued from Kāñchīpuram, and all containing the name of Skanda-varman with varying prefixes.[1] These prefixes are in order *Yuvamahārāja* Śiva, *Dhammamahārājādhirāja* Śiva, and Siri Vijaya. The words Śiva and Vijaya, like Siri, are only auspicious honorofics, and do not militate against our considering the Skanda-varman of all the three charters as one and the same person ; the palaeography of the records affords strong support to this view. Thus the earliest of these grants was issued by Skanda-varman when he was still Yuvarāja and the two others when he was the ruling monarch ; one of these bears a date in his eighth regnal year, and the year of the other is lost by the action of time.

As Yuvarāja, Skanda-varman is described as belonging to the Bharadvāja gotra and the Pallava family. As monarch, he is called in addition the performer of the Agnishṭoma, Vājapeya and Aśvamedha sacrifices and supreme king of kings devoted to Dharma. It appears from these inscriptions that the Pallava kingdom had Kāñchī for its capital and extended up to the Tuṇgabhadra and the Krishna rivers. There is no direct evidence on the location of its western frontier ; but considering the traditions that the Kadamba Mayūraśarman got the country between the Western sea and Prehārā from a Pallava monarch, and that the Gaṅga kings continued to occupy a feudatory relation to the Pallavas for some generations, it seems probable that Pallava dominion extended right up to the Western sea in this

[1] Mayidavolu, *EI.* VI. 84-9; Hirahadagalli, *Ibid.* I, 2; also II, 480-5. British Museum plates of Charudevi. *Ibid.* VIII, 145-6.

early period. The steps by which this empire was built up are not now traceable, but its wide extent shows that Skanda-varman could legitimately claim imperial position as he did by his title *Dharma-mahārājādhirāja.* He had also performed the Aśvamedha sacrifice. Obviously, he was not the first Pallava ruler of Kāñchī ; his title Yuvamahārāja in the Mayidavolu plates indicates that clearly enough ; but at present we have no definite knowledge of his predecessors. Skanda-varman had a son, Buddha-varman, who was Yuvarāja as we learn from a grant issued by his queen Chārudevī, who calls herself mother of Buḍdhyaṅkura. Skanda-varman flourished in the latter part of the 3rd century. We have no historical information about the reign or achievements of any of his successors.

There is total darkness for a century more or less after the records of Skanda-varman's time, and the only direct evidence so far known for the continuance of Pallava rule in this period in Kāñchīpuram is the well-known reference in the Allahabad pillar inscription of Samudra gupta to Kāñchī. Samudra-gupta's invasion of the South took place about the middle of the fourth century A.D. There can be no reasonable doubt that is opponent Vishṇugopa was a Pallava ruler of Kāñchī; but none of the kings of this name mentioned in the Pallava Sanskrit charters can be considered sufficiently early to be identified with the enemy of Samudra-gupta. There is no evidence that Samudra-gupta reached as far South as Kāñchī, though he met its ruler in battle somewhere.[1]

The next stage in the annals of Pallava rule known to history is represented by ten copper plate charters[2] and the

---

[1] Cf. p. 146 above.

[2] They are : (1-2) Omgodu—two sets A and B, *EI.* XV, 246-55; (3) Uruvapalli *IA.* V, 50-53; (4) Neḍuṅgarāya, *Bharatı*, (Vṛsa) Jyestha, pp. 699-713; (5) Mangadur, *IA.* V, 154-7; (6) Pikira, *EI.* VIII, 159-63; (7) Buchireddipalem, *Jl. Mad. Univ.* XII, 129-59; (8) Chendalur, *EI.* VIII, 233-36; (9) Udayendiram, *EI.* III, 142-7; (10) Chūra, *EI.* XXIV, 137-43.

Darsi fragment, all of them in Sanskrit. There is besides a unique stone inscription of Siṁha-varman in Prākṛit discovered recently in the Guntur district. The charters are all dated in the regnal years of the kings ruling at the time of their issue without reference to any well-known era, and for chronology we depend mainly on palaeography; a western Gaṅga copper plate charter, to be dated likewise on palaeographic grounds, mentions a couple of synchronisms with Pallava rulers, and there is a Śaka date in a Jaina manuscript which confirms the chronology suggested by these rather vague indications.

The Sanskrit charters are none of them issued from Kāñchīpuram except the Chendalur and Udayendiram plates. Several writers have maintained that the Pallavas lost Kāñchī during this period ; they find support for this view in the statement of the Vēlūrpalaiyam plates that Kāñchīpura was seized by Kumāravishṇu, and argue that Kāñchī passed into the hands of the Cholas, Karikāla and his successors for a time. We have assigned Karikāla to an earlier age ; and there is little tangible evidence of his having ever conquered Kāñchīpuram. Even if the Chendalur and Udayendiram plates of the Pallavas issued from Kāñchī are set aside on the score of doubts about their genuineness, the jumbled traditions of the Velūrpalaiyam plates cannot offer reliable guidance to occurrences which took place about four or five centuries earlier. The theory that Kāñchīpuram ceased to be the Pallava capital for a time cannot be accepted without more tangible evidence.

The genealogy and chronology of the Pallavas of the Sanskrit charters may be arranged in the following manner,

---

The last three have been suspected on palaeographical grounds; they are at best copies of originals no longer accessible, if not altogether spurious, and their evidence should be treated with reserve. The information supplied by the Pallava records about the cultural conditions of the times has been utilised in the general account of the Administration, Religion and Social and Economic condition of our period given in Chaps. XIV, XVIII & XIX.

accepting the data from all known records as genuine, but marking off the doubtful ones from the rest.

Kumāravishṇu I (Om. A), 325-50
|
Skanda-varman I, 350-375
|
Vīra-varman (Vīrakorcha-varman of Darśi), 375-400
|
Skanda-varman II (Om. A), 400-436
|

Siṁha-varman I (436-60)	Yuvamahārāja Vishṇugopa-varman I (Uruvapalli, Nedungarāya)	Kumāravishṇu II
Skanda-varman III 460-80	Siṁha-varman II (Om. B. Mangaḷūr, Pikira, Buchireddipalem), 480-500	Buddha-varman
Nandi-varman (Udayēndiram)	Vishṇugopa-varman II (Chūra)	Kumāravishṇu III (Chendalur)

The dates given against the monarchs are approximate, based on a rough calculation of twenty to twenty-five years for each reign with the date from the *Lokavibhāga* and the Gaṅga synchronisms as the starting points.[1] This scheme, it will be noticed, renders it probable that Samudra-gupta's Pallava opponent was either Kumāravishṇu I himself, or a brother of his named Vishṇugopa. Siṁha-varman II must be taken to have had a prosperous reign as he is found issuing the largest number of grants. Yuvarāja Vishṇugopa-varman I may or may not have reigned, though he is called *Mahārāja* in the Chūra plates ; perhaps he did not. We are by no means sure what happened after Simha-varman II ; the grants have all been suspected as their palaeography is not of the period to

[1] The Penukoṇda plates or Mādhava-varman II, for which A.D. 475 is considered a very good date, state that Mādhava himself, who had another name Siṁha-varman, was annointed by the Pallava Mahārāja Skanda-varman, and earlier, his father Ayya-varman was annointed by the Pallava Mahārāja Siṁha-varman, who is generally taken to be Siṁha-varman II. The manuscript of *Lokavibhāga* gives the information that Sarvanandin finished copying or composing the work on a day corresponding to 25th August D.A. 458, which fell in the twenty-second regnal year of Siṁha-varman, the ruler of Kāñchī.

which they purport to belong. There is no room in this scheme for Siṁha-varman, the father of Siṁhavishṇu, who starts the line of Pallava rulers whose history is best known from the end of the sixth century A.D. Here is another gap in the line of succession which cannot be bridged at present.

The political history of the Pallava kingdom during this period is almost a blank, as the conventional epithets applied to the different kings in different charters on their performance of sacrifices success in many fields of battle, honouring gods and Brāhmaṇas, and protecting their subjects, are not of much value to the historian and do not deserve detailed discussion. The contemporary inscriptions of the Kadambas and Gaṅgas, however, mention a few facts bearing on the relations of the Pallavas with these dynasties and these are best considered with the history of these lines of rulers.

3. THE KADAMBAS.

The rise of the Kadambas is narrated in some detail in the Tālaguṇḍa pillar inscription[1] engraved within a century of the events. There was a Brahmin family who derived their descent from Hāritī and belonged to the Mānavya gotra ; they were devoted to the study of the Veda and the performance of Vedic sacrifices ; they were regular in the performance of rituals, daily and periodical, and kept an open house where guests were always welcome ; they were called Kadambas as they tended with care a unique blossoming *Kadamba* tree that had come up near their dwelling. In this family was born Mayūraśarman who after a good education, went to the capital of the Pallava ruler with his *guru* (teacher) Vīraśarman, to complete his studies and entered the *ghaṭikā* (college) with a view to learn the entire Veda. There he had a fierce quarrel

1 *EI.* VIII, 24-36; *EC.* VII, Sk. 176.

with a mounted guard (*aśvasaṁstha*), and in his wrath, he felt: 'Alas! in this age of Kali, Brahmaṇahood is helpless against the Kshatra; for what can be more pitiful than this, that even after I have given full satisfaction to my *gurus* and studied my *śākhā* with great effort, the realisation of my spiritual aim should depend on the king?' So with his arm deft in handling *kuśa* (a kind of holy grass), *samidh* (fuel) and other ingredients of sacrifice, he grasped the shining weapons of war wishing to conquer the world. He soon overpowered the Pallava officials of the frontier in battle, and occupied the dense forests round about Śrīparvata (in the Karnul district). He also levied tribute from the Bṛihad-bāṇas and other rulers to fulfil his avowed project and to rouse the anger of the Pallava kings. When these rulers of Kāñchī came at the head of their vast forces to engage him in battle, he surprised them in their camps by nocturnal attacks, and kept on harassing them, while avoiding an open battle in the field. The Pallava rulers admired his prowess, and thinking that no good can come out of the destruction of so eminent a warrior, they readily courted his friendship, employed him as commander in their wars and in due course crowned him with their own hands sole monarch of the territory between the western sea and Preharā. Preharā, the eastern limit of the Kadamba kingdom which thus came into existence, has not been identified; it has generally been taken to be a river, either the Tungabhadra or Malaprabha; but at present this is no more than a plausible guess.

Now there is nothing incredible in this account; on insult, real or imagined, leads to a successful rebellion, terminated by a peace on the basis of mutual regard and friendship. But the details are far from clear; the nature of the original quarrel that followed Mayūraśarman's entry into the *ghaṭihā*, the place where he lived and studied at first and whence he went over to Kāñchī, the reason for his selecting the Śrīparvata region for the base of his operations against the Pallavas, or for the

Pallavas making over the western marches of their dominions to Mayūraśarman are all unknown. And it seems that the description of the family of Mayūraśarman as Hāritīputras of the Mānavya *gotra* who derived their family name from tending a *Kadamba* tree is a myth connecting the family with well-known local traditions of the Chūṭus and other lines of rulers to whom the country belonged in earlier times. Several myths gathered round the name and family of Mayūraśarman in later ages, and there was invented a three-eyed four-armed eponymous ancestor of the family. There is no need to reproduce all these legends, but a sample may be given ; an inscription of A.D. 1189[1] states that being born in a *Kadamba* forest the founder of the line was called Kadamba Rudra, and as he bore on his limbs the reflections of a peacock's feathers, he came to be called Mayūravarman,—note the change of *Śarman* to *Varman*.

Epigraphy is our only guide to the chronology of Kadamba history. The Talagunda pillar inscription may well be assigned to the middle of the fifth century A.D.; this would indicate the middle of the fourth century as the date for Mayūraśarman. The suggestion has been made that Samudra-gupta's inroad about this time must have given a rude shock to the power of the Pallavas, and that Mayūraśarman took advantage of the resulting weakness and confusion to establish his kingdom in the West. However that may be, the fact that the earliest Kadamba inscription known[2] is in the Prākṛit language and has features in common with the Hirahadagalli plates, shows that the foundation of Kadamba power cannot be later than the first half of the fourth century. This inscription is found engraved on a pillar in Malavalli, below a shorter record of the Chūṭas. The inscription does not give the name of the Kadamba king, but it may be assigned to the first ruler of the line as it confirms and amplifies an earlier gift of Śivaskanda-varman a

1 *EC*. VIII, Sk. 179.
2 *Ibid*. VII, Sk. 264; *IA*. XLVI, 154-55.

Hāritīputra of the Mānavya *gotra* and ruler of Vaijayantī—obviously a Chūṭu king ; the Kadamba king (*Kadambānām rājā*) is described as *Vaijayantī-dharma-mahār ājādhirāja* devoted to the study of the Veda—*patikala-sojjhāyi-chachchāparo*, a phrase which recalls a part of the set *praśastis* of the later Sanskrit inscriptions of the Kadambas. Another Prākṛit inscription from Chandravalli,[1] much shorter than the Malavalli record, names Mayūraśarmān, states that he dug a tank (*taṭākam*), ascribes to him conquests in Traikūṭa, Ābhīra, Pallava, Pariyātrika, Śakasthāna, Sayindaka, Punāta, Mokari, and then stops abruptly at this point. This impossible record has all the appearance of a modern fake, and its evidence should await confirmation before being accepted as history.

The genealogy of the Kadambas to be gathered from the inscriptions is as follows ; the dates given under each ruler being approximations of Jouveau-Dubreuil.

- Mayūraśarman A.D. (345-60)
  - Kaṅga-varman (360-85)
    - Bhagīratha (385-410)
      - Raghu (410-25)
      - Kākustha-varman (425-50)
        - Sāntī-varman (450-75)
          - Mṛigeśa-varman (470-488)
            - Ravi-varman (500-538)
              - Hari-varman (538-50)
            - Bhānu-varman
            - Śivaratha
        - Kumāra-varman
          - Māndhātṛi-varman (488-500)
        - Kṛishṇa-varman I
          - Vishṇu-varman
            - Siṁha-varman
              - Kṛishṇa-varman II (550-65 A.D.)
                - Aja-varman etc.
          - Deva-varman

---

[1] *MAR.* 1929, No. 1 pp. 50 ff.

What services Mayūraśārman rendered to the Pallavas after he became friends with them and before they gave him independent and sole charge of the kingdom of Vanavāsī (Vaijayantī), is not stated either in the Tālaguṇḍa pillar inscription or elsewhere. But the inscription says that Mayūraśarman was appointed as Senāpati by Shaḍānana and the mothers, a statement which finds a permanent place in the standard *praśasti* of the Kadambas ever afterwards in the phrase: *Svāmimahāsena-matṛigaṇ-ānudhyātābhishiktānām*; we have already shown reason to hold that this was an instance of the adoption of local myths and legend by the new line of rulers. Mayūraśarman, as he came to be known later, was credited in mediaeval times with the performance of eighteen horse-sacrifices, and the distribution of 144 villages among the 32,000 Brahmins of the primeval village—*anādi agrahāra*—of Sthānakuṇḍūra (Talgundā), but there is no mention of Mayūraśarman having performed even one Aśvamedha, not to speak of eighteen, in the contemporary inscriptions. The Halsi plates[1] of Yuvarāja Kākustha-varman, the great-grandson of Mayūraśarman, are dated in the eightieth *Saṁvatsara* of an unnamed epoch ; the reckoning may be taken to have started from the coronation of Mayūraśarman as monarch, but it does not appear in any other inscription.

Of Kaṅga-varman and Bhagīratha we learn little from the Talagunda inscription. The former is said to have won fame in fierce wars; the Vākāṭaka ruler Vindhya-seṇa of the Basim branch (*c.* A.D. 340-90) is said to have conquered Kuntala, and it seems probable that Kaṅga-varman had to face an invasion by the Vākāṭaka ruler which, while it tested the military strength of the Kadamba kingdom, does not to have had any permanent results.[2] To the reign of Bhagīratha may have to be assigned the embassy of Kālidāsa from Vikramāditya to

[1] *IA*. VI, 22-4.
[2] *JRAS*. 1914, pp. 324-25, 328. *EI*. *XXVI*. 148.

Kuntaleśvara.[1] Raghu, the elder son of Bhagīratha, who succeeded him, 'subdued his enemies by his valour' his younger brother Kākustha was *Yuvarāja* under him, holding his court perhaps in Palāśikā (Halsi) ; a grant issued by him from that town hands over some land to a general, Śrutakīrti by name, for the use of the venerable *arhats* of the place in order to secure his spiritual welfare in the next world (*ātmanas-tāraṇārtham*).[2] At the end of Raghu's reign Kākustha-varman became king ; the Talgunda pillar inscription bestows great praise on him and describes the prosperous condition of the country under his rule and the splendour of his numerous palaces adorned with *gopuras*. He is said also to have brought joy to many a royal household like that of the Guptas by means of his daughters. The details of the marriage alliance with the Guptas are not forthcoming, unless the surmise is accepted that Kālidāsa's embassy to the ruler of Kuntala, referred to above, had something to do with it. But a princess of Kuntala, Ajitabhaṭṭārikā by name is said to have been the queen of Vākaṭaka Narendra-sena and mother of Pṛithvī-sheṇa II,[3] and it seems probable that she was a daughter of Kākustha-varman. This king made a large fresh water tank within the precincts of the celebrated Śiva temple of Talagunda, and the fact was recorded on a pillar by his son and successor Śānti-varman in the inscription that has so far guided our exposition of Kadamba history.

An inscription from Talagunda mentions a prince Kākustha of the Bhaṭāri line, son of a beautiful Kadamba princess ; this

[1] The embassy is attested to by two rather later works, *Kāvya-mīmāṁsā* of Rājaśekhara and *Auchityavichāracharchā* of Kshemendra. There however is no unanimity among the scholars about the identity of the Kuntala king.

[2] *IA.* VI, 23. The phrase cited in the text was misunderstood by Fleet, and some history has been made by Moraes in his *Kadambakula* p. 23 out of Fleet's mistaken translation.

[3] *EI.* IX, 271, vv. 30-1. Kielhorn's date for the Balaghat plates is clearly far too late. J. Dubreuli *AHD*. pp. 75, 100. Cf. V.V above.

prince is said to have attained the headship of ten *māṇḍalikas* with control over customs duties—a statement which is interesting, as another inscription states, as we shall see, that Vaijayantī had eighteen *māṇḍalikas* in charge of its customs revenue. It seems not unlikely that the Kadamba princess mentioned here was also a daughter of the famous Kadamba Kākustha, and that his namesake of the Bhaṭarivaṁśa was a grandson of his.

Śānti-varman is described as a ruler of great fame, the beauty of whose fine person was enhanced by the wearing of three crowns (*paṭṭatraya*); this seems to indicate fresh accession of territoy, but the details are unknown. A record of his son Mṛigeśa from Halsi also says, without specifying details, that Śānti-varman dragged to himself by main force the Lakshmī from the palaces of his enemies.[1] He was apparently served in a subordinate capacity by his younger brother Kṛishṇa-varman and the latter's son Vishṇu-varman. The position of Kṛishṇa-varman is, however, involved in some obscurity. While there are no inscriptions directly emanating from him, in those of his sons he is credited with ruling the southern country with great efficiency and popularity and with having performed the Aśvamedha.[2] While Deva-varman calls himself Yuvarāja and issues his grant from a place called Triparvata (not identified) his elder brother Vishṇu-varman dates his grants in his own regnal years (third and fifth); in one grant he takes the permission of his uncle Śānti-varman for making the gift and describes him as "his elder father, lord of the entire Karnāṭa country of which Vaijayantī with its eighteen māṇḍalikas was the *tilaka*", but in another grant, two years later, there is no mention of Śānti-varman, and Vishṇu-varman announces that he was anointed by the Pallava ruler Śānti-varma-mahārāja.

1 *IA*. VI, 24-5.
2 Birūr plate of Vishṇu-varman *EC*. VI. Kd. 162; Hebbaṭa grant of same *MAR*. 1925, p. 98; Devagiri plates of Deva-varman *IA*. VII, 33.

Some light on this puzzling set of facts may be got from two other inscriptions of the time. From the Barnahalli plates of Kṛishṇa-varman II,[1] the great grandson of Kṛishṇa-varman I, the subject of our present discussion, we learn the fact that he had for his queen a Kekaya princess who was the mother of Vishṇu-varman. Secondly, a stone inscription from Anaji[2] (Davanagere *tāluq* in the Chitaldurg district of Mysore) makes the important statement that Śivananda-varman, a scion of the renowned line of Kekayas, witnessed the ravages to which his country became subject during the battle between Nāṇakkāsa, the Pallava king, and Kṛishṇa-varman in which Kṛishṇa-varman's forces were shattered ; the sight of so much suffering stirred Śivananda to the depths of his being, and he resolved to renounce all wordly ambition and seek his peace and the eternal fame of his family by fasting unto death. Now it seems very probable that Śivananda was the brother of the Kekaya queen of Kṛishṇa-varman.

In the light of all these facts the course of events may by reconstructed somewhat as follows. Duriug Śānti-varman's reign, the hostility of the Pallavas spelt danger to the Kadamba power ; the situation was met by the southern part of the kingdom being constituted into a separate charge under Kṛishṇa-varman and his sons with independent status, a virtual division of the kingdom accentuated by the performance of a horse-sacrifice by Kṛishṇa-varman; all the same, the blow from the Pallavas fell heavy on this boastful ruler and perhaps cost him his life, besides ruining the principality of the Kekayas, the home-land of his queen; as a result of their victory the Pallavas claimed the allegiance of Vishṇu-varman who had to accept investiture from them. If this view of the events is correct, the Kadambas must be held to have suffered a tangible set-back in their position in this period; a part of their territory and a

[1] *EI*. VI. 16-20.
[2] *EC*. VI, 162-0.

branch of the royal family passed under Pallava suzerainty at least for a time. The names of the Pallava rulers concerned, Nāṇakkāsa and Śānti-varman, are otherwise unknown, a sharp reminder of how little we know at present of the history of those times.

Śānti-varman was followed on the throne by his son Mṛigeśa-varman who is known from several records.[1] He ruled from Vaijayantī, had Palāśikā under his control, and waged successfull wars against the Gaṅgas and Pallavas ; in the Halsi plates he is described as the destroyer of the eminent family of the Gaṅgas and the destructive fire (*pralayānala*) to the Pallavas. But no details of these wars are forthcoming. His learning and wisdom, his proficiency in the riding of horses and elephants and all other manly exercises, his ability as a soldier and capacity as a ruler of men receive high praise in the Devagiri plates of the fourth year. He built a Jaina temple in Palāśikā in memory of his father and endowed it liberally (Halsi plates). The queen of Mṛigeśa-varman was called Prabhāvatī ; she came of the family of the Kekayas with whom the Kadambas had several matrimonial connections, and she was the mother of Ravi-varman.[2]

Māndhātṛi-varman is the next ruler to be considered. While editing one of his two records Kielhorn expressed the opinion that Māndhātā was more closely connected with Mṛigeśa than any other ruler of the Kadamba line, and that he might have been a younger brother of Śānti-varman or of Mṛigeśa himself, and thus, his immediate predecessor or successor. The discovery of the Shimoga plates[3] has shown, however, that the name of Māndhātā's father was Kumāra-varman ; and he might have been a third son of Kākustha-varman. Māndhātā is called ruler of Vaijayantī in the Kudigere plates of his second year,

[1] Devagiri plates Yr. 3 *IA*. VII, 35-7; Devagiri plates Yr. 4. *IA*. VII 37-8; Hitnahebhāgilu Yr. 7 *EC*. IV, Hs. 18; Hire Sakuna Yr. 8 *EC*. VIII Sb. 33; Halsi plates Yr. 8 *IA*. VI, 24-5.

[2] *MAR*. 1911, pp. 33, 35.

[3] *Ibid*. p. 32.

while the other grant is issued from Uchchangi (Uchchhṛingi) in his fifth regnal year. Possibly Māndhātṛi-varman ruled during the minority of Ravi-varman (son of Mṛigeśa) who succeeded him and had a long reign of about forty years.

Of Ravi-varman's reign we have quite a number of records, ranging from the fifth to the thirty-fifth regnal year, and a damaged stone record in Kavadi in the Sorab *tāluq* of Shimoga district[1] seems to record the *satī* performed by his queen on his death. Of the two undated records from Halsi[2], one deals with the institution of a Jaina festival at Halsi and the other makes the important statements that having killed in battle Vishṇu-varman and other kings the conquered the whole earth, and occupied Palāśikā after driving out the lord of Kāñchī, known as Chaṇḍadaṇḍa; probably, the title Kāñchīśvara applied to Chaṇḍadaṇḍa is only a synonym for Pallava, and does not necessarily imply his rule in Kāñchīpura, and Chaṇḍadaṇḍa might have belonged to the same branch of the Pallavas as Śānti-varman who appointed Vishṇu-varman. However that may be, we have clearly a further stage in the hostilities between the Kadambas and the Pallavas, and the former seem to have got the best of it in this round. The words of the inscription lead us to suppose that Chaṇḍadaṇḍa and perhaps Vishṇu-varman also had invaded the territory of the Vanavāsī kingdom, and penetrated into it as far as Halsi; Ravi-varman succeeded in disposing of his collateral uncle on the battle field, and throwing out the Pallava intruder. This perhaps restored the original unity and extent of the Kadamba dominion. The Nilambur plates are dated in the fifth year of the reign, and issued from Vaijayantī (Vanavāsī),[3] and so too the Sirsi grant of the thirty-fifth year,[4] which mentions a temple of Mahādeva

[1] *EC.* VIII, Sb. 523.
[2] *IA.* VII, 25-7, 29-30
[3] *EI.* VIII, 146-9.
[4] *Ibid.* XVI, 264.

erected by a favourite minister of the king who was the *amātyā* of the division (*deśa*) of the kingdom called Nīlakaṇṭha, the Nelcynda of the Greek writers.

Ravi-varman was followed by his son Hari-varman who ruled from Vaijayantī, as is seen from the Sangoli plates of his eighth year,[1] which contain astronomical details yielding a date in A.D. 538 for his accession to the throne. The Halsi plates of the fourth year[2] state that he enjoyed the rule of his kingdom in peace—(*nirupadravām rājyaśriyam*), ann this is confirmed by the general tone of anothor record of the next year from the same place, which mentions a Sendraka ruler Bhānuśakti, as a feudatory. But the end of the reign was by no means so happy or peaceful. About A.D. 545 Pulakeśin I established his power in Badami ; and this meant not only the loss of the northern parts of the Kadamba kingdom, but the emergence of a new danger to the very existence of Vanavāsī as an independent kingdom. And the Kadambas were by no means a strong and united power. The feud between the elder and younger branches was hushed for a time after the resounding successes of Ravi-varman, and Siṁha-varman, the son of Vishṇu-varman, took a warning from the fate of his father and was content to remain in obscure subordination. Not so, however, his son Kṛishṇa-varman II who strengthened himself by alliances with his neighbours and actually undertook a military expedition against Vaijayantī as we learn from his Bennur plates—*Vaijayantī-vijayayātrām-abhiprasthitaḥ.*[3] We may well suppose that this expedition put an end to the reign of Hari-varman, the last known ruler of the elder branch, and brought Kṛishṇa-varman II to the throne of Vaijayantī. His Bannahalli plates issued in his seventh year[4] confirm this view

---

[1] *EI*. XIV. 163-8.
[2] *IA*. VI, 30-2.
[3] *EC*. V, Bl. 245.
[4] *EI*. VI, 16-20.

of his progress by hinting at the contrast between his father's obscurity and his own prominence and saying that he obtained the status of monarch by the strength of his own mind and arms. An inscription of his nineteenth regnal year records a memorial grant for the spiritual benefit of his parents. Either Kṛishṇa-varman II himself or his son Aja-varman must have been ruling Vanavāsī at the time of its definite conquest by Kīrtti-varman, the son of Chaḷukya Pulakéśin I.

Other early Kadamba princes are known from stray records, like Madhu-varman of the Tadagani inscription,[1] and Dāmodara, whose name with the designation of king is inscribed twice on a rock near a water-fall of the Ghataprabha in Konnur, might have been a Kadamba too. But their place is uncertain, and their names are a warning that our knowledge of the history of the period is far from complete.

4. The Gangas.

We must now complete the main outlines of the political map of south India during the period by the history of the Gaṅgas whose territory lay between those of the Kadambas and the Pallavas in the southern part of the modern Mysore territory which came to be known to history as Gaṅgavādī by its long association with Gaṅga rule. Early Gaṅga history has suffered much and suffered in equal measure from scepticism as well as credulity. That a good number of copper-plates bearing unusually early Śaka dates are palpable forgeries is clear ; until about 1915 when Fleet admitted the Penukonda plates of Mādhava-varman as the first genuine early Gaṅga record, all was confusion and no record seemed to be free from suspicion. Since then, the tendency has been to reconsider the whole position, and fresh discoveries of clearly genuine copper-

---

[1] *EC*. VII, Sk. 66.

plates have aided in the work of reconstructing the history of the line in this period. But there is still room for different views even about the genealogy of the dynasty, and we must proceed with caution, aiming only at tentative conclusions from definite data.

The Gaṅgas, like many other dynasties, developed in course of time a legendary history of the achievements of their ancestors of which the early records know nothing, and the account that follows is based on records that turn out to be early by this test, though the later legends will be briefly adverted to in so far as they concern individual rulers. One of the earliest of these legends is the cutting of a stone pillar into two by a lusty blow of his sword by the founder of the line, and records mentioning even this feature should be treated separately from those which do not.

The earliest record so far known is a grant by the second ruler of the line, Mādhava-varman I, the son of Koṅkaṇi-varman, recorded in the Sasanakota plates and relating to a *brahmadeya* (gift to Brāhmaṇas) in the Paru-*vishaya*.[1] The next genuine record is found in the Penukonda Plates of Mādhava-varman II, the grandson of Mādhava I, referring to a *brahmadeya* in Paruvi-*vishaya*.[2] Paru and Paruv are clearly variants of the same name, and are represented by modern Parigi, seven miles north of Hindupur in the Anantapur district. The genealogy of the line yielded by these two records is as follows :

Koṅkaṇi-varman Dharmamahādhirāja (A.D. 400)
|
Mādhava Mahādhirāja (A.D. 425)
|
Gaṅgarāja Āyya-varman (A.D. 450)
|
Mādhava Mahādhirāja, alias
Siṁha-varman A.D. 470

[1] *EI*. XXIV, 234-9.
[2] *Ibid*. XIV, 331-6.

The dates suggested against each name are in accordance with Fleet's chronological scheme based upon the data of the Penukonda record.

The origin of the Gaṅgas is even more obscure than that of the Pallavas and Kadambas. The early inscriptions only say that the first ruler Koṅkaṇi-varman belonged to the Jāhnaveyakula, the family of the Ganges, and the Kāṇvāyana *gotra* ; that by the force of his victorious arms he carved out a prosperous kingdom for himself ; and that he distinguished himself on many a field as the many scars on his body witnessed. The invocation which occurs uniformly at the beginning of all Gaṅga plates shows them to have been worshippers of Vishṇu. The title *Dharma-mahādhirāja* may indicate that Koṅkaṇi-varman was an independent ruler ; but if that was so, the condition did not last long, and throughout their long history of seven or eight centuries, the Gaṅgas found themselves compelled to acknowledge the suzerainty of one or other of the greater dynasties of South India by turns. The elephant was the emblem of the family.

The capital of the early kingdom is nowhere named in the contemporary inscriptions ; later tradition, current among the Gaṅgas of Mysore and Kaliṅga, avers that it was Kuvalāla, modern Kolar, at first, and afterwards Talakād, nearer the hostile frontier of the Kadambas against whom they waged war in campany of the Pallavas in this early period. The view that a branch of the Gaṅgas ruled at Parigi rests on no more evidence than the location of the property that forms the subject of the gifts in the two grants just mentioned.

Of Mādhava I the early grants say that he inherited all the great qualities of his father, and that he had a well cultivated mind proficient in all the Śāstras, particularly in the exposition and practice of the science of Politics (*Nītiśāstra*) ; later tradition follows this up by attributing to him the authorship of a *vṛitti* (gloss) on the *Daṭṭakasūtra*, a treatise on adoption.[1] The next ruler Āyya-varman (Ārya-varman)[2] was a great warrior and proficient in the Sāstras, *itihāsas* and Purāṇa, and was appointed duly by the Pallava Siṁha-varman, the first ruler of the name known to have reigned in Kāñchi according to our chronological scheme. The reason of the coronation by the Pallava is not apparent, but probably the Gaṅgas had reason to fear the power of the Kadambas and entered into a subordinate alliance with the Pallavas and sought their protection. Or more likely there was a succession dispute between Āyya-varman and his brother Krishṇa-varman, who is known from at least three early records.[3] The Penukoṇḍa plates say that Āyya-varman was consecrated by Siṁha-varman 'according to his deserts' (*yathārham*), and later grants, which give his name as Hari-varman, state that he removed the capital to Talakād on the Kaveri in the Mysore district. So it may be that the brothers had a dispute, which was settled by Siṁha-varman's mediation which ended in a virtual division of the kingdom between them. We have the Chukuttur grant of Siṁha-varman, the son of Krishna-varman, in which he calls himself Mahādhirāja and makes a memorial gift after the death of his heroic younger brother *Yuvarāja* Vīra-varman. Let us note also that both Āyya-varman and Kṛishṇa-varman name their sons Siṁhaa-varman, in recognition of their political relation to the Pallava ruler.

Later genealogies introduce a Vishṇugopa as the son of Hari-varman, making Mādhava the son of Vishṇugopa. This looks much like a fabrication calculated to stress the Pallava

---

[1] This occurs in the Keragalur plate of Mādhava II (*MAR*. 1930 p. 113, No. 3). which contains the whole gamut of legends like Avani stone inscription (*EC*. V, Mb. 263). Such records do not seem to have the same claim to authenticity as the simpler ones used in our account in the text.

[2] Gudlur grant, *MAR*. 1930, p. 259, No. 88.

[3] Bendiganhalli plates of his first year, *MAR*. 1915, p. 40; Kudittiyan plates of his second year, *MAR*. 1932, p. 124; Chukuttur grant of his son Siṁha-varman. *MAR*. 1924. p. 79.

connection by borrowing one more Pallava name. The Penukonda plates do not know him, and Rice's attempt to explain the omission as due to accident or error is not convincing.

From the beginning of Āyya-varman's reign then, the Gaṅga kingdom was ruled in two parts by two branches of the family from Talakād and Kuvalāla, and the same arrangement seems to have continued under the sons and successors of Āyya-varman and Kṛishṇa-varman, viz., Mādhava II alias Siṁha-varman, and Siṁha-varman of the Chukuṭṭūr grant. The former was anointed by Pallava Skanda-varman, a fact which finds more prominent mention in the Kudalur grant than in the Penukonda plates, for the grant opens with a formal benediction of Skanda-varman, his family and *gotra* being duly mentioned. Mādhava II, called Taḍangāla Mādhava in later records, has for his queen a sister of Kadamba Kṛishṇa-varman I, i.e. a daughter of Kākustha-varman who is said to have bestowed his daughters on many royal families including the Guptās. The child of this union was Avinīta according to the later grants.

Our view of early Gaṅga history may be presented in a single conspectus thus :

Koṅkaṇi-varman (A.D. 400)
- Mādhava I—Sasanakota plates, Yr. 1 (A.D. 425)
  - Āyya-varman, crowned by Siṁha-varman (A.D. 450)
    - Mādhava II alias Siṁha-varman = Kadamba Kṛishṇa-varman's sister ; crowned by Skanda-varman —Penukoṇda plates (A.D. 475)
      - Avinīta (anointed as a baby in his mother's lap) (c. A.D. 500)
  - Kṛishṇa-varman—Bendiganhalli plates, Yr. 1; Kudittiyam plates (A.D. 450)
    - Siṁha-varman Chukuttūr grant (A.D. 475)
    - Vīra-varman Yavarāja

CHAPTER XIII

HISTORY OF CEYLON

The first dynasty of Sinhalese kings of the island of Ceylon came to an end with the death of Yasalālaka Tissa. This gave occasion for various adventurers to contend for the throne. An imposter named Sabha[1] ruled for six years, but was outed by a prince named Vaṣabha (66-110)[2] who not only established himself securely on the throne but also succeeded in founding a dynasty which lasted for more than three hundred years.

As is usual with the founders of new dynasties, stories of a romantic nature have been told of this prince. His future greatness, it is said, was foretold by soothsayers and he was protected by Providence from dangers which threatened him. He belonged to a clan called the Lambakaṇṇa, members of which had already made a bid for the throne before the accession of Vasabha.[3] Nothing certain is known about the origin of this clan. Later writers connect it with the imperial Mauryas of North India and state that the Lambakaṇṇa family was founded by Aśoka's kinsmen who accompanied the branch of the sacred Bodhi tree to Ceylon, but the *Mahāvaṁsa* and the other early Pali chronicles are silent about the origin of the Lambakaṇṇas. Whatever his origin, Vasabha succeeded in making his authority universally acknowledged in the island as

---

[1] The name occurs as Subha in the *Mahāvaṁsa*, but in inscriptions he is called Saba (*EZ*, 166).

[2] The proper names are in their Pali forms as given in the *Mahāvaṁsa*. For dates, see note on the chronology at the end of the chapter.

[3] See the account of Ilanāga's reign in the *Mahāvaṁsa*, Chap. xxxv, vv. 16 ff.

is attested by numerous inscriptions of his reign found in various parts of Ceylon. His long reign was a prosperous one and his benefactions to the Buddhist religion made his rule acceptable to the *saṅgha.*

The death of Vasabha was followed by a brief period of divided rule. The chronicles record that he was succeeded by Tissa 'of the Crooked Nose' ; but inscriptions attest to the fact that two brothers of Tissa set themselves up as independent rulers in various parts of the island, while he was reigning at Anurādhapura.[1] The weakness resulting from this state of affairs was taken advantage of by the Chola king Karikāla who raided the island and took away many thousands of Sinhalese as captives to South India. Tissa's son Gajabāhu I (113-135) unified the kingdom and felt himself strong enough to satisfy Sinhalese honour by undertaking a counter-invasion of the Chola country. In this enterprise, which has passed into legend, he is said to have been eminently successful. Not content with liberating the Sinhalese taken away as captives in the previous reign he, it is said, brought with him an equal number of the Chola king's subjects to Ceylon.

Gajabāhu's personal name was Gāmaṇi Abhaya, by which he is referred to in numerous inscriptions of his found in various parts of the island. The epithet by which he is universally mentioned in Sinhalese literature as well as in the chronicles is found in one record only.[2] The fact that he bore such a title indicates that he was noted for his prowess during his life-time. The stories of his exploits in South India may therefore be taken as based on fact, notwithstanding that they are found, overladen with details of a fictitious and marvellous character, in writings of a comparatively recent date and do not find mention in the *Mahāvaṁsa* and other early sources. Gajabāhu is mentioned in the Tamil poem *Silappadikāram* as

[1] *EZ*. IV, 214 ff.
[2] *AIC*. No. 5.

one of the kings present at the court of the Chēra king on the occasion of the consecration of a shrine to Kannagi, the heroine who has been deified as the ideal of a chaste and faithful wife. The cult of this goddess, Pattini, which is now obsolete in South India, is still widely prevalent among the Sinhalese villagers and has given rise to a considerable folk-literature in which Gajabāhu occupies a prominent position as the ruler who was instrumental in introducing it to the island. In the folk-lore of the Sinhalese, Gajabāhu takes a place second only to that of Duṭṭhagāmaṇī, the national hero.

The settled conditions established in the reign of Gajabāhu prevailed for over half a century after his demise. He was succeeded by his cousin Mahallaka Nāga (135-141) who was also his brother-in-law.[1] Two of Mahallaka Nāga's sons, Bhātika Tissa (141-165) and Kaniṭṭha Tissa (165-193) reigned one after the other. The period covered by the reigns of these three kings saw the construction of many irrigation works and the foundation and endowment of numerous Buddhist *vihāras*. Scores of inscriptions of these rulers, recording grants to Buddhist shrines, have been discovered in various parts of the island.

The death of Kaniṭṭha Tissa was followed by discord in the royal family, which, however, was not of long duration. Kaniṭṭha Tissa was succeeded by his son Khujjanāga who, after a reign of two years, was murdered by his younger brother Kuñcanāga. The last named in his turn, was ousted by Sirināga his *senāpati*. Sirināga I (196-215) is stated in the *Mahāvaṁsa* to have been the brother-in-law of Kuñchanāga. From inscriptions, however, we can glean the additional information that he was a son of Bhātika Tissa and had, therefore, a prior claim to the throne than his two predecessors.[2]

---

[1] For the relationship between these two monarchs, see *JRAS*. CB. XXX, 452.

[2] *EZ*. IV, 220.

Sirināga I was succeeded by his son Tissa who, on account of his concern for the proper administration of justice, earned the epithet of Vohārika (Skt. *uyavahārika*).

It was during the reign of Vohārika Tissa (215-237) that a sect of Buddhists called the Vetullaka in the *Mahāvaṁsa* and the Vitaṇḍa-vādins in the *Dīpavaṁsā*, is mentioned for the first time in the historical records of Ceylon. There is little doubt that the Vetullakas were Mahāyānists,[1] particularly of the Mādhyamika persuasion. The Vetullakas seem to have had considerable success in their propaganda and the inmates of the Abhayagiri *Vihāra* were ready to give them a respectful hearing. But the orthodox fraternity of the Mahāvihāra did not brook any compromise with them and persuaded the king to have an inquisition made into their doctrines. This task was entrusted by the king to a learned minister named Kapila, who, after due investigation, pronounced the views of the Vetullakas to be not in harmony with the genuine teachings of the Buddha. They were, therefore, banished from the island, but not for a long period, for we find them disturbing the peace of the orthodox Mahāvihāra monks time and again.

In spite of his just rule and his concern for the purity of the Church, the end of Vohārika Tissa was not happy. His younger brother, Abhayanāga, carried on an intrigue with the queen and fled abroad when the affair came to the notice of the king. The partisans of Abhayanāga, by wily stratagems, alienated the people from Vohārika Tissa, and when he was assured that the time was ripe, Abhayanāga returned to the island and raised the standard of revolt, backed by a numerous band of Tamil soldiers whom he had enlisted in his service. Realising that he had no chance in an armed struggle, Vohārika Tissa attempted to escape to the mountains with the queen, but was pursued, captured and put to death by

[1] See Paranavitana, Mahayanism in Ceylon, *CJS* Sec. G, Vol. II.

Abhayanāga. The latter married the woman who was the cause of this fraternal discord and ascended the throne at Anurādhapura. Abhayanāga's reign of eight years was not memorable for any outstanding events. So were the brief reigns of his two successors, Sirināga II and Vijaya, the son and grandson respectively of Vohārika Tissa.

After Vijaya, the throne was occupied in succession by two princes who came from Rohaṇa. Their relationship to their predecessors is not given in the chronicles, but they are stated to have been of the Lambakaṇṇa clan to which the rulers of Ceylon during this period all belonged. Saṁgha Tissa, the first of these two intruders, ruled for four years and came to an untimely end. He was succeeded by Sirisaṅghabodhi whose extreme devotion to the Bodhisattva ideal made him unfit for the duties and cares of kingship. The commander-in-chief of the army, Goṭhābhaya, rose in revolt and Sirisaṅghabodhi, in order to avoid bloodshed, left the palace and resorted to the forest where he adopted a hermit's life. Goṭhābhaya mounted the vacant throne and, fearing that Sirisaṅghabodhi might be restored by the people who loved him for his rare virtues, proclaimed a large reward for his head. The story continues that Sirisaṅghabodhi, on learning of this from a peasant, himself made an offering of his own head so that the peasant, the new king and he may all be benefitted, the first by obtaining the prize set on his head, the second by being firmly established on the throne and he himself by practising the virtue of supreme self-sacrifice thus qualifying for Buddhahood in the future. The place where Sirisaṅghabodhi is said to have performed this heroic action is marked by a temple built in his honour by Goṭhābhaya and is even now a popular place of pilgrimage. Sirisaṅghabhodhi will no doubt be counted a failure by modern historians, but that was not the judgment of the peole of ancient Ceylon. He is considered to have shed great lustre on the island's royal line and his name was born as a title by every alternate ruler of Ceylon for a thousand years after his death.

Goṭhābhaya (254-267) appears from the chronicles to have been an adventurer who mangaed to seize the throne by questionable means. From an inscription of his[1], however, it appears that he was a son of Sirināga II and had, therefore, a legitimate right to the throne. During his reign, the heterodox Vetuḷḷakas (the Mahāyānists) again came into prominence and were able to gain many followers among the members of the Abhayagiri community. Following the example of Vohārika Tissa, Goṭhābhaya proscribed them. He went further ; he selected sixty of their leading members, placed brand marks on their bodies and banished them. The disgraced Vetullaka monks went to Kāverīpaṭṭana in South India, where one of them had a pupil named Saṅghamitta who, having learnt of the barbarous treatment accorded to his teacher and others of his persuation, resolved to come to Ceylon in order to teach a lesson to the Mahāvihāra monks at whose instigation the king had acted in this wise. Saṅghamitta managed to win royal favour and was appointed tutor to the two sons of the king. The elder prince, Jeṭṭha Tissa, was not impressed by his teachings but the younger, Mahāsena, became a ready convert. Saṅghamitta realised that he could carry out his plans when Mahāsena, in due course, came to the throne.

When Goṭhābhaya died, there seems to have been a dissatisfied faction among the dignitaries of state. But Jeṭṭha Tissa (267-277) took effective, though drastic, action and nipped in the bud any possible schemes against him. Jeṭṭha Tissa was succeeded by his younger brother Mahāsena (277-304) who was one of the most outstanding among the rulers of ancient Ceylon. Saṅghamitta, who had left the shores of this island during the reign of Jeṭṭha Tissa, returned with Mahāsena's accession

[1] *EZ.* V, 223-28.

and did not lose any time in starting his campaign against the orthodox community. Acting on his advice, the king ordered the Mahāvihāra monks to accept the Vetulla or Mahāyāna doctrines. They refused and the king issued an edict prohibiting the townspeople to give alms to them. The inmates of the Mahāvihāra, rather than submit to the king in matters spiritual, left their monastery and took refuge in Rohaṇa. The king appropriated their properties, destroyed many of their establishments and utilised the material to embellish the Abhayagiri *Vihāra*. This persecution of the most important religious community in the island gave rise to popular resentment and the leaders of the anti-Mahāvihāra faction were murdered by the orthodox partisans. A civil war was narrowly averted by the personal friendship, which existed between Mahāsena and the leader of the insurgent forces ; but the king had perforce to change his religious policy and make peace with the Mahāvihāra.

Later, however, Mahāsena again quarrelled with the Mahāvihāra when he founded a new monastery, the Jetavanārāma, encroaching on the grounds of the ancient institution. Jetavana *Vihāra* developed into the headquarters of the third great sect among the three into which the Buddhist church of ancient Ceylon was divided. The *stūpa* built in this *vihāra* by Mahāsena was the largest in Ceylon and perhaps surpassed in size any other monument of its class anywhere in the world. Mahāsena also constructed a number of large irrigation reservoirs, one of which, the Minnēri, covers an area of nearly 5000 acres. His public works which were designed to benefit the land by ensuring a regular supply of water to irrigate the rice fields, so impressed the people with their magnitude that he was deified after his death. He still receives worship from the peasants in some parts of the island.

The reign of Sirimeghavaṇṇa (304-332), the son and successor of Mahāsena, is noteworthy for the arrival in Ceylon of the Tooth Relic of the Buddha from Dantapura in Kaliṅga. This became, in course of time, the palladium of the Sinhalese kings and, housed now in Kandy, is still an object of great devotion to the Buddhists of the island. Sirimeghavaṇṇa was a contemporary of Samudra-gupta, the great Gupta emperor of North India, and we learn from Chinese sources that the Sinhalese monarch sent envoys to the Indian potentate and obtained from him permission to build a convent at Buddha Gayā for the benefit of pilgrims from Ceylon to that holy place.[1]

Sirimeghavaṇṇa's younger brother, Jeṭṭha Tissa II, who was known for his proficiency in ivory carving, ruled for nine years and was succeeded by his son Buddhadāsa (341-370). This monarch was famous for his skill in medicine and surgery and a number of marvellous cures are attributed to him. He established hospitals all over the island, not only for human beings but also for animals, and maintained physicians in charge of them. He also provided for the mental uplift of his subjects by appointing preachers to expound the religion to them. Buddhadāsa's son, Upatissa II (370-412) was a man of a benevolent disposition and, though wearing a crown, practised the virtues of a Bodhisattva. This, however, did not protect him from his younger brother Mahānāma, who had adopted a religious life and developed an intimacy with the queen. Mahānāma persuaded the queen to murder Upatissa and himself ascended the throne.

Mahānāma's reign (412-434) was memorable for the labours of the great Pali commentator Buddhaghosha, whose writings have settled the doctrines of the form of Buddhism now prevailing in Ceylon as well as in Burma, Siam and Cambodia. Buddhaghosha's literary output has so impressed later generations that legends have grown around his name and it is now difficult to have a really historical account of his career.

[1] See p. 149 above.

Ceylon tradition asserts that he was a Brahmin of North India who, after his conversion to Buddhism, was entrusted by his teacher with the task of translating into Pali the vast exegetical literature on the Theravāda canon which then existed in the Sinhalese language. Buddhaghosha himself testifies to his connection with the Tamil country and mentions Kāñchī as a place where he resided for some time.[1] Buddhadatta, another Pali commentator, who is believed to have been a contemporary of Buddhaghosha, wrote at Kāverīpaṭṭana when the Kalabhra king Achyuta was ruling over the Chola country.[2] In Buddhaghosha's writings the Sinhalese king of his day is mentioned as Siripāla, Sirinivāsa or Sirikuḍḍa. In some of his inscriptions, Mahānāma is referred to by the name Tiripali which is equivalent to Siripālita in Pali.[3] Chinese annals record that an envoy sent by a king of Ceylon named Mohanan arrived in that country in the year 428 A.D. The king referred to is no doubt Mahānāma.

Mahānāma's death was followed by the extinction of the dynasty which, founded by Vasabha, continued to hold sway over the island for more than three hundred years. A son of his, named Sotthisena, born of a Tamil consort, ascended the throne but was immediately ousted in favour of the husband of Mahānāma's daughter born of the consecrated queen. The latter died after one year and an impostor named Mittasena held the sceptre for a similarly brief period when an invasion from South India imposed foreign rule on Ceylon for about twenty-five years.

The leaders of this Tamil invasion seem to have hailed from the Pāṇḍya country, for the first of them to rule Ceylon was called Pāṇḍu. He was succeeded, in turn, by five of his confederates, namely Pārinda, Khudda Pārinda, Tirītara

[1] See the Colophone of the *Manorathapūraṇī*
[2] See the Colophone of the *Vinaya-vinicchaya* (P.T.S.), p. 229.
[3] *CJS*. Sec. G. II, 18.

Dāṭhiya and Pīṭhiya. Though these rulers were of South Indian origin they seem to have patronised Buddhism and adopted Sinhalese institutions. Inscriptions of three of them, Pārinda, Khudda Pārinda and Dāṭhiya, have been discovered in various parts of the island. These records are in old Sinhalese and register donations to Buddhist shrines.[1] Khudda Pārinda bore the epithet of Buddhadāsa.[2]

Many Sinhalese nobles, however, did not submit to Dravidian rule and maintained themselves in various parts of the island to which the Tamils were unable to penetrate. The national movement against the Tamils found a leader in the person of Dhātusena, who is said to have belonged to the Maurya race. He spent his boyhood in a Buddhist *vihāra* where one of his uncles, who was a member of the Order, protected him from many dangers. Arrived at man's estate, Dhātusena rallied the national forces round him and started the campaign for the liberation of his people when Khudda Pārinda was in power. The three Tamil rulers who succeeded Khudda Pārinda were all killed in battle by Dhātusena who, after vanquishing his enemies in a protracted series of compaigns, ascended the throne of Anurādhapura about 463 A.D.

Dhātusena was a liberal patron of Buddhism and founded many *vihāras* and repaired dilapidated ones. He is, however, best remembered for the great contribution he made to the wonderful irrigation system of ancient Ceylon. One of the reservoirs constructed by him, the Kalāväva, is an immense work covering an area of over 4000 acres and irrigating a vast tract of paddy fields.

Dhātusena's end was tragic. At the instigation of his son-in-law, the commander-in-chief of the army, Kassapa, a son of Dhātusena by a wife of inferior status, usurped the throne and murdered the old king by walling him in the

[1] *CJS.* Sec. G. II, 181.
[2] *EZ.* IV. 113.

chamber in which he was imprisoned. The rightful prince, Moggallāna, fled to India vowing to avenge the foul crime. The parricide Kassapa I (479-497) betook himself to the impregnable rock fortress of Sīgiri, on the summit of which he built a magnificent palace and reigned for eighteen years. The remnants of the paintings with which he adorned the precipitous side of the Sīgiri rock are well-known and are counted among the most precious relics of the ancient pictorial art of India and Ceylon. Moggallāna eventually returned from India with an army and Kassapa, instead of waiting for the invader in his great stronghold, went forward with his forces to give battle to Moggallāna. In the encounter which ensued, Kassapa's army broke its ranks and fled, and the parricide, finding everything lost, committed suicide on the battle-field.

Moggallāna I (497-515) gave vent to his wrath by slaying all who had taken Kassapa's side and had a hand in the murder of his father. After a reign of eighteen years, he was succeeded by his son Kumāradāsa (515-534) who, for several centuries, has enjoyed a reputation, to which he had no claim, as the poet who composed the *Jānakiharaṇa*.[1] Kumāradāsa's son, Kittisena, came to an untimely end after a reign of nine months and with him the direct line of Dhātusena became extinct.

The elements of culture with the Aryan-speaking immigrants from North India brought to Ceylon in the fifth or sixth century B.C. and in the religious and artistic movements which arrived in Ceylon in the third century B.C., through the missionary zeal of Asoka, attained, in many respects, to a high degree of efflorescence during the period dealt with in this chapter. The largest *stūpa* in the island was built during

[1] A manuscript of this poem discovered some years ago in Malabar contains evidence to show that Kumāradāsa, the author of the *Jānakīharana*, was a scion of the Sinhalese royal family but was a personage distinct from the King of that name.

this period and the irrigation reservoirs and channels then constructed evoke the admiration of modern engineers. The sculpture attributable to this epoch is of high merit and bears affinity to that produced by the schools of Amarāvatī and Nāgārjunīkoṇḍa. The height to which the art of painting attained can be judged from the Sīgiriya frescoes.

In spite of occasional palace intrigues, which hardly affected the life of the people, and an interlude of Tamil rule, which lasted for only a quarter of a century, the social and economic conditions of the island during this period seem to have been of a settled character. Trade flourished between the island and various parts of the Indian continent and further afield ; envoys were dispatched by Sinhalese kings to the courts of powerful Indian monarchs, to Rome and to China. There was lively intercourse between the Buddhists of Ceylon and their co-religionists in India. Sinhalese convents were established at Buddha Gayā and Nagārjunīkoṇḍa and the Sinhalese monks and nuns had some share in the attempts made during these centuries for the propagation of Buddhism in East Asia. The reputation enjoyed by the great religious establishments of Anurādhapura as strongholds of the Theravāda Buddhism attracted to them seekers after the Truth from distant lands and a considerable commentatorial and exegetical literature in Pali, produced during this epoch by the Mahāvihāra of Anurādhapura, is still extant.

APPENDIX

NOT ON THE CHRONOLOGY.

The dates given above are in accordance with the chronological table appended to L. C. Wijesinha's translation of the *Mahāvaṁsa.* They have been computed, on the basis of the Buddhist era starting 543 B.C., current in Ceylon, by adding up the lengths of reigns given in the chronicles and taking into consideration the traditional dates in the Buddhist era given in literary sources for certain important events. Wickremasinghe (*E.Z.* III. 1-47) and Geiger (*Cūḷavaṁsa*, translation, Vol. II, Pp. 1-47) have both elaborated chronological tables prepared on the assumption that a Buddhist era with 483 B.C. as its epoch was current in Ceylon during the earlier period of its history. Wickremasinghe holds that such an era was in use for the whole period dealt with in this chapter while Geiger opines that its use extended up to the end of Mahāsena's reign.

The theory has landed both these scholars in considerable difficulties in effecting the transition from one Buddhist era to the other. Chinese references to Ceylon during the period between the fifth and eighth centuries published by Sylvain Levi (*JA*. 1900, pp. 297 ff, 401 ff) furnish us with indisputable evidence to prove that Wijesinha's dates are preferable to those of Wickremasinghe and Geiger. *Pien-e-tien*, chap. 66, records that in the fifth year of Iuen-kia (428 A.D.). the king of Ceylon, Mo-ho-nan by name, sent an embassy to the Chinese court. There is no difficulty in recognising the name Mahānāma in "Mo-ho-nan" and there was only one king of Ceylon by this name. According to Wijesīnha's tables, Mahānāma reigned from 412 to 434. The date of the Chinese embassy falls correctly within this period. Computing on the basis of a Buddhist era beginning 483 B.C. Wickremasinghe makes Mahānāma ascend the throne in 468 A.D., forty years after his envoy arrived in China.

The *Nikāya Saṅgraha*, a work of the fourteenth century, gives 818 B.E. as the date of Mahāsena's accession. Adding up the lengths of intervening reigns as given in the *Mahāvaṁsa*, the first year of Mahānāma would fall in 953 B.E , *i.e.*, 410 A.D. which enables the latter to be on the throne in 428 A.D. when his envoys were received by the Chinese emperor. On the same computation Sirimeghavaṇṇa should have ascended the throne in 845 B.E. (302 A.D.) and this is not in conflict with the fact that he was a contemporary of Samudra-gupta, as we learn from the Chinese writer Wang-Hieun-t'se.

There is no valid ground to doubt the general accuracy of the chronicle for the three or four centuries preceding Mahānāma's reign. The great majority of the kings of this period are mentioned in contemporary records and when regnal years are given in these records, they do not come in conflict with the data furnished by the chronicles. Sylvain Lévi, who has tested numerous dates from the fifth to eighth centuries by means of Chinese references, concludes that "the accuracy of the Sinhalese annals is triumphantly vindicated by this test". Vincent Smith, than whom there was no severer critic of the Sinhalese chronicles, confesses that 'there is not, I believe, any reason to doubt the substantial accuracy of the Ceylonese dates even for the much earlier time of Duṭṭhagāmaṇī, about B.C. 161' (*IA*. XXI, 195). The question is not whether the *Parinirvāṇa* of the Buddha actually took place in 483 or 543 B.C., but whether a Buddhist era with 483 B.C as its starting point was current in Ceylon at any period. The evidence available not only disproves the contention of Wickremasinghe, Geiger and others that such an era was in use during the period covered by this chapter, but establishes that dates were computed during this period in the traditional Buddhist era of Ceylon having 543 B.C. as its epoch.

CHAPTER XIV

THE ADMINISTRATIVE ORGANISATION

The prosperity of a country and the happiness of its inhabitants depend to a great extent upon the efficiency of its government and the ideals which inspire its administration. Let us, therefore, now review the administrative machinery of our period and find out how far it was well developed and efficient, and how far it could succeed in promoting the moral and material progress of the people of the country.

In the Vākāṭaka-Gupta period, there were two types of states in the country, monarchical and non-monarchical or republican. Monarchies existed throughout the country, but republics were flourishing only in certain parts of northern India. Democracy was better developed in the sphere of the village government in south India than in the north; it is, therefore, rather surprising to find that its application in the higher branches of government should not have resulted in the development of republics to the south of the Vindhyas as it did to its north.

1. Republican States.[1]

Let us first consider the non-monarchical states of our period. The chief ones among these were those of the Madras in the Central Punjab, the Kuṇindas in the Kangra valley, the Yaudheyas in the south-eastern Punjab, the Arjunāyanas in

---

[1] Standard works and authorities on political science define republic as a state, where the sovereign power rests, not with a single person as in monarchy, but in a group or college of persons, more or less numerous. Oligarchies, aristocracies and democracies have all been labelled as republics. Thus Sparta, Athens, Carthage, Rome, medieval Venice, the United Netherlands and Poland have all been described by political writers as republics, though none of them possessed that full representative character which some are inclined to consider as the

the Agra-Jaipur area and the Mālavas in the Central Rajputana. In Central India also there were some small non-monarchical states like those of the Prārjunas, Sanakānīkas,[1] Kākas and Ābhīras. Their earlier history is not known. These tribes had a non-monarchical form of government since early times and it continued to prevail among most of them down to the end of the 4th century A.D.

The Allahabad inscription of Samudra-gupta associates no kings with headships of these states; it describes how the Mālavas, the Yaudheyas etc., and not their kings, came forward to offer submission to the great Gupta Emperor. It is, therefore, clear that they had no kings and were non-monarchical states. The sovereignty, however, does not appear to have been vested in the whole population. The evidence of the early Buddhist literature and the accounts of the Greek writers tend to show that in the non-monarchical states of the 4th century B.C. the Central Assembly consisted mostly of the members of the landed military aristocracy of the Kshatriya class. The same was very probably the case in our age also. The towns and villages, however, had their own popular councils consisting of the elders hailing from all classes and professions.

The Central Executive of the republics was originally elected by the Central Assembly, but it was tending to become hereditary in our age. The Nandsa Yūpa inscription shows that in times of difficulties the government of the Mālavas used to be vested in aristocratic families, whose heads hereditarily used to lead the state armies in times of war and organise the civil administration in times of peace. They however enjoyed

---

distinguishing mark of a republic. With this theoretic background and historical evidence, we can safely call the *gaṇa* states of ancient India as republics, since sovereignty was vested in a fairly numerous group of persons, who elected the executive. We have no sufficient evidence to accurately describe the constitutions of the different *gaṇa* states, which appear to have differed considerably from one another.

[1] But cf. p. 144 above.

no regal titles like the *Rājās* and *Mahārājas*.[1] The headship of the Sanakānīka state had become hereditary and the regal title *Mahārāja* had also been associated with it[2]. The head of the Yaudheya state was permitted the regal title *Mahārāja* ; but his post was elective[3] and he was not permitted to put his name on the state coinage.[4] How precisely the Yaudheyas elected their *Mahārāja*,—who was also their commander-in-chief,—we do not know. Probably only the members of their aristocracy and perhaps the presidents of the city councils and village *Pañchāyats* took part in the election, the choice being confined to the rival claimants from a few leading families. The Kuṇindas; the Yaudheyas and the Arjunāyanas had probably formed a confederation in *c.* 200 A.D., the military and the foreign affairs being in the hands of a triumvirate representing the federating units. We do not hear anything further about these republics from the 5th century A.D. Their distinctively republican (*gaṇa*) coinage also comes to an end by *c.* 400 A.D.

The circumstances that led to the disappearance of the republics from northern India are not yet fully known. Dr. Jayaswal has attributed this phenomenon to the imperialism of the Guptas. 'Samudra-gupta like Alexander killed the free spirit of the country. He destroyed the Mālavas and the Yaudheyas, who were the nursery of freedom, and many others of their class'.[5] This does not seem to be true. The Mālavas and the Arjunāyanas, the Yaudheyas and the Madras had only accepted in a general way the imperial position of Samudra-

---

[1] It is however interesting to note that the Mālava ruling families had started the claim that their stock was as respectable as that of the royal family of the Ikshvākus; cf. इक्ष्वाकुप्रथितराजर्षिवंशे मालववंशे प्रसूतस्य । Nandsa Yūpa Inscription (unpublished).

[2] *CII.* III, 25.

[3] यौधेयगणपुरस्कृतस्य महाराजमहासेनापतेः *CII.* III, 252.

[4] The legend always is यौधेयगणस्य जयः; it never mentions the name of any Yaudheya *Mahārāja*.

[5] *HIJ*. p. 210.

gupta. They offered him tribute but retained their autonomy. Their territories were never directly administered by the Guptas, and so their administrative procedure and institutions could not have been much affected. It should be remembered that their independence had been completely eclipsed under the Mauryas and the Kushāṇas, but they once more emerged as republics when the above imperialisms declined. The Gupta imperialism had not interfered with their autonomy and it is, therefore, difficult to understand how it could have been fatal to their democratic institutions.

The Nandsa inscription shows that early in the 3rd century the leadership of the Mālavas had already begun to pass into hereditary families which were claiming to be as respectable as the Ikshāku-*rājarshis*. The leaders of the Yaudheyas and the Sankānīkas had assumed the titles of *Mahārājas* and *Mahāsenāpatis* in the 4th century A.D. The same probably was the case with the ancient state of the Lichchhavis, for Kumāradevī was an heiress to its dominions. When the headships of states thus passed into the hands of hereditary presidents, who were military leaders and claimed royal titles, they could no longer be distinguished from monarchies. Why the democratic traditions were allowed to be weakened by permitting the posts of presidents to become hereditary, we do not know. It may be that the growing tendency to regard monarchy as divine may have induced the republics to accept the leadership of hereditary presidents, styled as *Mahārājas*. Probably it was also realised that the monarchical state, which could easily develop into an empire, was a better protection against aggression than the republican one, which usually could not expand beyond its homeland.

2. Monarchical Governments : The Position of the King.

Hereditary monarchy was the prevailing type of government in our period. In the South, even great kings were usually content with the title of *Mahārāja*;[1] in the North, however, the Scythian title *Rājātirāja* was transformed into *Mahārājadhirāja*,[2] and it soon became popular with great conquerors and imperial rulers. The doctrine of the divinity of king, which has been already started earlier under the joint auspices of Hindu thinkers and Scythian rulers,[3] was becoming more and more popular in our period. Samudra-gupta is described as a god come down to live upon this earth,[4] and Kadamba and Sālaṅkāyāna rulers as fifth *Lokapālas* or divine protectors.[5] The divinity of king, however, was not taken too literally either by the rulers or by the ruled. No one among the former came forward to openly claim infallibility for himself or for his decrees on account of his theoretical divinity. Political thinkers and statesmen only conceded a certain functional resemblance between the king and the divine guardians, when they gave a qualified assent to the theory of king's divinity. They expressly point out that divinity does not invest the king with infallibility. Both the Smṛitis and the inscriptions of our age emphasise that a king can become a successful ruler, only if he waits upon the elders, studies the art of government, cultivates religiousness and protects his subjects as efficiently as the divine guardians.[6] He must make assiduous efforts to master the political science, to cultivate fortitude and to acquire leadership ; otherwise he would fail in his task.

---

[1] It is on very rare occasions that some southern rulers have used the title *Mahārājādhirāja* and *Dharmamahārājādhirāja*. See also *ante*, p. 106.

[2] The title *Mahārājādhirāja* no doubt occurs in the Brāhmaṇa literature, but its popularity in Northern India at this period was due to the cognate title *Rājatirāja* brought into vogue by Scythian rulers.

[3] The *devakulas* of the Kushāṇa rulers at Mathura and their title *Devaputra*, 'the son of heaven', show that they subscribed to the doctrine of the divinity of kings, which is guardedly accepted by *Manusmṛiti*, ch. VII, 4-7.

[4] *Lokadhāmno devasya* : Allahabad *praśasti*, *CII.* III, 8.

[5] *IA*. V, 151; *EI*. VIII, 234; *EC*. V, Belur No. 245.

[6] *IA* V, 155; see also *EI*. VIII, 161, 235, etc.

Kings who were haughty, irreligious, immodest and tyrannical, were never regarded as divine, nor was their right to oppress their subjects ever conceded; they are held to public opprobrium in the epigraphs of our period.[1]

Smṛitis continue to emphasise the necessity of training princes in the political science and military arts, and inscriptions show that their views were generally followed in practice. The Kadamba king Mṛigendra-varman is, for instance, described in one record as a ruler whose intellect was sharpened and viewpoint liberalised by the study of different sciences, and whose body was built up by various military exercises including riding and controlling horses and elephants.[2] We do not get such details about the training of the Gupta, the Vākāṭaka or the Pallava princes, but we can safely conclude that a similar course was followed in their case also. Literary education was often entrusted to the most famous scholars of the age; thus Vasubandhu, it seems, was one of the tutors of Samudra-gupta and Kālidāsa that of Pravara-sena II. Fine arts like music were also taught to princes; Samudra-gupta was a good connoisseur of music and the Kadamba king Siṁha-varman enjoyed a similar reputation.[3]

3. Other Members of the Royal Family.

The crown usually passed to the eldest son, who was installed to the office of the heir-apparent when he had come of age and finished his training. Sometimes, however, a junior son was specially selected by the father to succeed him when

---

[1] आविर्भूतावलेपैरविनयपटुभिर्लंघिताचारमार्गं-
म्मोहादैदंयुगीनैरपशुभरतिभिः पीड्यमाना नरेन्द्रैः ॥ *CII.* III, 146.

[2] अदेकशास्त्रार्थतत्वविज्ञानविवेचनविनिविष्टविशालोदारमति हस्त्यश्वारोहण-
प्रहरणादिषु व्यायामिकीषु भूमिषु यथावत्कृतश्रमः । *IA.* VII, 37.

[3] *EI*, VI, 18.

he was convinced that the interests of the state demanded that step.[1] Such cases were, however, rare and exceptional. Among the Western Kshatrapas, however, a peculiar mode of succession was established from *c.* 200 A.D., and the crown passed from the eldest brother to the younger ones in succession. When the youngest brother died after having his turn to rule, he used to be succeeded by the surviving eldest son of the eldest brother.[2]

Younger brothers of the crown prince were usually appointed to the post of provincial governors. Thus Govinda-gupta, a younger brother of Kumāra-gupta I, was a governor of Mālava under him. *Rājakumāras* or junior princes were ruling as provincial governors under the Pallavas.[3] If a king had no sons, the younger brother used to act as heir-apparent. Cases of kingdoms being divided among royal brothers in order to accommodate their rival claims are very few. This happened in the Vākāṭaka dynasty at the death of the emperor Pravarasena I, when his empire was divided among his four sons. In the Gupta dynasty a division of the kingdom seems to have taken place during the closing decades of its existence. In both the cases, the consequences were far from beneficial; the personal ambitions of the rival princes were no doubt satisfied, but at the cost of the prestige and the power of the dynasties concerned. It is, therefore, no wonder that the political theory and practice of our period should have disapproved of this procedure.

The heir-apparent used to be invested with several administrative power, but their precise scope is not known. Probably they varied in different cases according to personal factors. Under the Guptas, the *Yuvarāja* had his separate

---

1 This was most probably the case with Samudra-gupta. See pp. 137-38.

2 *Ante*, p. 50.

3 *EI.* I, 5. ff.

military establishment ;[1] under the Kadambas he used to make even important appointments.[2] Under the Pallava administration, we find him making land grants and issuing orders to provincial officers apparently on his own reponsibility.[3] If the king was old, a good deal of the administrative work would fall upon the heir-apparent, as was the case towards the end of the reign of the Gupta emperor Kumāra-gupta I, or the Kadamba ruler Kṛishṇa-varman.[4]

Queens of reigning kings and princesses do not appear to be taking any active part in the administration during our period. Kumāradevī, the wife of Chandra-gupta I, who figures on her husband's coins, was probably a regnant queen; but there is no evidence to show that she was taking any active part in the Gupta administration. The same seems to have been the case with Dhruvadevī, the famous queen of Chandra-gupta II. A number of queens and princesses figure in the Ikshvāku records from Andhradeśa, but they too do not seem to be entrusted with any administrative duties. A queen of king Mahāsenadeva of Kośala gave a coper-plate charter, but it was confirmed by her husband. *Yuvarājñī* Chārudevī of the Pallava dynasty is, however, seen granting a charter without the sanction of either her husband or her father-in-law.[5] The omission of this permission may be accidental in this case, or it may be that the queens in the Dravidian south took a more active part in the administration in this period also, as they undoubtedly did later under the Chālukyas. Dowager queens, however, were often assuming the reins of administration in our period even in the North ; the instance of the Vākāṭaka queen Prabhāvatī-guptā is well known in this connection.

---

1 A seal of a general belonging to the establishment of the heir-apparent has been found at Vaiśālī; *ASI*. 1903-4, p. 108.

2 *IA*. VII. 34.

3 *EI*. VI, 84.

4 *Ibid*. IX, 172.

5 *Ibid*. VIII, 146.

4. Powers of the King.

Kings were, as usual, the centre of all military, political, administrative and judicial powers. They no doubt governed with the assistance of a ministry, but the ultimate responsibility of a final decision rested with them. They were often their own commanders-in-chief and used to lead important military campaigns. All viceroys, governors and important military and civil officers were appointed by, and responsible to, them. The secretariat at the capital worked under their personal direction and supervision, and the provincial governors and their officers were under their control and guidance. They distributed titles and favours in recognition of meritorious service or literary and artistic works of distinction. To all appearance, kings were thus almost autocratic rulers, but in reality the case was considerably different. They shared their powers with ministers and other high officers[1] who, though not theoretically responsible to the people, were expected to control the king, if he was acting against the established laws and costoms. Kings had also no legislative powers and were expected to carry out rules and laws framed not by themselves but by the wise *ṛishis* (sages) of the bygone ages. Large powers were also delegated to local bodies like the village *Pañchāyats* and town councils; almost all functions of the government, except that of organising the army, determining foreign policy and declaring and conducting a war, were discharged through the agency of the local bodies, where the representatives of the locality had a powerful voice. No doubt, there was no central popular assembly like the modern parliament ; nevertheless people did not suffer from the evil consequences of autocracy owing to the above delegation of

[1] *Purohita* (chief priest), *Senāpati* (commander-in-chief), ministers, ambassadors and spies are referred to as constituting 'The Great Five-fold Group' in early Tamil literature; *Muduraikkañji*, II, 499, 510. They must obviously have exercised considerable influence over the king.

large powers to the local bodies. Smṛitis and epigraphs of our period emphasise that a good king should be particularly careful in winning popularity among his subjects by respecting their wishes and promoting there welfare,[1] and there is every reason to believe that the rulers ordinarily lived up to this ideal. The Chinese pilgrim Fa-hien seems to be paraphrasing the language of some of the inscriptions of our age when he describes how the people under the Gupta rule were virtuous, happy and prosperous, and had no occasions to complain against the autocracy or high-handedness of the government.[2]

5. Ministry.

As stated already, the king carried on the administration with the help of a ministry. Smṛitis and inscriptions often refer to ministers as *Mantrins* or *Sachivas*,[3] but do not give us any information either about the strength of the ministry or about the portfolios held by its different members. It is only the foreign minister who is frequently referred to in our records. We may, however, be not wrong in assuming that the ecclesiastical, military, revenue, land and trade departments were under the charge of different members of the ministry. It appears that the administrative heads of the different departments were often not distinguished from ministers, nor were the ministerial posts always regarded as superior to those of the departmental heads. Thus, for instance, Pṛithvīsheṇa was first a minister (*mantrin*) of Kumāra-gupta I ; he was later

[1] Cf. प्रजासंरजनपरिपालनोद्योग सतत सत्रव्रतदीक्षितस्य । *IA*. V, 51; see also *EI*. VIII, 235.

[2] Cf. Legge : *A Record of Buddhist Kingdoms*, Chap. XVI with vv. 6, 21-23 of the Junagadh inscription of Skanda-gupta. *CII*. III, 58 ff.

[3] The form *amātya* is not generally used in the sense of a minister in the records of our period. It denotes officers of a low grade in Śālaṅkāyana, Gupta and Parivrājaka records; see *ASI*. 1911-12, p. 52; *CII*. III, 96; *IA*. V, 126.

promoted to the post of a general (*mahābalādhikṛita*).[1] Military leadership was one of the important qualifications necessary for a minister. Harisheṇa, who was a foreign minister under Samudra-gupta, was a military general (*mahābalādhikṛita*). The same was probably the case with Śāba, who held the same office under Chandra-gupta II; he is known to have accompanied the emperor in his campaign against the Western Kshatrapas. Provincial governors under the Vākāṭakas and the Ikshvākus were military commanders and the same may have been the case with their ministers as well. Besides possessing a proficiency in the military art, ministers were expected to be well grounded in the political science as well; some of them like Śāba and Harisheṇa were also poets and authors. There was often a tendency for the ministerial office to become hereditary. The families of Śāba[2] and Pṛithvīsheṇa, referred to above, were holding the ministerial posts for more than one generation. Sūryadattā was a foreign minister under the Parivrājakas in 482 A.D. and his son Vibhudatta 28 years later.[3] Under the Uchchakalpa administration Gallu was foreign minister in 496 A.D. and his younger brother Manoratha in 512 A.D.[4] Learning and ability often descend for a generation or two in undiminished quantity and quality, and so the occasional transmission of office in the same family is often to the advantage of the state.

6. The Machinery and Departments of Central Government.

It is unfortunate that we have no direct and detailed information about the machinery of the Central Government,

---

1 पृथ्वीषेण: मंत्री···अनन्तरंच महाबलाधिकृत: । *EI.* X, 71.

2 Cf. अन्वयप्राप्तसाचिव्य: used as an epithet of Śāba; *CII.* III, 35.

3 *Ibid.* pp. 104 & 108.

4 *Ibid.* p. 128.

either of the Guptas, or of the Vākāṭakas, or of the Pallavas. The details of the district administration under the Guptas and some other evidence that we get from the contemporary seals and inscriptions enable us, however, to reconstruct, to some extent, the picture of the central administration during our period. The capital of the kingdom was the headquarters of the central secretariat, whose chief officer was called *Sarvādhyaksha*, or the general superintendent of the administration, in the Pallava, Vākāṭaka, and Kadamba inscriptions.[1] This officer conveyed the orders of the central government to the provincial and district officers through special messengers and inspectors who were often described as the carriers of royal orders.[2]

The central secretariat accommodated the offices of the different ministers and the heads of departments. Each office had its own seal with which its communications were invariably stamped for authentication. Routine business was transacted by each minister on his own responsibility, but important matters were referred to the whole council, which was presided over by the king himself. If the king was absent from the meeting, the practice was to refer the council's conclusion to him for final approval and disposal.[3] Kings often went on tours of inspection, when they were sometimes requested to make grants for religious purposes. It is on such occasions that they often passed oral orders, referred to in some of our grants.[4] There is, however, no doubt that these orders were noted by their private secretaries and communicated to the central secretariat for proper recording and appropriate action.[5] The private secretaries were called by the term *rahasi-niyuktas*;

[1] *IA.* V, 155; VI, 25; *EI.* XXII, 172.

[2] सर्वाध्यक्षवल्लभशासनसचारिण: । *EI.* VIII, 162.

[3] *Mālavikāgnimitra*, Act V.

[4] *EI.* VI, 38; *CII.* III, 155.

[5] स्वमुखाज्ञयाभिलिखित: रहसिनियुक्त न चुल्लेन । *EI.* XIX, 103.

the English term is almost a literal translation of the corresponding Sanskrit expression.

Pratīhāras and *Mahāpratīhāras*, who figure in the records of our period, were important officers in the royal court. They regulated its ceremonial and granted the necessary permits for admission to the royal presence. They do not seem to be taking any other part in the administration.

The military department was undoubtedly the most important department at the centre. The king was its head in all the states of our period, except when he happened to be a minor. He was assisted by the heir-apparent, if he was old enough to bear this responsibility. There were a number of *Mahāsenāpatis* under the king in the Gupta empire and it is quite possible that they and their armies were posted in its different provinces to overawe the neighbouring powers and prospective local enemies. *Mahādaṇḍa-nāyakas* appear to have been the subordinates of *Mahāsenāpatis*.[1] The army had different quarter-masters in different places, the seals of some of whom have been found.[2] The fighting force was divided into infantry, cavalry and the elephant corps. Each branch had its different cadre of officers and they bore significant titles like *aśvapatis*, *mahāśvapatis*, *pīlupatis* and *mahāpīlupatis* (captains and brigadiers in the cavalry and elephant corps). Weapons used in the army were bows and arrows, swords, battle-axes, spears, javelins, barbed darts, etc. and the soldiers were provided with armours and helmets.[3]

The police department must have had its own chief but his designation is not known. The *daṇḍapāśikas*, referred to in the seals from Basarh, were probably of the status of the modern district superintendents of police. Ordinary members of the police force were known as *chāṭas* and *bhāṭas*.

---

[1] *ASI.* 1911-12, p. 52.
[2] *Ibid.* 1903-4, p. 108.
[3] *Raghuvaṁśā*, VII, vv. 48-9.

The revenue minister supervised the collection of taxes and revenues. These were paid partly in kind and partly in cash, and so the government had to make elaborate arrangements for the proper administration of its granaries. Forests and mines of salt and metals were the state property and their administration also was most probably in the charge of the revenue department. The administration of the waste lands, which also were owned by the state, was left in charge of the municipal board or the village council, in whose jurisdiction they were situated.[1]

Hindu tradition required the king to administer justice himself when he was present at the capital. If ill-health or pressure of other work prevented him from discharging this duty, the Chief Justice presided over the court at the capital, and decided cases with the help of jurors. The Supreme Court tried important local cases and also entertained appeals against the decisions of the lower courts in the moffusil. The evidence of the contemporary Smṛitis like *Nārada* and *Bṛihaspati* shows that the judicial procedure was very well developed in the Gupta period. We may well presume that the sound rules which have been laid down in these Smṛitis about restraint, *res judicata*, the relative importance of the oral and the documentary evidence, etc., were evolved in the Gupta, Vākāṭaka and Pallava law-courts. The class of professional pleaders had not yet come into existence ; the jurors were expected to analyse the case, ascertain the points favourable for either party and weigh them impartially for coming to a proper decision. Brāhmaṇa Durdhara, who proceeds to plead the cause of the defendant against his creditors in the famous case from Pāṭaliputra described by Asahāya in his commentary on *Nārada-Smṛiti*, IV, 5, no doubt plays the role of the pleader ; but he is rebuked by the judge for advocating the cause of a third

---

[1] *EI.* XV, 130 ff.

party in return for a fee. So even in the 8th century the pleader class had not acquired a respectable status.

The Ecclesiastical Minister was in charge of *Dharma* and morality of the realm. He had his own subordinates at the provincial and district headquaters, who were designated as *Vinayasthitisthāpakas* (establishers' of the moral standard)[1] This department advised the king about the promotion of *Dharma* in its different aspects and suggested suitable objects and occasions for charity. It also supervised the administration of public temples. Promotion of learning by grants to learned Brāhmaṇas and Buddhist and Jaina monasteries carrying on the work of education probably fell within the purview of this department. Officers in charge of villages thus alienated were known as *Agrahārikas*.

Trade and Industries were prospering in our period, bringing considerable revenues to the royal treasury. Their affairs were probably under the charge of a separate minister, though he is not referred to in our records. *Drāṅgikas* or octroi officers, who figure in Valabhī and other records,[2] must have worked and collected the duties under his direction. This department was probably in charge of roads ; the rest-houses with which they studded and which excited the admiration of Fa-hien, were probably administered by its subordinate staff.

The foreign minister, *Mahāsāndhivigrahika*, worked in close co-operation with the king and the military department. He must have been one of the busiest officers in the early Gupta period, when Samudra-gupta was planning his famous campaigns in the North and the South. Which kingdoms were to be annexed and which were to be permitted to remain as feudatory states was to be determined by this department. In later times the kingdoms of the Deccan are known to have

---

[1] *CII.* III, 50.
[2] *Ibid.* p. 165; *EI.* XII. 339.

employed several *Sāndhivigrahikas*, each being in charge of a particular region. Probably the Vākāṭakas and the Guptas had done the same. Foreign ministers were required to be great diplomats ; their reputation would spread far and wide if they could gain by negotiations what seemed to be achievable only by the war.

7. The Feudatories.

There were a large number of feudatory states, owing allegiance to the Pallavas and the Guptas, and much of the time of the foreign minister and his staff must have been spent in supervising the poilcy and plans of the rulers of these states, many of whom were usually cherishing the secret hope of becoming independent one day by overthrowing the imperial yoke. In later times, the suzerain power and its feudatories are known to be entertaining each other's representatives at their courts ; the same was probably the case also in our period. The foreign department, as usual, employed a large number of spies.

It will be convenient to describe here the relations between the Imperial Power and its feudatories. These varied with different states. Feudatories, who had been permitted to rule after a smashing defeat, or who were very near the heart of the imperial kingdom, or whose resources and powers were insignificant, enjoyed little internal autonomy. They were not even the full masters of the revenues of their kingdoms. Nārāyaṇa Mahārāja and Śatrughna Mahārāja, who were the Vākāṭaka feudatories, king Rudradatta, who was a feudatory of Vainya-gupta, and the Sendraka king Bhānuśakti, who owed allegiance to the Kadambas, felt the necessity of getting the imperial sanction for alienating some revenues of their own states.[1] Bigger feudatories like the Parivrājakas, the Uchcha-

[1] *CII.* III, 236 ff; *IHQ.* VI, 53; *IA.* VI, 31-2.

kalpas, and the Varmans (of Mandasor) could, however, make land grants without the permission of the Imperial power, Some of them like the Uchchakalpas do not even refer to their suzerain lords in their records, but others like the Parivrājakas and the Varmans (of Mandasor) make a passing reference to the Imperial power. Important and powerful feudatory chiefs had their own sub-feudatories; thus king Mātṛivishṇu of Eran was a subordinate of king Suraśmichandra, who in his turn was a feudatory of Budha-gupta.[1] The Parivrājakas also had their own feudatories.

The Foreign Department insisted upon due obedience to the imperial orders by the feudatories. They were, as a general rule, required to pay tribute and come to the imperial court at suitable intervals for offering personal homage. Under the Gupta administration kings, who had been reduced to the feudatory status after a conquest, were granted imperial charter regranting them their territories under such conditions as were agreed upon or imposed. They had also to offer their daughters in marriage to the emperor, if the latter was inclined to accept them. It seems that the Guptas did not permit their feudatories to issue any currency of their own[2]; diplomatic-pressure also seems to have been exercised to induce them to use the imperial era.

8. Kumārāmātyas.

Before we conclude the survey of the Central Government, we have to refer to a class of officers known as *Kumārāmātyas* who figure very prominently both in the seals and inscriptions of the Gupta period. It was once believed that *Kumārāmātya* was a minister to the prince of the blood royal, who was

---

[1] *CII.* III, 89.

[2] Coins of the Gupta feudatories have not been found, but the same is the case with their independent contemporaries like the Vākāṭakas and the Pallavas.

appointed as an heir-apparent or a viceroy. But a careful analysis of the epigraphical evidence shows that such was not the case. Harisheṇa, who was the foreign minister of Samudragupta, and Śikharisvāmī and Pṛithvī-sheṇa, who were ministers of the emperors Chandra-gupta II and Kumāra-gupta I, are all called *Kumāramātyas.*[1] These officers were ministers serving directly under emperors ; still they are called *Kumārāmātyas.* The latter term, therefore, surely did not indicate a minister to a prince or an heir-apparent. *Kumārāmātyas* are often seen to be working as district officers,[2] and sometimes as subordinates of even *Mahādaṇdanāyakas.*[3] The post of a *Mahābalādhikṛita* or a *Mahādaṇḍanāyaka* was no doubt a higher one than that of a *Kumārāmātya,* for *Kumārāmatya* Pṛithvīsheṇa was promoted to it after some approved service.[4] It seems that *Kumārāmatyas,* to a great extent, resembled the modern I.C.S. officers, who sometimes work in the district, sometimes in the provincial or central secretariat and sometimes become members of the government itself. Higher posts of ministers and generals were filled by promotion from their cadre. Seals refer to *Yuvarājapādīya-Kumārāmātyas* and *Paramabhaṭṭārakapādīya-Kumārāmātyas* ; they seem to be *Kumārāmātyas* attached to or working in the office of the *Yuvaraja* and the emperor.[5] The designation *Kumārāmātya* became fairly popular in cousre of time ; we find officers of this designation existing under the Maitrakas of Valabhī and some local dynasties in Kalinga and Orissa.[6] The *Amātyas,* who figure under the Pallavas, were probably discharging functions similar to those of the *Kumārāmātyas.*

[1] *EI.* X, 52.
[2] *Ibid.* XV, 133.
[3] *ASI.* 1911-2, p. 32.
[4] *EI.* X, 52.
[5] *ASI.* 1903-4, p. 107. Prof. R.D. Banerji interpreted these expressions differently. See *AIG.* pp. 72-5. His view is, however, untenable.
[6] *CII.* III, 165; *EI.* XXIII, 201; XI, 28.

9. Provincial Administration.

Let us now survey the provincial and district administration. It would be first necessary to find out the different territorial divisions that prevailed in our period. Our records show that their nomenclature and extent varied with the different kingdoms. Big empires like those of the Guptas were first divided into provinces like Surāshṭra and Mālava. They were probably known as Deśas.[1] The names of all the provinces of the Gupta empire have not yet come to light, nor do we know the designation of the officers entrusted with their government. Only a few details of the provincial administration are known.

Viceroys of provinces were appointed by the emperor and were responsible for protecting their territories against external invasion and maintaining internal order. They were to help and watch over the feudatory rulers situated within their territories. They were to develop their provinces by constructing or repairing works of public utility like irrigation tanks, and strengthen the foundation of the empire by promoting good government and public confidence. They could appoint their subordinate officers. Almost all the departments that existed at the imperial capital probably had their replicas in the provincial headquarters.

Provinces were divided into *bhuktis* which were about the size of the Commissioner's divisions in modern times. *Bhuktis* were subdivided into *vishayas*, roughly corresponding to a modern district. Tīra-*bhukti* was about the size of the modern Darbhanga division; one of the districts included in it was that of Vaiśālī. Puṇḍravardhana-*bhukti* comprised the districts of Dinajpur, Bogra and Rajshahi in northern Bengal, and Magadha-*bhukti* of the districts of Gayā, Rājagṛiha and Pāṭaliputra. The *bhuktis* were in charge of officers known as *Uparikas*, who were

[1] Cf. *Sarveshu deśeshu vidhāya goptṛin*; *CII.* III, 66.

appointed by, and responsible to, the emperor himself.[1] *Vishayas* were governed by *Vishayapatis*, who were usually appointed by the *Uparikas*, but sometimes directly by the emperor himself. Often they had the status of a *Mahārāja*. Several sealings of the offices of *bhuktis* and *vishayas* have been found, which had once closed confidential despatches sent from their offices. It does not appear that in the Gupta empire there was any administrative division intervening between the *vishaya* and the towns and villages comprised within it.[2]

Rāshṭra, *rājya* and *bhukti* are the territorial administrative divisions to be met with in the Vākaṭaka records. Their extent is not known, but since no other territorial division is usually mentioned between them and the villages granted in their jurisdiction, we may well presume that all these different names were used to denote the same administrative division, usually equal in size to the modern district. Districts were often divided into eastern and western section;[3] sometimes groups of villages in them were known after the name of the important town situated in the area concerned.[4]

The early Pallava kingdom was divided into *rāshṭras*, *madavas* (?) and *deśas*, which appear to have been territorial divisions in the descending order of dimensions. Their precise extent, however, is not known.

In the smaller states of our period, like those of the Kadambas, and the Sālaṅkāyanas, administrative divisions larger than districts did not exist. Districts were known some-

---

[1] It is difficult to state what control was exercised over the *Bhukti* officers by the viceroys, since the former seem to have been directly responsible to the emperor.

[2] The spurious plates of Samundra-gupta mention the villages granted immediately after the *vishayas* in which they were situated; no intermediate division is mentioned.

Official designations of *Uparika* and *Vishayapati* continued to exist in the post-Gupta period also in Bengal and Kalinga. *JASB*. VII, 476-7; *EI*. III, 45.

[3] As was the case with Bennākaṭa district : *EI*. XXII, 172.

[4] *Ibid*. XXIV, 264.

times as *rāshṭras*, sometimes as *vishayas* and sometimes as *aharaṇis*. Their sub-division were known as *sthalis* in Kathiawar and *pāṭhakas* or *peṭhās* in Gujarat and Central India[1].

10. The Non-official District Council.

Let us now survey the district administration under the Guptas. It was presided over by an officer of the Central Government, who was usually called a *Vishayapati*. He often belonged to the cadre of the *Kumārāmātyas*. His office was well organised and used to keep careful records and files. The officer in charge of records was called *Pustapāla*; his records could show the precise dimensions of lands, both cultivated and uncultivated, situated within the district. His subordinates in the moffusil were called *Akshapaṭalikas*.

There was certainly no over-centralisation of government under the Guptas. The district administration enjoyed considerable powers. Even when waste lands owned by the central government were to be sold, the district authorities had to be consulted. In some cases, copper-plates granting such lands bore even the seal of the district administration as a proof of its approval.

The popular element had a large voice in the district administration. The chief banker, the chief trader, the chief artisan and the chief *Kāyastha* (writer), figured prominently in the council which helped the *Vishayapati* of Koṭivarsha in Bengal in *c*. 450 A.D. The members of this council were known as *Vishayamahattaras*. It should not, however, be supposed that only the big business dominated the district administration; the persons mentioned above were only the prominent members (*puroga*) of the district council, which consisted of a large number of other members as well. The Faridpur plate III shows that there were about twenty members of the district

1 *CII*. III, 136, 173.

council, some of whom, like Kulasvāmin and Subhadeva were Brāhmaṇas, and some, like Ghoshachandra and Guṇachandra, were non-Brahmins.[1] Seals of *Vishayamahattaras* have also been found at Nālandā. They functioned in the district council under the Vishṇukuṇḍins also.[2]

There is no direct evidence to show that similar popular councils existed at the district headquarters in other contemporary states; but probably we shall not be wrong in assuming that they functioned in our period under all administrations.

Unfortunately we have no information as to how the members of the district council were selected or elected. As fas as the bankers and traders are concerned they were obviously represented by the presidents of their guilds, as the terms, *prathama-śreshṭhin* and *prathama-sārthavāha*, show. The same was the case with the writers' class. As far as the remaining members of the council are concerned, we shall not be wrong in assuming that persons of different classes, who had, by their age, experience and character, acquired a pre-eminent status, were co-opted on the council by a general consensus of the opinion of the locality. Most probably the district council was dominated by the urban interests. It does not seem likely that it included any representatives of the villages situated in it.[3]

11. District Administration

Officers in charge of districts were responsible for maintaining law and order and collecting government taxes and revenues. They were assisted in this task by a large staff with different qualifications. The names of the subordinate officers of the revenue department under the Guptas are not known, but they were called *Dhruvas* in Gujarat, and were required to

[1] *IA.* XXXIX, 195 ff.

[2] *JAHRS.* VI, 17 ff. *Rāshṭragrāmamahattarādhikārins*, who figure in a record of Śaṅkaragaṇa, probably include *Rāshṭramahattaras*, who formed a council at the headquarters of a *rāshṭra*; *CII*, III, 216.

[3] But some councils, with headquarters in villages, and different constitution, cf. *HBR.* 268.

see that the state got its fair share of the standing crop in each field. Most probably *Yuktas*, *Āyuktas*, *Niyuktas*, *Vyāpṛitas* and *Adhikṛitas* who figure in some of our records were also subordinate revenue officers serving as links between the district administration and the village. The district administration is definitely known to be administering waste lands; it is therefore very likely that the forest officers, who frequently figure in our records, worked under the guidance of the district officers. *Daṇḍanāyakas*, whose seals are found in large numbers at Bhita, and who also figure in Bṛihatphalāyana records,[1] were probably the captains of military units stationed in the different districts to help the local authorities in maintaining law and order. *Daṇḍapāśikas* or *Choroddharaṇikas*, who figure in the records of most of the northern dynasties of our period, and the *Ārakshādhikṛitas* and the *Gaulmikas*, who figure in the Pallava records, were obviously the police and C.I.D. officers appointed to apprehend criminals and to haul them before the law courts.[2] *Chāṭas* and *Bhāṭas* were policemen working under their direction. Administration of justice in important towns and cities was carried on by specially appointed officers with the assistance of jurors trained in law (*Dharmaśāstra*). The seals of the office of *Nayādhikaraṇa*, *Dharmādhikaraṇa* and *Dharmaśāsanādhikaraṇa* that were found at Nālandā and Vaiśāli were obviously the seals of courts of justice functioning at important provincial and district centres like these places.[3]

We have no information about the administrative machinery of the *pāṭhaka*, which denoted the sub-division of the district in some parts of the country,[4] but probably it was similar to that of the district outlined above.

---

[1] *EI*. VI, 38.

[2] It is interesting to note that the seals of the officers of this department often bore the emblem of a standing policeman, with a staff in his hand. *ASI*. 1903-4, p. 108.

[3] *MASI*. No. 6, pp. 52-3; *ASI*. 1913-4, p. 128; *EI*. XI, 107.

[4] *e.g.* Gujarat and Central India; *CII*. III, 136, 173.

12. POPULAR COURTS.

In addition to the official courts at the headquarters of districts and provinces, there existed a number of popular courts in our period. Guilds of traders and caravans had their own courts, which took cognisance of disputes arising among their members. There were also *Pañchāyat* courts in towns and villages, which tried all civil and petty criminal cases. All parties had to refer their cases in the first instance to these popular courts, and their decrees were regularly enforced by the state, unless they were reversed in appeal by the royal courts. This policy of decentralisation reduced the congestion in the official courts and afforded leading citizens and villagers an opportunity to compose amicably the quarrels arising in their respective localities. Truth is always easy to discover when a case is tried locally with the help of local juriors.

13. VILLAGE AND TOWN ADMINISTRATION.

Let us now review the machinery of the government of the village, which was the pivot of administration. The jurisdiction of the village authorities extended over houses, streets, *bazars*, burning grounds, temples, wells, tanks, waste lands, forests and cultivable lands. The area of the lands included in different villages varied with local conditions. All lands, cultivated and uncultivated, were very carefully measured by officers known as *Simākaras*, as becomes clear from the data supplied by inscriptions found both in the South and the North.[1] Village settlements were usually protected by wells and ditches; the latter often figure in the description of the village boundaries.[2] Agriculture was the main occupation of the

---

[1] *IA*. V, 53 (for the Pallava administration); *EI*. XV. 130 (for the Gupta administration); *Ibid*. XVII, 53 (for the later Gupta period); *CII*. III, 236 (for the Vākāṭaka kingdom).

[2] *EI*. XIX, 130.

villages, but each of them had usually its own compliment of weavers, potters, carpenters, oil-pressers and goldsmiths.

The village headman, designated as *Grāmeyaka* in some places, and *Grāmādhyaksha* in others, was at the head of the village administration.[1] *Vallabhas* and *Govallabhas* were other officers that worked under him in the Pallava administration, but their precise function is not known The headman was assisted in his work by a non-official local council, the members of which were usually known as *Mahattaras* under the Pallava and the Vākaṭaka administration.[2] The same designation prevailed in western India. The council existed in the Gupta administration as well, and was known as *Pañchamaṇḍalī* in Central India and *Grāmajanapada* in Bihar.

The village council discharged almost all the functions of government. It looked after village defence, settled village disputes, organised works of public utility, acted as a trustee for minors, and collected the government revenues and paid them into the central treasury. A large number of the seals of the village *janapadas* have been found at Nālandā belonging to the later Gupta period.[3] They would show that the popular village councils in Bihar were known as village *janapadas* ; they met regularly to transact the village business. Letters sent to outsiders communicating their decisions were invariably stamped with their official seals.[4] We have no information as to how the members of the village councils were elected or

---

[1] *IA*. V, 155; *CII*. III, 256. The headman was called *Munuda* or *Miluda* under the Śālaṅkāyanas; *EI*. IX, 58; *JAHRS*. I, 101.

[2] *EI*. VIII, 145 (for the Pallavas); XIX, 102 (for the Vākāṭakas).

[3] *MASI*. No. 66, pp. 45-9.

[4] The village councils of our period were administrative bodies and have to be distinguished from *Mangrams* and *Podiyils*, mentioned in early Tamil literature, which were folk-gatherings, meeting mainly for religious and social purposes, and occasionally transacting some administrative work that may crop up. There is, however, no doubt that they were evolved out of the latter in south India.

19

selected. There is no hint of any elections of the modern type in our records and the term *Mahattara*, the elderly one, suggests that senior persons of different classes, who had acquired a pre-eminent status by their age, experience and character, were elevated to the village council by general approval.

The town administration was carried on by an officer, usually known as *Purapāla*. He had often the status of a *Kumārāmātya* under the Guptas. If the town or the city happened to be the headquarters of a district, the council of the *Vishayamahattaras* prabably carried on its administration along with that of the district. When such was not the case, we can reasonably assume that the towns, like the villages, had their own popular councils, which assisted the town prefect in the work of the administration. Town councils used to discharge most of the functions of the village councils. Citizens were naturally particular that their towns should have good water supply, fine gardens, imposing temples and spacious halls for public meetings and debates,[1] and town councils had to take the necessary steps in the matter. Most of the towns and cities were protected by walls and moats.

We have no information about the sources of revenue of the village and town councils. Very probably an appreciable percentage of the land revenue was handed over to them by the Central Government for financing the different projects and meeting the normal expenditure of the local administration. It is also likely that the local bodies imposed taxes on shops and houses and obtained a fair portion of the octroi duties in their jurisdiction, which were mostly collected in kind. Some Pallava records show that barbers, metal-workers and other artisans were taxed.

---

[1] *CII.* III, 75.

The Taxation.

Let us now consider the question of the Central taxation. From some of our records it appears that the traditional number of taxes was 18,[1] but their names are nowhere given. Among them, the land-tax of course was the most important. It was called *Bhāgakara* in some localities and *Udraṅga* in others, and its incidence seems to have varied from 16 to 25 *per cent* according to the quality of the land. It was usually collected in kind as the term *Bhāgakara* clearly suggests and so the question of granting remissions for failure of crops to some extent solved itself. If the yield was less, the government share, which was a certain fraction of it, automatically became less.

Octroi duties, mentioned both in the Smṛitis and inscriptions of our period, were the next important sources of revenue. Some of them were collected in kind and were assigned to the village and town officers as part of their remuneration. These seem to be referred to as *Bhogakaras* in our records.[2] Vākāṭaka and Pallava inscriptions refer to the tax on flowers, milk, curd and bullocks ; we may presume that octroi duties had to be paid on these and other important articles imported in towns and villages. Most probably excise duties were imposed on articles manufactured in the kingdom ; the expression *Bhūta pratyāya,* 'tax on what has come into existence', which occurs in some Maitraka and Traikūṭaka records, probably refers to them.

The State claimed ownership in waste lands, forests, pastures and salt-mines, and derived considerable income by letting them out or selling their produce.

The villagers and citizens had to pay additional imposts, when officers of the Central Government came for inspection.

---

[1] *EI.* I, 6; XV, 25.

[2] *CII* III, 193, 198; *EI.* XXII, 23.

They had to provide them, free of cost, with boiled rice, curd, milk, vegetables, grass, fuel, flowers and other necessities or luxuries of life, and supply labour, bulls and carts necessary for their transport.[1] When police and military officers had to visit a locality to detect crimes or apprehend criminals, their expenses also had to be met by the local residents ; donees of the *brahmadeya* grants are in many cases seen exempted from this impost.

It is unfortunate that we should possess no details whatsoever of the taxation under the Gupta empire.[2] Their inscriptions are all silent upon the point. We may however presume that most of the above taxes and sources of revenue existed under the Gupta administration as well.

15. General Review.

We shall conclude this chapter with a general review of the administration and its achievements. In the small kingdoms of our period, like those of the Kadambas of the Gaṅgas, the administrative machinery was no doubt simple, but it was fairly complex and well developed in larger states, like those of the Pallavas or the Guptas. We possess fairly detailed information about the Gupta government and its achievements and can well conclude that it was very well organised, both at the centre and in provinces. The central secretariat worked efficiently and could keep itself well informed about the happenings in districts and villages. Orders of kings, when oral, were noted by their private secretaries and communicated to the central secretariat for proper recording. Many of the plates of our period show that they were verified by government authorities after they were engraved. Lands were carefully measured by

---

1 *EI.* I, 6; VI, 14.

2 The spurious plates of Samudra-gupta simply refer to customary dues *samuchitigrāma-pratyāya*, but do not enumerate them.

a specially trained staff and detailed records were kept about their boundaries and ownership in the headquarters of the village and district.

Government could secure safety to its subjects both from foreign invasions and internal disturbances for a long time. It did not however put any restrictions in the movements of people, unless they were undertaken for the fraudulent purpose of avoiding taxation.[1] In the administration of criminal law there was a happy combination of justice and humanity; criminals were punished promptly, but the punishments were not inhuman. The police and C. I. D. were quite efficient in detecting crimes and bringing the delinquents before the law.

The maintenance of law and order however was not the sole concern of government. It was anxious to develop the resources of the country as well. Its trade department no doubt collected octroi duties, but also promoted commerce by securing safety of roads and establishing a gold currency of international standard. Mines and forests were developed. Agriculture was promoted by the construction and repairs of tanks and reservoirs, and the state afforded facilities for bringing waste lands under cultivation.

Government, however, was not content merely with promoting material prosperity of its citizens; it tried to promote their moral and spiritual welfare also by appointing special religious inspectors. Donees of *Brahmadeya* villages were particularly required to set high moral standards, so as to become an example to others. State extended its patronage impartially to Hinduism, Buddhism and Jainism.

There was no central parliament to control the king and ministers, but traditional rules about the duties of kings and ministers and the high ideals that were placed before them in semi-religious works were sofficiently effective to curb tyranni-

---

[1] *EI*. XXV, 52; Fa-hien p. 43.

cal tendencies. Government, moreover, was remarkably decentralised, and most of its functions were transferred to district administration. In the district headquarters, the officers of the central government were assisted and controlled by popular councils of *Mahattaras*, whose sanction was necessary even if the state wanted to sell the waste land of its own. Villages had their own councils, which functioned as corporate bodies and administered all the branches of its administration, including the settlement of disputes and the collection of taxes.

People were virtuous, rich and prosperous ; cities were teeming with population. The poor and sick were offered free relief and medicine in hospitals and charitable institutions. Peace and prosperity secured by the government led to a rich and remarkable development of art, literature, philosophy and science, as will be shown in later chapters. We may, therefore, be well proud of the Gupta administrative system, which served as the ideal for contemporary and later states.

CHAPTER XV

THE COINAGE.

In this chapter we shall consider the coinage current in our age. Owing to want of space, it is not possible to describe in detail all the coin-types issued by the different rulers of our period. We can only refer to the main types issued by each dynasty, the different metals used for them, the weight standards followed, and the relative value of the different denominations. The question of the origin and development of the different types with special reference to foreign influence, if any, will engage our special attention, and brief reference will also be made to the light thrown by important types on the contemporary history.

1. The Coinage of the Punjab and Afghanistan.

In the Punjab the Later Great Kushāṇa rulers, Kanishka III and Vāsudeva II, continued to issue gold coins (Pl. I, 1 & 2), closely resembling some of the earlier Kushāṇa types. On the obverse, there is the king offering oblation at the altar, with a legend in Greek, which becomes progressively more and more degenerate. Brāhmī letters are introduced in the field, the probable significance of which has been already discussed (*ante*, pp. 14-16). The reverse has two types ; in one there is Śiva standing by his bull (Pl. I, 2), as on the coins of Vāsudeva I, and in the other there is Ardoksho seated on the throne, as on the coins of Huvishka (Pl. I, 1). The first type was common in the Kabul valley and the second in the Western Punjab.

When the Later Kushāṇas lost Afghanistan to the Sassanians, the latter introduced a new series of coinage in that province, which is known as Scytho-Sassanian. The coins of the new series are thin and large ; they bear on the obverse the figure of the standing king, and on the reverse, that of Śiva standing by his bull. The Greek legend on the obverse and the Pahlavī legend on the reverse are both corrupt. (Pl. I, 3). The weight of these pieces is about 120 grains.

The Scythian successors of the Later Great Kushānas continued their Ardoksho type in the Central and Western Punjab with the same weight standard (Pl. I, 4). The Greek legend on their coins became too corrupt and degenerate to be intelligible. The names of the kings, therefore, began to be written in Brāhmī characters under their left arm. A number of Brāhmī letters make their appearance in the field, the significance of which has been described already in Chapter I. The weight standard of the later Kushāṇa and Scythian coins is the same as that of the earlier Imperial Kushāṇas. They weigh 120 grains on the average, but are often debased.

The currency of the Kidāra Kushāṇas or the Little Kushāṇas, who rose to power in *c.* 350 A.D., is entirely Sassanian in its type. There is the bust of the king on the obverse, usually supporting the globe on his crown. On the reverse there is Fire-altar with an attendant on either side. The legends are in Pahlavī characters (Pl. I, 5).

2. The coinage of the Western Kshatrapas.

The Śaka Kshatrapas of Western India continued their earlier coin-type during this period. Two revolutions took place, one in 304 A.D. and the other about forty years later, which put rival Śaka chiefs on the throne, but they brought no change in the coin-tape. The Ābhīra ruler Iśvara-datta, who got a temporary hold of the Kshatrapa kingdom for about two years, is also seen issuing coins in substantial agreement with the established type. The same was the case with the Guptas, who supplanted the Kshatrapas in *c.* 400.

The Śaka silver coins have the bust of the king on the obverse. In the earlier period, the bust is a portrait of the ruler, showing on different coins even the changes of features produced by age (Pl. II, 3 & 4). Later on it became stereotyped. The obverse has meaningless traces of the circular Greek legend, borrowed from the Indo-Bactrian prototype. Kshatrapa rulers possessed a remarkable historic sense. The circular Brāhmī legend on the reverse of their coins carefully mentions the name and the title, not only of the ruler but also of his father. But this is not all. From the reign of Jīva-dāman, (*c.* 175 A.D.)[1] each coin issued from the mint began to bear the date of its issue, given behind the bust of the king. This has enabled the modern historian to determine very accurately the reign-periods of most of the Kshatrapa rulers. It may be observed here that no other dynasty in ancient India, Indian or foreign, has issued such a long series of dated coins.

The crescented three-arched Hill with the Sun and the Moon on either side is the reverse symbol on the Kshatrapa coins. In course of time the Hill in the centre dominated the other two, which dwindled almost into insignificance. The average weight of the silver coins of the Western Kshatrapas is about 35 grains. They are obviously hemidrachms of the Persian weight standard. The Gupta and the Hūṇa silver coins, based upon the Kshatrapa prototype, are of the same weight. The purchasing power of these silver pieces was equal to that of two rupees in 1930.

A few Kshatrapa rulers issued copper coins also, but they are usually anonymous. Generally they have Elephant on the obverse and the three-arched Hill on the reverse, with the Sun and the Moon on either side and the date of issue below.

---

[1] For coins of Jiva-dāman see Pl. II, 3 & 4.

The latter enables us to attribute these coins to the Saka Kshatrapas.

3. The Coinage of the Republics.

The later Kushāṇa and Scythian rulers of the Punjab issued no copper coins. The money market had been so overflooded by the copious copper currency of the Great Kushāṇa rulers, that there was no necessity to issue any fresh coins. Many of the Indian republics, which overthrew the Kushāṇa overlordship and regained their independence, resumed their coinage by *c.* 200 A.D. Among these the Yaudheyas were the most powerful and prominent, and their coinage is most widespread and abundant. As may be expected, the Yaudheya copper coins bear a close resemblance to those of the Kushāṇas both in weight and fabric. The figures on their obverse and reverse bear a general resemblance to those on the Kushāṇa coins, but the standing king on the prototype is replaced by Kārtikeya, who was the tutelary deity of the Yaudheyas. The figure on the reverse recalls no doubt that of Helios or Mao on the Kushāṇa coinage, but the accompanying symbols of *Kalasa* and Conch make it clear that it is intended to stand for Lakshmī, (Pl. I, 6). The new Yaudheya coinage discards the foreign Greek and Kharoshṭhī alphabets and introduces the indigenous Brāhmī one. The legend on the obverse, *Yaudheya-gaṇasya jayaḥ*, undoubtedly refers to the victory of the issuers over their erstwhile overlords.

The coinage of the Kuṇinda republic, resumed in *c.* 200 A.D., also bears a general resemblance to the Kushāṇa coinage in weight and fabric. The standing king on the obverse is, however, replaced by the figure of Śiva, holding the trident in his hand. The reverse shows most of the symbols that we find in the pre-Kushāṇa Kuṇinda coinage, *e.g.*, the Deer, six-arched Hill, Tree-in-railing, Banner, Serpentine line, etc. The Brāhmī script replaces the Kharoshṭhi and the Greek.

The average weight of the copper coins of the Yaudheyas and the Kuṇindas is about 160 grains.

The Mālavas of Central Rajputana continued their coinage during our period down to *c.* 400 A.D. As before, they issued only copper coins, and they are surprisingly small and tiny. The heaviest of them do not exceed 40 grains in weight, and the lightest are as light as 1·7 grains. The average weight is about 10 grains, which is less than half the weight of the modern silver two anna piece. On the earlier coins, the old legend *Mālavānāṁ jayaḥ* continues to make its appearance (Pl. I, 7) and on some pieces it appears reversed owing to the mistake of the die-cutter. Later Mālava coins of our period have mysterious legends like, *Majupa*, *Mapojaya*, *Magajaśa*, etc., which have not yet been satisfactorily explained. It cannot be argued that these are the names of the kings of foreign extraction, because the contemporary inscriptions show that the Mālava stock was at this time regarded as equally respectable with the Ikshvākus.[1]

The Madraka republic of the Punjab very probably issued coins like its neighbours the Yaudheya and the Kuṇinda republics, but they have not yet come to light. The Arjunāyana coinage of our period has also not been discovered. The Kākas and the Sanakānīkas of Central India probably issued no coins, as coinage was not common in their territory.

4. The coins of Vīrasena and Achyuta.

In northern U.P. the coins of a king named Vīrasena have been found, having Tree-in-railing on the obverse and a rude

[1] The view that these words are abbreviations of *Mālava-gaṇasya jayaḥ*, initial letters alone being taken, can explain some legends like *Magaja*, but not others like *Mapojaya*, *Bhapaṁyana* or *Mapaya*. The mystery can be solved only by future discoveries.

figure of Lakshmī with king's name on the reverse. (Pl. II, I). At Ahichchhatra in Bareily district, king Achyuta was ruling by the middle of the 4th century A.D. He issued a copious copper currency, with the letters *Achyu* on one side and a wheel on the other (Pl. II, 2),

On some of his rare coins, there is his bust in the centre and the letters *a* and *chyu* on either side. This king was overthrown by Samudra-gupta in *c.* 350 A.D.

5. The Nāga coinage.

The Nāga rulers of Padmāvati[1] who are the Bhāraśivas of the inscriptions, have left an interesting series of copper coins, which are small in size and light in weight like those of the Mālavas. On the obverse of these coins there is a legend giving the name of the king, and on the reverse there are various symbols, like the Peacock, Trident, recumbent Bull and Wheel, which are mostly Śaivite (cf. coin of Bhava-nāga, Pl. I, 8). The coinage of Gaṇapati, the last Nāga king who was overthrown by Samudra-gupta, was very extensive; even now hundreds of his coins can be seen with the coin dealers of Mathura. The weight of the Nāga coins varies from 18 to 36 grains.

6. The coinage of the Maghas.

The Maghas of Kauśāmbī issued a copper currency which is crude and inartistic. The coins are irregular in size and their symbols badly executed. The weight varies from 45 to 60 grains. As may be expected, the symbols on these coins are borrowed from those on the earlier Kauśāmbī currency. They are the Bull, three-arched Hill and Tree-within-railing. The

---

[1] Padmāvatī is modern Padam-Pawaya, about 130 miles south of Mathurā.

coins of Bhadra-magha, Śiva-magha, Vaiśravana, Bhīma-varman, Vijaya-magha and Śata-magha have been discovered so far.

7. No Vākāṭaka coinage.

The Vākāṭakas succeeded the Sātavāhanas in the sovereignty of the Deccan, but did not continue their tradition of coinage. No coins of the Vākāṭakas have been discovered so far.[1]

8. the coinage of the Imperial Guptas.

We now proceed to consider the coinage of the Guptas. With the assumption of the imperial title *Mahārājādhirāja*, Chandra-gupta I started his gold coinage. The view of Allan[2] that the coins bearing the figures of Chandra-gupta and his queen Kumāradevī on the obverse are commemorative medals struck by his son Samudra-gupta is untenable. Chandra-gupta I owed his imperial status, to a considerable extent, to the valuable assistance that he had received from the Lichchhavi rela-

---

[1] The view of Dr. Jayaswal that the coins attributed to Vīrasena are really the coins of Pravara-sena I is quite untenable. The letter *Pra* does not at all occur in the lower left hand corner of these coins, as alleged by Jayaswal. Several specimens make it quite clear that the reading of the legend at the top is *Vīrasena* and not *Varasena*. (Cf. Pl. II, 1). Similarly Jayaswal's attribution of the Lankey Bull type to Rudra-sena I is untenable. What he read as Rudra is really part of the Triratna symbol, as is made quite clear by better preserved specimens (cf. Pl. II, 5).

Further it is worth noting that the coins of Vīrasena are found only near Mathura and those of the Lankey Bull type only at Kauśāmbī; they are never found anywhere within the boundaries of the Vākāṭaka kingdom. This circumstance is quite fatal to their attribution to any Vākāṭaka rulers. The contention that the coins so long attributed to Pavata should be regarded as the issues of Pṛithvi-sheṇa I, is equally untenable. Letters *pa*, *va*, and *ta*, are quite clear and cannot be read as Pṛithvī-sheṇa (cf. Pl. II, 6). For further discussion see *JNSI*. V, 130-4.

[2] *CGD*, pp. lxiv-lxviii.

tions of his wife; it was, therefore, but natural for him to issue throughout his reign a joint coinage, whose type would be acknowledging the Lichchhavi help in a suitable manner. Had Samudra-gupta issued these coins as commemorative medals, the name of the commemorator would naturally have appeared somewhere upon them, as it does on the admittedly commemorative issues of Agathokles and Eukratides. As it is, Samudra-gupta's own nâme is conspicuous by its absence on these coins.[1]

On the obverse of the coins of Chandra-gupta I, we see the king and his queen Kumāradevī standing and facing each other ; the king is probably giving the marriage ring to his consort. The names of both are engraved by their sides. On the reverse there is Durgā seated on a lion (Pl. II, 7). The legend is *Lichchhavayaḥ*, which is probably in acknowledgement of the help the Guptas had received from their Lichchhavi relations.[2]

In the realm of numismatics, conservatism was a very strong force in ancient times ; the early gold issues of the Guptas, therefore, closely resembled those of the later Kushāṇas to whose imperial position they succeeded in north. The obverse of the Kushāṇa prototype, the king standing and offering incense at the altar, is very common in the earlier stages of the Gupta coinage. The Hindu king is also to be seen wearing the Kushāṇa overcoat and trousers. His name is written perpendicularly under the arm, as on the Kushāṇa prototype. The reverse is again a close copy of the Kushāṇa type, which has Ardoksho seated on a high-backed throne. The Kushāṇa monograms also reappear with only slight variations (cf. Kācha-type, Pl. II, 8).

There was, however, a definite move to Hinduise the type soon afterwards. The Greek legend on the Kushāṇa prototype

---

[1] For a detailed discussion of this controversy see Altekar in *Num. Suppl.* XLVII. 105-111.

[2] See *ante*, pp. 128-29.

was replaced by the Brāhmī one from the very outset. The peaked Kushāṇa cap was never put upon the head of the Gupta emperor. Ardoksho on the reverse was hinduised usually by transforming her into the goddess Lakshmī and seating her on a lotus. Lakshmī, that was thus introduced on the reverse, was destined to figure on the gold coinage for more than a millennium; we find her not only on the coins of the Chedis and Gāhaḍavālas, but also on some coins of Mahmud bin Sam (Pl. II, 9).

The Kushāṇa prototype, king offering incense at the altar, lingered on for a few decades, but side by side with it, the Gupta mint masters introduced a number of original artistic types. Samudra-gupta's new types were the Archer type, the Battle-axe type, the Couch type, the Tiger-slayer type and the *Aśvamedha* (Horse sacrifice) type (Pl. III, 1). Chandra-gupta II added the Lion-slayer (Pl. III, 2), the Horseman and the *Chhatra* (Royal umbrella) types. The coins of most of these types are quite original in their conception and show no foreign influence whatsoever. Their execution is generally very fine, and the high-water mark of Hindu numismatic art may be seen in the *Aśvamedha* type of Samudra-gupta and the Lion-slayer type of Chandra-gupta II (Pl. III, 1 & 2), which are by far the best specimens of coins struck in ancient India. The art, however, began to decline in the reign of Kumāra-gupta I. The latter no doubt introduced two new types, the Peacock type and the Elephant-rider type, but his coins show a definite artistic deterioration, which was later accentuated by the declining fortunes of the empire. Skanda-gupta was content to issue coins of two types only, the King and Lakshmī type and the Archer type. His gold coins are heavily debased, a natural consequence of the depleted condition of the imperial treasury due to prolonged wars. The successors of Skanda-gupta were usually content to issue gold coins only of one type, the Archer type being the favourite one.

The Gupta gold coins at first followed the Kushāṇa weight standard of 120 grains, but in the reign of Chandra-gupta II it was raised to 124 gr. Some types of Kumāra-gupta I weigh as much as 132 gr. Skanda-gupta raised the weight to 144 grains and thus transformed his gold coins into *suvarṇas* of the traditional Indian standard of eighty *ratis*. Later Gupta rulers usually followed this standard.

The poetic renaissance, which was gathering strength in the Gupta age, is seen reflected in the coin legends, the majority of which are metrical and possess considerable poetic merit. One of them, introduced by Kumāra-gupta I, viz. '*Vijitāvaniravanipatiḥ Kumāragupto divaṁ jayati*' was destined to have a long life of more than two centuries. It was copied with the necessary change of the proper name not only by later Gupta kings, like Skanda-gupta and Budha-gupta, but also by the Hūṇa invader Toramāṇa and the Maukhari kings, like Iśānavarman and Avanti-varman. Even king Harsha requisitioned the same line for his coin-legend.

Silver coinage was started by the Guptas towards the end of the reign of Chandra-gupta II, when they came into contact with the silver currency of the Western Kshatrapas. The size, weight and fabric of these coins are closely similar to those of the Kshatrapa ones; and no wonder, for they were originally intended to circulate only in those provinces which were once included in the Kshatrapa kingdom. They, therefore, bear the Kshatrapa bust on the obverse, as also the meaningless traces of the once significant Greek legend. The year of issue is however given in the Gupta era and the *Garuḍa*, the emblem of the conquering dynasty, replaces the three-arched-Hill on the reverse (Pl. III, 3).

In the reign of Kumāra-gupta I, silver coinage was started also for the home provinces of the Gupta empire, and a new type was introduced which was naturally free from all foreign influences. The meaningless traces of Greek letters were discarded and the Kshatrapa bust was discontinued. The *Garuḍa* on the reverse was replaced by the peacock (Pl. III, 4), which is the mount (*vāhana*) of god Kumāra, after whom Kumāra-gupta himself was named. Towards the middle of the 5th century financial stringency compelled the Guptas to issue silver-plated coins; they have the Trident on the reverse. Among the later Gupta rulers only Skanda-gupta and Budha-gupta continued the silver coinage of the Peacock variety, but both its type and legend were continued by the Hūṇas, the Maukharis and the Pushyabhūtis, as observed above already.

9. The coinage of the Hūṇas.

The Hūṇas issued several coin types in silver and copper, but none of them is original. Their earliest coins, intended for currency in the conquered provinces of the Sassanian empire, closely imitate the Sassanian prototype. They are thin and large and have the Sassanian bust on the obverse and the Altar and Fire-attendants on the reverse. When the Hūṇas annexed Afghanistan and entered the Punjab, this type was gradually Indianised by the introduction of Hindu symbols like the conch, wheel, and trident; the legend was written in Brāhmī, instead of Pahlavī. (Pl. III, 5).

When the Hūṇas conquered the Punjab and Kashmir, they issued a copper currency closely imitating the Kushāṇa prototype with the standing king on the obverse and the seated goddess on the reverse. This type continued to prevail in Kashmir in a progressive deteriorating form till the end of the Hindu period. With the conquest of Central India, the Hūṇas came into contact with the Gupta coinage. They issued no gold coins, but were content to issue silver and copper pieces only, closely imitating those of the Guptas. The silver coins have the bust of the king on the obverse and the Peacock on the reverse, the legend being the same as that on the coins of Budha-gupta, with the proper name changed (cf. coin of Toramāṇa, Pl. III, 6). The copper coins have the bust of the king on the obverse, the reverse showing a symbol in the upper half and the name of the king in the lower (Pl. III, 7).

The thin broad pieces of the Sassanian type, which have the legend *Shāhi Javula*, are usually attributed to Toramāṇa (Pl. III, 8). Mihirakula, the successor of Toramāṇa, did not issue any coins imitating the Gupta coinage, a clear evidence that he did not retain a hold on the Gupta provinces for a long time. The reverse of his copper coins testifies to his faith in Śaivism; they have Bull in the upper half and the legend '*Jayatu Vṛishaḥ*' in the lower (Pl. III, 9).

10. Coinage in South India.

Among south Indian States, coinage was practically unknown during our period. The Sātavāhanas of the earlier age had issued some coins, which were current in their territory; the Roman coins, which frequently came as Roman imports, were also known. It seems that some of the Roman traders, who had settled down in the country, used to issue inferior imitations of the original Roman coins.[1] The southern States of our age however did not care to issue any coinage. We have so far come across no coins issued by the Pallavas, the Gaṅgas, the Ikshvākus of the Kadambas. The only exception in this connection is the petty Sālaṅkāyana dynasty, which ruled over a district or two in Andhradeśa. Six copper coins of only one of its rulers, Chandra-varman, have so far come to light.[2]

The apathy of south Indian states to issue its own coinage need not however cause any surprise. For coins were not very necessary for ordinary daily transactions and did not figure

[1] *JRAS.* 1904, pp. 609-614.
[2] *D.R. Bhandarkar Volume*, pp.213-6.

much even in the markets of northern India, the States in which used to have their own coinage. During our age things were about eight times cheaper than what they were in 1930. The Gupta gold coins, weighing about two thirds of a *tolā*, were therefore naturally twice as rare in the market as a hundred rupee note in modern times. Silver pieces (weighing about 35 grains) and copper coins could be used in daily transactions, but even the states in northern India did not care to issue them in abundant quantity. The copper coins of the Guptas are rarer than their gold issues.

The absence of small coins or change did not inconvenience the public, because ordinary daily trade transactions were carried by barter in villages and *cowries* in towns and cities.[1] Things being extremely cheap, a handful of *cowries* was quite sufficient for making purchases for the daily needs of life. They were the only currency of daily market transactions among all but the richest people down to the 16th century. Coins as a matter of fact figure in our records only in large transactions like the purchase of land or the creation of permanent endowments.

11. Relative values of Different Coins.

Let us now consider the question of the relative value of the different denominations of coins in different metals. The problem is very difficult to deal with, firstly because the data are meagre, and secondly because no fixed weight standard was followed, especially in the copper currency.

The average gold and silver coins of our period weighed 120 and 30 grains respectively. Towards the middle of the 5th century, the weight of the gold coins was raised to about 148 grains by the Guptas, and a record belonging to this period

[1] Fa-hien, p. 43.

suggests that 16 silver pieces were equal in value to one gold coin.[1] This would show that the ratio between the prices of gold and silver was as high as 7 : 2. The Gupta coins of 148 grains were however heavily adulterated and contained only about 50 per cent of gold. The real ratio between the prices of the two metal[2] seems to have been 7 : 1 which is somewhat higher than that in the Sātavahana age, which was 9 : 1.

Some Smṛitis of our period state that 16 copper *paṇas*, weighing 144 grains, were equal in value to 16 silver *kārshāpaṇas* weighing 56 grains. In our period however the normal silver coins issued by the Kshatrapas and the Guptas weighed only 30 grains, and they may have been equal to 16 copper *paṇas*, which weighed about 80 grains. The Guptas however have issued copper coins, apparently intended to weigh 100, 90, 75, 60, 50, 40, 30, 20 and 10 grains. The copper coins of the Nāgas vary from 20 to 40 grains, and those of the Mālavas from 2 to 40 grains. The coins of the Yaudheyas were on the other hand as heavy as 160 grains. It is not possible to state at present how many copper coins of these different denominations were equal to the silver coin of 30 grains. The ratio between the prices of silver and copper varied between 50 : 1 and 70 : 1.

---

1 *EI.* XXI, 81-82.

2 See *JNSI.* II, 1-15 for a detailed discussion of this subject.

CHAPTER XVI

COLONIAL AND CULTURAL EXPANSION.

I. COLONIAL EXPANSION IN INSUL-INDIA.

1. Hindu Colonial Kingdoms.

The early centuries of the Christian era are marked by an outburst of maritime and colonial enterprise in India, specially in the direction of the East Indies. Its beginnings may be traced to a much earlier period, but between 200 and 550 A.D., with which this volume deals, we have positive evidence of its scope and nature, and are in a position, for the first time, to trace its course with definiteness and some detail.

Indian literature, particularly the stories narrated in the Buddhist and Jaina books for purposes of edification, contain frequent references to merchants sailing to the east for purposes of trade.[1] The various islands and other localities mentioned in them cannot be always identified, but the stories leave the general impression that the eastern coast of Bay of Bengal and the islands in the East Indies were regarded in ancient India as the veritable *El dorado* which constantly allured enterprising traders by promising immense riches to them. This idea is also reflected in the name Suvarṇadvīpa or Suvarṇabhūmi (Land of Gold) which was used as a general designation for this vast region.[2]

By the end of the second century A.D. this commercial

---

[1] *Champā*, pp. xi ff. *Suvarṇadvīpa*, I, 37 ff. Similar stories are also found in Jaina works of later date, *e.g.*, in *Samarāichcha-kahā* by Haribhadra (*c.* 750 A.D.).

[2] *Suvarṇadvīpa*. I, 37 ff.

intercourse had not only led to the settlement of Indians in various parts to Suvarṇadvīpa, but also to the establishment of political authority by them in some regions. For the Chinese Annals and epigraphic evidence refer to states in Malay Peninsula, Java, Cambodia and Annam, with rulers bearing India names, as having existed in the second century A.D.

We may get a more definite idea of the nature of Hindu colonisation in this region by dealing with one or two specific kingdoms which have left behind positive memorials of Hindu culture and civilisation.

2. FU-NAN.[1]

One of the oldest Hindu kingdoms in this region was situated in Cambodia, and comprised nearly the whole of it along with Cochin-China. The Chinese call it Fu-nan and have preserved many details of its early history. According to the Chinese accounts the primitive people of this country hardly possessed any elements of civilisation, as both men and women went about naked. Civilisation was first introduced among them by Huen-tien (Kauṇḍinya), a follower of the Brahmanical religion. In particular he made the women wear clothes.

Huen-tien's descendants ruled for nearly a century when the throne passed to a new dynasty founded by Fan-Che-man, the general of the last king. The original form of this royal name cannot be restored, though Fan probably stands for *Varman*. Fan-Che-man laid the foundations of the greatness of Fu-nan. He built a powerful navy and conquered ten neighbouring kingdoms. Nearly the whole of Siam and parts of Laos and Malay Peninsula were brought under the supremacy of the kingdcm of Fu-nan, which may thus be regarded as the first Hindu colonial empire in this region.

---

1 *Kambuja-deśa*, pp. 26 ff.

Fu-nan established diplomatic relations both with India and China. Towards the end of the fourth or the beginning of the fifth century A.D., a Brahmin named Kauṇḍinya went from India to Fu-nan and was elected king by the people. This second stream of colonists, coming direct from India, completed the Brahmanical culture which was introduced more than three hundred years before.

Jaya-varman, a successor of Kauṇḍinya, sent Nāga-varman as ambassador to China in A.D. 484. It appears from the report of this ambassador, preserved in Chinese chronicles, that the dominant religious cult in Fu-nan was Śaivism, but Buddhism was also followed by many. During the reign of Jaya-varman two Buddhist monks of Fu-nan settled in China and translated canonical texts.

Jaya-varman's chief queen was Kulaprabhāvati. Both she and her son have left Sanskrit inscriptions, which show how thoroughly Indian culture and civilisation were implanted in this far-off colony. In addition to Śaivism and Buddhism the inscriptions refer to the prevalence of Vaishṇava cult.

Jaya-varman was succeeded by his elder son Rudra-varman. Of him also we possess a Sanskrit inscription. He sent several embassies to China between 517 and 539 A.D. and is the last king of Fu-nan referred to in the Chinese texts. During or shortly after his reign Fu-nan was invaded by the rulers of Kambuja, which was originally a vassal state in Northern Cambodia, but had grown very powerful under able rulers and had thrown off the yoke of Fu-nan. Before the end of the sixth century A.D. Fu-nan was conquered by Kambuja which now took its place as the dominant power.

3. CHAMPĀ.[1]

Another powerful Hindu kingdom was established in the country immediately to the east of Cambodia. The Hindus

[1] *Champā*, Chs. I-III.

called it Champā, and the country was known by this name until the nineteenth century when the Annamites finally drove away the king of Champā from his last stronghold in the south, and the whole country was called after them Annam.

The first historical Hindu king of Champā, so far known, is Śrī-Māra, who is mentioned in a Sanskrit inscription, and probably reigned in the second century A.D. The Chinese empire at this time extended up to Tonkin immediately to the north of Champā. The early Hindu kings of Champā made naval raids against the Chinese province and gradually extended the northern boundary of the kingdom at the expense of Tonkin.

A constant struggle with the imperial Chinese authority in Tonkin marks the first century of Hindu rule in Champā, and although we are wholly dependent upon the Chinese chronicles for an account of the struggle, it reflects great credit upon the brave sons of India. In 340 A.D. the king of Champā, called Fan-Wen by the Chinese, sent an envoy to the Chinese emperor, demanding that the Hoan Sonh mountains be recognised as the frontier between the two States. As this meant the cession of the district of Nhut-Nam, a vast extent of fertile territory, the Chinese emperor refused. But in 347 A.D. Fan-Wen led an expedition and conquered Nhut-Nam. In A.D. 349 he again defeated a vast Chinese army. Although he was himself wounded in the fight and died the same year, he had the satisfaction, before his death, of carrying the northern boundary of Champā to its furthest limits in the north.

During the reigns of the next two kings, Fan-Wen's son Fan-Fo (349-380) and grandson Fan-Hu-Ta (380-413), there was a continual war with the Chinese. The latter scored some success at first and recovered Nhut-Nam, but Fan-Hu-Ta not only reconquered it, but even carried his arms further to the north, as far as Than Hoa. This king is almost certainly identical with the king of Champā whose full name is given as

Dharma-Mahārāja Śri-Bhadra-varman in his Śanskrit inscriptions. He was a great scholar and was versed in the Vedas. He erected a temple of Śiva and called the image Bhadreśvara-svāmin, after his own name, following a well-known Indian practice. This Śiva temple, at Myson, became the national sonctuary of the Chams (the name by which the people of Champā are known).

Bhadra-varman's death was followed by a period of troubles which ended in the overthrow of the dynasty about 420 A.D. During this period a king Gaṅgārāja abdicated the throne in order to spend his last days on the Ganges.

The new dynasty continued the raids against Chinese territory. At last the Chinese emperor decided to send an expedition on a large scale. The preparations took three years, and in 446 A.D. the Chinese army invaded Champā. The Chams opposed a brave resistance and scored some success at first, but the vast Chinese army bore down all opposition, and at last the capital city Champā-purī fell into their hands.

The Chinese returned with a rich booty. The king of Champā now pursued a policy of peace, and sent embassies to the Chinese emperor with rich presents which the latter regarded as tribute.

In spite of some internal troubles Champā remained at peace with China for the next century. The last two kings Vijaya-varman (527 A.D.) and Rudra-varman (534 A.D.) sent regular embassies with tributes.

4. Other Kingdoms.

In addition to the two kingdoms in Annam and Cambodia, there were many other Hindu kingdoms in Indo-Chinese peninsula during the first five centuries of the Christian era. Unfortunately their political history for this early period is not known with definite details, and we can only refer to them in a general way.

Beginning from the north-west, Burmese traditions refer to the establishment of kingdoms by Hindu immigrants, both in Upper and Lower Burma, long before the beginning of the Christian era. Although we have no positive evidence in support of this, archaeological and other evidences leave no doubt that there were important Hindu settlements in various parts of the country during the early centuries of the Christian era. The kingdom of Śrīkshetra, with its capital near modern Prome, was an important Hindu kingdom, and is referred to in Chinese Annals as early as 3rd century A.D. The Hindu kingdom of Dvāravatī in Siam was also a powerful one, and served as the centre from which Hindu culture penetrated into the interior of the peninsula. It did not come into prominence till after the fall of Fu-nan, to which it was subject, but probably existed from an earlier date.[1]

Further south, in the Malay Peninsula, we have definite references to several Hindu States. One of these, founded in the second century A.D., is called by the Chinese Lang-kia-su. According to the Chinese chronicles a prince or a member of the royal family, having incurred the displeasure of the king, fled to India and was there married to the daughter of a king. When the king of Lang-kia-su died all on a sudden, the great officers of the state called back the prince and made him king. He died after a reign of 20 years and was succeeded by his son Bhagdato (Bhagadatta) who sent an envoy named Āditya to China in 515 A.D.[2]

Hindu kingdoms were also established in various islands in the East Indies during the first centuries of the Christian era.

---

[1] R. C. Majumdar, *Hindu Colonies in the Far East*, p. 222.
[2] *Suvarṇadvīpa*, I, 73.

In Java[1] the local tradition refers the first Hindu colony to the first century A.D. But there is no doubt that a Hindu kingdom was established by the beginning of the second century A.D.; for we learn from Chinese chronicles that king Deva-varman of Java sent an embassy to China in 132 A.D. Four Sanskrit inscriptions, found in West Java, refer to a king Pūrṇa-varman and his two ancestors. The inscriptions are not dated, but may be referred, on palaeographical grounds, to the sixth century A.D., though some would refer them to the fourth. We have thus got evidence for the existence of a thoroughly Hinduised kingdom in Western Java. Fa-hien, who stayed in Java for five months in 414-415 A.D. during his return journey from India, has also described the country as a stronghold of Brahmanical religion.

The neighbouring island of Bali[2] was also a rich Hindu kingdom, and one of its kings sent an envoy to China in 518 A.D.

The Hindu kingdom of Śrīvijaya[3] was founded in Sumatra in or before the fourth century A.D. It rose to great power and eminence in the seventh century A.D. as will be related later, but not much is known of its early history. Even in the island of Borneo,[4] the home of the head-hunting Dayaks, Hindus established a kingdom as early as the fourth century A.D., if not before. Four Sanskrit inscriptions, which may be dated about 400 A.D., record the rich donations and sacrifices of king Mūla-varman, son of Aśva-varman and grandson of king Kuṇḍunga (Kauṇḍinya). The stone pillars on which the inscriptions are engraved were the *Yūpas* (sacrificial pillars) set up by Brāhmaṇas to commemorate the great sacrifice called *Bahu-suvarṇakam* (large quantity of gold) performed by king

---

[1] *Ibid.* Ch. VI, pp. 91 ff.
[2] *Ibid.* Ch. IX, pp. 132 ff.
[3] *Ibid* Ch. VII, pp. 116 ff.
[4] *Ibid.* Ch. VIII, pp. 125 ff.

Mūla-varman and his gift of 20,000 cows to the Brāhmaṇas in the holy field of Vaprakeśvara.

The establishment of kingdoms by Hindus in different parts of the East Indies and the Indo-Chinese Peninsula may not be regarded as the deliberate expansion of political authority by any Indian State or States. There is nothing to suggest that an Indian monarch planned or equipped any expedition to effect any conquest in these far-off lands. They seem to have been the result of individual enterprise,—successful efforts of men of superior ability, by virtue of their higher culture and military skill, to impose their authority upon primitive peoples. There is nothing to indicate that the Indian States derived any political advantage from this extensive colonisation. It is even doubtful whether the colonial powers maintained any regular contact with the political powers in India, though the claims of Samudra-gupta that he exercised suzerainty over all the islands might have reference to some of them. But the most outstanding effect of the establishment of these Hindu colonies was the spread of Hindu culture and civilisation in these regions.

5. Hindu Civilisation in Sūvarṇadvīpa.[1]

It seems almost to be a universal law, that when an inferior civilisation comes into contact with a superior one, it gradually tends to be merged into the latter, the rate and the extent of this process being determined solely by the capacity of the one to assimilate, and of the other to absorb. When the Hindus first appeared in Malayasia, and came into close association with her peoples, this process immediately set in, and produced the inevitable result.

[1] The facts relating to any particular colony, as stated below, will be found in the chapter in *Champā* or *Suvarṇadvīpa* dealing with its history to which reference has been given above; cf. also *Suvarṇadvīpa*, I, 138 ff.

The inscriptions discovered at Borneo, Java, Annam, Cambodia and Malay Peninsula lead inevitably to the conclusion that the language, literature, religion, and political and social instiutions of India made a thorough conquest of these far-off lands, and, to a great extent, eliminated or absorbed the native elements in these respects.

The inscriptions of Fu-nan and Champā show a thorough acquaintance with the Puranic religion and mythology. The inscriptions of Mūla-varman hold out before us a court and a society thoroughly saturated with Brahmanical culture. The inscriptions discovered in Western Java also present before us a strongly Brahmanized society and court. We have reference to Hindu gods like Vishṇu and Indra, and Airāvata, the elephant of Indra. The Indian months and attendant astronomical details, and Indian system of measurement of distance are quite familiar to the soil. Besides, in the river-names Chandrabhāgā and Gomatī we have the beginnings of that familiar practice of transplanting Indian geographical names to the new colonies.

The images of various gods and goddesses discovered in Borneo and Malay Peninsula corroborate the evidence of the inscriptions. Images of Vishṇu, Brahmā, Śiva, Gaṇeśa, Nandi, Skanda and Mahākāla have been found in Borneo, and those of Durgā, Gaṇeśa, Nandī and Yoni in the Malay Peninsula. The thorough preponderance of the Puranic form of the Hindu religion is also proved by the remains at Tuk Mas in Java. Here we get the usual attributes of Vishṇhu and Śiva,—the *Saṁkha* (conch-shell), *Chakra* (wheel), *Gadā* (mace), and *Padma* (lotus) of the former, and the *Triśula* (trident) of the latter. Besides, the inscription refers to the sanctity of the Ganges.

The images and inscriptions prove that in addition to the Brahmanical religion Buddhism had also made its influence felt in these regions. Taken collectively, the inscriptions prove that the Sanskrit language and literature were highly cultivated. Most of the records are written in good and almost flawless Sanskrit. Indian scripts were adopted everywhere. The images show the thorough-going influence of Indian Art.

The archaeological evidence is corroborated and supplemented by the writings of the Chinese. First of all, we have the express statement of Fa-hien that Brahmanism was flourishing in Yava-dvīpa, and that there was very little trace of Buddhism. The 200 merchants who boarded the vessel along with Fa-hien were all followers of the Brahmanical religion. This statement may be taken to imply that trade and commerce were still the chief stimulus to Indian colonisation. As the merchants belonged mostly to the Brahmanical religion, we get an explanation of its preponderance over Buddhism in the Archipelago.

But that Buddhism soon made its influence felt in Java appears clearly from the story of Guṇa-varman, preserved in a Chinese work compiled in 519 A.D. Guṇa-varman, a prince of Kashmir (Ki-pin), was of a religious mood from his boyhood. When he was thirty years old, the king of Kashmir died without issue and the throne was offered to him. But he rejected the offer and went to Ceylon. Later he proceeded to Java and converted the Queen-mother to Buddhism. Gradually the king, too, was persuaded by his mother to adopt the same faith. At this time Java was attacked by hostile troops, and the king asked Guṇa-varman whether it would be contrary to the Buddhist law if he fought against his enemy. Guṇa-varman replied that it was the duty of everybody to punish robbers. The knig then went to fight and obtained a great victory. Gradually the Buddhist religion was spread throughout the country. The king now wished to take to the life of a monk, but was dissuaded from this course by his ministers, on the express condition, that henceforth no living creatures should be killed throughout the length and breadth of the kingdom.

The name and fame of Guṇa-varman had now spread in all directions. In 424 A.D. the Chinese monks requested their emperor to invite Guṇa-varman to China. Accordingly, the Chinese emperor sent messengers to Guṇa-varman and the king of Java. Guṇa-varman embarked on a vessel, owned by the Hindu merchant Nandin, and reached Nanking in A.D. 431. A few months later he died at the age of sixty-five.

In addition to religion, the influence of Hindu civilisation is also clearly marked in the political and social ideas and the system of administration. We may refer in this connection to a State called Tan-Tan, the exact location of which it is difficult to determine. This kingdom sent ambassadors to China in 530, 535, and 666 A.D. We get the following account in the Chinese annals : "The family name of its king was Kchsatriya (Kshatriya) and his personal name Silingkia (Śṛiṅga). He daily attends to business and has eight great ministers, called the 'Eight Seats' all chosen from among the Brāhmaṇas. The king rubs his body with perfumes, wears a very high hat, and necklace of different kinds of jewels. He is clothed in muslin and shod with leather slippers. For short distances he rides in a carriage, but for long distances he mounts an elephant. In war they always blow conches and beat drums."

The following customs of Ka-la, referred to by the Chinese, are also Indian in origin. "When they marry they give no other presents than areca-nuts, sometimes as many as two hundred trays. The wife enters the family of her husband. Their musical instruments are a kind of guitar, a transversal flute, copper cymbals, and iron drums. Their dead are burned, the ashes put into a golden jar and sunk into the sea."

Two of the three inscriptions of Fu-nan,[1] referred to above, are fairly long compositions and indicate, more than

[1] These inscriptions have been edited by Coedès; the first two in *BEFEO*. XXXI, 1 ff and the third in *JGIS*. IV, 117.

anything else, the deminance of Indian literary style and Indian social and religious ideas in these colonies. They refer to large settlements of Brahmins, versed in the Vedas, the Upavedas and Vedāṅgas and also to the Kshatriyas and their high ideals. They faithfully reflect the Indian outlook on life and society and may be regarded as undying memorials of the triumph of Hindu civilisation in these far-off colonies.

6. The Malay Peninsula[1].

From a very early period, the Malay Peninsula played a very important part in the maritime and colonising activity described above. Indeed, its geographical position made it the centre of the carrying trade between China and the western world. It must have been known to India from very early times, probably long before the Christian era.

Actual remains of early Hindu civilisation in the Malay Peninsula, though scanty, are not altogether lacking. There are the remains of a Hindu temple and a few stone images at Sungai Batu Estate at the foot of Gunong Jerai (Keddah Peak). The remains of a brick-built Buddhist shrine, discovered in its neighbourhood, at Keddah, may be dated approximately in the fourth or fifth century A.D. on the strentgh of a Sankrit inscription found in it. Similarly remnants of pillars, which once adorned some Buddhist temples, have been found in the northern part of Province Wellesley. These also may be dated in the fourth or fifth century A.D. on the strength of inscriptions engraved on them. A gold ornament, bearing the figure of Vishṇu on his Garuḍa, was unearthed at Selinsing (Perak), and also in a hole left by the roots of a fallen tree, a Cornelian seal engraved with the name of a Hindu prince Śrī Vishṇu-varman, in characters of the fifth century A.D.

---

[1] *Suvarṇadvīpa*, I, Ch. V, pp. 65 ff.

Ruins of shrines exist in the region round Takua Pa, which has been identified with Ptolemy's Takkola. Opposite Takua Pa, on the eastern coast, round the Bay of Bandon, are the remains of early settlements, specially in the three well-known sites Caiya, Nakhon Sri Dhammarat, and Vieng Sra. The temples and images of these places may be of somewhat later date, but the inscriptions found at Ligor and Takua Pa, and the Sanskrit inscription on a pillar at Caiya show that these settlements could not be later than the fourth or fifth century A.D.

A large number of inscriptions have been discovered in different parts of the country. They are written in Sanskrit and in Indian alphabets of about the fourth or fifth century A.D. Two of them reproduce a well-known formula of the Buddhist creed, and this proves the spread of Buddhism in that region. These inscriptions clearly testify to the fact that the Indians had established colonies in the northern, western and the eastern sides of the Malay Peninsula by at least fourth and fifth centuries A.D., and that the colonists belonged to both northern and southern India.

One of these inscriptions refers to "the captain (*Mahā-nāvika*, the great sailor) Buddhagupta, an inhabitant of Rakta-mṛittikā". Rakta-mṛittika, which means 'red-clay', has been identified with a place still called Rāṅgāmāṭi (red clay) 12 miles south of Murshidabad.

The archaeological remains in the Malay Peninsula confirm what might have been deduced on general grounds from literary evidence. Takkola (modern Takua Pa) was the first landing stage of the Indian traders and colonists. Form this port some crossed the mountain range over to the rich wide plain on the opposite coast round the Bay of Bandon. From this centre they could proceed by land or sea to Siam, Cambodia, Annam, and even further east. This trans-peninsular route, marked by the remains of Indian settlements, was followed by many who wanted to avoid the long and risky voyage through the Straits of Malacca. That this second route was also very popular and largely used is indicated by the archaeological remains in the Province Wellesley This all-sea route was naturally preferred by many traders who wanted to avoid transhipment, and offered a shorter passage to Java and southern Sumatra. On the whole the Malay Peninsula may be regarded as the main gate of the Indian colonial empire in the Far East. The report of the Archaeological Mission in the Malay Peninsula contains interesting observations regarding Hindu colonisation in this land which may be summed up as follows :—

"The colonies were large in number and situated in widely remote centres, such as Chumphon, Caiya, the Valley of the river Bandon, Nakhon Sri Dhammarat (Ligor), Yale (near Patani), and Selensing (in Pahang) on the eastern coast; and Malacca, Province Wellesley, Takua Pa, and the common delta of the rivers Lanya and Tenasserim, on the western. The most important of these was unquestionably that of Nakhon Sri Dhammarat (Ligor). It was an essentially Buddhist colony which probably built the great *stūpa* of Nakhon Sri Dhammarat and part of the fifty temples which surrounded it. A little to the north was the colony of Caiya, which appears to have been at first Brahmanical, and then Buddhist. These two groups of colonies were mainly agriculturists. The others which occupied Selensing, Panga, Puket, and Takua Pa, prospered by the exploitation of tin and gold-mines.

"The available evidence justifies the assumption that the region around the Bay of Bandon was a cradle of Further Eastern culture, inspired by waves of Indian influence spreading across the route from Takua Pa. There is a strong persistent local tradition in favour of an early migration of Indians across the route from the west. At the same time persons of an Indian cast of features are common on the west coast near Takua Pa, while colonies of Brahmans of Indian descent survive at Nakhon Sri Dhammarat and Patalung, and trace the arrival of their ancestors from India by an overland route across the Malay Peninsula."

II. CULTURAL RELATIONS WITH EASTERN TURKESTAN AND CHINA.[1]

The whole of Eastern Turkestan, from Kashgar right up to the frontier of China, had grown into a sort of Greater India by the beginning of the 4th century A.D. The slow but regular infiltration of Indian civilisation in this area during the preceding centuries, and the contact that was being constanly maintained between China and India by the routes of Eastern Turkestan, led to the establishment of Indian civilisation in almost all corners of this region. The kingdoms in the southern part of this region were from west to east—Śailadeśa (Chinese—Shu-lei, Kashgar), Cokkuka— (Chinese—So-kiu, Yarkand), Khotaṁna (Chinese—Yu-t'ien, Khoṭan), and Calmada (Chinese—Che-mo-tang-na, Shan-shan); and in the northern part—Bharuka (Chinese—P'o-lu-kia, Uch-Turfan), Kuchi (Chinese—Kiue-tse, Kuchar), Agnideśa (Chinese—Yen-ki, Karasahr) and Kao-ch'ang (Turfan). Among these kingdoms Khotan in the south and Kuchi in the north were playing the most important rôle in the dissemination of Indian culture in Central Asia and China.

In some of these localities, specially in the south, there was a strong Indian element is the native population. This was due mainly to a regular Indian immigration in an earlier period and the consequent foundation of Indian colonies.

---

[1] The following works may be used as general references for this subject :

(i) Hoernle—*Manuscript Remains of Eastern Turkestan.*
(ii) *Travels of Fa-hien*—translated by H. A. Giles.
(iii) P. C. Bagchi—*Le Canon Bouddhique en Chine*, Vol. I.
(iv) P. C. Bagchi—*India and China.*

Brisk trade relations between North-Western India and some of the kingdoms in this area also led to Indian colonial expansion. Evidence of the existence of such colonies is available not only from the currency of a Prākṛit dialect, akin to the North-western Prākṛit, in certain areas in the southern part of Eastern Turkestan, but also from the deep cultural influence of India in the whole of Eastern Turkestan.

This influence was further strengthened by the introduction of Buddhism in early centuries of the Christian era. Buddhism became the established religion practically in all kingdoms of Eastern Turkestan in the beginning of the Gupta period. It brought to many of the local people a religion and a literary culture for the first time. Indian script was adopted in most of the localities,—Kashgar, Khotan, Shan-Shan, Kuchar and Karasahr. In the earlier period it was the Kharoshṭhī script which got currency in the southern region, but in the Gupta period it was the North Indian Brāhmī that was adopted in all the localities both in the south and the north. The Gupta script, as modified in this area, is generally styled "Slanting Gupta". The language of culture was also in many places Sanskrit. Fa-hien is the first to speak about it. He says : "From this point (Lob region) travelling westwards the nations that one passes through are all similar in this respect (*i.e.* in the practice of the religion of India), and all those who have left the family (*i.e.* priests and novices) study Indian books and the Indian spoken language". That Sanskrit was seriously cultivated by the Buddhist monks of Eastern Turkestan is also proved by the very large number of Sanskrit Buddhist texts discovered in various parts of the country. There are also bilingual texts in Indian script consisting of Sanskrit texts and their translations in local languages. These bilingual documents furnish the oldest and sometimes the only remains of some of the ancient local languages of which no other race has as yet been found.

It was customary for the Buddhist scholars of India, specially from Kashmir, to travel to Eastern Turkestan in those days. Many of them even settled down in the monasteries of the principal cities in this region. They were mainly responsible for the dissemination of the knowledge of the Sanskrit Buddhist texts. They were a source of attraction and inspiration not only to the local monks but also to the Chinese. The latter were drawn to them with the expectation of getting a first-hand knowledge of Buddhist lore. As early as 260 A.D. a Chinese Buddhist monk named Chu She-hing, who was probably the first to come out of China for education in the Buddhist lore, came to Khotan to study Sanskrit and the Buddhist texts with Indian scholars of Gomati-*vihāra*, which was the principal religious establishment there. When Fa-hien passed through Khotan he found the place equally important as a centre of Buddhist culture. In the middle of the 5th century, a Chinese noble, Ts'i-kiu King-sheng, who had become a convert to Buddhism, passed sometime in the Gomati-*vihāra* of Khotan studying Sanskrit with Indian scholars. It was therefore considered by the outsiders as good as an Indian centre of Buddhist learning.

It was not merely Buddhism, but along with it other elements of Indian culture also had migrated to Eastern Turkestan. The discovery of a number of Indian medical texts of the early Gupta period, and of fragments of other medical texts, translated in the local languages, specially in the ancient language of Kuchar, clearly testifies to the currency of Indian medical system in this region.

A still more important Indian influence may be observed in the field of Art. The numerous remains of Buddhist images, monasteries and grottoes in various parts of the country contain relics of Indian sculpture and painting of this period. Apart from the question of Indian influence by the side of other influences such as Western Asiatic, Iranian and Chinese, there is also the problem of pure Indian tradition of art being carried to Eastern Turkestan. In some places the art-relics point out to an extension of the Gandhāra school without any modification. The influence of Gupta art, specially in the fresco paintings of the Buddhist grottoes, is not small. In sculpture, too, the influence of this classical Indian art sometimes assumes a dominating character.

A somewhat detailed account of some of the principal kingdoms in Eastern Turkestan will make the position clearer. Two at least, Khotan in the south and Kuchar in the north, exercised the most preponderating rôle in the history of Ser-Indian culture in the period under consideration. Fa-hien has left a full account of Buddhism in Khotan. He says : "They have all received the faith, and find their amusement in religious music. The priests number several tens of thousands, most of them belonging to the Greater Vehicle. They all obtain their food from a common stock. The people live scattered about ; and before the door of every house they build small pagodas, the smallest of which would be about twenty feet in height." Fa-hien further tells us that during his stay in Khotan he was lodged in the Gomati-*vihāra*. The priests of this *Vihāra* also were followers of Mahāyāna. The monastery accommodated about 3000 monks. "At the sound of a gong, three thousand priests assemble to eat. When they enter the refectory, their demeanour is grave and ceremonious : they sit down in regular order ; they all keep silence : they make no clatter with their bowls etc. ; and for the attendants to serve more food, they do not call out to them, but only make signs with their hands." There were then fourteen large monasteries in Khotan and, besides, numerous small ones. An annual procession of images like Indian *Ratha Yātrās* also used to take place in Khotan in those days. On this occasion streets used to be swept and all the houses decorated. In this procession the Gomati-*vihāra* had the first place. "At a distance of three or four *li* from the city, a four-wheeled-image-car is made over thirty feet in height, looking like a movable 'Hall of Buddha' and adorned with the seven preciosities, with streaming pennants and embroidered canopies. The image of Buddha is placed in the middle of the car, with two attendant Bodhisattvas and Devas following behind. These are all beautifully carved in gold and silver and are suspended in the air. When the images are one hundred paces from the city gate, the king takes off his cap of State and puts on new clothes ; walking barefoot and holding flowers and incense in his hands, with attendants on each side, he proceeds out of the gate. On meeting the image, he bows his head down to the ground, scatters flowers and burns the incense." Fa-hien next speaks of the second large monastery in the city which he calls "the King's New Monastery." It took eighty years to build it and three generations of kings helped in its construction. It was 250 feet in height and was ornamentally carved and overlaid with gold and silver. The hall of Buddha behind it was splendidly decorated. Its beams, pillars, folding doors, and windows are all gilt. Besides this, there are appartments for priests, also beautifully and fitly decorated, beyond expression in words. The kings of the six countries to the east of the Bolor Tagh range (*i.e.* Eastern Turkestan) make large offerings of whatsoever most valuable things they may have, keeping few for their own personal use."

The account of Fa-hien which belongs to the closing years of the 4th century A.D. gives a true picture of Buddhism as practised in Khotan in those days. It shows that the king and the people were devout followers of the faith ; they lavishly spent for the maintenance of the church and showed personal respects on occasions of public ceremonies. The priests also were not yet unworthy of the true traditions of their faith and were strict followers of the Buddhist rules of decorum. Besides, the monasteries still enjoyed high prestige as centres of learning. Contemporary Chinese accounts of Indian Buddhist scholars who had gone to China also tell us that the Buddhist monasteries of Khotan possessed Sanskrit manuscripts which could no longer be found in India. Thus one of the Indian scholars, Dharmakshema, who was working in China in the beginning of the 5th century, proposed in 433 A.D. to go to Khotan in search of the manuscript of the *Mahāparinirvāṇa-Sūtra* of Mahāyāna which could be found only there.

The remains of ancient Buddhist culture have been discovered mainly in the abandoned sites of Yotkan, Rawak, Dandan-Uilik and Niya in the neighbourhood of modern Khotan. Fragments of manuscripts, images, paintings etc. all go to confirm the fact that Indian Buddhist culture was prevalent in this area till the eighth century, the most flourishing period being that which corresponds to the Gupta age.

It was from Khotan that this culture spread eastwards along the southern route up to the frontier of China via Shanshan (Lob region). Khotan was also connected with Karasahr region by a direct route through the Tarim desert which was however rarely followed by the travellers. Fa-hien followed this route while coming from Karsahar to Khotan. Indian travellers might have followed this route while going eastwards from Khotan, but the more usual route, at least in the later period, was from Kashgar towards Kuchar by way of ancient Bharuka (Uch-Turfan).

The kingdom of Kuchi played the same immportant rôle in the north as that of Khotan in the south. The people long settled in the country were a white race and spoke a language of the Indo-European family. This lost language has now been deciphered and interpreted with the help of old Buddhist texts. It has been variously styled by the scholars—Tokharian Kuchean, Arśi etc. The people of Kuchi had adopted Buddhism very early. The Chinese records tell us that in the beginning of the fourth century the number of *stūpas* and temples in the country was nearly 10,000. This figure may not be taken too literally. It probably means to say that the number was very high. The history of the first Tsin dynasty gives a more faithful account of the state of Buddhism in Kuchi in the 4th and 5th centuries A.D.

The account says : "The kingdom of Kuchi possessed numerous monasteries. Their decoration is magnificent. The royal palace also had standing images of Buddha as in a monastery. There is a convent named *Ta-mu* which had 170 monks. The convent named *Che-li* on the northern hill had 50 monks. The new convent of the king named *Kien-mu* had 60. The convent of the king of Wen-su 70. These four convents were under the direction of Buddhasvāmin. The monks of these convents change their residence in every three months. Before completing five years after ordination they are not permitted to stay in the King's convent even for one night. This convent has 90 monks. There is a young monk there named Kiu-kin (? mo) -lo (Kumārajīva) who has great capacity and knowledge and has studied the Mahāyāna. Buddhasvāmin is his teacher but he has changed as Buddhasvāmin is of the Āgama school.

"The convent of *A-li* has 180 nuns, that of *Liun-jo-kan* has 50, and that of *A-li-po* has 30. These three convents are also under the direction of Buddhasvāmin. The nuns receive regular Śikshāpadas ; the rule in the foreign countries is that the nuns are not allowed to govern themselves. The nuns in these three convents are generally the daughters or wives of kings and princes (of countries) to the east of the Pamirs. They come from long distances to these monasteries for the sake of the law. They regulate their practices. They have a very severe rule. They change their residence once in every three months. Excepting the three chief nuns they do not go out. They observe five hundred presciptions of the law."

Buddhist culture therefore had a stronghold in Kuchi.

Both the rulers and the people were devout followers of the faith. The literary remains of ancient Kuchi amply confirm this supposition. Apart from Buddhist religion and art, the people of Kuchi had also adopted other elements of Indian culture. The kings had adopted Indian names, such as Swarnate (Svarṇadeva), Arte (Haradeva), Suvarṇapushpa, Haripushpa, etc. Indian system of music was known in Kuchi and it was taken to China by the musicians of that country. It is probable that Indian families had also migrated to Kuchi and intermarried with the local people. There is at least one striking example of such an intermarriage of which the issue stands as a sort of symbol of Ser-Indian intercourse. As the biography of this man throws a fiood of light on how this intercourse was taking place at least in the 4th century it may be treated here in some details.

The father of this famous man was Kumārāyana. He belonged to a family of ministers in India but abandoned his claim when his turn of succession came, adopted a religious life and left for foreign countries. He was cordially received by the king of Kuchi and was appointed his *Rājaguru*. This king was king Po-shun. Kumārāyana was not, however, destined to lead a monastic life. The sister of the king of Kuchi, Jīvā by name, fell in love with Kumārāyana and the two were married. The first issue of this marriage was a boy who was given the name of Kumārajīva after the names of the father and the mother. After the birth of a second son, who was named Pushyadeva, Jīvā embraced the Buddhist faith and become a nun. Kumārajīva was then only seven years old. He was, however, a boy of extraordinary intelligence. He soon learnt from his mother to recite the holy texts. His mother soon realised the need of taking him to India for further education. At the age of nine the boy started with his mother, and after travelling in different places at last reached Kashmir. He was placed under a famous teacher named Bandhudatta who was a cousion of the king of Kashmir. He studied the Āgamas and other texts under the latter's direction.

After three years of study in Kashmir Kumārajīva started on his return journey with his mother. They stopped for sometime in Kashgar where Kumārajīva studied the four Vedas, the five sciences, the Brahmanical philosophy and astronomy. They then went to Cokkuka (Yarkand). Kumārajīva was initiated there in Mahāyāna Buddhism and studied the works of famous Mahāyāna teachers like Nāgārjuna, Āryadeva, etc. After travelling in a few other places they at last returned to Kuchi where Kumārajīva took his residence in the "King's new monastery."

Kumārajīva's reputation had by then spread to different parts of Eastern Turkestan and both nobles and common people soon began to flock round him for instruction in the law. He used to recite the *Sūtras* in the largest monastery of Kuchi, the Tsiao-li monastery, and also explain the texts to the people. He thus started playing a great rôle in the dissemination and interpretation of the Buddhist religion in Eastern Turkestan. Kuchi now faced a Chinese invasion. All kingdoms to the west of Kuchi helped the Chinese invader and Kuchi stood alone. The king turned down a proposal for surrender and fought bravely. But the town fell to the invader. The Chinese general set up a new king on the throne in 383 A.D. and returned to China with a number of prisoners among whom was also found Kumārajīva. But his worth was known to the Chinese and he was obliged to remain with the local chief of Ku-tsang in Kan-su till 398 A.D. He had the highest regard for Kumārajīva.

In spite of repeated invitations from the emperor Kumārajīva was not allowed to proceed to the capital before 401 A.D. On his arrival at capital a number of scholars was placed under him to help him in the work of translations of Sanskrit texts into Chinese. Scholars from various parts of China came to him for study. His knowledge of Chinese and Sanskrit was perfect and that is why his translations are of a high literary value. He translated within a few years about 106 Sanskrit texts into Chinese and some of these texts were quite extensive. He was the first to interpret the Mahāyāna philosophy to the Chinese. Kumārajīva died in 412 A.D. but the service which he rendered to the cause of Buddhism in China was lasting. His Chinese disciples gave a new orientation to the faith. Their interpretation made Buddhism acceptable to the Chinese and it ceased to be looked upon as a foreign religion.

Kumārajīva was also responsible for attracting best Indian scholars to China. In number of Indian scholars who had gone to China before his time was not considerable and Buddhist missionaries of foreign nationalities were then more active. Kumārajīva had personal touch with the Buddhist scholars of Kashmir, and it was through his intervention that some of the Kashmirian scholars were induced to go first to Kuchi and then to China. One of them as Puṇyatrāta who came to China most probably in 403 A.D. and worked there in collaboration with Kumārajīva. The other was Buddhayaśas who was also a Kashmirian scholar settled at Kashgar. It was probably there that he came in contact with Kumārajīva. The attachment was so great that when Kuchi was invaded by the Chinese army Buddhayaśas exercised all his influence with the king of Kashgar and induced him to march with his army to the help of Kuchi. But it was already too late and the town had fallen before he could render any help. Later on Buddhayaśas went to Kuchi and then to the capital of China at the special request of Kumārajīva. During his stay in China he collaborated with the latter in the work of translation. Of other Kashmirian scholars who had gone to China in the 5th century mention may be made of Gautama Saṅghadeva, Dharmayaśas, Guṇavarman, Guṇabhadra, and Buddhavarman. A few other Indian scholars from other parts of India had also been to China in this period. Most of them remained in China and died there. They were responsible for numerous translations of the canonical texts from the Sanskrit Tripiṭaka, specially of the Sarvāstivāda school of which the largest centre was then in Kashmir. They contributed the most to the interpretation of Indian culture of the Chinese and the establishment of a relation of amity between the two countries which for many centuries yielded a fruitful result.

CHAPTER XVII.

INTERCOURSE WITH THE WESTERN WORLD.

It has now been established on good authority that from remote antiquity India had trade relations with western countries both by land and sea. The overland route passed through Khyber to the Upper Kabul valley, and thence across the Hindu Kush to Balkh, which stood on the great highway connecting the East and the West. There were several routes from Balkh both towards Central Asia and China on the east, and to the Mediterranean and Black Sea on the West. One of the western routes went down the Oxus to the Caspian, and the wares were then carried, partly by land and partly by river, to the Black Sea ports. The other skirted the Karmanian desert to the north, and having passed through the 'Caspian Gates' reached Antioch by way of Ctesiphon and Hekatompylos.

The sea-routes from the mouth of the Indus lay, in ancient times, along the coast to the mouth of the Euphrates. Then ships either proceeded up the Euphrates and touched the overland route at the point where it crossed that river ; or continued the coastal voyage along the shores of Arabia and through the Red Sea to its head near Suez. From this point goods were carried by land to Egypt on the west and to famous ports like Tyre and Sidon on the north. It must not be understood, however, that Indian traders travelled direct from the beginning to the end of these routes, for the merchandise often changed hands at important towns and harbours.

But even when direct sea-voyage was made the sailors had to keep close to the coast. The great discovery, made by Hippalus about 45 A.D., of the "existence of the monsoon winds, blowing regularly across the Indian ocean", enabled the ships to sail straight across the Indian Ocean.[1] From Okelis, the port at the mouth of the Red Sea, the monsoon winds would carry a ship in forty days or even less to Muziris (Cranganore on the Malabar coast). Thus Alexandria was now less than three months' journey from the Indian coast. Henceforth the ships from Southern India could avoid the long coastal voyage.

The establishment of the Roman empire gave a great impetus to the Indian trade. The *Pax Romana* secured the trade routes, and the articles of luxury from India were in great demand in Rome. The volume of trade was, therefore, increased to an unprecedented extent. According to Pliny nearly fifty million *sesterces* flowed every year from Rome to India to pay for the balance of trade. This statement is borne out by the huge hoards of Roman coins unearthed in Indian soil. Sewell, who has made a special study of these coins, is of opinion that the Indo-Roman trade flourished in the early days of the Roman empire, culminated about the time of Nero, who died in A.D. 68, and declined from this time till it almost ceased after Caracalla (A.D. 217). It revived again, though slightly, under the Byzantine Emperors.[2]

The general conclusion of Sewell about the large volume of trade between India and Rome during the first century A.D. admits of no doubt. But his more detailed statements regarding the condition of trade in different periods do not stand on the same ground, being based merely on the negative evidence of Roman coins in India. These coins, mostly discovered in South India, are undoubtedly the result of direct maritime trade between Roman empire and India. But other coins are also known[3] and we have to consider also the overland trade,

---

[1] This is the general view, but Kennedy maintains that the monsoons must have been known from the earliest times (*JRAS*. 1898, pp. 272-3).

[2] *JRAS*. 1904, pp. 591 ff.

[3] According to Cunningham, "Roman gold coins are plentiful down to the time of Caracalla". (*JASB*. LVIII, 158). Four Roman coins have recently been discovered in Bilaspur and Vizagapatam districts, of which

which, though for a time partly deflected from its course, and perhaps reduced in volume, by the rise of Parthian and Sassanid kingdom, continued as an important factor for several centuries. It flourished so much in the 4th century A.D. that "silk, worth in Aurelian time its weight in gold and a luxury of the rich and noble, was in the reign of Julian sold at a price which brought it within every man's reach."[1]

In addition to the old land-route across Iran and Mesopotamia, we find two new routes coming into favour, leading to the two famous trade centres, Palmyra and Petra. In the first, the goods were brought by sea from India to the head of the Persian Gulf, then along the Euphrates to Vologesia and thence by land to Palmyra. In the second, Indian ships coming up the Red Sea unloaded their goods at the two ports on the Arabian coast of the Red Sea, *viz.* Aelana (ancient Ezion Geber) and Leuke Kome, and being carried by land to Petra were thence transported to Mediterranean ports Ghaza and Rhinokolura. Fine muslins, pearls, beryls, precious stones, incense, and drugs, among others, formed, as before, the cheif articles of trade. After the overthrow of the Nabataean kingdom of Petra in A.D. 105, Palmyra gained the commercial pre-eminence on the principal land-route between Roman Empire and India, and retained this position till it was sacked by Aurelian in A.D. 273. After the destruction of Palmyra, Indian trade was continued for a time through Batne, near the Euphrates, and a day's journey from Edessa. About the close of the third century A.D. Alexandria, too, fell into decay, and the Indian trade was carried on through Arab vessels. Adule, a petty village on the African coast, grew into a great centre of commerce. Roman trade with the east revived under Constantine (306-337 A.D.) but even then Roman vessels did not proceed

one is of Commodus (189-90 A.D.) and the other, an imitation of a coin of Maximus (216-18) (*JNSI.* V, 171).

[1] Priaulx, *The Indian Embassies to Rome*, p. 252.

beyond Adule, then the chief port of Ethiopia. The Arabs and Indians now carried on the principal part of the trade between India and the western world. Accoding to the Chinese chronicles, there was a great trade between India and the Roman empire even in the sixth century A.D.

If we bear in mind this brief account of Palmyra and Alexandria, the two chief emporiums of active commerce between India and the Roman empire, we may reasonably conclude that it flourished till the third century A.D. and its decline commenced much later than the time suggested by Sewell. Priaulx observed 'that it was during the reigns of Severus, his son Caracalla, and the pseudo-Antonines, that Alexandria and Palmyra were most prosperous, and the Roman intercourse was at its height'.[1] Sewell rejects this view, but it was fully endorsed by V. A. Smith.[2] Priaulx very truly remarks, in support of his contention, that during this period "Roman literature gave more of its attention to Indian matters, and did not, as of old, confine itself to quotations from the historians of Alexander or the narratives of the Seleucidan ambassadors, but drew its information from other and independent sources." The truth of this observation will be apparent when we discuss this topic later in the section ; and the conclusion is strengthened by the enumeration of Indian embassies of Rome, and the further important historical fact that the oriental expeditions of the Roman emperors in the third century A.D. brought them into close and sometimes almost direct contact with India.

The increased trade between India and Rome led to political intercourse between the two. When Augustus finally came out triumphant from the Civil War and established the Principate, one or more Indian States sent embassies. Other Indian embassies also visited Rome during the first four centuries of

---

1 *Ibid.* p. 132.
2 *JASB.* LVIII, 158.

the Christian era, and no less than seven are expressly referred to as having been sent to Trajan (A.D. 98-117), Hadrian (117-138), Antoninus Pius (138-161), Heliogabalus (218-222), Aurelian (270-275), Constantine (323-353) and Julian (361-363). Two more Indian embassies were probably sent to Justinian in 530 and 552 A.D.

The commercial and political intercourse must have brought an increasingly larger number, both of Indians and Roman subjects, to visit each other's country. Alexandria, which occupied almost the central position, was the great meeting ground between the East and the West, and must have been visited by large numbers of Indians. An interesting evidence of such visit, even in Ptolemaic days, is preserved in an inscription on the temple at Dedesiya near the Nile river which contains the name of an Indian.[1] Even so late as 470 A.D. some Brahmins visited Alexandria and lodged in the house of Consul Severus. This personal contact between the Indians and the peoples of the west must have improved the knowledge of each about the other.

A more accurate knowledge of India is reflected in the western literature of the third century A.D. Clement of Alexandria, who died about 220 A.D., gives us highly interesting accounts of both Brahmins and Buddhists. In particular he refers to the former's belief in transmigration and the latter's worship of relic-*stūpas*. Bardesanes, the Babylonian (3rd century A.D.), wrote a very interesting work on Indian Gymnosophists. Though the work itself is lost, some passages that have been preserved in quotation show a remarkably intimate knowledge of India, particularly of its two religious sects, Brāhmaṇas and Buddhists. Archelaos of Carrah (278 A.D.) and

[1] Rawlinson, *Intercourse between India and Western World* p. 99. Cf. also Warmington, *The Commerce between the Roman Empire and India.*

St. Jerome (340 A.D.) both mention the Buddha by name and narrate the tradition of his birth.[1]

Among other writers may be mentioned Philostratus, Callistratus and Dio Cassius. It is interesting to note also that Roman art employed itself on Indian subjects as we gather from Callistratus' description of the statue of a drunken and reeling Hindu.

The intimate intercourse between India and the western world naturally affected the culture of both. It is difficult to estimate the scope and nature of their influence upon each other, but some of its aspects can be broadly stated.[2] There is no doubt that Indian art and coinage were profoundly affected by that of the West. The influence of Roman astronomy on the progress of that science in India is also undeniable. *Ramaka Siddhānta* is freely alluded to by Varāhamihira and the *Paulisa Siddhānta* is based on the astronomical works of Paul of Alexandria (*c.* 378 A.D.). On the other hand Indian medical science, astronomical terms and the system of numerals were adopted by Western countries. Some Indian books like *Pañchatantra* were also very popular there and translated in many languages.

The same reciprocal influence is noticed in the domain of religion and philosophy. It is generally agreed that Indian philosophy exercised a great influence on the development of Neo-Platonism. The rise of Christianity affected Indian religion which had still some hold in the West. The Syrian writer Zenob gives us a very highly interesting account of the iconoclastic zeal of Christian missionaries which led to the destruction of two Hindu temples in the Canton of Taron (Upper Euphrates, west of Lake Van). The temples are said to have been built by an Indian colony

[1] For an account of the writers named, cf. J. W. McCrindle, *Ancient India as described in Classical Literature*.

[2] *JASB*. LVIII, 107 ff; *JBBRAS*. XXIII, 217.

settled in that region in the second century B.C. About A.D. 304 St. Gregory appeared before these temples, and in spite of heroic defence by the Indians, defeated them and broke the two images of gods which were 12 and 15 cubits high.[1] St. Gregory, who thus anticipated Mahmud of Ghazni and his successors, must have been instrumental in destroying to a large extent the traces of Indian religion in the West. But the fact remains that Indian religion, both Brahmanical and Buddhist, was still a living force in the region where Christianity arose and had its early field of activity. It strengthens the belief that the similarities noticed between the two may not be accidental, but the effect of the old religion upon the new. The resemblance of the interior of the Christian church to a Buddhist *Chaitya*, the extreme and extravagant forms of asceticism in early Christian sects, such as the Thebaid monasticism, metempsychosis, relic-worship and the use of the rosary might all have been borrowed by Christianity from Indian religious ideas. It is also very likely that the Manichaeans and the Gnostics were influenced by Indian ideas. Certain it is that several religious leaders of the West took the name of Buddha.

It is, of course, always difficult to define precisely the extent of the influence that one religion exercised upon the other, but of the general influence of Indian ideas upon Christianity there cannot remain any possible doubt. It is more difficult to estimate the effect of Christianity on India. That Christian missionaries visited India from an early period, and small Christian communities were established there, may be easily accepted. We have reference to progress of Christian church in south India in the 'Nations of India', a pamphlet included in the *Romance History of Alexander* of the Pseudo-Kallisthenes (5th Century) and in the *Christian Topography* of

---

[1] *JRAS*. 1904, p. 309.

Cosmas Indikopleustes, a Christian monk who visited India in the first half of the sixth century A.D.

We have described above, in a very brief outline, the relations between India and the Western World between 200 and 550 A.D. The facts, definitely known, are few, and hence the picture is vague and incomplete. But the little that we know is enough to show that India did not lead an isolated life but kept contact with the great civilisations of the West through trade and commerce, and this led to political and cultural relations. Such relations which began much earlier and continued in later periods, were fairly constant and active during the period under review.

CHAPTER XVIII.

SOCIAL AND ECONOMIC CONDITIONS.

I. SOCIAL CONDITION

1. CASTE SYSTEM—INTER-MARRIAGES.

The caste system in one form or another has characterised Hindu society in most of the epochs of its history ; it, therefore, naturally existed in the society of our age as well. It had not yet assumed, however, that rigidity, which we associate with it at present, in respect either of inter-marriage, or of inter-dining or of the professions. Marriages were usually endogamous, but inter-caste marriages of bridegrooms of higher caste with brides of lower ones, which were technically known as *Anuloma* marriages, often took place. The Smṛitis of our age, while recognising the validity of such marriages, were not prepared to recommend them. But a record of our age, which refers to the marriage of a Brāhmaṇa bride-groom with a Kshatriya bride, describes it as perfectly in consonance with the rules of Śrutis and Śmṛitis.[1] We need not then wonder how the Vākāṭaka king Rudra-sena, a scion of an orthodox Brāhmaṇa family, should have married Prabhāvatī-guptā who belonged to the Vaiśya Gupta family. It is interesting to note that contemporary Smṛitis permit the wife of a lower caste to participate in religious rituals, if the husband had no wife of his own caste.[2]

---

[1] सोमस्ततः सोम इवापरोऽभूत्स ब्राह्मणक्षत्रियवंशजासु ।
श्रुतिस्मृतिभ्यां विहितार्थकारी द्वयीसुभार्यासु मनो दधार ।। *ASWI.* IV. 139.

[2] *Yāj*, I, 88.

Pratiloma marriages of brides of higher class with the bride-grooms of lower ones have been recognised as legal by Yājñavalkya,[1] and they often took place in society. Thus Kadamba rulers, who were Brāhmaṇas, had married their daughters in the family of the Guptas, who were Vaiśyas.

Inter-racial marriages were also taking place. The Ikshvāku kings, who were orthodox Brāhmaṇas, had no objection to accepting a bride from the Śaka royal family of Ujjayinī. The Sātavāhanas had done the same in an earlier period. Inter-marriage seems to have been one of the ways by which foreign tribes were absorbed in Hindu society.

The marriage with a Śudra girl has been vehemently condemned by the Smṛiti writers of our period. They, however, did take place in our society, for the same Smṛiti writers, who taboo this union, provide for a share for the sons of such wedlock. Yājñavalkya permits the son of a Śūdra woman to inherit the property of Brāhmaṇa father (II. 134) though Bṛihaspati, who wrote at the end of our period, refuses to recognise this right (*Putrabibhāga* section, 44).

As our period advanced, inter-caste marriages began to become more and more unpopular. But they continued in society for a few centuries more.

When inter-marriages were allowed, inter-dining could naturally excite no opposition. Smṛitis of our period have an objection only to the practice of taking a meal with the Śudras, but even among the latter an exception is made in favour of one's farmer, barber, milkman and family friend (*Yāj.* I, 166).

2. Caste System—Professions.

Professions also were not very rigidly determined by caste during our period. Contemporary Smṛitis afford ample evidence to show how some Brāhmaṇas were following non-Brahmanical professions, and their evidence is confirmed by the data

[1] *Ibid.* I, 93.

of inscriptions, showing how some Brāhmaṇas were traders, others architects[1], and still others government servants. Many like Vindhyaśakti and Mayūra-śarman, the founders of the Vākāṭaka and Kadamba dynasties respectively, used to exchange the sacrificial ladle for the sword. The case of Mātṛi-vishṇu, who was a Gupta feudatory in Central India, shows how ambitious Brāhmaṇa families gradually made their way to the throne. Indra-vishṇu and Varuṇa-vishṇu, the great-grandfather and grandfather respectively of the donor, are described as pious Brāhmaṇas who spent their time in religious sacrifices. The father of the donor is, however, described as the cause of the greatness of the family; obviously it was he who gave up the priestly life and entered the army, where he eventually made a mark, that enabled him to found a principality. The grantor is described as one, who had humbled his enemies on the battlefield and thereby spread his fame to the four corners of the earth[2]. Had our records stated the castes of the military officers mentioned in them, it would probably have been found that some of the Vaiśyas and Śūdras also, who had the necessary martial fervour and ambition, used to take to a military career. The Gupta emperors were Vaiśyas, and it is very likely that a large percentage of the infantry was recruited from the Śūdra caste.

The Kshatriyas in their turn are often seen following commercial and industrial pursuits. The chief officers of the guild of oilmen at Indore in U.P. are expressly described as Kshatriyas in a fifth century record.[3] Very probably this was not an exceptional case of Kshatriyas preferring the cosy commercial career to the risky military one.

The Vaiśyas were never a homogeneous group even in earlier ages, and the same was the case in our period. The

---

1 *CII.* III, 119.
2 *Ibid.* p. 89.
3 *Ibid* p. 70.

agriculturists, the merchants, the cattle-rearers, the smiths, the carpenters, the oil-mongers, the weavers, the garland-makers, etc., had developed into full fledged caste-groups. They were more conscious of their own sub-groups than of their being members of the theoretical Vaiśya caste. Inter-marriages between members of these sub-castes probably took place occasionally, though we have no definite evidence on the point.

A number of mixed (*saṅkara*) castes, like Mūrdhāvasikta, Ambashṭha, Pāraśava, Ugra, Karaṇa, are mentioned in contemporary Smṛitis.[1] It is interesting to note that only Karaṇa among them is mentioned in the records of our period, and it is quite possible that the expression is used there to denote an office rather than a caste. It is clear that the Smṛiti view that the inter-caste marriages give rise to mixed castes of low status had not yet become popular in society. And no wonder, for inter-caste marriages were often taking place even in respectable Brāhmaṇa families, as shown above. A Vākāṭaka record shows that the sons of a Brāhmaṇa father and a Kshatriya mother were not known as Mūrdhāvasiktas, but as Kshatriyas,[2] as suggested at one place in the *Manu-smṛiti*.[3] The Smṛiti nomenclature of the mixed castes was gradually becoming popular only towards the end of our period, when inter-caste marriages tended to become less and less popular.

Kāyasthas frequently figure in contemporary epigraphical records, usually as professional writers. It is however doubtful whether they had developed into a caste during our period. This may account for the non-reference to them as a case in the contemporary Smṛitis.

The pre-historic view that the Śūdras should be content merely to become the servants of the twice-born was not accepted in theory or followed in practice. Smṛitis of our

---

[1] *Yāj*. I, 91 ff.

[2] *ASWI*. IV, 140.

[3] X, 5.

period like that of Yājñavalkya permit them to become traders, artisans and agriculturists, and there is no doubt that they availed themselves of this concession. Many of them also enlisted in the army and rose to the position of captains and generals.

Contemporary Smṛitis and the account of Fa-hien show that untouchability existed in society more or less in its present form. The untouchables lived outside the main settlements and used to strike a piece of wood as they entered them, so that men might note their arrival and avoid their contact. They used to follow hunting, fishery, scavenging and similar despised professions.

Among the castes referred to above, Brāhmaṇas and Kshatriyas enjoyed the highest status. Though some Brāhmaṇas used to follow secular and un-Brahmanical professions, the number of those who followed religious and literary pursuits was fairly large. The class as a whole, therefore, continued to inspire respect as in earlier days. The Kshatriyas also were held in high esteem on account of the prestige and power they enjoyed. The relations between these two castes were usully cordial ; we find several Kshatriya kings of our period describing themselves as devout worshippers of Brāhmaṇas.[1] Occasionally however pelf and power produced their natural consequence and kings or their officers were sometimes disrespectful to the needy Brāhmaṇa. It was the affront which he had received from the insolent Kshatriya officers of the Pallava government that induced the Brāhmaṇa Mayūraśarman to exchange his sacrificial ladle far the steel sword.[2]

Brāhmaṇas were divided into different *śākhās* (classes) bosed upon the Vedas which they studied, and our epigraphs enable us to get a fairly accurate idea of their distribution.

---

[1] *IA*. V, 155; *EI*. VIII. 161, *CII*. III, 96.
[2] *EC*, VII, 200 ff.

There is sufficient evidence to show that Orissa, Teliṅgana,[1] Kośala[2] and Central Province[3] were the stronghold of Yajurvedin Brāhmaṇas and the same was probably the case with U. P., though the evidence is rather inadequate. The donees of most of the numerous grants given to the Brāhmaṇas of the above provinces are usually described as the followers of one of the *śākhās* of the *Yajurveda*. Kathiawar seems to have been a stronghold of the *Sāmaveda*, for the donees of several Valabhī plates of our period are described as Sāmavedins.[4] The followers of this Veda are to be occasionally but rarely seen among the donees residing in Indore (in U.P.), Belur (in Karṇāṭaka) and Mangdur (in Telingana).[5] The Atharvavedins figure rather rarely in our period and their number, we may presume, was not large. We come across one follower of this Veda in Mysore, another in the Belgaum district, a third one at Valabhī and a fourth one in the Kangra valley.[6] Brāhmaṇas of all the four Vedas living together in one place figure rather rarely. This was a natural consequence of the discontinuance of the Vedic sacrifices, which usually required the co-operation of the Brāhmaṇas of all the Vedas.

It is interesting to note that the Ṛigvedins figure very rarely in our records. Why this should be so cannot be explained satisfactorily at present.

The Kshatriyas continued to enjoy the status of *Dvijas* (twice-born) and had the privilege of *Upanayana* and Vedic studies. The same also was probably the case with the majority of the Vaiśyas. All of them had not yet been reduced to the status of the Śūdras. It is interesting to note that at least in

---

1 *IA*. V, 155; *EI*. XII, 135.
2 *Ibid* VIII, 287; IX. 173-5.
3 *CII*, III, 96, 103, 193.
4 *EI*. XI, 108; XVII, 107, 118, 348 XV, 257.
5 *CII*. III, 70: *EC*. V, Belur 245; *IA*. V. 155.
6 *EC*. IV, Hs. No. 18; *EI*, X, 74; XIV, 165.

some cases they knew their *Gotras* and *Pravaras*.[1] As in almost all periods of Indian history, the great Vaiśya community was famous for its charitable disposition. The hospitals in Pāṭaliputra and Magadha, where free relief was given to the needly and the sick, were financed by the charity of this community. The same was the case with many temples, monasteries and free feeding houses. The Vaiśyas were organised into guilds, which were dominating the trade and industry of the country. They also occupied position of honour and responsibility on the town councils.[2]

3. Slavery.

Slavery is not referred to by contemporary foreign writers, but it is described in minute details by Nārada, who belongs to our period.

Prisoners of war were often reduced to slavery ; debtors unable to pay their debts or gamblers unable to pay off their stakes had to become the slaves of their creditors. Sometimes, when there was acute famine, people would voluntarily sell themselves to rich persons, who would undertake to feed them. Slavery in India, however, was not lifelong. Gamblers, debtors and famine-slaves could regain their liberty, if their dues were paid either by themselves or by their relations or friends. Prisoners of war could do the same by finding a substitute. If a slave saved his master's life, he could not only become free but also get a son's share. If a female slave bore a child to her master, she became free. It was thus relatively very easy for slaves to regain their freedom ; they also received much better treatment in India than they did in the West. These circumstances would explain how foreigners like the Greek writers and Chinese pilgrims failed to detect the existence of slavery in India.

---

[1] *Ibid.* VI. 18.

[2] *Ibid.* XV, 129 ff. See *ante*, pp. 285-86.

The emancipation procedure of slaves[1] was interesting. The master was to take away a jar from his slave's shoulder and to smash it. Then he was to sprinkle his head with water containing gram and flowers, and to declare him a free man three times.

4. The Family.

Let us now turn to the family life.

As in earlier centuries the joint family continued to be the characteristic feature of Hindu society. Smṛitis of our period disapprove of partition of the family in the lifetime of the father, and epigraphs also often disclose patriarchs living together with their eight grown-up sons and numerous grandsons and brothers often continuing to live jointly even after the death of their father.[2] In one record we find the donor making a grant for the spiritual welfare of himself, his mother, wife, one son, one daughter, his brother, two nephews and two nieces.[3] It will thus appear that even after the death of the father, brothers and their sons and daughters often continued to live together. Cases of separate shares being allotted to the father and sons in land-grants are rather rare.

The ownership of the family property was vested in the father, but the rights of the different sons and brothers to their separate shares were recognised ; they are separately mentioned in the land-grants in a few cases. What later on came to be known as the *Mitākshарā* system of inheritance was prevailing ; the Smṛitis exclude from *Śrāddha* a Brāhmaṇa who had enforced partition on his father against his will. This presupposes son's right by birth in the ancestral property and is not possible under the *Dāyabhāga* scheme of inheritance.

---

1 *Nārada*, Chap. V. 25-43.
2 *EI*. I, 6; XII, 2; XIX, 120.
3 *IA*. XI, 258.

Most of the twelve subsidiary sons mentioned in the early Dharmaśāstra works were getting more and more unpopular. Of the 12 subsidiary sons, the *putrikāputra* or the daughter's son, was the most popular.[1] It is interesting to note that one who offered himself in adoption was treated with contempt in our age. 'One who leaves his family and goes to another is undoubtedly guilty of sin', says Bṛihaspati.[2] The son by levirate (*nīyoga*) was still regarded as superior to him. Opinion, however, was divided upon this point. Yājñavalkya and Nārada had no objection to *niyoga*, but Bṛihaspati was opposed to the practice. He represented the reform school.

By birth right, sons had shares in the family property, which were usually equal. On rare occasions we see eldest sons receiving larger shares,[3] as recommended by some earlier Smṛitis. These cases are, however, exceptional. Opinion in our period was divided as to whether the widow should have the right to inherit the share of her husband. If he was a member of the joint family at the time of his death, the widow got only a maintenance, but if he had separated, Yājñavalkya and Bṛihaspati argued that she should be given her husband's share as a life estate. This view of the reform school had not yet become popular, and other jurists of our age, like Nārada, were opposed to it. That reformers had not yet made much headway in society would appear clear from the sixth Act of the *Śakuntalā*, where we find the property of a widow, having no son, was liable to escheat to the crown. Daughters, having brothers, had no share in father's property. The latter was expected to spend liberally, usually to the extent of one-fourth of the son's share, at the time of their marriages.

---

1 *Yāj*. II. v. 128.

2 *Dāyabhāga*, v. 75.

3 श्रीवापिका ज्येष्ठ इति कृत्वा नागवत्सस्वामिने ग्रामार्द्धस्याधिका दत्ता ।
(*CII*. III, 199).

Pre-puberty marriages became the order of the day in our period. Writers of the earlier period, like Manu, permitted a father to keep his daughter unmarried up to any age, if a suitable bride-groom was not available; Smṛitis of our period like *Yājñavalkya* and *Nārada* condemn a guardian to hell, if he does not marry his daughter before the time of puberty. When girls were married at the early age of 12 or 13, naturally they had hardly any voice in the settlement of their marriage.[1] Their *Upanayana* ceremony also became impossible owing to early marriages. Yājñavalkya explicitly declares that women were ineligible for the privilege of the *Upanayana* and the Vedic studies. Vedic *mantras* also were not to be recited at the time of the rituals exclusively intended for them. Our age, therefore, denied the Vedic education to women. In well-to-do families, however, literary and cultural education was imparted to them, and several women figure as authoresses and poetesses in our age.[2] Nārada and Parāśara permit remarriage of widows and Chandragupta II had probably married his widowed sister-in-law in *c*. 375. But the puritanical section of seciety was frowning upon widow marriage and it was becoming more and more unpopular among the higher classes as our period advanced.

Widows, who did not marry, led a simple and ascetic life. They wore no ornaments and used no ointments. They did not decorate their hair, but it was not shaved either. The custom of the *Satī* was, no doubt, known to our age and is occasionally referred to by Bhāsa, Kālidāsa and Śūdraka in their works. We have, however, only one historical case of a *Satī*, which took place when king Goparāja died on the battle-field in 510 A.D. and his wife immolated herself on his funeral

[1] When Kālidāsa or the writers of some inscriptions refer to *Svayaṁvara*, they clearly have the old tradition and not the contemporary practice before their mind.

[2] Altekar, *Position of Women*, pp. 19-20.

pyre.[1] It, therefore, appears that it was only on rare occasions that widows became *Satīs* during our period. Among the Smṛiti writers of our age, only Bṛihaspati refers to the possibility of a widow following her husband on the funeral pyre ; others lay down detailed rules about the ascetic life which the widow was expected to lead and are altogether silent about the possibility of her becoming a *Satī*. The custom, therefore, had neither become popular nor acquired a religious sanction.

Sculptures and paintings of our period show that women could move freely in society and were not immured in *harems*. Ladies of aristocratic families, however, used to put on a veil over their face when they were out on a journey.[2]

5. Food and Drink.

Hindu society was partly vegetarian and partly non-vegetarian in our period. When Fa-hien refers to the absence of meat shops in the Madhyadeśa in *c*. 400 A.D., he is obviously referring to the Buddhist sections of the population. The Smṛitis of our period, like *Bṛihaspati*, lay down that only those women, whose husbands are away, should refrain from meat and wine. They expressly permit meat-eating in the case of sick persons and enjoin it at the time of *Śrāddha*. In south India, meat dishes were popular in royal courts and fashionable society. As a result of the Bhakti and Māhāyāna movements, which were against meat-eating, the Buddhists and Brāhmaṇas of our age had gradually begun to eschew meat except at the time of *Śrāddha* and sacrifices.

The evidence of the *Śakuntalā* shows that non-Brāhmaṇas had no compunction against drinking wine.[3] In south Indian

---

[1] *CII*. III, 92: see *ante*, p. 190.
[2] *Śankuntalā*, Act V.
[3] Act VI.

courts rich liquors, imported from the west, were served at the royal table and country wine was drunk by the poor.[1] Brāhmaṇas, however, eschewed wine ; Hiuen Tsang's statement that Brāhmaṇas drank syrup while the Kshatriyas took wine[2] was probably true of our period as well.

The use of betel leaves after dinner was quite common.

6. Dress and Ornaments.

The old Indian dress consisting of an upper garment and a lower *dhoti*, neither of which required any stitching, continued to be the costume of the vast majority of the male population. The Scythians had, however, introduced coats, overcoats and trousers, and they were often worn by Indian kings also as can be inferred from the effigies of the Gupta emperors on some of their coins. The official court dress of the kings, however, was the old national one and we find Gupta emperors hunting the lions and tigers with *dhotis* and sashes. Head-dress was worn on auspicious occasions. Shoes were not very common ; most people went without them.

The dress of women was more or less the same as it is today. In some part of the country they wore a petticoat below and the *sāri* over it; in other parts a long *sāri* served both the purposes. A bodice was used below the *sāri* to cover the bust ; its two ends were usually tied together between the breasts. Jackets, blouses and frocks were used by Scythian women. They did not become popular in Hindu society except among the dancing girls. Cotton garments were used for daily purposes, but silken ones were worn by rich and fashionable persons on festive occasions.

Contemporary sculptures and paintings give us a graphic idea of the variety and gracefulness of women's different orna-

1 *Porunar*; ll. 84-93, 101-121.
2 Watters, I, p. 178.

ments.[1] A large number of them was used over the forehead. The designs of the ear-rings were graceful. The variety in the necklaces of gold and pearls was striking. More than half a dozen types of zones (*mekhalās*) were in vogue. A gauzy pearl ornament was used over the breasts as well as the thighs. The arms were adorned with *keyūras* of which there were several varieties. A large number of bangles, often set with pearls or jewels, figured on the forearms. Rings were quite common but the nose-ring was still unknown. The number of bangles used on the feet was not small. Men were not much behind women in their fondness for ornaments.

The fashions of dressing the hair were as numerous as graceful.[2] An examination of the paintings at Ajanta will be an eye opener even to the most fashionable ladies of the present generation. False hair was often used to increase the volume of the braid in order to give it different artistic shapes. The use of paints, pastes and lipsticks was not unknown.

Water clocks (*nāḍikās*) were used in government offices, temples, monasteries and cultured families to ascertain the time of the day. The clock consisted of a small pot, kept floating in a larger vassel filled with water. The pot could be filled in twenty-four minutes (*ghaṭikā*) by water slowly coming into it through a hole made at the bottom. An attendant was necessary to empty it out and float it again the moment it was filled.

Dice and chess were the favourite indoor pastimes and hunting, ramfights and cockfights were the principal outdoor amusements. Ball game (*kandukakrīḍā*) was popular with childern and women ; the latter used to gather together on festive occasions and have a variety of physical games. Fairs, shows and dramas also provided a variety of entertainment.

---

[1] Altekar, *Position of Women*, pp. 358 ff.

[2] *Ibid*. Pl. VIII.

II. ECONOMIC CONDITION

I. Guild.

Let us now survey the economic conditions of our times. The organisation of trade and industry in guilds was a feature of ancient Indian economic life since very early times, and it continued to be the same in our period as well. Contemporary inscriptions and seals refer to the guilds not only of merchants and bankers, but also of the manual workers like weavers, oil-men and stone-cutters.[1] It is thus clear that trades and industries, both high and low, were organised in guilds. In order to secure capital they were also doing banking business and receiving permanent deposits guaranteeing regular payment of interest to be utilised for the specific charitable objects which the donors had in view. Even if the members of the guild migrated in a body to another place offering better trade prospects, the public had full confidence that they would honour their obligations.[2] The affairs of the guild were managed by a president and a small executive committee of four or five members.

The peace and prosperity that prevailed in our age gave a great impetus to inter-provincial and inter-state trade, and it had its own repercussions on the development of the guilds. As Basarh, the ancient Vaiśālī, which was a seat of provincial government under the Guptas, 274 sealings were found of a joint guild of bankers, traders and transport merchants, having its membership spread over a large number of towns and cities in northern India.[3] These sealings, which belong to the end of the 4th century A.D., had closed the letters that were received by the provincial government of Vaiśālī from the different

---

[1] *ASI.* 1903-4, pp. 101 ff; *CII.* III, 81 ff; *EI.* XXIV, 56.
[2] *CII* III, 70.
[3] *ASI.* 1903-4, pp. 101 ff.

branches of this great organisation. No clay tablet contains the sealing of the guild alone ; it is always accompanied by the sealing of another private individual. As the great guild had its branches in a number of cities, duplicates of its seal must have existed in a number of places; it was, therefore, naturally felt necessary that the common seal should be used along with the seal of the president or the secretary of each local branch to authenticate its letters. It is interesting to note that the seal of Īśānadāsa appears along with the seal of the great guild in 75 cases, that of Mātṛidāsa in 38 cases, and that of Gomisvāmī in 37 cases. These three merchants must have been the presidents or the secretaries of the guild at some of its important branches like those in Pāṭaliputra, Gayā or Allahabad. Ghosha, Harigupta, Bhavasena, etc., whose sealings figure jointly with that of the great guild only five or six times, were probably managing its branches in less important towns, which had no occasions to communicate frequently with the provincial government of Vaiśālī. In some places the branches of this guild managed the affairs of local temples.[1] The guild had a great reputation and status ; for it often entered into transactions jointly with the office of the heir-apparent of the great Gupta empire.[2] If excavations are carried at other places, it is quite likely that seals may be discovered of other great guilds, operating over wide areas.

Guilds were autonomous bodies, having their own rules, regulations and bye-laws, which were usually accepted and respected by the state.[3] Disputes among their members were settled by their own executive and not by the state tirbunals.

---

[1] In some cases the guild sealing is accompanied with another bearing inscriptions like *Jayatyananto bhagavān*, *Jitambhagavatā*, *Namaḥ Paśupataye*. These were obviously sealings of Vaīshṇava or Śaiva temples, which probably wanted their financial transactions at Vaiśālī to be done through the agency of the great guild.

[2] In one case the sealing of the guild is accompanied by the sealing of *Yuvarājapādīyakumārāmātyādhikaraṇam*.

[3] *Yāj.* II, 191-2.

They had their own funds and properties. Many of them were rich enough to excavate a cave or build a temple.[1] Individual members of a guild were both rich and cultured ; thus the weavers' guild at Daśapura or Mandasor in Central India had some members well versed in folk lore, some in astrology and some in the military profession. It would appear that in the case of emergency a guild could raise a militia from among its own members and employees to afford protection to the person, property and merchandise of its members.

Partnership transactions were also widely prevalent in the Gupta period. At Vaiśāli letters bearing the joint sealings of two merchants were very frequently received, clearly attesting to their partnership in different transactions. The Vaiśya community enjoyed great prestige and wealth. Its senior members usually figured prominenty in the town and district councils.

2. Trade

Unfortunately we have no detailed evidence about the principal itmes of trade carried on by our merchants and guilds. Different varieties of cloth, food-grains, spices, salt, bullion and precious stones were most probably the main articles of internal trade. It was carried both by the road and the river. Principal towns and cities like Broach, Ujjayinī, Paithan, Vidisā, Prayāga, Benares, Gaya, Pāṭaliputra, Vaiśālī, Tāmralipti, Kauśāmbī, Mathura, Ahichchhattra, Peshawar, etc. were connected by roads, which were fairly well protected during the Gupta rule. Goods were transported in carts and on the backs of animals, including elephants where available. Rich riverrine traffic was carried along the Ganges, the Brahmaputra, the Narmadā, the Godāvarī, the Kṛishṇā and the Kāverī. River traffic in fact was more convenient and less costly. Good pro-

[1] *CII.* III, 81 ff; *ASI*, 1937-8; p. 38 (in press).

gress had been made in ship-building and Indians could build ships big enough to carry 500 men on high seas.

Tāmralipti (modern Tamluk), which is now landlocked, was the principal port in Bengal and carried on an extensive trade with China, Ceylon, Java and Sumatra. The Andhra country was studded with a number of ports at the mouths of the Godāvarī and the Kṛishṇā, of which Kadūra and Ghaṇṭa-śāla are mentioned by Ptolemy. Kāverīpattanam, modern Puhar at the mouth of the Kāverī, and Tondai were the principal ports of the Chola country, Korkai and Saliyur of the Pāṇḍya country and Kottayam and Muziris (modern Crangnore) of the Malabar coast. They were carrying a progressively increasing traffic with the Eastern Archipelago and China, which helped the spread of Indian culture in eastern Asia.

Most of these ports had also brisk commercial relations with the West. There is sufficient evidence to show that sometimes Roman and other foreign traders used to settle down in them to facilitate trade transactions. Early Tamil literature has preserved for us some vivid accounts of the port of Puhar, —how Yavana ships used to enter it with swan-shaped lamps at their tops, how they used to unload their precious cargo, how customs officers, 'as vigilant as the horses of the sun', used to seal it with the tiger-signet ring of the king, pending the settlement of the customs duties, and how it was subsequently sold off in big shops, which had their own distinctive flags flying over their buildings. Kings tried to facilitate trade by building and maintaining light houses at necessary points and also by keeping the sea routes free and safe. We have got an interesting account of how kings, like the Chēra ruler Imaiya-varamban Neduñjeral, used to take effective steps to apprehend and punish Yavana and other pirates.

Kalyan, Chaul, Broach and Cambay were the principal ports of the Deccan and Gujarat, but we do not get any contemporary account of their activity. An account of the export trade carrid by these and other ports has been already given. The land and sea routes to the west have also been decribed there. The principal items of export were pearls, precious stones, cloths, perfumes, incense, spices, indigo, drugs, cocoa-nuts, and ivory articles, and the main items of imports were gold—bullion and coins—, silver, copper, tin, lead, silk, camphor, corals, dates and horses.

3. Wealth of the Country.

We get very little information from contemporary sources about the natural wealth and products of the country during our age. We may, however, safely assume that rice, wheat, sugarcane, jute, oilseeds, cotton, *jwar*, *bajra*, spices, betel-nuts, betel-leaves, medicinal durgs, incense and indigo were the main agricultural products. Forests also contributed considerably to the national wealth, and supplied teak, sandal and ebony wood. It does not seem that the mines of the country produced much gold or silver ; these two metals were mostly imported into the country and represented the excess of our exports over imports. Mines of precious stones were most probably worked in the Deccan, Central India and Chotanagpur.

Cloth manufacture was the principal industry of the country and offered employment to millions of peope, both male and female. Cloth was manufactured all over the country, but its famous centres were located in the different towns and cities of Gujarat, Bengal, Deccan and Tamil country. Sculpture, inlaying, ivory work, painting, smithy, and ship-building were other crafts and industries that offered employment to thousands.

4. Cost of Living.

Rates of interest varied between 12 and 24 per cent according to the solvency of the debtor. If we assume the former rate on permanent endowments, it will follow that one *dīnāra* (¾th of a *tola* of gold) was sufficient for the feeding of one monk throughout the year.[1] The monthly cost of feeding one individual sumptuously was thus about Rs. 2/-. Living, therefore, was very cheap in the Gupta period and we can well understand how *cowries* could serve the purpose of daily transactions. Barter also was extensively resorted to, especially in rural areas. Some of the governments of our age, like those of the Ikshvākus, the Vākāṭakas and the Pallavas, did not care to issue any currency, probably because it was not required for daily transactions.

5. Agrarian Problems.

Let us now consider the agrarian problems. It does not seem that anything like the modern *zemindari* system of Bengal or the United Provinces existed in the country. It is referred to neither in the inscriptions nor in the Smṛits. Occasionally, Brāhmaṇas, temples and monasteries were assigned entire villages, but the donees acquired only the right to receive the royal revenues and could not dispossess any tenants. The donees were often required to stay in villages alienated to them, which discouraged absentee landlordism.

Landlords, not tilling their own lands, used to lease them to tenants ; the latter used to receive as the return for their labours a share which varied frcm 33 so 50 per cent of the gross produce.[2]

Bhūmi, *Pāṭaka*, *Paṭṭikā*, *Droṇavāpa*, *Kulyavāpa*, *Khaṇḍukāvāpa*, *Nivartana and Veli* are the different land measures referred to in our period, but the precise dimensions of most of them are not known. It seems that a *Kulyavāpa* was slightly larger than an acre and a *Nivartana* was equal to about 2½

[1] *CII.* III, 261.

[2] *Yāj.* I, 166; *Br. Sm.* XVI, 13; *EI.* IX, 59.

acres. A *Veli*, which produced about a thousand *Kalams* of paddy, was most probably equal to six acres.

The price of land varied according to its nature. In Bengal fallow land was sold at the rate of two to three *dīnāras* (Rs. 50 to 75) per *kulyavāpa* ;[1] land under cultivation was about 35 per cent dearer.[2]

Land was regarded as a very valuable piece of property and its transfer could be effected only through the consent of the fellow villagers of the permission of the village or town council.[3] The actual transfer of ownership was effected in the presence of the village elders, who formally demarcated the piece.

Let us now very briefly consider the question of the ownership of land. The fallow and waste lands belonged to the state, but their actual disposal was made with the assent and through the agency of the local village *Panchāyat* or town council.

In several villages, the State owned small fields of cultivable land, which are expressly described as *rājyavastu*[4] i.e., Crownlands or the property of the state, in some of our records. These fields used to come under the state ownership usually on account of want of heirs or failure to pay the land-tax. Kings are often seen granting them in charity.[5] Donees in such cases acquired full ownership or the land, and not a right to its land-tax, in fact they were often not exempted from it. When however entire villages were given away in charity, what was donated was the right to receive the royal dues. The inhabitants of these villages were never exhorted to quit their private lands in favour of the donee, but to pay him the different taxes and to show him proper courtesy ; future kings were besought to desist not from evicting private owers but from

---

[1] *EI*. XV, 129 ff.
[2] *IA*. XXXIX, 200.
[3] *Ibid*.
[4] *EI*. VIII, 235.
[5] *IA*. IX, 103; VII, 36.

collecting the royal dues.[1] Cases are also on record where an entire village was granted to a donee along with specific fields or plots in it.[2] It is clear that in such cases the state was the owner of only some small plots of land in the villages concerned, which it could easily transfer to the donee. As far as the rest of the cultivable land was concerned, it was owned by private individuals ; the state could not dispossess them, but could only direct them to pay the usual taxes to the donee. The available evidence thus makes it clear that the ownership of the cultivable land vested in private individuals or families, and not in the state.

---

[1] *CII.* III, 118; *EI.* II, 364.
[2] *EC.* VII, Sb. 33; *Ibid.* VI, Kadur, 162.

CHAPTER XIX

RELIGION AND PHILOSOPHY

1. General Background

The Vākāṭaka-Gupta period is an important and interesting age in the history of Indian religion and philosophy. The portestant movements, Jainism and Buddhism, which got a great impetus in the Mauryan age, gave rise to a counter-reformation among the Hindus, who began to remedy the situation in right earnest without losing much time. By *c.* 100 B.C. the *Bhārata* had been expanded into the *Mahābhārata* and Hindu society was presented with an encyclopaedia of religion, philosophy and ethics, in which the main principles of the neo-Hinduism were presented in a popular and attractive form. A little later the philosophical side of Hinduism was strengthened by the systematic exposition of the teachings of its various schools that was attempted in the *Mīmāṁsā-*, *Brahma-*, *Yoga-* and *Nyāya-sutras*.

As against agnostic and atheistic Buddhism, which maintained that salvation was possible only through self-exertion, Hinduism offered a religion where God was presented to the masses in the theistic form of Kṛishṇa, Vishṇu, or Mahādeva, always ready and anxious to save genuine devotees, who threw themselves upon his mercy. This led to the rise of a new school in Buddhism in the form of the *Mahāyāna* movement at about the beginning of the Christian era. This school also began to aver that Gautama Buddha was only one incarnation of the *Dharmakāya* and that the latter will reincarnate Himself as often as may be necessary. Nay, it was maintained that the Bodhisattvas are always present and ready to help the weaker brethren and that they would voluntarily transfer their own *puṇya* (merit) to them in order to effect their release.

Considerable thought ferment was created in the domain of religion and philosophy during the period 200 B.C. to 200 A.D. by the reformation movements referred to above ; and it continued unabated during our period (200 A.D. to 550 A.D.). Nay, it is during this period that for the first time we find the controversies between the rival movements reflected in the religious and philosophical literature. The Hīnayāna conon does not attempt any systematic refutation of the Hindu position, nor does the *Mahābhārata* deliver any frontal attacks on Buddhism. The new sections that were added to the *Brahma-sūtras*, the *Yoga-sūtras* and the *Nyāya-sūtras* during our period are however keen in refuting the philosophical views of the different schools of Buddhism and Jainism. Vātsyāyana in his Nyāyabhāshya attempts to combat the views of Nāgārjuna and is criticised in his turn by Dignāga, who seeks to defend the Buddhist view-point. Vātsyāyana, however, soon found a defender in Udyotakara, who tried to refute the position of Dignāga. We would have got more instances of the conflict of mind with mind and ideas with ideas, had the whole of the extensive Buddhist literature, produced in our period, been preserved in its original language.

2. The Spirit of Tolerance and Harmony.

Hinduism and Buddhism were more or less evenly balanced during our period and so philosophical conflicts (*Śāstrārthas*) were very frequently taking place between the followers of the two systems. They are often referred to in our epigraphs ; thus Mahānāman's inscription at Bodhagaya describes how the heretical philosophers, who opposed the views of the Buddha, were completely overthrown.[1] An epigraph at Ajanta exultingly

---

[1] *CII*. III. 276.

observes that Kṛishṇa, Śaṅkara and other gods have beat a precipitate retreat before the advance of the doctrine of the Buddha.[1] There is no doubt that considerable heat was generated during the philosophical tournaments between the followers of the different religions, but there is no evidence to show that it appreciably disturbed the even tenor of life of their ordinary followers. During the succeeding age (550 to 900 A.D.) the Buddhists, the Jains, the Śaivas and the Vaishṇavas suffered to some extent from mutal persecution in south India, but during our period the relations of the followers of these sects were fairly cordial throughout the length and breadth of the whole country.

In spite of the controversies that were frequently taking place between the ambitious philosophers of the different schools,[2] society as a whole had come to take the commonsense view that there was a substantial uniformity underlying their fundamental principles ; an individual may make such synthesis of their principles as appealed to his temperament and extend his patronage to all without any distinction. Thus king Dāmodara-varman of the Ānanda dynasty (*c.* 375 A.D.) was a Buddhist and yet he believed in the efficacy of the Hiraṇyagarbha ceremony recommended by the neo-Hinduism of the Purāṇas, for ensuring a celestial body after one's death.[3] Brāhmaṇa Nāthaśarman and his wife Rāmī of Puṇḍravardhana (in Bengal) were pious Hindus, but they felt that they could promote their spiritual welfare by giving a land-grant in order to make a permanent arrangement for the proper worship of Jain Arhats.[4] Emperor Samudra-gupta was no doubt a staunch

---

[1] Burgess and Indraji, *Inscriptions from the Cave Temples of Western India*, p. 77.

[2] It was customary in some places in South India to hoist permanent flags, announcing a standing challenge for debate on behalf of celebrated scholars. *Perumbān*. I. 142.

[3] *EI*. XVII, 328 ff.

[4] *Ibid*. XX, 62.

Hindu, who took peculiar pride in resuscitating the Aśvamedha sacrifice, but he entrusted the education of his son to Vasubandhu who was a famous and erudite Buddhist scholar. King Śāntamūla of the Ikshvāku family was an enthusiastic follower of the Vedic religion, but his sister, daughters and daughters-in-law were all Buddhists. Some of them, however, had given donations to Brāhmaṇas as well[1]. In the Kadamba family, kings Kṛishṇa-varman and Mṛigeśa-varman performed Aśvamedha sacrifice out of their respect for the Vedic religion, and made grants to a Jain establishment out of their reverence for Mahāvīra.[2] There are many records in our period which show that the Jains used to respect the Hindus and their teachers.[3] The Guptas were orthodox Hindus, but the best tribute to their administration has been paid by some contemporary Jain records.[4] It is well known how the Buddhist University at Nālandā owed most of its prosperity to the patronage it received from the Hindu Gupta emperors. Among the latter's officers also there were some who were Buddhist, and one of them is seen making a donation to the Buddhist establishment at Sanchi for the spiritual benefit of his Vaishṇava sovereign Chandra-gupta II.[5] Vainya-gupta, one of the later Gupta kings, was a Śaiva and yet he gave a donation to a Mahāyāna Buddhist establishment known as Vaivartika *Saṅgha*.[6] It is quite possible that this Mahāyāna *Sagṅha* bore

[1] *Ibid*. p. 16.
[2] *IA*. VI, 24.
[3] *CII*. III. 47.
[4] श्रीसंयुतानां गुणतोयधीनां गुप्तान्वयानां नृपसत्तमानाम् । *Ibid*. p. 258.
गुप्त।नां वंशजस्य प्रविसृतयशसस्तस्य सवो त्तमर्घे:
राज्ये शक्रोपमस्य क्षितिपशतपते: स्कन्दगुप्तस्य शान्ते । *Ibid*. p. 67.
[5] *Ibid*. p. 31.
[6] *IHQ*. VI, 53 ff. Dr. Dutt's view that the name of the *Saṅgha* is *Avaivartika*, and that the expression has the same sense. as that in the phrases *avaivartika samādhi* and *avaivartika bodhisatva* (*Ibid*. p. 572) is untenable. An individual Bodhisatva or his *samādhi* may be believed

this interesting appellation because it preached the *Vaivarta* or the *Māyā* doctrine. If such was the case, this donation of a Hindu king to the followers of the Buddhist Vaivartika philosophy may have helped its popularisation in Bengal. We should not forget in this connection that Gauḍapāda, one of the earliest exponents of the *Māyāvāda* among the Hindu philosphers, most probably belonged to Bengal.

When there was so much of harmony even between the followers of the orthodox and heterodox schools, there is no wonder that the different sects of Hinduism should have lived in perfect accord. During its earlier career, the Bhāgavata religion used to excite a certain amount of opposition in orthodox circles owing to its veiled opposition to the Vedic sacrifices. In our period, however, we find a staunch Bhāgavata like Kumāra-gupta I performing the Vedic Aśvamedha sacrifice. In the 3rd century A.D. there was another ruler, named Rājamitra, who performed a number of Vedic sacrifices and marked their conclusion by a donation for a Śaiva temple.[1] These instances show how a complete harmony had been established among the followers of the Vedic, Bhāgavata and Śaiva sects by the 4th century A.D. This became possible because of mutual adjustment and accommodation. A staunch follower of the Bhāgavata religion of the earlier period would never have, like Kumāra-gupta I, performed an Aśvamedha sacrifice involving the slaughter of a horse. Nor would an out-and-out Vaidika like Kāśakṛitsna have given at the end of a sacrificial session a donation to a shrine of Mahādeva, who had destroyed the Vedic sacrifice of Daksha. Hinduism of our age however felt that even a *paramabhāgavata* may occasionally perform a Vedic sacrifice, and a staunch Vaidika may signalise the termi-

to be *avaivartika* or infallible; a whole *Saṅgha* of monks at different stages of spiritual progress cannot claim this proud title.

[1] *EI.* XXIV, 245.

nation of his sacrificial session by a donation even to a Śiva temple.

Among the followers of the Puranic deities also, there was complete harmony. Families changed their principal deity of devotion according to individual inclinations. First three Valabhī rulers were Māheśvaras. The fourth was a Bhāgavata and the fifth was an Ādityabhakta (worshipper of the Sun). The Naḷa ruler Bhavatta-varman was a Śaiva, but, his son Skanda-varman, who constructed a Vishṇu temple, was a Bhāgavata.[1] In the Parivrājaka dynasty, Hastin was a Śaiva but his son Saṅkshobha was a Vaishṇava.[2] How people regarded Brahmā, Vishṇu and Śiva as the different aspects of one and the same God would become clear from the opening verse of a 5th century inscription from Mysore.[3]

3. Vedic Religion.

In *c.* 200 B.C. the *Mahābhārata* and the *Manusmṛiti* made a determined effort to defend the Vedic sacrifice. The *Mīmāṁsā-sūtras* of Jaimini were also composed at about the same time to expound and defend the same cause. This advocacy was not without an effect during our period. Even in Dravidian south the sacrificial post (*Vēḷvittuṇa*) of the Vedic ritual figures as a thing of common knowledge in popular Tamil literature. Down to *c.* 400 A.D. the Vedic religion was fairly popular in society. A number of Vedic sacrifices were performed by the rulers of our period, the Aśvamedha among them being very popular. It was celebrated not only by big emperors like Pravara-sena I, (*c.* 275 A.D.), Samudra-gupta (*c.* 375 A.D.) and Kumāra-gupta I (*c.* 430 A.D.) but also by small kings like Śāntamūla of the Ikshvāku dynasty (*c.* 250

---

1 *Ibid.* XIX, 102; XXI, 155.

2 *CII.* III, 106, 114.

3 हरनारायणब्रह्मत्रितयाय नमः सदा। *EC.* VI, Kadir, 162.

A.D.), Vijayadeva-varman of the Śālaṅkāyana family (*c*. 320 A.D.) and Dahrasena of the Traikūṭaka house (*c*. 460 A.D.). Even the Kadamba ruler, Kṛishṇa-varman, who was a mere feudatory, is known to have performed it. There is no wonder that the Bhāraśivas and the Pallavas, who claimed to be powerful rulers, should have performed it several times. The available data show that the Vedic sacrifices were never more popular since the revival of Hinduism than during the 3rd and the 4th centuries. The great Vākāṭaka emperor Pravara-sena I not only celebrated four Horse-sacrifices, but also performed *Agnishṭoma*, *Āptoryāma*, *Ukthya*, *Shoḍashin*, *Bṛīhaspatisava* and *Vājapeya*. The last mentioned one was celebrated to proclaim the formal assumption of the imperial title of *Samrāṭ* by the Vākāṭaka emperor. The early Pallavas performed so many sacrifices that they claim to have become *Śatakratukalpa*, 'almost similar to Indra' in their greatness.[1] According to the popular belief Indra owes his position to the successful performance of a hundred sacrifices, and the implication of the above expression is that the Pallavas had almost reached that limit. Agnishṭoma, Vājapeya and Aśvamedha figure prominently among the sacrifices performed by them as well as by the Ikshvākus.[2] The Maukharis of Gaya were a petty ruling family, but they had performed a large number of Vedic sacrifices in the 4th century. Indra had to come down to earth so frequently to accept their oblations, that his poor consort became lean and thin owing to her enforced and prolonged separation from her husband. The Maukharis of Badva in Kotah state were by no means less enthusiastic in the cause of the Vedic religion. Sacrificial pillars have been recently discoved com-

---

[1] IA. V, 155.

[1] *EI*. XX, 16; XV, 251.

[3] यस्याहूतसहस्रनेत्रबिरहक्षामा सदवाध्वरे पौलोमी चिरमश्रु पातविरह
घत्तकपोलश्रियम् ।। *CII*. III. 224.

memorating the Trirātra sacrifices performed by four of them.[1] Two other chiefs in Jaipur State performed the same sacrifice towards the end of the 3rd century A.D.[2] The Mālava chief who regained independence for his country in 226 A.D. signalised the event by the celebration of the Ekashashṭi-rātra-sattra, which was quite an appropriate one for the occasion.[3] The Puṇdarika sacrifice was performed by another local ruler in Bharatpur State in 372 A.D.[4]

4. Growing Popularity of Puranic Hinduism.

The popularity of the Vedic sacrifices during our period was no doubt due to special pleading in their favour by the *Mahābhārata*, the *Manusmṛiti* and the Mīmāṁsā school, as a reaction to their condemnation by the Buddhists and the Jains. It did not, however, last long. People were gradually veering round to the view of the *Bhagavad-gītā* that the Vedic sacrifices, though good in their own way, do not constitute the best method to secure spiritual progress and divine favour. From the 5th century A.D. we find them definitely on the decline. The Vākāṭaka emperor Pravara-sena and the Ikshvāku king Sāntamūla performed several Vedic sacrifices ; Samudragupta and Kumāra-gupta I were content with only one of them. Stone *Yūpas* commemorating their performance were fairly common in the 2nd, 3rd and the 4th centuries A.D.; they disappear subsequently.

It must be further noted that the Vedic sacrifices were in

---

[1] *EI.* XXII, 52.

[2] *Ibid.* XXVI, 118.

[3] When the gods first offered this sacrifice, everything around them had become sapless; trees had lost their freshness and kine their strength; as a result of the sacrifice nature regained its original vigour and brilliance and there ensued a period of all-round prosperity like the one which must have begun in Mālava when it got its freedom from the foreign rule.

[4] *CII.* III, 253.

vogue only among the richer sections of society. The Smṛitis of our period[1] expressly state that they should be performed only by those who had provisions in their stores sufficient for three years. We hardly come across commoners performing them. The general population had definitely veered round to the Smārta religion dominated by devotion, thanks to the teachings of the *Bhagavad-gītā*. On private seals of individuals discovered at Bhita, Nalanda and Vaiśālī, Vaishṇava and Śaiva emblems like *Śaṅhka* (conch), *Chakra* (wheel), *Triśūla* (trident) and *Nandi* are quite common; fire altar or *Yūpa* rarely makes its appearance. Puranic deities like Vishṇu and Śiva appealed more to the heart of the general population than the Vedic gods. The Bhāraśivas no doubt performed ten Horse-sacrifices, but they constantly carried on their person an emblem not of *Yūpa*, but of Śiva. Kumāra-gupta I performed a Horse-sacrifice, but was anxious to call himself not a *Parama-vaidika* but a *Parama-bhāgavata*. Vākāṭaka Rudra-sena II attributed his prosperity to Chakrapāṇi; the Naḷa ruler Bhavatta-varman felt that his restoration was due to the favour of Mahāsena. We do not come across the case of a single individual ascribing his greatness or luck to the favour of a Vedic deity. It is clear that Vedic gods had become far and distant figures, to be formally invoked at sacrifices and religious functions; they had ceased to appeal to the average individual.

The available evidence tends to show that during our period Vaishṇavism was becoming popular. In South India this was due to the work of the first three Āḷvāras, Seroyogin, Bhūtayogin and Mahadyogin, whose impassioned devotional songs in Tamil, which could he understood even by the man in the street, naturally made Vaishṇavism very popular. The growing prevalence of Vaishṇavism in northen India cannot be attributed to any vernacular devotional poetry. It seems to

[1] *Yāj*. I, 123-5.

be due to the efforts of the remodellers of the Purāṇas, the majority of which hold up Vishṇu as the highest god. A very large number of the epigraphs of our period refer to the temples of Vishṇu[1]. Among his ten incarnations epigraphic evidence shows that Varāha[2] and Kṛishṇa wer most popular. This was probably due to the country being recently rescued from foreign yoke. The achievements of Kṛishṇa often figure in our epigraphs by way of similes, and sculptures have been recovered at Paharpur in Bengal illustrating some of his feats in his childhood.

It is interesting to note that the cult of Rāma had not become popular in our period. Kālidāsa no doubt refers to him as an incarnation of Vishṇu, and there was a temple dedicated to him at Ramtek near Nagpur. But there is no evidence to show that Rāma had become the object of popular worship down to the end of the 6th century A.D. No king or minister of our period describes himself as a devotee of Rāma, nor does his name figure in *Amarakosha* as that of a deity. His temples also were very rare in our period.

Śiva has also been held up as the highest god in several Purāṇas of our period, though their number is relatively small, and we find Śaivism almost equally popular with Vaishṇavism. If the Gupta, Pallava and Gaṅga kings were mostly Vaishṇavas, the rulers of the Bhāraśiva, Vākāṭaka, Naḷa, Maitraka, Kadamba and Parivrājaka dynasties were usually Śaivas. Śāba and Pṛithvīsheṇa, who were both officers under the Vaishnava Guptas, were themselves Śaivas.

The custom of establishing a Śiva temple to commemorate

---

[1] Meharauli inscription refers to the erection of a *Vishṇu-dhvaja*; Gangdhar and Eran records mention the temples of Vishṇu and Junagadh and Bhitari epigraphs describe the construction of the temples of Chakrabhrit and Śārṅgin. There was a temple of Vishṇupāda at Nagari.

[2] At Udayagiri a beautiful Gupta sculpture vividly represents the rescrue of the earth by Vishṇu in this Vaarāha incarnation. In Puṇḍravardhana, there was a Varāha temple, as also at Eran.

the name of oneself or one's ancestor was fairly popular in our period. Pṛithvīsheṇa and Vishṇuvarman, who were the generals under the Guptas and the Pallavas, both founded temples to commemorate their names.[1] The custom prevailed in the Punjab also. Īśvarā, the wife of Chandragupta, a petty ruler at Jālandhar, built a Śiva temple in memory of her husband, and Mihiralakshmī dedicated a temple in Kangra district to Mihireśvara.[2] Śiva was worshipped in our period in different forms. His human form can be seen on the later Kushāṇa coins. His earliest phallic emblem goes back to a remote antiquity. The majority of the Śiva images of the Gupta period combine the phallic with the human form; they are either *ekamukha-liṅgas* or *chaturmukha-liṅgas* with one or four faces of Śiva carved upon them. Other emblems of this god like trident and bull figure frequently on common seals.

At Mathura, the Lakulīśa sect of the Pāśupatas was fairly popular. Kuśika, one of the four main disciples of its founder Lakulīśa, who is regarded as the last inca nation of Śiva, appears to have established himself at this place in *c*. 150 A.D. The Pāśupata doctrine was preached by him and his disciples for more than ten generations at this place. The followers of the sect used to erect a temple in memory of each departed teacher, who used to be honoured with the divine epithet *bhagavān* after his death. Parāśara, Upamita, Kapila and Udita were the Pāśupata teachers, who flourished in the Gupta period.[3] As a result of their teachings, the worship of Lakulīśa became popular; an image of the deity was discovered in the precincts of Mathura in 1945. It belongs to the Gupta age.

What precisely was the nature of the Śiva worship advocated by the Pāśupatas of Mathura, we do not know. But

---

1 *EI*. X, 60; *IA*. V, 32

2 *EI*. I, 13; *CII*. III, 289.

3 *EI*. XXI. 8.

there is a sculpture at Mathura belonging to our period showing a devotee offering his own head to Śiva. When the illness of king Prabhākara-vardhana of Thanesvar became critical, his relatives and courtiers began to offer oblations of their own flesh to secure the king's recovery. It therefore seems that the Pāśupata religion in the Mathura region was preaching some of the extreme practices associated with it. It is not unlikely that even human sacrifices may have been offered by a few fanatics of the sect on rare occasions. Hiuen Tsang was about to be immolated before Durgā, when he was miraculously saved by the sudden occurrence of an unexpected storm. Temples or images of Mahishāsuramardinī, another form of Durgā, have been found at Udayagiri and Bhumra in Central India.[1] Śiva had two sons, Kārtikeya and Gaṇeśa. Of the former, we get one temple in the Gupta period, but of the latter none has so far been found. Some Gaṇeśa images attributed to the Gupta age have however been recovered.

Temples of the Sun are extremely rare at present. Such was however not the case in our period. There was one solar temple at Mandasor (in Malwa), a second one at Gwalior, a third one at Indore (in northern U.P.) and a fourth one at Āśramaka in Baghelkhand. The images of the Sun-god have also been found in Bengal. One of the tutelary deities of the Śālaṅkāyanas of the Andhra country was Chitraratha or the Sun. The epigraphical references show that the Sun was specially invoked for curing diseases. Devotees of the Sun used to have either the solar orb or an *agnikuṇḍa* on their seals.[2]

The worship of Nāgas, as also of Yakshas, was fairly common among the lower classes of the population. There was a Yaksha temple at Padmāvatī near Gwalior and a Maṇināga shrine at Rajgir.

---

[1] *ASC.* X, 50.
[2] *ASR. W.C.* 1919, pl. 26.

Worship in public temples became fairly common in the Gupta period and remnants of several shrines of the age have been found in Central India. Temples were gradually becoming centres of Hindu religion and culture. Their construction and decorations encouraged the sculptor, the architect, and painter; their service at public worship required the musician and the dancer; and the public sermons delivered in their pandals in the evening afforded a scope to the services of the Paurāṇika and the philosopher. It was but natural that temples, which were thus contributing to the cause of culture and religion, should have been richly endowed. It is pleasing to note that temple authorities spent a part of their income in poor relief by founding free feeding houses; these are, for instance, known to have existed in the Kārtikeya temple at Bilsad in U.P. and in the Pishṭapurī temple at Manapur in Central India.[1] Hindu temples had not however yet become centres of education in our period as they did later on.[2] The ritual of the temple worship was almost similar to what it is now.

5. Popular Beliefs.

Let us now turn to some of the popular religious notions of the age. A number of epigraphs of our period, both from south and north India, describe it as the Kali age, where Dharma declines and immorality prospers ; pious kings are usually described as making an effort to restore the standard of the Kṛita age.[3] Prayāga was regarded as a holy place, death at which was regarded as highly meritorious. Persons suffering from incurable diseases would often valuntarily terminate their life at the confluence of the Ganges and the

---

[1] *CII.* III, 44, 115; *EI.* XVI, 19.

[2] The *Ghaṭikā* (college), located in a Kāñchī temple, seems to be an exceptional case.

[3] *IA.* V, 57; *EI.* VIII, 163, 235; *CII.* III, 44, 145.

Jumna.[1] Kings from the Deccan would often visit it on pilgrimage and make suitable grants in charity to commemorate the event.[2] The non-reference to the pilgrimage to Benares in the records of our period is probably accidental.

In his daily life, the average Brahmaṇa of our period used to perform the religious rites and rituals prescribed in the contemporary Smṛitis like those of Yājñavalkya and Bṛihaspati.[3] He offered his *Sandhyā* prayers morning and evening; the noon-time *Sandhyā* had begun to be advocated,[4] but probably it had not yet become popular. *Prāṇāyāma*, *Sūryopaṣṭhāna* and *Gāyatrījapa* formed the main features of the *Sandhyā*;[5] it is doubtful whether it included the modern Puranic verses tacked on to it. When we remember how Vaishṇavism made great strides in our period, it will be permissible to conjecture that the twenty-four names of Vishṇu, with which the modern *Sandhyā* begins, were added on to it in the Gupta age. The morning *Sandhyā* was followed by *devapūjā*, the worship of tutelary deities, and *pitṛipūjā*, the oblations to the manes. A perusal of the contemporary Smṛitis and inscriptions would show that Smārta sacrifices like the *Pañcha-mahāyajñas* were daily performed by the pious people,[6] though it is not likely that the *Smarta-agni* was maintained by many outside the priestly classes. Sixteen *Saṁskāras* were regularly performed in all the Dvija families and our age was particular in offering the *Śrāddha* to the ancestors once every month, and not once in the year. Sacrifices like the *Chāturmāsyeshṭi* and *Agrahāyaṇeshṭi* were performed only in priestly families.[7]

---

[1] *CII.* III; *Raghu,* VIII, v. 95.

[2] *EI.* XIX, 102.

[3] One epigraph of our period, dated 532 A.D., describes ideal kings as following *smārtam vartma,* the Dharma of Smṛitis. *CII.* III, 59.

[4] *Yaj.* III, 307.

[5] *Ibid.* I, 22.

[6] *Ibid.* I, 126; *EI.* XV, 130, 133.

[7] *Yāj,* I, 124-26.

6. Rites and Ceremonies

The Purāṇas in their present from recommend a number of *vratas* on numerous occasions in the year and prescribe one religious rite or another almost on every day of the month. They are particularly insistent on recommending charity on the occasions of eclipses, equinoxes and *Saṁkṛāntis*. The Purāṇas were no doubt remodelled in the Gupta age, but it seems that the chapters that were added at this time did not include those which recommend the above practices. Contemporary epigraphic evidence shows, for instance, that the theory, that gifts on the occasions of eclipses and *Saṁkrāntis* are particularly efficacious, had not yet gained ground in society. Among the scores of grants that were made during our period, it is interesting to note that only two were made on the occasions of eclipses[1] and one only on the occasion of the *Uttarāyana*.[2] This is rather surprising when it is noted that about eighty per cent of the grants subsequent to *c.* 600 A.D. were made on the days of eclipses, equinoxes and *Saṁkrāntis*. Purāṇas recommend *Rathasaptamī*, *Mahāvāruṇi*, *Kapilāshashṭhī* etc. as particularly appropriate occasions for charitable gifts and their advice has been followed by the donors of the latter half of the 1st millennium A.D. But during our period we come across no grants made on such occasions. The numerous *vratas*, mentioned in the latest redactions of the Purāṇas, had not yet become popular in Hindu society. It was following the simple and few religious practices mentioned in the Smṛitis only. The *vrata* of *Ekādaśī*, however, had become fairly popular among the Vaishṇavas of our period ; a number of grants made by them are to be seen given on this occasion or on the day previous or subsequent to it.[3] A few grants were

---

[1] Omgodu grant, *c.* 350 A.D. (*EI.* XV, 255) and Polamuru grant, *c.* 550 A.D. (*JAHRS.* VI, 17).

[2] *CII.* III, 198.

[3] *Ibid.* pp. 75, 246; *EI.* XXIII. 174; XXIV, 261; *Bṛihaspatismriti*, *Āchāra*, vv. 66-70, also recommends this *vrata* very strongly.

also made on the occasion of the full moon day.[1] But the majority of grants were given on days which are not recommended as particularly holy either in the Smṛitis or in the Purāṇas. Astronomical-cum-astrological notions had not yet got an ascendancy in society[2] and almost any day was regarded as equally good for performing a meritorious act or giving a charitable donation.

Many of the grants given after 600 A.D. describe how the donor proceeded to make the grant in question on realising the transitoriness of the mundane glory and prosperity. It is interesting to note that this motive is conspicuous by its absence in most of the grants of our period.[3] This would show that our age was able to keep an even balance between *Artha* and *Kāma* on one side and *Dharma* and *Moksha* on the other.

7. Hinduism and Foreigners.

The Aryan and Dravidian religion had become completely fused much before the beginning of our period. It is on very rare occasions indeed that we get survivals of pre-Aryan deities or practices even in the popular Tamil literature.

The assimilative power of Hinduism continued unabated during our period and it went on admitting foreigners of diverse cultures and religions within its fold. In bygone centuries it had absorbed the Greeks, the Scythians, the Parthians and the Kushāṇas ; in our age it could completely Hinduise the Hūṇas,

---

[1] *EI.* X, 75; *IA.* VII, 28.

[2] In the *Saṁskāra* section of the reconstructed *Brihaspatismṛiti* great importance is attached to the astrological auspiciousness of the days to be selected for the different *Saṁskāras.* This section of the *Smriti* would appear to be later than the Gupta period. Some of the modern astrological notions can be seen in the *Brihajjātaka* and *Bṛihatsaṁhitā* of Varāhamihira, but these works were composed towards the end of our period.

[3] It is mentioned only in the Mandasor inscription of Nara-varman; dated 405 A.D. *EI.* XII, 320.

who invaded and settled down in the country during *c.* 450 to 550 A.D. The Kushāṇa rulers of the Punjab had been already Hinduised by *c.* 150 A.D. The same was the case with the Śakas of Western India. It is doubtful whether during our period they were regarded as religiously or culturally differant from the bulk of Hindus. We find the Ikshvāku king Śāntamūla (*c.* 250 A.D.), who was an orthodox Hindu, had no objection to marry his son to a princess of this Śaka family (*ante*, p. 66). The Hinduisation of the Hūṇas also took place in less than a generation. Toramāṇa was probably not much influenced by the Hindu view of life and philosophy, but his successor Mihirakula became a devoted Śaiva. A record of his enemy, which states that he never bowed down his head before anybody with the exception of Sthāṇu or Śiva, is confirmed by the testimony of his coins, which have the symbols of Trident and Bull, and the legend '*jayatu vṛishaḥ* 'victory of the bull', mount of Śiva (cf. Pl. III, 9).

It may be added that Hinduism was prevailing in Java, Sumatra and Borneo during our period (*ante*, Ch. XVI) and it is quite possible that its followers included not only the descendants of the first immigrants but also some converts made by them. It has been already shown how Hindu temples were flourishing in Mesopotamia and Syria down to the 4th century, when they were destroyed by St. Gregory (*ante*, p. 340). Indian religion was thus a living force in parts of western Asia down to *c.* 300 A.D. and may have influenced Christian religious dogmas and practices to some extent (*ante*, p. 340).

Unfortunately we do not know the precise process by which non-Hindus were absorbed in the Hindu fold. Probably they were attracted by the Hindu religion and philosophy and began to worship Hindu gods. Brāhmaṇas of our age did not only not believe that Hinduism was intended only for those who were born within its fold, but they had no objection to act as priests to the new-comers and to perform the different *saṁskāras* for the various members of their families. The Sanskrit language was taught and the Smṛitis and the Purāṇas were expounded to them ; and so within a generation, they used to become almost *pucca* Hindus. Inter-caste marriages were still taking place in society and even orthodox Hindus had no objection to establish marriage connections with the new converts. Their absorption in Hindu society would thus become complete.

8. Hindu Philosophy.

Let us now survey the march of Hindu philosophy during our period. This task is not very easy because the dates of many of the philosophical works are not yet satisfactorily datermined. The available indications, however, show that the six system of the Hindu philosophy were systematised in our period and most of their standard works were given their present form. The *Mīmāṁṣā-sūtrās* of Jaimini were no doubt composed in the earlier period, but the *Śabara-bhāshya*, which is the standard commentary on them, was composed in *c.* 300 A.D. This work contains a systematic exposition of the Mīmāṁsā philosophy and occupies the same position in the sphere of Mīmāṁsā, which the *Bhāshyas* of Patañjali and Śaṅkara occupy in the realm of grammar and Advaita Vedānta respectively. The *Śabara-bhāshya* shows that the Mīmāṁsā had ceased to concern itself only with the rules about the exposition of rituals, but had entered into the whole field of philosophy, advocating its own views about the nature of soul, God, salvation, etc. Upavarsha, who is quoted both by Śabara and Śaṅkara, probably lived by the beginning of the 3rd century A.D. The development of the Vedānta in our period cannot be properly gauged ; there was controversy going on between the followers of the Vedānta and those of the new schools of Buddhism, which is partially echoed in the new sections added to the

Brahma-sūtras refuting the views of the Mādhyamika and the Yogāchāra schools. The problem of the interpretation of the *Upanishats*, the *Brahma-śūtras* and the *Gītā* must have given rise to several controversies in this period, as it did in later times, resulting in the advocacy of *Jñānavāda*, *Karmavāda*, and *Jñānakarmasamuchchayavāda*. But the works produced in our period on these topics have not been preserved. It is not unlikely that some of the predecessors of Śaṅkara, like Upavarsha, Bhartṛiprapañcha and Baudhāyana, may have flourished in the Vākāṭaka-Gupta age.

It was in our period that the Sāṅkhya philosophy was given its classical form by Iśvarakṛishṇa in his well-known work *Sāṅkhyakārikā* composed early in the 4th century A.D. This is the earliest, the most authoritative and the most popular work on the Sāṅkhya system and determines its main features once for all. In the realm of Yoga, our period witnessed the composition on *Vyāsa-bhāshya* of the *Yoga-sūtras* of Patañjali in *c.* 300 A.D. This work for the first time gives the standard exposition of the Yoga philosophy and is quite indispensable to understand its main principles.

The Nyāya-Vaiśeshika school of philosophy was also very active in our period. It was engaged in constant controversies with the Mādhyamika and Yogāchāra schools of Buddhist philosophy ; the sections in the *Nyāya-sūtras* of Gautama, which seek to refute the views of these philosophers, were probably added in our period. Vātsyāyana, a scholar of Kañchī, composed the *Nyāya-bhāshya*, the most authoritative commentary on the *Sūtras*, towards the end of the 4th century A.D. He criticises the views of the Mādhyamika school about inter-relation (*opekshā*) and void ((*śūnyatā*) (IV, 1, 39-40 ; IV, 1, 31-2) and attacks the theory of idealism of the Yogāchāra philosophy (IV, 2, 26-27). A little later flourished Praśastapāda, who, under the guise of writing a commentary upon the *Vaiśeshika-sūtras*, has really given us the earliest independent and systematic exposition of the Vaiśeshika philosophy in his *Padārthadharma-saṁgraha.*

A remarkable change was taking place gradually in our period in the works on the Nyāya ; they were devoting themselves more and more to the discussion of the problems connected with *Pramāṇas* (mechanism of knowledge) and syllogism ; the treatment of other heterogeneous topics included in the sixteen categories was gradually falling into background.

9. Buddhism.

The development of the Mahāyāna religion and philosophy had already started by about the 1st century A.D. During our period both the Mahāyāna and Hīnayāna schools continued to prosper. Ceylon, as before, was the stronghold of the Hīnayāna. In the 3rd century the Mahāyānists tried to get foothold in the island, but did not succeed in their effort (*ante,* chap. XIII). The Ceylonese started writing their own commentaries on the sacred texts. These were first composed in Sinhalese, but that language was soon given up in favour of Pali. Our period undoubtedly marks a brilliant epoch in the history of the Pali literature of Ceylon. The *Dīpavaṁśa* and *Mahāvaṁśa*, composed in *c.* 350 A.D. and 475 A.D. respectively, are valuable for reconstructing the ancient history of Ceylon and India. The output of the religious and philosophical literature of the age is, however, still more remarkable. In the first half of the 5th century, Buddhaghosha, who according to tradition was a Brāhmaṇa Buddhist from Gaya, composed at Anurādhapura his famous work *Visuddhimagga*, which lucidly expounds how *śila* (immaculate character), *samādhi* (meditation) and *prajñā* (true knowledge) lead a person to *Nirvāṇa.* He has also written many valuable commentaries on the Tripīṭakas and some other works. The present day Buddhism, not only of Ceylon but also of Burma, Siam and Cambodia, has been considerably influenced by the theories and views propounded by Buddhaghosha in his different works. A little later, Buddhadatta, another immigrant from India, wrote comprehensive works on Abhidhamma and Vinaya, viz., *Abhidhammāvatara*, *Rūpārūpavibhāga* and *Vinayavinichchaya*.

Ceylonese Buddhists during our period began to pay back their spiritual debt to India by sending their own missionaries to preach the gospel of the Master in the land of his birth. In the 3rd century A.D. they were active not only in Andhra and Tamil provinces, Karṇāṭaka and Koṅkana, but also in Bengal, Kashmir and Gandhara.[1] Ceylon sent her missionaries also to China[2] and they translated a number of Hinayāna texts into Chinese. Pious Ceylonese pilgrims continued to visit the holy places of Buddhism in large numbers, and a rest house was built in *c.* 350 A.D. for their convenience at Buddhagayā by king Meghavarṇa of Ceylon.

Kashmir, Gandhāra and Afghanistan continued to be the strongholds of the Hinayāna down to the 5th century A.D. Its Sarvāstivādin school was strong in Kashmir and its Sanskrit canon was completed in our period. It was due to its missionary activity that Hīnayāna continued to be strong in the North-West of India.[3] Vasubandhu in the earlier part of his life was the most authoritative exponent of its philosophy. His famous work *Abhidharmakosha*, written from the point of view of the Vaibhāshika school, expounds the fundamental principles of Buddhism in such a masterly fashion, that it is regarded as authoritative by all schools of Buddhism.

The Mahāyāna was however getting gradually stronger as our period advanced. This is shown by the Mahāyāna garb which the Buddha biography assumed in the *Mahāvastu*, the

---

1 *EI*, XX, 22.
2 Farquhar, *Outlines*, p. 155.
3 Fa-hien, pp. 29-34.

Lalitavistara, the *Jātakamāla* and the *Divyāvadāna*. Of these the last two works were composed certainly in our period.[1]

The growing popularity of the Mahāyāna was due partly to the greatness of its philosophers and partly to the attractiveness of the philosophy they propounded. Nāgārjuna, Āryadeva, Asaṅga, Vasubandhu and Dignāga have not many equals among Indian philosophers. The creed they preached appealed much more to the ordinary mind than the philosophy of the Hīnayāna. Atheism was replaced by the gospel of a Divine Helper of men, and the apprehensions created by the doctrine of *anattā* (non-existence of soul) were practically all removed by the doctrine of *Dharmakāya*, through which an individnal could get eternal existence. *Nirvāṇa* was not the tranquilisation of human aspirations, but the fulfilment of human life ; one can live in the whirlpool of life and death and yet be above it as the Bodhisattvas do as a matter of fact. The latter are always ready and present to save the genuine devotees and can also transfer to them their good *karmà* to secure their salvation. What mattered was not a *Jnāna* so much as genuine *Bhakti* ; a single obeisance made to a *stūpa* or Buddha image by a pious devotee would secure his eventual salvation. Naturally, a religion which offered this simple way to attain the spiritual goal became more popular than its rival, which maintained that one must depend entirely on one's own exertions for getting the *Nirvāṇa*.

The Mahāyāna religion developed its two schools of philosophy, the Mādhyamika and the Yogāchāra, during our period. Of these the former had been already expounded by Nāgārjuna towards the end of the 2nd century A.D. His pupil Āryadeva composed *Chatuḥśataka* during our period (*c.* 250 A.D.) ; this in one of the most authoritative works upon the system. Two of

[1] Winternitz, *History* II, 276. Vasubandhu's disciple Sthiramati has written a commentary on the *Abhidharmakosha* and the other works of his master. Saṅghabhadra, a rival of Vasubandhu, has attacked the doctrines of *Kosha* in his work *Koshakāraka*.

the most famous Prajñā texts, the *Vajrachchhedikā Prajñāpāramitā* and the *Prajñāpāramitā-hṛidayasūtra* were also most probably composed during our age. Both these are of very high metaphysical value, and the latter one is the most widely read Buddhist text of Japan.

Our period is undoubtedly the golden age of the Yogāchāra school of the Mahāyāna philosophy. Its founder Maitreyanātha flourished in *c.* 200 A.D. The most authoritative works of the school, *Mahāyānasaṁparigraha*, *Yogāchārabhūmiśāstra* and the *Mahāyānaśūtrālaṅkāra* were composed at Peshawar in *c.* 300 A.D. by Asaṅga, who was a Brāhmaṇa convert to Buddhism. Asaṅga's younger brother Vasubandhu was, as observed already, a Hīnayānist till late in his life. But when he was converted to Mahāyāna by his brother, he helped the propagation of its doctrines by writing a number of important works characterised by independence of thought and depth of erudition. Two of his works, *Viṁśātikā* and *Triṁśatikā* give a masterly refutation or a belief in the existence of the external world, while defending the reality of *Vijñāna*. Vasubandhu was also a great controversialist and has attacked the Sāṅkhya position of Īśvarakṛishṇa in his work *Paramārthasaptati*. The *Laṅkāvatāra-sūtra*, composed probably towards the beginning of the 5th century,[1] is also controversial and shows how the Buddhists were trying to refute the views and theories of the Sāṅkhyas, the Naiyāyikas, the Vaiśeshikas and the Mīmāṁsakas. But its main importance lies in the further development of the *Vijñānavāda* which it records. It maintains that all pluralism and differentiations in this world are due to ignorance. *Vijñāna* is the only reality and constitutes the essence of the *Dharmakāya*. When once it is realised, all differences in the empirical world appear no more

[1]The translation of this work into Chinese, made by Guṇaprabha in 443 A.D., does not contain the Chapters I, IX and X. It is therefore clear that they were added to it later on, probably towards the end of the 5th century A.D.

substantial than a magical show. In order to explain the non-reality of the external world, the *Sūtra* compares it to the horns of the hare, the son of a barren woman and the cirle of fire produced when a burning stick is twirled round,—conceptions which were destined to loom large in the development of the Advaita philosophy. The *Sūtra* practically assumes the Advaitic position when it declares that Ātman or the Individual Soul is identical with Tathāgatagarbha, the Cosmic Soul. It will be thus seen that the development of the *Vijñānavāda* in our period paved the way to the enunciation of the Advaitic Vedanta by Gauḍapāda and Śaṅkara about two centuries later.

The Mādhyamika and the Yogāchāra schools, though branches of the Mahāyāna, were drifting further and further away towards the end of our period. This development was not welcomed by some Buddhist thinkers and one of them, the younger Aśvaghosha, attempted a synthesis of their view-points in his *Mahāyānaśraddhotpāda* composed in the 5th century A.D.

The foundations of the Buddhist logic were laid-down in our period by Vasubandhu in his work *Tarkaśāstra*. Its further development is to be seen in the works of Dignāga,[1] who flourished in Kāñchī towards the end of the 4th century A.D. In his works on logic Dignāga maintains that the syllogism should have only three members, and not five, as maintained by Gautama and Vātsyāyana ; being an out and out subjectivist he also gives his own definitions of *Pratyaksha* and *Anumāna*. His attacks on the Hindu logicians evoked counter-attacks on his position by Udyotakara and Kumārila in subsequent centuries. In fact the activity of the Mediaeval school of Indian logic has largely centred round the theories of Dignāga, which are accepted and implemented by some of his successors, and rejected and refuted by others. Dignāga is undoubtedly one of the greatest thinkers and foremost figures

[1] *E.g. Pramāṇasamuchhaya*, *Pramāṇaśāstranyāyapraveśa*, etc.

in Indian philosophy, and it is a great pity that one alone among his works, *Nyāyamukha*, should have been preserved, only in Chinese and Tibetan versions. *Nyāyapraveśa* by his disciple Śaṅkarārya[1] has, however, been preserved in Sanskrit and also been published.

10. Extent of Buddhism.

The general view that Buddhism was on the decline in the Gupta period owing to the revival of Hinduism under the Guptas is not supported by the above survey of its philosophical activity and output. Nor is it confirmed by the artistic evidence. That the Vākāṭāka-Gupta age was the golden age of the Buddhist art will be easily conceded by any visitor to Sarnath, Paharpur, Ajanta and Nagarjunikonda.[2] It is true that Kapilavastu, Rāmagrāma, Śrāvastī, and Vaiśālī, which were important places connected with the life of the Buddha, were deserted when Fa-hien visited them early in the fifth century, but this circumstance was probably due to the shifting of the economic and political centre, rather than to the decline of Buddhism in the country around them. There is clear evidence to show that Kashmir, Afghanistan and the Punjab were the strongholds of Buddhism during our period ; Fa-hien saw thousands of monasteries and myriads of monks in these provinces. In the upper Gangetic plain, Hinduism and Buddhism seem to have been equally popular and the same was probably the case in Bihar and Bengal. Epigraphs have been found at

1 Some however ascribe this work of Dignāga himself.

2 Donations in favour of Buddhism mentioned in our epigraphs are no doubt relatively fewer than those recorded in favour of Hindu temples or gods and Brāhmaṇas. The withdrawal of the patronage by a section of the richer classes does not seem to have affected the popularity of Buddhism. No epigraphs have, however, been recovered from the Punjab, where the religion was most popular.

Mathura, Kauśāmbī and Kasia (the place of the Buddha's death) showing that these were sufficiently important centres of Buddhism. Numerous votive *stūpas* and Buddhist statues discovered at Sarnath show that it was a very important centre of Buddhism, visited by thousands of pilgrims coming from far and near. The same was the case with Bodhgaya, where a special rest-house was built in our period for the convenience of the Ceylonese pilgrims. In Bengal Mrigaśikhāvana was a famous centre of Buddhist religion and culture. Wo have no reliable information about the relative position of Hinduism and Buddhism in Central and Western India. In western Mahārāshṭra, the Buddhist cave temples and monasteries at Bhaja, Kuda, Mahar, Bedsa, Junnar, Kanheri, etc. were occupied at least down to the 5th century and were being patronised not only by the aristocracy, but also by smiths, carpenters, garland-makers, goldsmiths, traders and doctors.

The numerous caves at Ajanta and Ellora show that they were famous centres of Buddhism in eastern Mahārāshṭra, richly endowed by the State and society. Andhra country was studded with Buddhist *Stūpas* and *Vihāras*, but the most famous among them were those at Nagarjunikonda, which were discovered and excavated only in the thirties of the present century. It was most probably at this place that the famous Nāgārjuna lived, preached and wrote, and it is no wonder that the place should have been one of the most important, thriving and populous centres of Buddhism. During the 3rd century it was richly endowed by several members of the Ikshvāku royal family, and its description by Fa-hien shows that it continued to thrive down to the beginning of the 5th century A.D. In Tamil country, Kāñchī was a famous Buddhist centre since the beginning of the Chirstian era. During our period it produced the famous Buddhist logician Dignāga and supplied an abbot to Nalanda in Dharmapāla. In Kathiawar, Valabhī was a famous Buddhist centre having a number of monasteries richly endowed by the Maitraka rulers. Some of these had started building up libraries also.[1]

It would appear that the Buddhist monasteries just started their educational activities in the latter half of our period. Their description by Fa-hien does not show that any of them had yet become University centres. But soon after his departure both Nalanda and Valabhī started their career as University centres, when they began to receive rich endowments enabling them to offer free tuition, boarding and lodging to a large number of students. How they functioned as Buddhist centres of learning and disseminated the doctrines of religion throughout Eastern Asia will be described in the next volume.

The Buddhist monasteries were usually well-endowed and their residents were generally keen in following the rules of the Order. Foreigners like Fa-hien were well struck by the piety of conduct and strictness of behaviour of the Buddhist monks. Monastic authorities were very particular to look after the needs of strangers and guests coming to them.

Nuns were admitted into the Order early in our period. There was a nunnery at Junnar[2] in Western India and Fa-hien's account shows that there were others in the Punjab and the Gangetic plain at the beginning of the 5th century A.D.[3] The practice of admitting nuns into the Order was getting unpopular and Buddhaghosha observes that it was no longer sanctioned in his time (*c.* 500 A.D.).

The difference between the Hinayāna and the Mahāyāna were becoming more and more pronounced as our period advanced, and sometimes there was keen rivalry between the followers of the two schools. Their monasteries were therefore often separate. In smaller places, however, the followers of the two schools lived together.

---

1 *IA.* VII, 67 ; *JRAS.* 1895, p. 383.
2 *ASWI.* IV, 23.
3 Fa-hien, pp. 43-45.

Due to the growing popularity of the Mahāyāna cult, Buddhism became an attractive religion in our period. The Buddha image became quite common all over the country ; it used to be the centre of rich worship almost similar to that which prevails today in Hindu temples. There were magnificient *Stūpas* and *Chaityas* built everywhere and the image of the Buddha was carried in procession in special chariots during the week preceding the full moon of Vaiśākha, the date of his birth and enlightenment. The Buddhist estabishments were decorated with artistic sculptures and paintings, describing the scenes of the last and earlier lives of the Blessed One. Buddhism was quite free from Tantric practices during our period, but towards its end some Mahāyāna books like *Suvarṇaprabhāsa* and *Samādhirāja* began to introduce magic spells and charms which were destined to pave the way to later Tantrism.

Buddhism had made considerable headway in China, as has been already narrated in Chapter XVI ; and we find Chinese Pilgrims like Fa-hien coming to India in our period. Their objects were usually twofold, to visit holy places of Buddhism and to procure authentic texts of their sacred canon. The intercourse however was not one-sided, for Indian Buddhists also were going to China in large numbers to preach the gospel and to translate Sanskrit works into Chinese. The account of their work and activities has been already given in Chapter XVI.

11. Jainism.

The Vākāṭāka-Gupta period is undoubtedly an important epoch in the history of Jainism. The knowledge of the *Aṅgas* and *Pūrvas*, as determined at the council of Pāṭaliputra in *c.* 300 B.C., was again threatening to lapse into oblivion. Matters became worse owing to a long famine that occurred early in the fourth century A.D. In the year 810 of the Vīra era[1] (313 A.D. two councils were therefore simultaneously convoked by the Śvetāmbaras, one at Mathura under the presidency of Skandila, and the other at Valabhī[2] under that of (Jain) Nāgārjuna. These councils settled the correct texts of the sacred writings. The texts so determined were later committed to writing at the second council at Valabhī held in 980 of the Vīra era (453 A.D.) which was presided over by Devardhi Kshamāśramaṇa. The intellectual urge which characterised the Gupta period resulted in the Jains starting to write a number of commentaries upon their sacred texts, known as *niryuktis* and *chūrṇis*. The most important writer of this class is Bhadrabāhu II, who wrote *niryuktis* upon most of the important canonical works.

Sanskrit was getting the upper hand in our period and it is interesting to note that the Jains were also beginning to succumb to its charm. Umāsvāti's famous work *Tattvārthādhigamasūtra* is written in Sanskrit and not in Prākṛit. The same is the case with Siddhasena's *Nyāyāvatāra* and a number of his *Dvātriṁśikās*.

The precise following of Jainism is difficult to determine in our period. Mathura and Valabhī continued to be the strongholds of Śvetāmbara Jainism. In northern Bengal Puṇḍravardhana was a strong centre of Digambara Jainism. Epigraphs show that Jain establishments existed at Kahaum in Gorakhpur district (U.P.) and Udayagiri in Central India, and there is no doubt that many more existed in other places in northern India, though we know nothing about them today. In south India Karṇāṭaka and Mysore were strongholds of Digambara Jainism;

---

[1] This will correspond to 313 A.D. if we accept the orthodox Jain view that the death of Mahāvīra took place in 527 B.C. The time will be 50 years later, if we place this event in 477 B.C. as some scholars do at present.

[2] These councils are not so well known as the later council of Valabhī. But their meeting is attested to by the *Nandichūrṇi* of Jinadāsa (578 A.D.) and *Yogasāstravṛitti* of Hemachandra (1140 A.D.).

the religion was richly patronised both by the Kadamba and Gaṅga rulers. In Tamil country Jainism had gained a firm footing since the early centuries of the Christian era, and important Tamil works *Naladiyar*, *Palmoli Nanuru* and *Jīvakachintāmaṇi* had been witten by eminent Jain scholars. During our period in *c.* 470 A.D. Jains convened a special *saṅgam* of their own at Madura under the presidency of Vajranandi. In south Arcot district, in the village of Pāṭalikā, there was a famous Jain monastery, where *Lokavibhaṅga* was composed by Muni Sarvanandi in 458 A.D.[1] Kāñchī also was a famous centre of Jainism and some of the Pallava and Pāṇḍya rulers were its followers. There was a keen rivalry between Jainism on one side and Śaivism on the other, but it did not result in any mutual persecution during our period.

The ritual of public worship in Jina temples was rich and costly. Baths in perfumed oil and water were given, flower-garlands and scents were offered, and incense and lamps were burnt before the image of one who had preached renunciation in its extreme form. On special occasions, especially in the week preceding the full moon of Kārtika, the Jina image was taken out in a grand procession. Jain monasteries were richly endowed ; usually half the revenues were spent over the expenses connected with public rituals and the other half over the maintenance of the monks and nuns.

The rich patronage offered to the religion by the state and society was tending to introduce laxity in a section of the monks, who began to argue that they need not move throughout the year, but may settle down permanently in monasteries. Some began to wear coloured and scented clothes and others to use carriages and comfortable beds. Prophesying and selling of Jina images was started by others as a profession. Leaders of

---

[1] The original Prākṛit work is not available. Its Sanskrit rendering made much later gives the above date for the work.

the Jain religion came forward in time to condemn these tendencies. Their efforts were however only partly successful.

As is well known, the Digambaras do not accept the canon as finally determined at Valabhī. According to them the only surviving portions of the twelve *Aṅgas* have been preserved in the *Shaṭkhaṇḍāgama*, *Kashāyapahuḍa* and *Mahābandha*. The dates of these works, which are of course in Prākṛit, cannot be determined with certainty, but they seem to have been composed towards the end of the 2nd or the beginning of the 3rd century A.D. Our age therefore is as important in the history of the Śvetāmbara literature as in that of the Digambara one. The Digambara works referred to above deal with the doctrine of *Karman* and the causes of bondage which tie down the soul to *Saṁsāra.*

Jain religion and philosophy are remarkably conservative; we hardly notice any change or development in them, as we do in Hinduism or Buddhism. The historian can, therefore, hardly refer to any religious practices or philosophical dogmas as being evolved in our period. Towards its beginning, however, Umāsvāti composed (in *c.* 200 A.D.) his famous work *Tattvārthādhigamasūtra* which is a very useful manual for understanding the main features of Jain religion, philosophy, cosmography, ontology and ethics. It is in fact the most important and non-canonical work, and has the merit of explaining the fundamental principles of Jainism in a very lucid and effective manner. It is accepted both by the Digambaras and the Śvetāmbaras and has been extensively commented upon. It is interesting to note that it was in our age that Jain philosophers for the first time began to offer rational explanations for their religious dogmas and tenets. The most prominent among these was undoubtedly Siddhasena Divākara, who flourished in the 5th century A.D. In his famous work *Sanmati-tarka* he proceeds to support the scriptural doctrine of *Anekāntavāda* with cogent arguments based purely on logic;

he undoubtedly strikes us more as a philosopher than as a theologian.

The rational tendency of the age gave a great impetus to the progress of logic among the Jains. Siddhasena Divākara is also the father of Jain logic. His *Nyāyavatāra* is the first systematic Jain work on this topic and its merit lies in its not being sectarian in its outlook. It was Siddhasena who started the practice of writing works on logic in such a manner as not to clash with the religious dogmas either of the Hindus or of the Buddhists or of the Jains. This method was followed by a number of later Buddhist and Jain writers and helped the development of the science in the mediaeval times.

12. General View.

Let us now make a general résumé of the religious and philosophical condition. Self-complacency had not yet become the characteristic of the mental outlook of the leaders of our religious movements and philosophical thought. They were alert and on the look out to see and examine the new theories and movements that were coming into prominence. Every philosophical system was anxious to remain up-to-date and it added new sections to its traditional works, reviewing and refuting the theories of the opposing schools. It is in this period that we for the first time see the conflict of mind with mind and theory with theory in the sphere of Indian philosophy, for direct attacks and refutations of each other's systems did not take place earlier among the followers of Hinduism, Buddhism and Jainism. Philosophical controversies were however carried on with decorum and without creating any bitterness ; the followers of different religions continued to live in harmony.

Hinduism still knew how to adjust itself to new surroundings and abandon gracefully a position that had become untenable. It still continued to believe in the gospel of *Kriṇvanto viśvamāryaṁ* ; the spread of Hinduism in Indo-China and the East Indies in our period is a glorious example in this connection. At home it continued to absorb peacefully the foreign tribes like the Śakas and the Hūṇas, who had come as conquerors.

It was still keeping an even balance between *Dharma* and *Moksha* on one side and *Artha* and *Kāma* on the other. It was not yet overgrown with superstitions. Notions of astrology had not yet begun to sway the mind of average Hindu, nor was he prescribed an unending series of *vratas* and rituals to be performed almost on every day of the year.

The achievements af the Hindu systems of philosophy in our period were mostly critical, and consisted of readjustments necessitated by mutual studies and controversies. But our period was undoubtedly the most creative one in the case of the Mahāyāna school of Buddhism. The most original, the most daring and the most far-reaching contributions of this school to the progress of philosophy were made by its thinkers who flourished in our period.

CHAPTER XX

EDUCATION, LITERATURE AND SCIENCES.

One can hardly understand the spirit, importance and characteristics of an age without studying its educational institutions, understanding the nature of its literature, and ascertaining its achievements in the different branches of sciences and fine arts. We therefore now proceed to study the education, literature and sciences of our period in this chapter ; fine arts will be discussed in Chap. XXII.

I. EDUCATION.

Since very early times, private teacher was the pivot of ancient Indian system of education. He used to train students as a matter of duty, content with such honorarium as may be voluntarily paid to him by the guardians of his students. This uncertain income was supplemented by the teacher's professional earnings as a priest and by such grants and donations, which he occasionally received from the state or wealthy citizens. Holy places (*tīrthas*) and capitals of kingdoms thus tended to become educational centres from early times, because they offered the best chances to the teacher of supplementing his uncertain income from the above sources. The same was the case in our period. Of the capital cities Pāṭaliputra and Valabhī are definitely known to have been famous centres of education, and the same must have been the case of Ujjayanī, Padmāvatī Pravarapura, and Vatsagulma (Basim). To turn to *tīrthas*, we find that the Brāhmaṇas of Ayodhyā were famous for their skill in the exposition of *Mantra*, *Sūtra* and *Bhāshya*[1],

[1] Cf. स्वाध्यायमंत्रसूत्रभाष्यप्रवचनपारग *EI.* X, 72.

and the same must have been the case with those of other holy places like Benares, Mathura, Nasik and Kāñchī. The last-mentioned place was a centre of both Hindu and Buddhist learning, and one of its famous scholars Dharampāla became the head of the famous University of Nalanda in the 6th century.[1]

The fame of Taxila was on the decline ; the Shāka kings, who were ruling over it during our period, were almost barbarous, and they could not encourage the cause of education. When Fa-hien visited the place at the beginning of the 5th century A.D., he found there nothing of educational importance.

I. AGRAHĀRA VILLAGES AS CENTRES OF LEARNING.

Agrahāra villages, containing learned Brāhmaṇas enjoying shares in their revenues assigned to them for maintenance by the state, had become famous centres of learning in our period. King Umavarman of Kalinga used to take care to see that the number of the *Agrahāra* villages in his kingdom was never less than 36.[2] It is almost certain that other kings of our period also followed similar policy in order to encourage the cause of religion and education. The donees in the *Agrahāra* villages, however, were not merely devoted to their own studies, but many of them were celebrated teachers who could attract students from far and wide. Thus the Brāhmaṇas of the *Agrahāra* village of Pishṭapuram, modern Pithapuram in Godavari district, were famous both as scholars and teachers in the 6th century A.D.[3] The donee of the Pāṇḍuraṅgapallī grant (*c.* 500 A.D.) was a teacher of hundreds of Brāhmaṇas.[4] There is therefore no doubt that

[1] Watters, II, 168-9.
[2] *EI*. XII, 5.
विद्याध्ययनप्रवचनव्याख्यानशीलिन:; Tandiwada grant, *EI*. XVIII, 98.
[4] ब्राह्मणशतमध्यापकस्य; *MAR*. 1929, p. 197.

the *Agrahāra* villages in our period were usually centres of higher education. If a small ruler like Umavarman used to maintain as many as 36 of them, their numbers in larger kingdoms like those of the Vākāṭakas and the Guptas may well have been easily more than 100. Most of the rulers of these kingdoms were patrons of Brahmanism and many of them like Samudra-Gupta, Chandra-gupta II and Pravara-sena II were lovers of learning. *Agrahāra* villages, therefore, must have been very numerous in our period and they were the main centres of higher learning, apart from capital cities and *tīrthas*.

In South India centres of higher learning were known as *Ghaṭikās*. We have no detailed information about them during our period, but it seems that they were something like post-graduate colleges.[1] There was a famous *Ghaṭikā* at Kāñchī, drawing students from far and near. This institution was located in a temple and the same was probably the case with other *Ghaṭikās*. We can then well conclude that they were the precursors of the temple-colleges of the later period.

2. Rise of Monastic Colleges.

Buddhist monasteries began to develop into educational institutions during our period. When Fa-hien visited Nalanda in *c.* 410 A.D., there was no educational activity at the place; but by the end of the 5th century this Buddhist monastery became a famous University, thanks to the generosity of a number of Hindu emperors of the Gupta dynasty. Several nonasteries were built to accommodate the growing pupulation of monk-students. Particular attention was given to the development of the library, and the teachers of the University were beginning to get international reputation by the end of

[1] Mayūra-śarman started for the *Ghaṭikā* of Kāñchi along with his teacher. *EI.* VIII, 31.

our period. The establishment was a Mahāyāna one and must have naturally concentrated on the studies of the works of Asaṅga, Nāgārjuna, Vasubandhu and Dignāga. But Hindu and Jain systems of philosophy were also taught in the University in order to enable the Buddhist controversialist to meet his opponents on their own ground. Detailed information about the organisation and administration of this University will be given in Vol. VII.

We may well presume that other important Buddhist monasteries had also begun to become centres of learning during the latter half of our period (*c.* 400-550 A.D.). There is no direct evidence on the point, but since they had acquired the status of colleges in *c.* 625 A.D., the transformation, we may presume, must have started at least about a century earlier.

Let us now survey the curricula followed in our schools and colleges. The Vedic studies definitely fell into the background. Purāṇas were remodelled in our period and the Dharmaśāstra and the different branches of philosophy developed their literature with great rapidity. We may, therefore, well presume that Purāṇas, Smṛitis, logic and metaphysics must have been studied with great enthusiasm in the colleges of our period. Sankrit grammar, being the key subject, must have been studied everywhere. Astronomy-cum-astrology was gradually becoming popular.[1]

The general level of culture and learning was very high among the Brāhmaṇas during our period on account of the large number of *Agrahāras* and the assiduosness with which education was imparted in them. But the same was not the case with the Kshatriyas and Vaiśyas. Their *Upanayana* was being gradually discontinued, to the great detriment, not only of their Vedic studies, but also of their cultural education. Female education, suffered a definite set-back in this peried owing to

[1] See Altekar, *Education in Ancient India* (2nd edition) for more detailed information about this section.

the disappearance of girls' *Upanayana*. The situation deteriorated further owing to the lowering of their marriageable age to 12, which rendered any serious education worth the name impossible. In cultured families, however, special tutors used to be maintained for imparting higher education to girls, some of whom became poetesses and authoresses in later life.

3. Technical and Primary Education.

Technical education was imparted usually in the family itself, as most of the professions had become hereditary. When however this was not possible, young students used to indenture themselves as apprentices to artisan masters for an agreed number of years. During the earlier part of this period they used to learn the craft, free of charge, but during its latter half they were required to work gratis in their masters' workshops, as a compensation for their trouble in training them.[1]

We have not much information about primary education. In our period, *Upanayana* and Vedic studies presupposed the ability to read and write, and since it was obligatory for the Brāhmaṇas, literacy amongst them must have been very high. The gradual disappearance of *Upanayana* from the Kshatriyas and Vaiśyas tended to increase the illiteracy among them. We may however well presume that about 60% of the regenerated classes (*dvijas*) could read and write in our period. Most of the Śudras and untouchables were illiterates.

Primary education commenced at about the age of 5 and was imparted by teachers who were called *Dārakāchāryas*. Very often teachers who taught the Vedic hymns also initiated their students in the 3 R's. *Lipiśālās* or primary schools existed in several villages. Children of rich families used to write on wooden boards in some kind of colour. In poorer schools,

---

[1] *Nārada*, Chap. V, 16-21.

alphabets were written by the finger on the ground covered with sand or fine dust. The curriculum in primary schools consisted mainly of the 3 R's. In advanced schools, students were also encouraged to memorise primers of Sanskrit grammar.

II. Sanskrit Literature

Let us now take a survey of the literature of the period. The theory that Sanskrit language was in a state of abeyance during the post-Aśokan and pre-Gupta period has now been completely exploded. The early works of Buddhists and Jains were composed in Pali and Prākṛits, but their loyalty to vernaculars became eventually lukewarm. Sanskrit had a decided superiority over Pali and Prākṛits in the richness of its vocabulary, compactness of its form and expressiveness of its idioms. As Prākṛits, began to develop and differentiate more and more from one another, Sanskrit naturally attained the position of the *lingua franca*, and we find that the Mahāyāna Buddhists accepted it for their sacred canon more than a century before the rise of the Gupta empire.[1] The attraction of Sanskrit had become so strong even in the second century A.D., that a foreign ruler like Rudra-dāman I began to spend his leisure hours in its cultivation. If we are to trust his court poet, he had even composed a number of good and graceful poems in that language.

There can, however, be no doubt that with the rise of the Gupta empire, the progress of Sanskrit got an additional

[1] The *Jātakamālā* of Ārya Sūra, which describes the incidents in the past lives of the Buddha in the classical *Kāvya* style, is also a pre-Gupta work. The *Lalitavistara*, which narrates the life of the Buddha in Sanskrit, is a still earlier work. These two books show that the Buddhists had began to perfer Sanskrit to Prākṛit as early as the 1st or 2nd century A.D. even in the case of those works which were intended for the masses.

momentum. The Sātavāhana rulers were staunch followers of Hinduism, and probably they were Brāhmaṇas. But they used to patronise Prākṛit as their court language.[1] The same was the case with the Ikshvākus, the early Pallavas and the Vākāṭakas, who were the immediate successors of the Sātavāhanas in the South. Though the Guptas were Vaiśyas, they were so zealous admirers of Sanskrit that they are said to have enjoined its use even in their *harem.*[2] This encouragement undoubtedly resulted in a great and all-round development of Sanskrit literature.

As observed already, *Kāvya* (court poetry) was fairly popular even in the 2nd century A.D. Its development presupposes works on dramaturgy and poetics. The *Nāṭyaśāstra* of Bharata, composed in the earlier period, continued to guide the dramatists of our period ; no new work was composed. Rāmaśarmā, Medhāvin and Rājamitra, who flourished between *c.* 200 and 400 A.D., made important contributions to the development of the *Alaṁkāraśāstra* (poetics), but their works have not been preserved. The earliest extant works on this science were composed towards the end of the period by Bhāmaha, Rudraṭa, and Daṇḍin.[3] The science, however, was still in its infancy and was busying itself only with the figures of speech, fundamental problems connected with the essence of poetry or with *dhvani* and *rasa* were not yet engaging its attention.

---

[1] Hāla, one of the Sātavāhana kings, is the reputed compiler of the *Saptaśati*, an anthology of Prākṛit lyrical verses. It is however likely that this work was enlarged in our period to its present size. *Brihatkathā* of Guṇāḍhya was also composed at the Sātavāhana court.

[2] *Kāvyamīmāṁsā*, p. 50.

[3] De, *Sanskrit Poetics*, II, 40 ff. According to another view, however, Bhāmaha was not the predecessor but the successor of Daṇḍin. (Keith *History of Sanskrit Literature*, p. 375). In that case he would not fall within our period.

1. The Authors of the Age : Bhāsa.

The chronology of Sanskrit authors is still to a great extent unsettled, but it seems fairly certain that Bhāsa, Śūdraka, Kālidāsa, Viśākhadatta and Bhāravi flourished in our age. Inscriptious of our period reveal the names of some other poets, who will also be referred to later.

Curiously enough the opinion among scholars is sharply divided as to whether we have really discovered the plays of the poet Bhāsa, who has been so highly praised by Kālidāsa and Bāṇa. One school maintains that the thirteen Trivandrum plays do not really belong to Bhāsa, but to some second-rate dramatist. It points out that none of them gives Bhāsa as the name of its author, and that many of the verses attributed to that poet by mediaeval anthologies do not occur in them. The opposite school demurs to this conclusion, mainly on the ground that the *Svapna-Vāsavadattā* of the Trivandrum plays possesses most of the features noticed by the ancient critics and poets about Bhāsa's drama of that name. And as there is a marked similarity about the language and the dramatic technique of the thirteen Trivandrum plays, it is claimed that all of them should be ascribed to Bhāsa. This view seems to be the more probable one.[1]

Bhāsa seems to have flourished about a century or so before Kālidāsa, and his time may, therefore, be taken to be *c.* 300 A.D. So far thirteen plays of his have come to light and they are the *Madhyamavyāyoga*, the *Dūta-Ghāṭotkacha*, the *Karṇa-bhāra*, the *Urubhaṅga*, the *Pañcharātra*, the *Dūtavākya*, the *Bālacharita*, the *Pratimā*, the *Abhisheka*, the *Avimārka*, the *Pratijñā-Yaugandharāyaṇa*, the *Svapna-Vāsavadattā*, and the

[1] For arguments in favour of the authenticity of the plays of Bhāsa, see T. Ganapati Sastri, *Bhāsa's works, a Critical Study*; Keith, *Sanskrit Drama*, Pusalkar, *Bhāsa, a Study*. For the contrary view, consult Barnett, *JRAS*. 1919 pp. 233-4; Levi, *ZDMG*. LXXII, 203-8; Kane, *Vividhaijñānavistāra*, 1920, pp. 97-102 and Pisharoti *HIQ*. V, 552-558.

Chārudatta. The majority of these plays are based upon epic themes, but Bhāsa shows considerable skill in dramatising them. Characterisation is effective and the language and style are racy and direct.

2. Kālidāsa.

Kalidāsa, the most famous and gifted poet in Sanskrit literature, was most probably a contemporary of Chandra-gupta II, and may be taken to have lived between *c*. 360 and 420 A.D. Unfortunately modern research has not yet succeeded in conclusively fixing his date. One school holds that he flourished in the first century B.C., and the other maintains that he lived in the Gupta period. The first school points out how the tradition asserts that the poet was a contemporary of Vikrama, the founder of the Vikrama era, and how he gives minute details about the Śuṅga times, possible to be known only by a contemporary. Vikrama, the patron of Kālidāsa, can, however, also be Chandra-gupta II Vikramāditya, and even a poet of later times can give minute details of an earlier age from sources known to him, but no longer available to us. The advocates of the first school lay particular emphasis upon the admitted resemblance between some verses of Aśvaghosha and Kālidāsa, and point out that if we place Kālidāsa in the Gupta period, we shall have to suppose that the greatest among the Sanskrit poets had borrowed some of his ideas from the Buddhist author. This argument also is not very decisive ; for like other great poets in all countries, Kālidāsa may well have taken a few ideas from his predecessors. Almost in each case, however, Kālidāsa is seen improving upon the original.

Literary tradition states that Kālidāsa had revised the poem *Setubandha* of king Pravara-sena. We have shown already how the author of the *Setubandha* is none other than the Vākāṭaka king Pravara-sena II (*ante*, p. 114); very probably Kālidāsa was his tutor for some time. Rāmagirisvāmin of Ramtek was highly revered by the Vākāṭakas, and it is quite possible that it was during a visit to this place in the company of the royal family that the idea occurred to Kālidāsa to make this mountain the place of exile of his hero in the *Meghadūta*. It must be, however, admitted that we have so far no decisive, direct and definite evidence to place Kālidāsa in the Gupta age. The balance of evidence however suggests that the end of the 4th century A.D. is the most probable time of the poet.

The *Ṛitusaṁhāra*, the *Mālavik-Āgnimitra*, the *Kumārasambhava*, the *Meghadūta*, the *Śakuntalā* and the *Raghuvaṁśa* are the main works of Kālidāsa and they were probably composed in the stated order. *Kuntaleśvaradautya*, which was probably a drama, has also been attributed to him, but it has not yet been recovered. It is probable that the *Setubandha* of Pravara-sena may have been revised by him.

By a universal consensus of opinion, Kālidāsa has been regarded as the best poet in Sanskrit literature, and he well deserves this honour. His poetry is characterised by grace, simplicity and sentiment and is decorated by striking figures of speech. He is deservedly famous for his similes, which appeal to us by their beauty, appropriateness and variety. In characterisation he has few equals. He is superb in describing the emotions of love and pathos. His love of nature is as unequalled as his power of describing it. Works of Kālidāsa are not only noteworthy for their aesthetic beauty and poetic appeal, but they are equally valuable for the ideals which they place before the society. By studying them the reader knows the Hindu ideals about the duties and responsibilities of persons in the different grades of society and in the various stages of life. His writings abound with pithy sayings containing salutary advice couched in beautiful language, from which persons in all walks of life can derive immense benefit.

3. Other Poets.

Śūdraka, the author of the *Mṛichchhakaṭika*, also seems to have flourished in the 4th century A.D. The drama asserts that its author was a king, but no ruler of this rather unusual name is known so far. The *Mṛichchhakaṭika* is one of the most interesting dramas in Sanskrit literature, and its relationship to the *Chārudatta* of Bhāsa has given rise to several problems and controversies, which have not yet been satisfactorily solved.

Viśākhadatta most probably flourished in the 4th century. Some scholars, however, place him a few centuries later.[1] His play *Mudrā-Rākshasa* dramatises the revolution which placed Chandra-gupta Maurya on the throne of Magadha. This author had written a political drama, named *Devī-Chandra-gupta*, describing how prince Chandra-gupta killed the Śaka king in the guise of his sister-in-law and eventually ascended the Gupta throne. The entire drama, however, has not yet been recovered and we can get only an imperfect idea of its contents from the few extracts preserved in later works on dramaturgy and poetics.[2]

Bhāravi, the author of the *Kirātārjunīyam*, flourished towards the middle of the 6th century. The same may have been the case with Bhaṭṭi, the author of the *Rāvaṇavadha* popularly known as the *Bhaṭṭikāvya*, which illustrates the rules of grammar, while narrating the life of Rāma. Some scholars identify Bhaṭṭi with Bhartṛihari, the famous author of the three *Śatakas*. Others do not accept this view but are still inclined to place Bhartṛihari somewhere in the 6th century A.D. Whether the grammarian Bhartṛihari, the author of the *Vākyapadīya*, is to be identified with the author or authors of the *Bhaṭṭikāvya* and the three *Śatakas*, is still a moot question.[3]

---

1 Keith, *Sanskrit Drama*, p. 204.
2 *JA*. 1923, p. 203 ; see also *ante*, pp. 161-62.
3 Keith, *History of Sanskrit Literature*, pp. 116, 176.

Mātṛigupta and Bhartrimeṇṭha are other authors of our period[1], but their works have not been preserved. Bhartṛimeṇṭha was the author of the *Hayagrīvavadha* and tradition asserts that it was so highly appreciated by Mātṛigupta, the poet king of Kashmir, that he sent a golden dish to place below it, lest its flavour should ooze out on bare ground. Dramatists Saumilla and Kulaputra, who were popular in the days of Kālidāsa, are also known to us only by their names. They probably flourished in the 3rd century A.D.

Some epigraphs of our period have preserved beautiful specimens of classical poetry and it is necessary to say a few words about their authors. The foremost among them is undoubtedly Harisheṇa, who was a general and foreign minister under Samudra-gupta. His panegyric (*praśasti*) of Samudra-gupta, inscribed on the Asokan pillar at Allahabad, is undoubtedly a poem of great merit. Being partly in prose and partly in metre, it belongs to the variety of Kāvya known as *Champū.* The author shows himself to be a master of both the *Vaidarbhī* (simple) and *Gauḍī* (ornate) styles, the former being used for the metrical and the latter for the prose portions of the composition. Choice of words is judicious; figures of speech are beautiful. The power of the poet to give an effective and graphic pen-picture of a critical situation, like Samudra-gupta's selection as his father's successor from among aspiring princes, is indeed remarkable.

Vasula, the author of the panegryic of Yaśo-varman (*c.* 540 A.D.), was an equally able poet, though we have only a small poem of his preserved for us. Ravisānti, the author of the Ḥaraha *praśasti* of the Maukhari king, was his junior contemporary. Vatsabhaṭṭi, the author of the Mandasor *praśasti* of Kumāra-gupta and Bandhu-varman, was a poet of no high order, but we should be grateful to him for his neat poem;

---

1 *Rājataraṅgiṇī*, II, 125, 260.

it supplies us with valuable data showing that Kālidāsa could not have flourished after *c.* 475 A.D. Kubja, the author of the Talgunda *praśastī*, shows a remarkable mastery over complicated Sanskrit metres. Śāba was a poet in the court of Chandra-gupta II, but no works of his have been handed down to our time.

It is a matter of deep regret that the above poets should have been content only with writing small *praśastis*, instead of addressing themselves to the task of giving a detailed and systematic history of their patrons and their ancestors.[1] The Gupta age is undoubtedly the golden age of ancient Indian History and it is a great pity that we should have no adequate and comprehensive account of its achievements from a contemporary historian. No works on history were written in India during our period. Ceylon, however, produced the *Dīpavaṁśa* and the *Mahāvaṁśa*, which throw considerable light on the history of the island, and incidentally on some of the events in the history of India.

4. Fable.

To turn from history to fable, we have to note that the original *Pañchatantra* was composed by Vishṇuśarman, sometime during the Gupta period. This work is deservedly popular ; it narrates its attractive fables in a simple yet elegant style, and is full of salutary advice and worldly wisdom. The book has played an important part in the literature of the world; about two hundred versions of it are known to exist in more than fifty languages of the world; and about three-fourths of these are non-Indian. It was translated into Pahlavī before 570 A.D. and it reached Europe before the 11th century ; its versions into Greek, Latin, Spanish, Italian, German, English and old Slavonic languages had come into existence before the close of the 16th century.

[1] It is not impossible that some of these poets may have written historical poems, not preseved to our ages ; but this is a rather remote possibility.

5. Technical Literature.

Though there was a great boom in Sanskrit literature during our period, its output in works on Sanskrit grammar is disappointing. This was undoubtedly due to the great popularity of the works of Pāṇini, Kātyāyana and Patañjali, which rendered the acceptance of a new work extremely difficult, if not almost impossible. A Buddhist scholar from Bengal named Chandragomin, however, composed a book on grammar, called *Chāndra-vyākaraṇa* after him, which has been recovered from its Tibetan translation. The book seems to have become popular among the Buddhists. It omits Pāṇini's rules about Vedic accent and grammar, recasts some of his other *sūtras* and adds 35 new ones. The author flourished in the 1st half of the 6th century A.D. Amarasiṁha, the author of the *Amarakosha*, the most popular Sanskrit dictionary, flourished at about the same time. He was a Buddhist, yet his book has become most popular even among the Hindus. *Śrutabodha*, a handbook on metres, has been ascribed to Kālidāsa, but the attribution is very doubtful. Varāhamihira also deals with metres in one of the sections of the *Brihatsaṁhitā*. The section of the *Agnipurāṇa* dealing with metres probably belongs to our age. The same is the case with section of the *Vishṇudharmottara Purāṇa*, which deals with painting and gives detailed instructions about surface preparation in fresco paintings and the use of the different colours in them.

6. Religious and Philosophical Literature.

We now proceed to take a brief survey of the religious and philosophical literature. Purāṇas were in existence in India as early as the later Vedic period. They used to devote themselves to the theories about the creation and re-absorption of the universe, describe the history of important dynasties and give an account of the lives and achievements of famous sages.

Early in the Gupta age, the custodians of the Purāṇas made them up-to-date, by bringing the history of the dynasties of the Kali age down to *c.* 350 A.D. They also added a number of chapters in glorification of Śiva and Vishṇu and thus helped the popularisation of the *Bhakti* school. As we have shown already, the chapters in the Purāṇas, prescribing a number of *Vratas*, had not been added during our period (*ante*, p. 377).

The Smṛitis of Yājñavalkya, Nārada, Kātyāyana and Bṛihaspati most probably belong to our period. *Yājñavalkya-smṛiti* is perhaps the most systematic and evenly balanced work of its class, for it pays equal attention to the description of *Āchāra* (rituals), *Vyavahāra* (civil law), and *Prāyaśchitta* (penances).[1] Civil law and legal procedure were rapidly developing in our period and the work of Nārada, Kātyāyana and Bṛihaspati are devoted entirely to their discussion. In the realm of the Arthaśāstra, it is likely that the *Kāmandakīya Nitisāra* was written in our period, probably by a minister of the Guptas. It is however mostly a summary of the previous work of Kauṭilya.

The main authors of philosophical works have been already mentioned in Chapter XIX, where their contributions to Hindu, Buddhist and Jain metaphysics and logic have been discussed. They need not be, therefore, again discussed here.

7. Dravidian Literature.

Let us now turn to Dravidian literature. The literature of Tamil alone among them goes back to our period. As may be expected, it is mostly in poetry, prose being practically unknown. Metres used are characterised by great simplicity

---

[1] All these three topics are to be seen forming part of the reconstructed *Brihaspati-smṛiti* published as Gaekwad's Oriental Series, Vol. LXXXV; but it is doubtful whether these parts can be attributed to one and the same author.

of form, neither the number of lines to a stanza nor those of feet to a line being strictly determined. Complex metres from Sanskrit poetry had not yet become popular. The rhythm is generally good and the expression both compact and vivid. Love and war were the main themes of poetry. The poems are remarkably free from clogging literary conventions and replete with a simple realism that succeeds with a few bold strokes and a rare economy of words in recalling many scenes of daily life in town and country, shops and fields, temples and palaces, in Brāhmaṇa households and fishermen's huts. The Tamil literature of the Śangam age holds a unique place in the whole range of India's literatures in many languages, including Sanskrit, for this universal realism, but owing to the difficulty of the early idiom, even Tamilians are not alive to its beauties as one could expect.

The earliest attempts to translate the *Rāmāyaṇa* and the *Mahābhārata* into Tamil most probably go back to our age ; it must however be admitted that these early versions have not been preserved to our times.[1]

III. The Sciences.

We shall now proceed to consider the condition and progress of sciences during our period, and while doing so shall also refer to important authors and their works in this field. Mathematics, astronomy, medicine, chemistry, physics and metallurgy have to be mainly considered in this connection.

1. Mathematics.

Unfortunately no treatises that can be described either as textbooks, or as systematic and comprehensive works on these

[1] I am indebted to Prof. K.A. Nilkantha Sastri for the information about the Tamil literature given above. A. S. A.

subjects, have been handed down to us. A few books have been preserved, but they are usually of the nature of short class notes jotted down by a professor lecturing to advanced classes. We have, therefore, to draw our own inferences from these works as to the condition and progress of the different sciences in our age. Thus, to give one instance, the *Āryabhaṭīyam* refers to some of the important properties of circles and triangles ; we have therefore to conclude that most of the theorems included in the first four books of Euclid must have been worked out by this time. But we have not a single work handed down to us dealing with the whole geometry in a systematic manner.

The most epoch-making achievement of our age in the realm of arithmetic was the discovery of the decimal system of notation, now accepted and followed all over the world, based upon the principle of the place-value of the first nine numbers and the use of the zero. This notation system has immensely simplified arithmetical calculations and processes, and we can at present hardly imagine that there ever was a time when our ancestors all over the world were expressing a number like one thousand one hundred and eleven not as 1,111, but by four different and distinct symbols, the last one denoting one, the third one, ten, the second one, hundred, and the first one, one thousand. Symbols for ten, twenty, thirty, forty, etc. as well as those for hundred, thousand, etc. were all distinct and different. This method of expressing big numbers was very cumbersome, but even Europe was following it down to the 12th century when it learnt the decimal system of notation from the Arabs. The Arab authors like Ibn Washiya (9th century), Al Masūdi (10th century) and Alberuni (11th century), however, give the credit of the discovery of the new system to the Hindus.[1] It is therefore clear that there is no reason to doubt

[1] B. B. Dutt in *Bulletin of the Calcutta Mathematical Society*, XXIV, 194 ff.

as to who discovered the system. Kaye's view that the Hindus were not the discoverers of this notation is altogether untenable.

When exactly the Hindu mathematicians made the epoch-making discovery is however not known. Nor has the name of the discoverer been preserved. The new system of notation is followed by Varāhamihira (550 A.D.)[1] and is referred to by Āryabhaṭa (499 A.D.) in the *Aryabhaṭīyam* (II, 2).[2] The method of extracting square root and cube root which he describes in II, 4 and 5, is just the one now in vogue in India, and it distinctly presupposes the decimal place value of numbers. It is therefore clear that the new decimal system of notation was well established among the mathematicians in the 5th century and we may therefore place its discovery at least a century or two earlier.[3]

Though the mathematicians were using the new system of notation from the 5th century A.D., it took several centuries for the society as a whole to accept it. It is first used in epigraphs in the Samkheda inscription of 695 A.D. (*EI.* II, 20). Ordinary people probably looked askance for a long time at a system of notation where the same figure say, seven, would stand for seven, seventy, seven hundred, seven thousand, etc., according to its place. They probably preferred the old system where the symbols 7,000 700, 70 and 7 were all different and distinct.

---

[1] Varāhamihira expresses 584 as *veda* (=4), *ashṭa* (—8) and *bhūta* (=5) (*Pañchasiddhāntikā*, Act XVIII, 1); the figures mentioned are of course to be written from right to left. 427 is expressed as *saptāśvivedasaṁkhyaṁ* (*Ibid.* I, 8), *sapta aśvi*, and *veda* standing for 7, 2 and 4 respectively.

[2] Cf. एकं दश च शतं च सहस्रमयुते तथा प्रयुतम् ।
कोटयबदं च वृन्द स्थानात्स्थानं दशगुणं स्यात् ।

[3] The Bakshali arithmetic (*c.* 300 A.D.) uses the decimal system; but as its present Ms. belongs to the 9th century A.D., we cannot exclude the possibility of its transcriber having introduced the new decimal system that had become popular in the interval. Its original author may or may not have used it.

The Bakshali manuscript,[1] which is unfortunately fragmantary, is the only work that gives us a fairly comprehensive idea of the state of mathematics during our period. It not only deals with elementary topics like fractions, square roots, arithmetical and geometric progressions, etc. but also deals with advanced topics like summation of complex series, simultaneous linear equations and indeterminate equations of the second degree. It also shows that some work was being done on the theory of numbers in the direction of extracting the square root of a non-square number.

The next work we have to consider is the famous *Āryabhaṭīyam* written by Āryabhaṭa I in 499 A.D. at Pāṭaliputra. Problems of mathematics are only incidentally dealt with in this important work. Besides dealing with the rules of involution and evolution it deals with the arithmetic progression, both of numbers, as well as of their squares and cubes. In the realm of geometry the work describes several properties of the circle, discusses questions connected with projective geometry and gives a value for π, far more accurate than any suggested till then. In algebra simultaneous equations with four unknown quantities have been solved, and the problem of finding a general solution of the indeterminates of the first degree is successfully tackled. That trigonometry was also being cultivated at this time will become clear from the use of the sine functions made for solving the problems of astronomy.

In the realm of arithmetic and algebra, it is admitted on all hands that the Indians had the lead over the contemporary Greek mathematicians. In geometry no further progress was

[1] This manuscript has been preserved only in fragmentary condition, its greater portion being lost. It was found by a farmer in the course of digging at his village Bakshali near the city of Peshawar in the year 1881. Kaye's view that Bakshali arithmetic belongs to the 12th century A.D. is altogether untenable. The mixed Sanskrit and Prākṛit dialect, in which it is written, went out of vogue after the end of the 3rd century A.D. For a detailed discussion, see *Bulletin of the Calcutta Mathematcial Society* XXI, 1-60. Kaye ; *Bakshali Manuscript.*

recorded in our period, probably because neither the needs of ritualism nor those of astronomy gave an incentive to its study. The problem of squaring a circle, which was attempted by the *Sulva-sūtra* writers is, for instance, not taken up in our period.

2. Astronomy.

Let us now consider the state and progress of astronomy. Down to the beginning of the 3rd century the *Paitāmaha Siddhānta* was in use and its astronomy was almost the same as that of the *Vedāṅga Jyotisha.* It postulated a year of 366 days, added two intercalary months in a *yuga* of five years and operated with *Nakshatras* and not with the *Rāśis* (signs).

Vaśishṭha Sīddhānta (*c.* 300 A.D.) marks a further progress in astronomy. Signs (*Rāśis*) displace the *Nakshatras* and the idea of *Lagna* (*i.e.* the point of ecliptic that is on the eastern horizon at any time) is also adumbrated. Its year consisted of 365·2591 days, and was thus more accurate than that of the *Paitāmaha Siddhānta.* It however did not know how to work out eclipses.

Pauliśa Siddhānta[1] (*c.* 380 A.D.) represents a further progress in astronomy, for it lays down a rough rule for calculating the lunar and solar eclipses.

The *Romaka Siddhānta* (*c.* 400 A.D.) represented a further stage in the progress of the science. As its name suggests, it is based upon the astronomical theories that had reached India from the west. Its *Yuga* of 2850 years was obviously obtained by multiplying by 150 the period of 19 years, during which the Athenian astronomer Meton had postulated seve intercalary

---

[1] Alberuni says (I, 153) that this *Siddhanta* is based upon the works of Pauliśa (=Paulus) of the city of Alexandria (*c.* 378 A.D.). But the conjecture is based merely on the similarity of names. Its validity cannot be confirmed or contradicted, for no astronomical books of the Greek author have been handed down. Pauliśa can also be a purely Sanskritic name.

months. Its duration of the day is identical with that of Hipparchus. Its degree of anomaly closely follows those of Ptolemy.

The *Sūrya Siddhānta* is the next one to be considered. It was most popular before the time of *Āryabhaṭa*. It had formulated some rules for calculating eclipses and discovered solutions for some of the problems in spherical astronomy. But the precise nature of this *Siddhānta* is difficult to determine now, for it has undergone extensive modifications in later times.

The authorship of the above five Siddhāntas is either unknown or attributed to divine or semi-divine persons. The information given about them is based upon their summary, as given by Varāhamihira in the 6th century. We can get a definite and first hand idea of the progress in astronomy only from the *Aryabhaṭīyam* of Āryabhaṭa I, who was the earliest known historical person to write on the subject. He was born in Pāṭaliputra in 476 A.D. and he wrote his famous work when he was only 23. He is undoubtedly one of the greatest scientists produced by India. He was fairly well posted about the main theories and conclusions of the Greek astronomers of Alexandria, and he had carefully studied the works and methods of his Indian predecessors. He, however refused to follow either of them blindly. 'I dived deep', he says, 'in the ocean of astronomical theories, true and false, and rescued the precious sunken jewel of true knowledge by means of the boat of my own intellect'.[1] His conclusions were therefore independent, based upon his own observations and researches. He no doubt respected Śrutis, Śmṛitis and Purāṇas, but did not flinch from stating that eclipses are caused, not by the demons Rāhu and Ketu, as stated in some of the works, but by the moon coming within the earth's shadow or between the earth and the sun. He did not blindly accept the results of the Greek school of

[1] IV. 49.

astronomy at Alexandria, but improved upon them by his own observations and calculations.

Āryabhaṭa was the first Indian astronomer to discover that the earth rotates round its axis (IV, 9). He was the first to find out sine functions and utilise them in astronomy.[1] He worked out the accurate formula to measure the increase or decrease in the duration of two consecutive days (IV, 26). He obtained the correct equation for the orbit of a planet by taking the apse (III, 22-3). He postulated an epicyclic theory of his own to explain the variations in planetary motions (III, 21). His equations of spherical trigonometry to find out the right ascension and declination of any point of the ecliptic are also correct (IV, 25). He accurately expressed the angular diameter of the earth's shadow at the moon's orbit (IV, 39-40), and knew how to find half the duration of an eclipse and total obscuration (IV, 41-2). He has also given rules to ascertain what part of the moon will be obscured in an eclipse (IV, 43-4). The length of his year, 365·2586805 days (III, 1), is nearer its true duration (365·2563604) than that postulated by Ptolemy 365·2631579); the same is the case about his longitude of the sun's apogee and sidereal period of the moon's nodes.[2] All these represent striking advances in astronomy, and it is a pity that we do not know anything about the methods and experiments by which they became possible. Āryabhaṭa deservedly enjoys very high reputation as an astronomer. He had a number of disciples of whom Niśśaṅka, Pāṇḍuraṅgasvāmin and Lāṭadeva may be mentioned here. Of these the last became very famous ; he was known as the expert in the whole science (*sarvasiddāntaguru*) and is known to have expounded *Pauliśa* and *Romaka Siddhāntas*.

---

[1] Ptolemy has utilised chords instead of sines for this purpose. Before the discovery of the *Āryabhaṭīyam*, Europeans believed that the Arabian astronomer Al-Balani was the first to discover and utilise sines.

[2] P. C. Sengupta in *The Cultural Heritage of India*, II, 374-8.

The next writer on astronomy during our period is Varāhamihira, who flourished during the second and third quarters of the 6th ceutury. He has made no original contribution of his own to the progress of this science, but the historian will remain ever grateful to him for his *Pañchasiddhāntikā*, which gives a concise account of the five *Siddhāntas* that were in use in India during the 3rd and 4th centuries A.D. *Bṛihajjātaka*, *Bṛihatsaṁhitā* and *Laghujātaka* and his other works, but they are mainly astrological. The last two of these were later translated into Arabic by Alberuni.

A few words are necessary here about the controversy[1] of the Indian indebtedness to Greek astronomy. The horizon of Hindu scholarship and intellect was wide during our period and Hindu scholars were keen to note and study the advances made in other countries by both their contemporaries and predecessors. Varāhamihira pays a handsome compliment to the Greek astronomers. They are, he says, no doubt Mlechchhas, but nevertheless good experts in astronomy and therefore worthy of as high a respect as the sages of yore[2]. The technical terminology of Hindu astronomy contains some words like *kendra hārija*, *drekkāṇa lipta*, etc., which are clearly adaptations of the corresponding Greek terms κεντρον, οριζων, δεκανος, λεπτη, etc.; they cannot be derived from any Sanskrit roots. The *Romaka Siddhānta* clearly betrays Greek influence both in its name and contents.

It is therfore true that Āryabhaṭa and the unknown author of the *Sūryasiddhānta* knew some Greek results and methods, but they were not content to copy them blindly. A comparison of the astronomical constants of Hipparchus and Ptolemy on the one side and Hindu astronomers, like Āryabhaṭa, on the other shows that the Hindus had almost in all cases arrived at

1 Thibaut and Dvivedi (ed), *Pañchasiddhāntikā*, Introduction; *Encyclopaedia of Religion and Ethics*: Astronomy.

2 *Brihatsaṁhitā*, II. 15.

independent results, usually more reliable.[1] It has been generally admitted that only a very imperfect knowledge of Greek astronomy had reached India in the form of almanacs and rough summaries. Hindu astronomers of our age critically examined it in the the light of the knowledge handed down to them from the past, made their own observations, determined their own constants with the help of geometry and trigonometry as developed by themselves, and succeeded in formulating a system of their own, which was on the whole superior to the astronony as developed in contemporary times at Alexandria.

3. Medicine.

Let us now turn to the science of medicine. *Charaka-saṁhitā* and the *Suśruta-saṁhitā*, which had practically assumed their present form towards the end of the 2nd century A.D., continued to enjoy supreme reputation and confidence during our period. A systematic summary of the teachings of these works is presented in the *Ashṭānga-saṁgraha* by Vāgbhaṭa I, who seems to have flourished in the 6th century. Another work on medicine, that is known to have been composed in our period, is *Nāvanītakam*, a manuscript of which was luckily procured by Lieut. Bower in 1890 during his stay at Kuchar in Eastern Turkestan.[2] *Nāvanītakam* is not a systematic or comprehensive work on medicine, but a mere manual of recipes, formulae and prescriptions intended for the useof the busy practitioner. 12 of its formulae are taken from the *Bhela-saṁhitā*, 29 from the *Charaka-saṁhitā* and 6 from the *Suśruta-saṁhitā*. It is likely that some of its formulae, not attributed to the above three authorities, may have been based upon the lost *Saṁhitās* of Hārīta, Jātukarṇa, Kshārapaṇi and Parāśara, who also were,

[1] P. C. Sengupta, *op. cit.* pp. 374-8.
[2] Hoernle, *Bower Manuscript.*

according to tradition, disciples of Punarvasu like Charaka and Suśruta.

Though no new and original works were written during our period, there is no doubt that the medical science was assiduously cultivated. India enjoyed high reputation for its progress in this science in the contemporary world, as the discovery of the *Nāvanītakam* in the far off eastern Turkestan will clearly show. In her big cities, like Pāṭaliputra, there were well managed hospitals, which excited the admiration of Chinese visitors. Students were given regular practical training, and surgery was still practised within the natural limitations imposed by the non-discovery of anaesthetics. Buddhist educational institutions, like the Nalanda University, were taking keen interest in the study of medicine, for it was realised that physical healing was as important as spiritual healing.

The veterinary science was not neglected in our age. The *Hastyāyurveda* of Pālakāpya was probably composed during the later Gupta period. It is an extensive work of 160 chapters and deals with the principal diseases of elephants, their diagnosis and treatment, both medical and surgical.

4. Chemistry and Metallurgy.

Let us now briefly survey the Indian achievements in the realm of physics, chemistry and metallurgy. Unfortunately no books on these subjects, written in our period, have been handed down. According to Hiuen Tsang and Tārānātha Nāgārjuna, the famous Buddhist Mahāyāna philosopher, was a great student of chemistry and metallurgy, and it is not unlikely that his disciples at Nagarjunikonda may have continued to take interest in the subjects during our period also. There is no doubt that chemistry and metallurgy made striking progress in our period, but unfortunately we have no books preserved to enable us to estimate its nature. Not even the names of the workers in the field are handed down to us. The famous Iron Pillar near the Qutb-*minar* on the outskirts of Delhi, manufactured in our period, stands, however, as a silent witness to proclaim the striking metallurgical skill of the contemporary Hindus. At a time when the process of making iron was but imperfectly known even in the west, Hindu metallurgists manufactured this huge iron pillar so skilfully, that although it stands exposed to the sun and rain for the last 1500 years, it shows not the least sign of rusting or corrosion. How its iron was so skilfully treated is still a mystery, because modern scientists have admitted that iron of identical composition does not stand corrosive action. The pillar is 24 feet in height and six and half tons in weight ; even the simple forging of so large an iron column was out of the reach of human thought elsewhere not only at that time but for many centuries afterwards as well.

Metallic preparations are sporadically referred to by Charaka and Suśruta, but they had not yet begun to form regular ingredients of the Āyurvedic materia medica. The use of mercury and iron with proper treatment had begun to be advocated by some of the writers of our period, like Varāhamihira, and it is likely that the close association of medicine and chemistry, which was to achieve great progress in chemical knowledge in the later period, began towards the end of our age.

It must be here noted that Varāhamihira was a scientist of encyclopaedic interests, and his *Bṛihatsaṁhitā* is a veritable mine of useful information. Besides being an astronomer, mathematician and astrologer, Varāhamihira was also a student of metallurgy, and has given his own formulae and processes for sharpening swords (Chap. 50). He was a good jeweller and has supplied useful information for ascertaining the nature and value of gold, emerald, pearls, diamonds, etc. (Chaps. 80-3).

He was a student of botany and has offered his own suggestions about various topies of gradening, including, steps to be taken for making trees fruit out of season (Chap. 55). He was a critical observer of the animal world and has given useful information to ascertain the nature of good as well as bad horses, elephants, dogs, etc. (Chaps. 62-4). He had studied civil engineering and his book contains valuable information about the nature and structure of temples, palaces, mansions and houses that were in vogue in the sixth century (Chap. 53). He took great interest in water divining and his work supplies useful information on this topic (Chap. 54). Again, the science of meteorology had not escaped his attention ; what kind of clouds will bring us rain when accompanied with what king of wind coming from what quarter has been explained by him in great details (Chaps. 21-28). It is a great pity that Varāhamihira could not succeed in founding a school of his own to contiune a systematic study of these different branches of science. Had he been followed by a succession of students and followers as keenly devoted to these different branches as their master, India would certainly not have lagged behind the west in her contribution to the progress in the different branches of science during the mediaeval age and modern times.

CHAPTER XXI

ARCHAEOLOGICAL REMAINS OF THE GUPTA PERIOD

The Gupta period is regarded as the golden age of Indian history and its archaeology is sufficiently important to bear out this claim. The extent to which remains of this period are found all over Northern India, the artistic and distinctive character of the small antiquities associated with this period, the various new forms of architecture and the beautiful forms of pottery all bespeak the prosperity and high culture of the age. Gupta influence continued to dominate Indian culture for a sufficienly long period though its progressive deterioration can be marked in every succeeding century. The torch of culture lit in the spacious times of the Guptas was gradually diminishing in lustre, but its presence was felt in all nooks and corners throughout Northern India.

Beginning from the north-east, the province of Assam has hardly anything to show of its culture heritage before the Gupta period. The temple of Dah Parbatiya, a few miles down-stream from Tezpur on the north bank of the Brahmaputra, shows a typical door-frame of the Gapta period. The graceful river goddesses, Gaṅgā and Yamunā, flanking the entrance and the geese depicted on the door-frame would find place among the best creations of Indian art. The temple, of which these vestiges are preserved, was built of burnt bricks of the typical size of the Gupta period. In the secluded position of Assam the stimulus received in the Gupta period apparently lasted for a longer time than elsewhere, and the use of the Gupta era for a longer period (up to the 9th century) in the inscriptions of Harjjara-varman and the sculptures on the river bank at Gauhati and at Deopani are instances in point. The remains of the city of Prāgjyotishapura near modern Gauhati, as brought to light from time to time, mostly go back to the Gupta period.

Proceeding next to Bengal, it is clear that while stray finds of an earliar period have been found in different places, no structural remains of an earlier period than the Gupta have been unearthed. It was in this period that the style of brick temple evolved further west was brought into Bengal and the smaller antiquities from most of the earlier sites in Bengal are associated with the Gupta period. In the deltaic region the formation of new esturial or alluvial belts of land is a continuous process, and it is inconceivable that any large settlements were formed further south than the city of Tāmrolipti (modern Tamluk in Midnapur District) which was also the ocean port of North India for a long time. One monument, which if excavated, is likely to provide another example of the high terraced brick temple of the Nandangarh-Paharpur type is the lofty mound at Bharat Bhayna in a corner of the Jessore district surrounded by marshy-land. In North Bengal the ancient sites, almost entirely situated in the area of the older reddish loam, known as the Barind soil, in the districts of Dinajpur, Rangpur, Rajshahi, Bogra and Melda, were either established or flourishing in the Gupta period. The larger city sites like Puṇḍravardhana (present Mahasthan near Bogra) and Devkot or Kotivarsha (modern Bangarh in Dinajpur district) must no doubt have been founded in the Mauryan period or even earlier, but the most important artistic antiquities from these cities undoubtedly belong to the Gupta period. The fortifications of the city wall at Bangarh and Mahasthan approximately belong to the Gupta period or to a silghtly later date. As regards the architecture revealed by excavation, the Meḍh mound at a short distance to the south of Mahasthan has revealed an example of the high terraced temple type in which the terraces are not well defined, but the filled-up chambers rise in tiers or terraces one above the other.

The oldest temple in the isolated mound (Gobinda Bhiṭā) overhanging the river to the north-east of the main city of Mahasthan also belongs to the Gupta period, showing the shrine surrounded by cells. The remains of the Gupta city lie 10 to 15 ft. below the present field level. At Bangarh an elaborate system of ornamental brick reservoirs connected with properly constructed drains is assigned to the Gupta city. The gigantic temple at Paharpur was undoubtedly planned in the late Gupta period, the scheme of ornamentation including the ornamental brick mouldings and the stone sculptures being referable to the Gupta age. The temple mounds at Birat in Rangpur district, only partially cleared, show a group of high terraced shrines. A site of the Gupta period, presumably Buddhist, exists at Biharoil in Rajshahi District where a sandstone Buddha of the Sarnath type was brought to light. At Rangamati near Murshidabad, the ancient Karṇasuvarṇa, a Buddhist establishment of late Gupta period has been unearthed in which the long hall and a number of large chambers, presumably the remains of a *vihāra*, were unearthed.

In the province of Bihar it is clear that the city of Pāṭaliputra near modern Patna was restored to the dignity of a secondary, if not the main, capital by the Guptas. Here the excavations at Kumrahar and Bulandibagh yielded a number of antiquities of the Gupta period and even earlier. There does not appear to have been any considerable occupation on this site after the Mauryan except in the Gupta times.

At Rajgir (ancient Rājagṛiha), the most ancient capital of the historical period going back to the time of Buddha and beyond, a very interesting monument known as Maniyar Math was brought to light by excavation in the centre of the hill-girt valley. It is a cylindrical shrine having on the exterior face well perserved stucco images of the Gupta period in large niches or recesses separated by pilasters. Except for a *Linga*, a Vishṇu image and a Gaṇeśa, the rest consists of human figures with their heads covered by single or multiple heads of cobras, one of the figures being the well-known female figure or Nāgī. There is little doubt that this temple was dedicated to the Nāgas or in particular to Maṇi-nāga, the protector of Rajgir, as several terracotta snake-hoods and large numbers of jars, with multiple spouts of a unique shape, were found in the close vicinity of this shrine. These were no doubt the offerings of devotees who must have prayed for rain or other blessings at this shrine of Maṇi-nāga, whose connection is further evidenced by an inscribed Nāga stone image found in the same compound. Though the hey-day of Rajgir was gone, it was not the deserted city that it has remained ever since the Gupta times.

Nalanda was undoubtedly founded during the Gupta period and the earliest remains at this site belong to those times. At Bodhgaya it is very likely that the Buddhist establishment was not then in a flourishing state and that the original temple with the pyramidal *śikhara* was built in the Gupta period. The most extensive Gupta city in the province was, however, the city of Vaiśālī (modern Basaroh in North Bihar), a prosperous provincial metropolis of the Gupta empire. A number of disjoined but solid structures forming the rooms, brick-platforms, pavements, etc. were unearthed in course of the two excavations conducted here, and among the minor antiquities exhumed a large number of Gupta seals, throwing a good deal of light on the life of the times, are included. The artistic designs on the seals include Lakihmī sprinkled by flanking elephants, *kalasas* (vases), lions, trees, altars, all symbolic of the deities which were worshipped.

Manjhi on the Gogra in Saran District which yielded inscribed Gupta bricks, Belwa in the same District and Jahangira and Sultanganj near Bhagalpur (the find spot of the great copper Buddha image now in Birmingham Museum) are other important sites which have yielded Gupta antiquities.

In the Madhyadeśa, corresponding roughly with the present United Provinces, was situated the heart of the Gupta empire—a fact which stimulated the growth of cities and towns to an unprecedented extent. Thus in each of the provincial centres such as Benares, Kauśāmbī, Śrāvastī, Ahichchhatra and Mathura the new culture manifested itself in an unmistakable manner. Countless mounds and ruined sites scattered all over the province testify to the way in which Gupta culture spread all over the land, as antiquities of this period are the commonest of all those originating from the mounds. It is seldom indeed that a site or settlement founded in an earlier period was abandoned before the Gupta times, and also that a site exhibiting medieval antiquities on the surface does not go back at least to the Gupta period. The Gupta age therefore saw the culmination of the earlier art styles on the one hand and the starting point of their decline on the other. In Sarnath, the *stūpa* architecture found a new form as in the well-known Dhamekh *stūpa* ; small shrines like the ornamental temple (No. 136) in the passage between the main shrine and the Dhamekh *stūpa* were built ; the main shrine itself was reconstructed and votive *stūpas* were built by pious pilgrims attracted by the popularity of the site. The renowned Gupta shcool of sculpture was at its best in Sarnath, and the antiquities of the contemporary city on the river bank, recently unearthed near Rajghat, offer the most abundant material for the study of the minor arts of the period. Benares may perhaps be regarded as the geographical centre of the Gupta empire and further systematic work on sites such as Bairant in Benares and Masaon Dih and Sadipur Bhitri in the Ghazipur District is likely to yield much more important material for the reconstruction of this period. The city of Kauśāmbī (modern Kosam near Allahabad), which appears to have been deserted after the

Gupta period, seems to have been a continuously flourishing city from the Mauryan to the Gupta period, and the phenomenal number of coins, terracotta figurines and moulded animals, heads, etc. belonging to all these periods make this an exceptionally rich site, perhaps the richest in India. The site of Bhita, a rich trading city also in the Allahabad District, has yielded a great number of Gupta houses and antiquities. Garhwa Fort has yielded a number of inscriptions and sculptures of an early Gupta date. In the city of Śrāvastī in the Gonda and Bahraich Districts, the only area properly explored is the monastery at Jetavana (now Sahet). Here we find the remains of five brick-built monasteries with a temple and *stūpa*, the most important of which belong to the Gupta period. At Kasia (the ancient Kuśīnagara) the main shrines connected with the decease (*Mahāparinirvāṇa*) of the Buddha appear to have been rebuilt at this period, particularly the one known as the Mathakuvar-ka-kot.

Other sites of this period in Eastern U. P. are the Kahaum (old Kakubha), Khukhundu (old Kishkindhyā) and Sohnag in the Gorakhpur District. In the central Districts, the sites of Bilsad and Sankisa in the Farrukhabad District are primarily of Gupta date ; the vast site of Atranji in the Etah District represents a larger city that flourished in the Gupta period, though it came down from at least the Mauryan period ; the site of Chakranagar and the fort Kudarkot (ancient Gavīdhumat), both in the Etawah District, are important Gupta sites; Padham in Mainpuri District and Kampil in the Farrukhabad District are other ancient sites which promise to yield remains of the Gupta period. The Gupta brick temple at Bhitargaon in the Cawnpore District and others, probably belonging to the same period, in the Fatehpur District are associated with regular mounds representing contemporary settlements.

At the great site of Ramnagar (ancient Ahichchhatra) the Gupta period was one of the most floürshing in the history of the settlements there. The two highest mounds, which represent the remains of high terraced Hindu temples, were remarkable for the details of their planning, construction and scheme of decorations. Large-sized terracotta plaques of dimensions unknown before, showing scenes related to Śaiva worship, have been found, and were apparently used for decorating the walls and the different terraces which were approached by staircases. In the highest temple, which rises nearly 60 feet above the surrounding plain, one finds the expression of the lofty spirit of the Gupta architect. In the town planning of ancient Ahichchhatra the temple appears to have been the centre on which the principal roads of the city converge. Among the 8 successive strata unearthed at the site of Ahichchhatra, which range from the 2nd century B.C. to the 9th century A.D., the most solid constructions are those belonging to the Gupta period. Within the compound of a religious enclosure of the period have been found three smaller square temples with a row of niches or small shrines for housing images of deities. In the peculiar circumstances of the locality where stone is not available within a considerable distance the Gupta architects seem to have reached a high level of skill in the manufacture of burnt clay images, plaques, etc. The extent to which the citizens in the alluvial Gangetic plains depended on the brick-maker, potter and clay modeller for their daily life has only to be seen to be realized, but the artists of the Gupta period seems to have come out particularly successfully from this ordeal and shared in the high aesthetic and cultural sense of the citizen of the period for whom he produced an ever-increasing variety of objects.

The pottery finds from Ahichchhatra, systematically collected from the successive levels and carefully arranged and studied, now enable us to have an idea of the sequence of all types of pottery from the pre-Mauryan period to the early mediaeval period. The evolution of a cooking pot from the early rimless types to the lug-handled *hāṇḍis* of the last period, and the sequences of water jars, drinking vessels, basins, lids and other pottery types can now be established. The characteristic features of the pottery of the Pāñchāla and Gupta periods can be distinguished, while the older painted or polished wares of the pre-Mauryan or Mauryan periods are not to be found, nor do the grey wares of the Śuṅga period survive to the Gupta times. The pottery of the Pāñchāla period (2nd-3rd Century A.D.) stands distinctly apart both from its predecessors and its successors of the Gupta period, and it has been found in the greatest profusion in company with terracotta animal and human figurines in several of the Ahichchhatra sites. The finish and grace of design, as also the schemes of decoration, distinguish the handicrafts of the Gupta period. Hundreds of designs, mostly lotuses, rosettes and smaller vegetable patterns incised on the face or in relief among red ware which appears to have been used as dishes, bowls and caskets and similar other purposes, are abundant on the terracottas, bricks and pottery of the Gupta period.

A section of the excavated site was set apart from the early Gupta period for the use of the potters whose large cylindrical pits have gone to 10′ or 12′ in depth at the main site and must undoubtedly have intended for some special purposes, presumably ornamental pottery which required special kilns. It appears that the demand for the special kind of ornamental pottery continued during the late Gupta period. From specimens found in association with the debris covering these pits it also appears likely that in this period enamelled tiles and pottery were produced in large quantities. Another feature of the pottery of the Gupta period is the vast number of designs used for the pottery spouts. Thus the explorations at Ahichchhatra and Rajghat have yielded a large number of animal heads, such as the *makara*, horse, boar, elephant, lion, etc. Among the designs of pottery may be mentioned very graceful figures of the river Ganges occurring on the handles of drinking vases. These were undoubtedly fancied for religious motives as the association of the sacred river with a drinking pot gave the character of the pure and sacred Ganges water to any other water that may be put into the vessel. A number of such spouts have been discovered at the site of Naliasar-Sambhar (Śākambharī) near the Sambhar lake in Jaipur State.

In the Delhi-Mathura region vestiges of the Gupta period are not particularly abundant as compared with the exuberant productions of the Kushāṇa School, but it was hardly likely that the copious material available for sculpture in this region was not availed of by the Gupta artist. Some of the best images of Buddha known to exit are those that have come from Mathura in the Gupta period, but few structures of the period have been preserved there. The Mathura stone pillar of the year 61 of the Emperor Chandra-gupta (II) and the Meharauli iron pillar, which is a marvel of its kind, are the only relics left. On the ground of certain bricks of the Gupta period found inside the Purāṇā Qilā or Indrapat fort, it has been surmised that the antiquity of this place goes back at least to the time of the Gupas. The site of Tilpat (Skt. Tilaprastha), a few miles south of Tughlaquabad, is at present the only one of the ancient places ending with *prastha*, which has extant remains going back to the period under consideration.

In the Punjab, the third century after Christ witnessed the decline of the Kushāṇa Empire, though under their successors, the little Kushāṇas, the Punjab continued to flourish until the devastating invasions of the Hūṇas swept away what remained of the brilliant heterogeneous culture of the Śaka-Parthian-Kushāṇa epoch. Although the Gupta empire did not embrace the greater part of the Punjab, it is very likely that its influence will be found to have permeated that province as deeply as Sindh. The only historic site that has been excavated on a large scale in the Punjab is the great site of

Taxila. The least touched of the three successive cities is Sirsukh, the site of the last city, which was founded about the 2nd Century A.D., when the Bir and Sirkap cities had already been reduced to mounds. The great Buddhist establishment at the Dharmarājikā *stūpa* was the only part of the city which continued throughout the period, and we can trace here how monastic life changed from the early Scytho-Parthian times to the end of the 5th Century A.D. Numerous monasteries also grew up in the outlying hills, such as Jaulian, Mohra Moradu, Kalawan, and Bhamala where the second Gandhāra school with its beautiful and sensuous stucco figures unmistakably reflected the contact with the indigenous Gupta School. The clear traces of incendiarism in all these establishments leave no doubt as to their destruction at the hands of invaders, among whom were the Hūṇas under Toramāṇa and Mihirakula. Their antagonism to Buddhism, the prevailing creed of North-west, is probably responsible for their leaving behind them only the trail of destruction in this part, while their Śaivite leanings seem to have been responsible for some constructive activities in Central India. The find of some gold coins of the little Kushāṇas from mounds near Nankana Saheb and the excavation of some brick towers at Pattan Munara in the Bahawalpur State, indicate that more remains of the Gupta period are likely to be found in the Punjab on proper investigation. The sites of Bhera in Shahpur District, Sangla and Shorkot in Central Punjab, the great site of Sunet near Ludhiana, which has yielded a number of terracotta seals of the Gupta period, the site of Sugh (ancient Srughna) not far from Jumna bank in Ambala District, the site of Theh Polar near Kaithal and Amin both in Karnal District, the site of Agroha in Hissar District and the site near Rohtak town (known as Khokra Kot)—all these have been only partially examined; but what has been already found sufficiently proves that these sites were flourishing in the Gupta period. Such mounds as the Sar Deheri (in the Peshawar valley), Sahri Bahlol, Takhti-Bahi and Jamalgarhi and Bala Hissar, which have already been partially examined, have yielded ceramic and terracotta and stucco remains of several priods after the Kushāṇa, and other mounds such as the Akra mound near Bannu and the Kafir Kot in the Dehra Ismail Khan District are bound to add to our knowledge of the archaeology of the period, if examined.

In Kashmir, the Buddhist remains on the hill side at Harwan (Shaḍarhadvana) are the most striking monuments of the period under review. The vicinity of Hushkur (ancient Huvishkapura), Paraspur (Parihāsapura) and Pandrethan (Purāṇādhishṭhāna) are other important localities, which contain remains earlier than eighth century, the glorious age of Lalitāditya.

In Rajputana excavations in the Jaipur State have revealed the existence of a number of settlements of the Gupta period at places like the commercial and metallurgical centre of Rairh south-east of Jaipur, the site of Naliasar near the Sambhar lake, and Nagar of Karkoṭanagara (one of the ancient capitals of the Malavas in South Jaipur). At the last named place the recent excavations revealed that in spite of the continuance of this great city upto the 10th century, its most prosperous period was no doubt the Gupta period as judged by the excellent town planning. Similarly the city of Sambhar (old Sākambharī) continued up to the 9th or 10th Century ; but the strata associated with the Gupta period show the most solid constructions and the most artistic antiquities.

In Jodhpur, such ancient sites as Pokharan (ancient Pushkaraṇa), Bhinmal (the early seat of the Gurjaras) and Mandor (ancient Māṇḍavyapura) must have been founded in the Gupta period. In Bikanir, Hanumangarh has yielded a number of terracotta decorative tiles in the late Kushāṇa style, along with a number of coins. The excavations at Nagari (ancient Madhyamikā) in the Udaipur State have revealed the existence of remains from the Mauryan period up to the Gupta. The Kotah State has a number of early sites like Badwa and Antah which go back to the second or third century. Gangdhar in the Jhalawar State has a pillar recording an inscription of King Viśva-varman, the ruler of Malwa, dated 423-24 A.D., and mentioning a long series of public works such as irrigation wells, tanks, temples, causeways, etc.

In the province of Sindh there are practically no remains of any historic period except the Gupta. The whole archaeology of Śindh is thus reduced to the three periods, pre-historic, Gupta and Muslim, a gap of nearly three millennia separating the Indus Valley Civilisation from the Gupta, which terminated abruptly with the advent of the Arabs in the beginning of the 8th century. Thus although the original relics recovered from the Mirpurkhas *stūpa* indicate presumably a Mauryan date, the super-structure, ornamentation and figure sculptures clearly indicate the Gupta period for the great *stūpa*. At Mohenjo-daro the *stūpa* and monastery on the top of the highest mound have been assigned to the 3rd Century A.D., *i.e.*, slightly earlier than the Gupta period. The builders, however, made no attempt to manufacture any new bricks either for purposes of construction or ornamentation. On the other hand, the Gupta builders in Sindh left their mark at almost every place of antiquity and as the Arab conquest descended somewhat suddenly on Sindh before the influence of the Gupta period had waned or disappeared, the legacy of the Gupta was not completely wiped out by the Arabs, who were themselves not great builders. The vast city of Brahmanabad-Mansura in Northern Sindh was in a flourishing condition in the Gupta period, and although a large number of buildings were apparently occupied under the early Arabs, such features as the brick wells, drains, libation slabs connected with drains by means of earthenware pipes and the pottery and ornamental bricks with typical designs, shell inlay pieces and beads—all indicate the predominance of the

Gupta influence, which was hardly disturbed by the Arab occupants.

The best examples of Gupta art and architecture in Sindh come from Mirpurkhas on the border of the eastern desert skirting Sindh. The copper image of Brahmā, originating from this place and now in the Karachi Museum, is a fine work of art; the terracotta sculptures, decorating the exterior of the *stūpa* known as Kahu-jo-daro near Mirpurkhas town, are as impressive as the stone images from Mathura and Sarnath. Most of these terracotta panels show the Buddha seated in the attitude of meditation on a lotus with a large pillow at the back decorated with lotus resettes and floral patterns. Among the carved bricks that were used in the recess mouldings and niches such typical designs as the incised alternate square, quatre-foil, meander, interlocked chain, voluted scroll work, full blown flower, inverted lotus Petal and diamonds, are most noteworthy. Small dumpy squatting figures with stepped curls falling on either side on circular medallion, *kīrttimukhas* or lion faces and dwarfs are among the figure-sculpture designs. Some of the trellis work partterns on the panels of the *stūpa* are those which occur on the Dhamekh *stūpa* at Sarnath. The square plan of the Mirpurkhas *stūpa* with a triple chamber in the thickness was probably similar to what must have existed in the Mohen-jo-daro *stūpa*. Another extant *stūpa* which still preserves intact some of its exterior mouldings is the Thul. Mir-Rukan in which the capitals of the pilasters still retain some reminiscence of the Indo-Corinthian style. The *stūpa* known as Sudheranjo-dar near Tando Muhammad Khan shows a square plan of the plinth, but of the super-structure only the steep hard core of clay survives. Here again the carved bricks found in course of clearance leave no doubt about the Gupta date. Although the *stūpa* at Depar-Ghangro near Brahmanabad also discloses a basement 50 feet square and the date is indicated by carved bricks, it is possible that still earlier remains lie buried underneath. Jherruk near Tatta must also have been a place of importance in the Gupta period as indicated by the carved brick ornamentation found in the vicinity of the *stūpa* site on the top of the hill. The latest addition to our knowledge of the Gupta remains in Sindh comes from the site of Jhukar where remains showing a later phase of the Indus Civilization were found underlying a settlement of the Gupta period. The buildings include very few solid structures, but among them were found some remarkable earthenware, coins and sealings.

In Cutch, no definitely Gupta remains have yet come to light. In Kathiawar, the flourishing Valabhī kingdom, at first owing allegiance to the Gupta Empire, has left a larger legacy of copper-plate grants that any other dynasty, but their material remains are comparatively less common. The lake Sudarśana near Junagadh, last repaired under the Guptas, can now hardly be traced on the ground. In the ring of hills surrounding the main Girnar hill there are some sites of the Gupta period, notably the Buddhist site of Bori. The fame of the Somnath shrine at Prabhāsa Pattana is known to every student of medieval history, but the remains of the earlier period are yet to be investigated. Vala, the ancient Valabhī, has occasionally yielded relics of its former greatness and Hathab (ancient Hastāvapra) near Bhavnagar was an important site in the Gupta period. The temple at Gop in Western Kathiawar is a typical Gupta product ; and this site as also Ghumli, the provenance of some important copper-plates of a hitherto unknown dynasty and interesting temples, deserve to be better investigated.

We have enough evidence of the prosperity of Malwa and the adjoining region to the north and at Mandasor (ancient Daśapura) the local rulers, belonging to the Varman dynasty, have left a number of records covering the 5th and 6th centuries. The monuments and excavations at Bhilsa (ancient Vidiśā) and Sanchi have revealed the existence of a very strong centre of Gupta art and architecture in eastern Malwa and the excavations at Pawaya (ancient Padmāvatī) have brought to light a large temple and unique terracotta sculptures of the 3rd-4th Century. The poet Kālidāsa, admittedly assigned by most scholars to the Gupta period, has shown a close aquaintance with Malwa, and it is possible to locate many of the contemporary cities, countries and rivers and reconstruct contemporary life from the literary references checked by finds of contemporary objects. The excavations at Ujjain have yielded a cemetery of the Gupta period with a number of skeletons regularly deposited, the objects interspersed showing definitely their Gupta date. In the hilly country of Bundelkhand in Central India two prosperous feudatory kingdoms of the Guptas have left a number of relics. Places such as Bhumara, Nachna-Kuthara, Majhgawan, Kari-Talai (all in Central Indian States) and Eran in Saugor District offer a number of remains of this period in the shape of pillars, stone temples, images etc. The Vishṇu temple at Deogarh in Jhansi district and the ruined temple at Darrah or Mukandarah in the Kotah State offer very interesting examples of the types of Gupta temples characteristic of Central India. The peculiar feature of these temples is the existence of a raised square plinth with a parapet decorated with sculptures, the centre of the plinth being occupied by a square shrine. The Deogarh temple has many decorative reliefs from the *Mahābhārata* and the *Rāmāyaṇa*, which are described in the next chapter.

In the Central Provinces and Berar the greater part of which was under the powerful Vākāṭaka dynasty, such monuments as the world-famous rock-cut caves at Ajanta are the only extant remains, although important relics still lie buried. Ramtek, the ancient Rāmagiri, and the contiguous Mansar (or Mānasa-Sarovara) with its monastic establishment of the Gupta period and shell-character records on the adjoining hills deserve to be properly explored. Paonar in Wardha District (ancient

Pravarapura, one of the main capitals of the dynasty), situated picturesquely on high land between two rivers, has yet to be excavated. Paoni and Bhandak (already seriously despoiled) in the Chanda District and Deotek and Padampur in the Bhandara District are other important sites in Southern C. P., which ought to yield relics of the Vākāṭaka period. In the Mahākośala area Sirpur and Rajim in the Raipur District and Malhar and Chandrapur in the Bilaspur District are the principal places where relics of the period are found. In the Jubbulpore region the vicinity of Bheraghat has yielded two inscribed red sandstone images of the 3rd century A.D. Tripurī (modern Tewar) is a site which seems to go back to an early period though it later became the capital of the Kaḷachuris. In Berar, the most important ancient site of the period is Basim, ancient Vatsagulma. The site of Kundinpur on the bank of the Wardha, in Amraoti District, has several mounds, now largely scoured by river action. The southern part of the Buldhana District, specially the vicinity of the Lonar lake, is another promising region where remains of the early period of settlement of the Aśmaka country can be discovered.

In Orissa, the site of Sisupalgarh near Bhuvaneśvara (likely to be identical with the ancient Tosali) ss archaeologically the most imporant for the late Gupta period. The group of Buddhist monuments in the Jaipur hills, known as Udayagiri, Lalitagiri and Ratnagiri, has already yielded a number of sculptures, attributable to the sixth century ; and the ancient capital of Khiching in the Mayurbhanj State also dates back to the same period. The later caves in Khandagiri and Udayagiri, the earliest settlements at Bhuvaneśvara and Jajpur, and the earlier sites in the Orissa States, such as Baudh, may also go back to the same antiquity. The stimulus received by Orissa in the Gupta period is responsible for laying the foundations of the great architectural heights reached by that province during the subsequent periods.

In the Deccan, the four centuries beginning with the third witnessed great changes from the decline and end of the Sātavāhana empire, the period of the Vākāṭakas and Kaḷachuris and Kadambas, and finally the rise of the Chālukyas. Archaeologically the age of the great Buddhist caves of the Hīnayāna School was over, and the coming in of the Mahāyāna doctrines ushered many changes in the existing caves, particularly the introduction of Buddha and Tārā figures in relief. The idea that, apart from rock-cut caves, very few actual remains have survived in the Deccan has so far been responsible for the want of proper investigations in the subject. In the Nizam's Dominions, the recent excavations at places like Kondapur in the Bidar District and at Paithan on the Godavari, and the caves at Bhokardhan (ancient Bhogavardhana) in the Aurangabad District, have brought out abundant material for the study of the Sātavāhana and later periods in the Deccan. The upper Godāvarī and Kṛishṇā valleys have yet to be systematically surveyed for remains of the Sātavāhana empire. At Kolhapur the old Brahmapuri site on the banks of the river Panchganga has yielded structural remains, which show that the peculiar system of having a foundation of hard layers of beaten clay below the brick layers was in vogue in the South as well as in the North in the 3rd century A.D. The site of old Belgaum near Vadgaon Madhavpur has corroborated the same observation. Excavations at the sites of Chandravalli and Brahmagiri in the Chitaldrug District of the Mysore State have also yielded remains of the Sātavāhana and Kadamba periods. Halsi (ancient Palāśikā) in the Belgaum District and Vanavāsī (ancient Vaijayantī) in the Kanara District, the two capitals of the Kadambas, particularly the later, have some mounds which deserve to be excavated. On the whole, considerable work is needed to establish the proper sequence of material cultures in the Deccan.

The Andhra country, particularly the Kṛishṇā velley comprising the modern Districts of Guntar and Krishna, was the seat of the prosperous kingdom of the Ikshvākus in the beginning of the third century A.D. and the pious kings and their queens and other relatives have left ample vestiges of their zeal all over the lower Kṛishṇā basin. Amarāvatī and Nagarjunikonda (ancient Śrīparvata) were their principal centres, the sculptured marble reliefs from which have given us such a comprehensive idea of their religion, art and culture. The soft pink marble of the Eastern Ghats on the Palnad tract seems to have provided the Ikshvāku artists with an ideal medium for their work which was unavailable anywhere else in the peninsula. Among sites which have yielded their relics (mostly Buddhist monuments) and which are still awaiting systematic work are Goli and Rentala in Palanad, Chebrolu south of Guntur, Jagayyapetta, Ghantapalle and Bhattiprolu in the Kṛishṇā delta, Ramireddipalli (or Gummadidurru) and Alluru on the right bank of the Kṛishṇā. Chezarla near Narasaraopet, Guntur District, is another site which has a rare type of apsidal temple later converted into a Śaiva temple. The sita of Pithāpuram in the Godāvarī basin, along with other places like Koṭṭura and Eraṇḍapalla, Devarāshṭra and Veṅgi also in the Andhra country, is yet to be explored for relics of the period. Except the Buddhist establishment at Śankaram. Ramatirtham and Salihundam, all in the Vizagapatam District, the important maritime province anciently known as Kaliṅga has been very inadequately surveyed for ancient remains, and even the sites of the capitals of the various minor dynasties of the period, such as Vishṇukuṇḍins, Eastern Gaṅgas, etc. have not been determined.

In the extreme south of the country, the land of the Tamils, the city of Kāñchī or Conjeevaram in the Chingleput District has maintained its predominance throughout the historical period and was the capital of the Pallavas, the first of the historic dynasties of the South. There are mounds known as

Pallavamedu, likely to date back to the middle Pallava period, which is also the period of the well-known Kailāsanātha and Vaikuṇṭhaperumāl temples at Conjeevaram, as also of the seven Pagoda monuments. The vast programme of temple building in the Chola and later periods has hardly left any vestiges of the earlier period in the interior, but the marts on the sea-coast like Arikamedu near Pondicherry and Korkai in Tinnevelly District, which had commerical intercourse with the Roman empire, yield antiquities of the second and third century A.D. Systematic investigation of these sites is at present in progress and it is likely that the synchronism offered by dateable antiquities of the Imperial Roman period will enable archaeologists to lay out a sequence of material cultures in the South, by a comparative study of the results in different sites.

In conclusion, it may be stated that the Gupta period represents the climax and culmination of the native Indian genius in all spheres of intellectual activity found throughout the length and breadth of this land. If the period of the Mauryan empire showed a remarkable elevation of the Indian mind, it was under the stimulus of a strong central direction ; but in the Gupta epoch, it was a spontaneous exuberance which permeated every field and filled the entire sub-continent, spreading out in other lands beyond the seas.

CHAPTER XXII

FINE ARTS

In the present chapter, we shall take a survey of Fine Arts from *c* 200 to 650 A.D. This period falls into two convenient divisions, pre-Gupta, 200 to 320, and Gupta, 320-650. In northern India during the pre-Gupta, period the artistic activity may no doubt have continued aloı.g the old lines at famous centres like Mathura and Peshawar, but outstanding specimens have not been preseved. It should also be remembered that the unsettled political condition in the Punjab and the United Provinces, consequent upon the break-up of the Kushāṇa empire and the emergence of a number of small states (as described before in Chaps. I and II), was hardly favourable for progress in art. Pre-Gupta art can therefore be studied only in South India.

I. SOUTH INDIAN ART, *C.* 200—350 A.D.

1. Sculpture

South India has left a number of important and interesting monuments of art at centres like Amarāvatī, Nagarjunikonda, Ghantasala, Gummadidurru and Goli. The continuation of the Sātavāhana art, which was closely akin to the Śaka-Kushāṇa art, can be seen at Amarāvatī (Pl. IV, 1), where we see the last phase of its activity early in the 3rd century. The human figures sculptured at this time are a little more attenuated than those of the preceding period, but they have a beauty of their own. Long and lovely *yajñopavītas* in pearls, the lion head motif in the crown and *makarī* design for the coiffure of women are some of the innovations of this period worth mentioning here. The art of Chūṭukula Sātakarṇis of Vaijayantīpura also belongs to this period, but a sculptured *Nāga* is its only specimen handed down to us.

We shall now proceed to consider the religious monuments at Nagarjunikonda, Ghantasala, Gummadidurru and Goli.[1] These were mostly built under the patronage of the kings and queens of the Ikshvāku house to whom belongs the credit of keeping the torch of art alive in the Kṛishṇā valley during this dark period. The sculpture at the above place, which naturally continues the tradition of the earlier Amarāvatī school, shows considerable merit and vigour.

The *Stūpa*-casing slabs are richly carved. The Buddha is represented sometimes in human form and sometimes as a symbol—a flaming pillar surmounted by a wheel and *triśula.* In the human form he is often shown seated with legs hanging down and resting on a foot-stool as in the later Gupta-Vākāṭaka sculptures at Ajanta. Scenes from the life of the Buddha like Renunciation (Pl. IV, 2) and Enlightenment, Birth and Temptation are freely depicted in a style closely similar to that at Amarāvatī. The Jātaka stories also supply many of the themes, the Chhaddanta Jātaka being depicted at some length in the carvings from Goli. The story of Nanda and Janapadakalyāṇī, which was a pouplar theme both in Mathura and the Kṛishṇā valley, is most effectively rendered at Nagarjunikonda. The story of the Sasa Jātaka found at Amarāvatī is repeated at this place and Goli. While the full flush of power of Māndhātā is usually emphasised in sculptures from all these places, it is the fall of the emperor and his repentance which are selected for special treatment at Nagarjunikonda. Sometimes the art of this famous centre reveals closer parallels with that of Mathura. The visit of Indra to the Buddha at the Indasela-

[1] These places are situated in the Guntur and Krishna districts.

guhā, a favourite theme in Kushāṇa sculpture, is beautifully portrayed at Nagarjunikonda. The visit of Ajātaśatru to the Buddha found at Bharhut is also depicted at Amarāvati and repeated cerefully at Nagarjunikonda. As sculptures worthy of special mention we may refer to the lovely scene of temptation from Ghantasala, the finely proportioned flying figures over *stūpas* from Gummadiduirru, the magnificent penels depicting Vessantara's story at Goli, and the boy pulling a toy-horse on wheels, *mithuna* figures between the panels and the Yakshī figures at the end of the long rows of panels at Nagarjunikonda.

The Northern dress of a Scythian soldier wearing a coat and trousers at Nagarjunikonda (Pl. V, 1) shows some realistic influences from outside. Surprisingly, the bolt in the hand of the god Vajrapāṇi, which has three prongs at both ends in Amarāvatī, is at Nagarjunikonda, similar to the weapon in Gandhāra sculpture, where its ends are flat.

A comparative study shows that some of the motifs were particularly popular. The figure of the dwarf with the head on stomach is one among them. It occurs not only at Amarāvatī and Ghantasala during the 3rd century, but recurs later in the Gupta-Vākāṭaka sculptures and at Ajanta. Not only did this motif migrate from the south through the Vākāṭaka realm to the home provinces of the Gupta empire, as we find it occurring at Sarnath, but it also crossed the seas and found a place among the lovely carvings in Java.

2. Architecture

The architectural activity in the Kṛishṇā valley for the pre-Gupta period is mainly Buddhist and centres round the *Stūpa* ; naturally its earlier form at Amarāvatī served as the model. The *Stūpa* of the south, like that in the north, stood on a platform reached by a flight of steps. The plan of the solid *stūpas* in the Kṛishṇā valley shows two circular walls, one at the hub and the other at the outer end, the space between the two being partitioned by spoke-like walls and the space intervening between the walls being filled up with mud. The outer casing of the drum consisted of richly carved marble slabs. The hemispherical top of the drum was decorated with lime and mortar work. The four rectangular projections, one at each cardinal point, supported a row of five free-standing pillars labelled in the inscriptions on them as *Āyakakhambas* (*Āryakastambha*, i.e. a pillar for worship). The *āyaka* pillars together with the *āyaka* platforms on which they stood and the simple gateways guarded by lions are special features of the *stūpas* in the Andhra country not found elsewhere. The *pradakshiṇapatha* between the *stūpa* and the outer railing was approached by steps near the gateways; the first being semi-circular was known as the 'moon stone' and decorated with bands of animals and creeper designs executed in a lovely manner. The 'moon stones' at the lower end of the staircase becomes a regular feature of Gupta *stūpas* in Ceylon and are also found in the temple at Deogarh.

The *Chaitya* remains at Nagarjunikonda show that its plan was apsidal, the remote end towards the apse having a small votive *stūpa* for worship. The approach to the *chaityas* was, as in the case of large *stūpas*, by a flight of steps starting with a 'moon-stone'. These later structural *chaityas* are not different in plan and form the earlier rock-out ones in Karli and other caves in Western India.

The *Vihāras* or monasteries for the residence of monks were composed of a number of cells arranged, as usual, around a rectangular courtyard. The foundations of such monasteries have been laid bare in excavations at Nagarjunikonda, showing that the approach to the cells and some of the entrances was by small steps with 'moon-stones' and low flanking *makara* balustrades.

At Nagarjunikonda, there are many pillars in rows which have now fallen down, but once formed part of a hall. This is an example of one of the earliest halls in south India, later associated with temples, sometimes having as many as a thousand pillars.

II. ART IN THE GUPTA PERIOD.

The glories of the Gupta age proper (*c.* 350-650 A.D.) have been made permanent through the visible creations of its art. The age witnessed an unprecedented artistic activity all over India and synchronised with the growth and perfection of the most beautiful art definitions. Different forms of art, *e.g.*, sculpture, painting and terracotta, attained a maturity, balance and naturalness of expression that have for ever remained unexcelled. Some of our most beautiful monuments representing the very acme of India's artistic achievement, among which the immortal Ajanta frescoes take precedence, are a cultural heritage of the Gupta period.

This all-embracing artistic activity covered almost the whole country. Famous provincial centres like Mathura, Benares and Patna, besides many new ones, became the seats of the new intellectual and spiritual movement, and the economic prosperity of the age gave a refreshing outlook on life. Under ideal conditions of society and state art and culture flourished as never before. Owing to close alliance between art and life many details of Gupta life can be gathered from the objects of contemporary art, which appear like so many lovely documents of culture.

1. SCULPTURE.

Sculpture has contributed most of the high esteem in which the Gupta art is held. Under the stroke of the master's chisel the stone became malleable, as it were, and was transformed into figures of permanent beauty and grace. The success of Gupta sculpture lies in its balanced synthesis between the obtruding sensuality of the Kushāṇa figures and the symbolic abstraction of the early mediaeval work. The aggressive beauty, as seen in the figures on Mathura rail pillars, is no longer in accord with the spirit of the Gupta age; its sensuousness is restrained by a conscious moral sense. Nudity as a rule is eliminated in Gupta art. The effect of the diaphanous drapery in Kushāṇa art is to reveal the charm of the flesh; the Gupta artist on the other hand employs drapery to conceal those very charms.

The synthesis of the external form with the inner spirit is nowhere better illustrated than in Buddha images of this period. The three most outstanding examples are the seated Buddha image from Sarnath (Pl. VI), the inscribed image of the standing Buddha in the Mathura Museum, No. A. 5 (Pl. V, 2), and the colossal copper statue of Buddha (about 7½ feet high) from Sultanganj, now in the Birmingham Museum (Pl. V, 3). The spiritual expression, the tranquil smile and the serene contemplative mood of the Sarnath Buddha posed on a diamond seat in the attitude of preaching show us the highest triumph of Indian art—an attempt to visualise the superman endowed with the highest wisdoṃ (*anuttarjñāna*), detached and austere in his discipline, but radiating an almost divine influence. The other two Buddha images referred to above are also characterised by similar artistic qualities.

We notice some innovations in the Gupta age with reference to the Buddha statue. Usually it has beautiful curly hair ; the Kushāṇa Buddha type with a shaven head makes its appearance but once in the Gupta age at Mankuwar (near Allahabad). It was obviously rejected as it did not satisfy the aesthetic instinct of the age. A second feature consisted in bands of graceful ornamentation of different kinds introduced in the halo of the Buddha figure,[1] which in the previous age was almost plain. Transparent drapery, plain or with folds, clearly revealing the form, was introduced by the Gupta artist. Several Buddha images have webbed fingers (*jālāṅgulikara*); they also show a larger variety of *mudrās* (hand poses).

The Buddha image in the Gupta school provides important testimony as regards the freshness and vitality of that art. As Smith remarks in connection with the Sarnath figure, the Gupta Buddha is "absolutely independent of the Gandhāra school"[2]; it reveals the fullest fruition of the original Indian genius in carving out a figure in perfect harmony with its spiritual conceptions. Even the Gandharan Buddhas, in stucco and clay, of this period are profoundly Indianised and hardly show any foreign influence. The inspiration characterising the Gupta Buddha figure travelled to Greater India, towards the east and the north, where it is palpable as a living force in innumerable images of the succeeding centuries.

We have seen already in Chap. XIX how there was a remarkable revival of Hinduism in the Gupta period and it is naturally reflected in its sculpture. Śaivism and Vaishṇavism were equally popular, and the sculptures and temples of the age confirm this conclusion. Some of the most beautiful Śiva images, like the Śivaliṅga from Khoh (Pl. VII, 1) belong to the Gupta period. Both the *Liṅga* form and the anthromorphic image of Śiva existed in the Kushāṇa period, but their combination as evolved in *Ekamukhī* and *Chaturmukhī* Śivaliṅga was a characteristic feature of Gupta iconography. The Ardhanārīśvara form of Śiva, which represents a synthesis between the eternal pair of opposites by presenting the deity

[1] The halo on the Mathura Buddha with its foliated scroll, rosettes, geese designs, etc. imitates the full blown lotus and reminds us of *Raghu*, IV, v. 5, where Kālidāsa compares the halo of Raghu with a full blown lotus parasol (*padmātapatra*).

[2] *HFA*, p. 170.

as half-male and half female, was rendered by the artists of our age with masterly skill.

The sculptures of this period give ample evidence to the growing popularity of the worship of Vishṇu and his different incarnations. Perhaps the best qualities of the Gupta plastic art find expression in the superb example of Vishṇu from Mathura (Pl. VII, 2) with its face revealing a celestial contentment and serene spiritual contemplation, similar to that of the seated Buddha image in the Sarnath museum. For the first time Gupta statuary begins to show the images of the cosmic form of Vishṇu combining a human head with those of a boar and a lion. These are images of Nṛisiṁha-Varāha Vishṇu (M.M. 2525, D. 28). A different form of the cosmic aspect (*Viśvarūpa*) of Vishṇu in this period is that in which the central human figure is surrounded by a number of radiating heads, *e.g.*, the eight armed figure or the great architrave from Garhwa[1] (also on a recently found relief from Mathura).

The attributes of Vishṇu, *śaṅkha*, *chakra* etc., appeared in their natural form in Kushāṇa figures, but in Gupta images they are often personified as *āyudha-purushas*. These figures are generally dwarfish as compared with the tall stature of the main figure. This agrees with Kālidāsa's reference to the attendant figures of *Vāmanas* or 'short-statured persons'; he also says that each personified attendant was marked with its respective symbol (*Raghu*, X, v. 60).

The great Varāha image at Udayagiri (*c.* 400 A.D.) has been rightly regarded as a monument to the genius of the Gupta sculptors. Its volume and powerful execution furnish a happy contrast to the scenes of lesser dimensions forming the background. The two flanking scenes also are of unusual significance, representing the birth of the twin rivers Gaṅgā and Yamunā, their confluence at Prayāga and the final merging

[1] *ASC*. X, 13, Pl. VII, c.

of the combined waters into the ocean (cf. *Raghu*, XIII, v. 58). The whole scene is permeated with a lyrical feeling, and probably conveys an ideal representation of the Middle Country or the Madhyadeśa, which was the heart of the wide culture-empire built in this age. Its symbols were the two river goddesses Gaṅgā and Yamunā standing on their respective vehicles, the crocodile and the tortoise. It is only in Gupta art, as in the literature of this period, that the two rivers make their appearance for the first time in the scheme of temple architecture, and we cannot but infer that Kālidāsa, making a pointed reference to them as attendants of the deity, is referring to a principal feature of contemporary art (cf. *Kumārasambhava*, VII, v. 42).

The epigraphic evidence from this period shows that the sun worship was fairly popular. The images of the solar deity show that the sun-god was clad in the northern dress, wearing coats and trousers and long buskined boots. This form of the deity is found right from Afghanistan to Mathura and Madhyadeśa, and seems to have been adopted as the popular representation of this god. He is also shown as accompanied by his two attendants, Daṇḍa and Piṅgala.

Owing to the continuous progress made during the preceding few centuries, Gupta sculptors found themselves in possession of well-defined conventions and iconographic canons. With this heritage of well-understood forms of art the artists handled the complicated legends and myths of the many incarnations of Vishṇu and Śiva with an easy mastery. One is impressed with the genuine simplicity in which grand mythical conceptions of religious and metaphysical import are visualised by the engraver. The sculptural representations of the epic stories from the Rāma and Kṛishṇa cycles are delineated with effective success in the Deogarh temple belonging to this epoch. Here we find the details of the Kṛishṇa legend completely developed, and a few of the many panels bear scenes of Kṛishṇa's childhood exploits—his surreptitous transfer to Gokula, his kicking the milk-cart on which pots of milk have toppled over, and his seizing the demon Kaṁsa by the hair. On another beautiful panel we find a homely scene showing Kṛishṇa, Rukmiṇī and Sudāmā. The emaciated Brāhmaṇa is leaning on his crooked staff and in front of him stands Kṛishṇa, an elegant figure with the effect of his dignity heightened by the very elaborate and gorgeous coiffure spreading round his head, with the lady Rukmiṇī by his side steeped in astonishment at the measureless bounty of her husband in fulfilling the wishes of his friend. The iconographic wealth of this period is further illustrated in the scenes from the *Rāmāyaṇa* which once adorned the plinth of this temple. The redemption of Ahalyā, the departure of Rāma, Lakshmaṇa and Sītā to the forest, their visit to the hermitage of the sage Agastya and the mutilation of Śūrpaṇakhā by Lakshmaṇa are some of the major episodes preserved in these panel-reliefs. *Gajendramoksha*, Vishṇu reclining on Ananta (Pl. VIII, 1), and Nara and Nārāyaṇa in their Himalayan hermitage (Pl. VIII, 2), sculptured in the Deogarh temple, rank among the best specimens of Hindu sculpture.

The art critic can discern the full-fledged Gupta inspiration in the Hindu sculptures of the Deccan as well. This is particularly true of the beautiul sculptures in the caves at Mogulrajpura and Undavalli. The carvings at the latter place treat of a number of themes from Hindu mythology like Varāha raising the earth, Trivikrama taking three paces, Vishṇu rescuing Gajendra, Kṛishna lifting Govardhana, etc., all of which show unmistakable Gupta inspiration.

The sculpture of this period is also rich in charming ornamental designs. On a door-jamb from Garhwa we find the *Kalpalatā* motif treated in a very artistic style (Pl. IX, 1). The whole scroll, which is deeply sunk and very clearly and carefully carved, is one of the most pleasing and graceful specimens of Indian architectural ornament.[1] The foliated scroll is a special trait of Gupta art and the artists must have undergone prolonged and rigorous training in order to attain their admirable skill. In literary descriptions we find several names for this kind of work, viz., *patralatā*, *patrāṅguli*, *patra-bhaṅga-rachanā*, *anekabhaṅgakuṭila-patrāvalī*, etc. The curves and twists with an increasingly deep relief finally reached a logical sequence in the almost perforated work on the screens and reliefs of medieval temples (*c.* 11th-12th century) as seen in Chandella art and the Dilwara marble temples.

2. Architecture.

The wave of creative enthusiasm and intensely religious purpose behind it that swept the country at this time are seen at thair best in the architectural activity of the period which produced the Brahmanical temple. "In the art of building two progressive movements of fundamental significance are discernible, one relating to its aesthetic character, and the other to structural procedure. The former marks the begetting of a new sensibility, a change from the mere imitative to the infinitely creative, from the servile copying of meaningless from expressive of undeveloped mind and unskilled forces, to a reasoned application of the first principles of architectural compositions. The latter records the use for the first time of dressed stone masonry, a pronounced step in the technique of building construction, the introduction of which placed a new power in the hands of the workman. It was when the art was in such a formative state that there emerged the earliest known conception of the Hindu 'house of god'. And with the appearance

[1] This motif of the *nārīdāśāhkhā* (the girls springing from the Wish-fulfilling lilies) is as old as the Jātakas, (*Mahāvaṇija*, *Jāt* IV, 352), *Rāmāyaṇa* (Kishkindhyā, v. 43, 48) and *Mahābhārata* (Bhīshma, VII, v. 9). Cf. also Agrawala in *JISOA*. 1943, pp. 1-8.

of this type of building, architecture composed of stone masonry made its beginning."[1]

The chief surviving temples of the Gupta age are the following :—

1. Vishṇu temple at Tigawa in Jubbulpore district.
2. Śiva temple at Bhumara in Nagod State.
3. Pārvatī temple at Nachna-Kuthara in Ajaigarh State.
4-5. Buddhist shrines at Sanchi and Bodhgaya.
6. The Daśāvatāra temple at Deogarh.
7. A temple in a ruined state but of great merit, found at Dah Parbatia on the banks of the Brahmaputra in Darrang district of Assam.
8. A temple of Śiva at Khoh in Nagod State (the beautiful *Ekamukhī Liṅga* and a mass of sculpture showing lively *gaṇas* from this temple are now deposited in the Allahabad Museum).

Besides these we have temples made entirely of brick, numerous examples of which have been found from Bhitargaon in Cawnpore district to Paharpur in Bengal and Sirpur in C. P. Of these, the temple at Bhitargaon, conceived from top to bottom in terms of terracotta and brick, is particularly worth mentioning ; it is beautified with several courses of well-preserved friezes and moulded bricks with designs exceedingly varied and beautiful. The temple has a pyramidal roof and its walls were decorated on the outside with terracotta panels, depicting scenes from Hindu mythology. Architecturally, the temple is important as possessing the earliest true arch found in India.

Let us now revert to the Brahmanical stone temples of the age. They are the known Hindu shrines in stone and naturally show the early phases and features of stone temple architecture. They were small and unimposing structures with

---

[1] P. Brown, *Ind. Archit., Buddhist & Hindu*, p. 54.

a square sanctuary, about 10 feet in dimensions, and a portico of still smaller proportions. Obviously they were rather shrines for images, than places for congregations of the worshippers. The roof was usually flat and the stone masonry was finely dressed and held together without any kind of mortar. Gupta Hindu shrines therefore present a marked contrast to the later Hindu temples with high *śikharas* (pinnacles) and extensive *maṇḍapas* (halls). A transition to the later style had however begun towards the end of our period and can be seen in the Daśāvatāra temple at Deogarh, which had originally a *śikhara* of about 40 feet : its stones were secured together by dowels and its four porches afforded relatively more space for the worshippers to congregate.

The sanctum of this temple stood on a raised plinth, occupying the central square of the open terrace. It had a plain interior, but its doorway was exquisitely carved and decorated, the jambs showing the figures of Gaṅga and Yamuna carved on them (Pl. IX, 2). This was a typically Gupta feature and it is possible that the two river goddesses occupying the upper corners of the door-jambs were derived from the early *śālabhañjika* figures which once festooned the architraves of the Buddhist *toraṇas*.

In front of the richly carved doorway was usually a shallow porch, which in later Gupta examples developed into a pillared portico, and later still into a full-fledged *mukhamaṇḍapa*. Among other specific features should be mentioned the shape of the pillars and their capitals of the *pūrṇa-kalasa* design, the system of rendering the architrave of the doorway as a string course running round the entire building, and courses of fine *chaitya* window or more properly *gavākṣha-vātāyana* patterns, containing round medallions with figures of gods and goddesses or peeping male or female busts.

Most of these features are seen at their best in the beautiful Daśāvatāra temple at Deogarh. As observed by Percy Brown, when complete, this building was unquestionably one of rare merit in the correct ordering of its part, all alike serving the purpose of practical utility, yet imbued with supreme artistic feeling. Few monuments can show such a high level of workmanship combined with ripeness and rich refinement in its sculptural effect as the Gupta temple at Deogarh.

The doorway leading to the sanctum was the chief centre of attraction in a Gupta temple, serving as an elegant outer frame to set off the image installed in the cella. Looking in detail it was marked by the following decorative features:—

A projecting image in the centre of the lintel (*dvāra-lalāṭa-bimba*), attendant figures (*pratihārī*) occupying the lower one-fourth portion of the height of the jambs, auspicious birds on wings (*māṅgalya vihaga*) usually flying geese, auspicious tree more or less stylised (*śrīvṛiksha*), *svastika*, full vase or the pot and foliage design (*pūrṇa-ghaṭa*), amorous couples (*mithuna*), foliated scrolls (*patra-vallī*), and dwarfish figures (*pramathas*). All these motifs occur on the Deogarh door-frame except the lucky birds which adorn the door-jambs of the Dah Parbatia temple in Assam. Another typical feature of decoration consisted in the two auspicious symbols, conch and lotus, being either carved or painted on door jambs (cf. the reference in *Meghadūta*, II, v. 17 : *dvārcpānte likhita-vapushau śaṅkha-padmau cha dṛishṭvā*). These two symbols with rising arabasque designs are seen in the jambs of the beautifully farmed panels on the three outer walls at Deogarh.

The style of such panels or images in exterior wall niches (*rathika-bimba*) continued as a common feature into the mediaeval period. Originally it appears to be an adaptation from a *stūpa* having projecting Buddha figures in the four directions. Two other structural features point to the relationship of the temple with Buddhist *stūpas*, firstly, the high square platform corresponding to the terraces (*medhi*) with a stairway (*sopāeta*) in the centre of each side, and secondly, four small temples or sanctuaries at the four corners (cf. *Divyāvadāna*, pp. 243-44). Many earlier Indian *sṭūpas*, such as those of Bhallar (Taxila) and Mirpur Khas (Sind) or at Nagarjunikonda in the Krishna valley, stand on a single square or rectangular platform with axial approaches on one or four sides.[1]

South India has handed down to us very few structures of the Gupta period. Among these, the Kapoteśvara temple at Chezarla, built by the Ānanda kings of the 4th century, is the most interesting. It is the earliest known Hindu temple with an apsidal plan, similar to the Buddhist *chaityas* at Karli or Nagarjunikonda. The facade of the *vimāna* is shaped like a huge *chaitya* and the back top is curvilinear on an apsidal plan. The Durgā temple at Aihole (*c.* 6th century A.D.) and the Vaishṇava temple at Ter, which are both apsidal, seem to have been inspired by this earlier model.

Let us now turn to Buddhist structural buildings. *Stūpas*, chapels and monasteries have been found at Jaulian, Charsadda and other ancient sites near Pushkalāvatī. At Mohra Maradu an assembly hall, refectory, kitchen, store room, bath room and latrine, associated with a religious establishment, indicate the luxurious mode of life of the monk-residents. The Sarnath excavations have unearthed the remnants of a Buddha temple and a number of monasteries. The latter usually, consisted of a number of rooms round a court-yard, sometimes having chapels of their own.

One of the two *stūpas* at Jarāsandha-kā-Baiṭhak in Rajgir and the Dhamekh *stūpa* at Sarnath belong to the end of our period. The latter one is 128 feet in height and has four niches at the four cardinal points for Buddha images. The scroll work on this *stūpa* has evoked just praise and the structure is also remarkable for the variety of geometric patterns with which part of its area has been covered.

---

[1] *HIIA*. p. 205.

Narasiṁha-gupta Bālāditya had built a magnificent brick temple of the Buddha at Nālandā. It was 300 feet in height and evoked admiration of the Chinese travellers who later visited the University town. This majestic structure has entirely disappeared ; archaeolocial excavations have unearthed only its massive basement. The temple was probably similar to the well-known Buddha temple at Bodhgaya.

We now proceed to survey the cave architecture of the age. Excavation of caves (*leṇa*, skt. *layana*) was quite well-known in northern India and Deccan from *c.* 250 B.C., but was practically unknown to the extreme south till the 6th century.[1] The main cave structures of our period belong to Ajanta and the Andhra country.

Both *Chaitya* and *Vihāra* caves[2] continued to be excavated at Ajanta during our period. Among these, the *vihāra* caves Nos. XVI and XVII, excavated in the last quarter of the 5th century by a minister and a feudatory of the Vākāṭaka king Harisheṇa,[3] and the *chaitya* cave No. XIX, finished a little later, are the most important. From the artistic and architectural points of view these are magnificent monuments and no visitor can easily forget the grand impression produced upon his mind by their architecture, sculpture and paintings. They are undoubtedly among the best artistic monuments of the Gupta age and will therefore be briefly described here.

The *chaitya* cave No. XIX, like its earlier precursors, consists of a nave separated from aisles by a row of pillars, but

---

[1] King Mahendravarman proudly describes his cave temples, which were an innovation in the south, as built without bricks, timber, mortar and metal, *anishṭakam, asudham, alauham, adrumam, nirmāpitam* (Mandagapattu Inscription).

[2] The *Chaitya* cave is a cave temple enshrining a *stūpa* or Buddha image as the central object of worship. The *Vihāra* cave is primarily a monastery for the residence of monks; sometimes it also has a small chapel.

[3] Inscriptions on their walls give the names of the donors and the ruling king.

it also shows many new features. In the earlier *chaitya* caves considerable use had been made of wood for the purpose of completing the facade ; here it has been discarded altogether. The rail ornament also disappears from the facade and is replaced by a double row of cornice decorated with *chaitya* window motifs. The entrance is flat-roofed, supported by four pillars with a huge *chaitya* window above it separated by the cornice (Pl. X). The aisle pillars inside have fluted columns with pot and foliage capitals. But the most striking new feature of the *cha itya* is its zeal for the Buddha figure. In the earlier *chaityas* at Karli and Nasik, the Blessed One is nowhere to be seen in the human form ; at Ajanta he can be seen in the human form at the facade, in the frieze of niches above the brackets, and carved on the monolithic *stūpa* inside, which was the main object of worship. It was the new Mahāyāna belief which had brought about this transformation. The rock-cut *stūpa* of this *chaitya* consists of a high cylindrical drum, decorated with standing or seated Buddha figures between pilasters crowned by graceful *makara* arches. The drum supports the globular dome, with the usual pavilion (*harmikā*), and a series of three umbrellas (*tri-chhatra*) one above the other.

The *vihāra* cave Nos. XVI and XVII are justly famous for their paintings, which will be discussed a little later ; they are however equally interesting for their architecture. The cave No. XVI is a twenty pillared cave, 65 feet square, having six residential cells for the monks on either side, two at either end of the verandah and two at the back. Between these two cells there is a rectangular sanctuary with a large figure of the Buddha, seated in *pralambapāda* posture, *i.e.*, feet hanging down. The beauty of the pillars is remarkable as their variety, no two pillars being exactly alike. The general harmony of design and form, however, prevents variety from being obtrusive. The cave No. XVII is almost similar to cave No. XVI. It was long known as the Zodiac cave on account of the 'Wheel of Life' (*bhāvachakra*) painted on the walls of its verandah. On account of the famous fresco paintings, these caves produce an effect which can be better experienced than described. All the walls were once covered with painted scenes from the life of the Buddha or the Jātakas and the roof and the pillars beautified by arabesque and ornamental designs in bold outlines and pleasing colours.

The caves at Mogulrajapuram, Undavalli and Akkannamadanna, excavated under the Vishṇukuṇḍins, belong to the Gupta period. It is interesting to note that their plan is modelled on that of the Udayagiri caves in Central India, and not on that prevailing nearer home at Guntupalli near Bezwada. The architecture of these caves is simple. The facades at Mogulrajapuram show two pillars in the centre, two pilastes, one on either side, and a *Dvārapālaka* at each end beside the two pilasters. The pillars and pilasters are simple and massive, being square in section at the base and the top and octagonal in the central part. The corbels are rounded at either end, and judging from the less weathered ones, fluted. Right above the pillars are *chaitya* windows with heads introduced in them. The floral design flanking the *chaitya* windows with the head on top is the precursor of similar pattern on Pallava *chaitya* windows. Above this is sometimes a row of animals spiritedly carved. On entry the cave presents a verandah with or without an additional row of pillars beyond which is a single cell or triple cells forming the sanctuary. The Undavalli caves have similar architectural features, but are three-storied.

We must also make a passing reference to the Brahmanical cave temple at Udayagiri, near Bhopal, having an inscription, dated 401 A.D. and referring to the reign of Chandra-gupta II. It is thus the earliest dated Hindu temple known so far. The shrine is partly rock-cut and partly stone-built, as a shallow pillared portico has been added in front of the excavated cella. This style is just a transition from the pure cave shrines to the structural ones. The portico, the carved doorway and the pillars with their 'Bowl of Plenty' capitals show the typical features of the Gupta style.

3. Secular Architecture.

Secular buildings of our period are unfortunately not preserved,[1] but some idea of early palace can be formed by a study of their sculptural representation at Amarāvatī and Nagarjunikonda. They were imposing structures several storeys high. The types of windows included the arched one with finial, the rectangular one and the latticed. Different kinds of balustrades are shown ; pilasters and polygonal pillars have fine capitals, some on the model of the earlier bell-shaped ones with *kalasa* motif at the base. The roof was sometimes shaped after the hood of a wagon, sometimes after a simple rectangular hut, and sometimes circular with a curvilinear top and a single tapering finial. The second type was probably known as the *śālā* and the third *kūṭāgāra*. Both are known and described in early literary accounts of palaces. Terraces and balconies were sometimes open and sometimes canopied, the latter being known as *valabhīs*. There were separate entrances and exits with fine arched *toraṇa* decoration, as in the case of the gateways at Sanchi, which were decorated with fresh garlands on occasions. These entrances cut a boundary wall much in the same way as in some of our modern high class residential buildings.

The paintings at Ajanta show that sometimes moderate sized royal pavilions were raised on four cylindrical pillars (*maṇidaṇḍikāchatushṭaya* according to Bāṇa), decorated with

---

[1] It is possible, as suggested by Dr. Coomaraswamy, that the two-storeyed pillared hall excavated in rock at Uparkot in the Junagadh state, may have been an underground summer chamber of a palace. It has a bath attached to it.

golden festoons. The royal seat was placed under the canopy of this audience hall, which was tastefully decorated. Halls of audience, both private and public (*āsthānamaṇḍapas*), are also referred to by Bāṇa. Literary evidence further shows that the palace apartments were usually decorated with paintings ; not only palaces but even the houses of rich citizens were furnished with separate picture galleries (*chitrasadma*) and concert halls (*saṅgītaśālā*).

4. Terracotta.

Terracottas formed another important branch of Gupta art. In this modest medium gifted clay modellers created things of real beauty and achieved a wide popular basis for their art. The modeller compared favourably and at a par with the builder, the painter and the engraver.[1] Clay figurines served as poor man's sculpture and contributed largely to popularise art and culture. As small objects easy to reproduce mechanically from moulds they were capable of mass production and were used both for religious and secular purposes. Men and women, passionately fond of recreating beautiful forms, employed the terracotta medium with great zeal and success. In their home, the drawing room, and the lover's bed-chamber, terracotta figurines showing amorous scenes or forms of exquisite beauty were displayed. On the exterior walls of houses plaques, depicting deities, dwarfs and animals, or narrative scenes from epics and mythical stories, were fixed in friezes. In the temples and the *stūpas* also, bigger plaques and statues in clay were freely used. On festive occasions terracotta figurines were specially in demand. At the time of

[1] Bāṇabhaṭṭa skilfully compares these four branches of art. Vaiśampāyana seated statesquely in a love-smitten condition is said to appear as static as a pillar in a building, a figure in painting, a carved statue is sculpture or like a figure modelled in clay (*stambhita iva, likhita iva, tukīrṇaiva, puslamayaiva*; *Kādambarī*, p. 276).

Rājyaśrī's marriage multitudes of modellers moulded clay figures of fishes, tortoises, crocodiles, cocoanuts, plantains and betel-trees.[1] Bāṇa speaks also of female clay figurines holding auspicious fruits and technically named *añjalī-kārikā* as fixed in the sides of the altar.

The terracotta figures may be classified under three heads (*a*) gods and goddesses (*b*) male and female figures, (*c*) animal figurines and miscellaneous objects.

Most of the Hindu deities are represented in the terracottas of the age; we have figures of Vishṇu, Kārtikeya, Sūrya, Durgā, Gaṅgā and Yamunā found all over the Gangetic plain. Some of these, as those of Gaṅgā and Yamunā from the terraced brick temple at Ahichchhatra, are almost life-size; their baking must have presented a difficult technical problem, tackled with success by the expert potters of the age.

The group of detached male and female figures shows a great variety of forms, including charming representations of aristrocratic men and women, figures of foreigners from Persia and Central Asia whose influx in the population introduced new facial types too conspicuous to be ignored, and ordinary figures of attendants of all classes as grooms and elephant-riders, jesters and dwarfs (*vāmanaka*), etc. A scientific study of the physiognomy of the Śakas, Pahlavas Kushāṇas, Hūṇas, and other races entering India during the early centuries is needed to identify the various facial types from amongst hoards of terracotta figurines exposed in numerous excavations at the ancient sites in north India.

The group of heads made of fine well-baked clay originally belonged to smaller plaques which were completely pressed out of moulds. The faces, combining elegance of features with gorgeous coiffure,[2] constitute a veritable gallery for the

---

[1] *Harshacharita*, tr. by Cowell and Thomas, p. 124.

[2] Kālidāsa often describes *alaka* to be the mark of a beautiful face, the hair of Indumatī being referred to as *valī-bhritaḥ*, i.e., frizzled or

study of beautiful types admired in that art-inspired age. Hundreds of specimens hold up to our eyes even now the charming ideals of feminine beauty immortalised by the classical poets like Kālidāsa and Bāṇa who strive so often to paint visions of loveliness as familiar to men and women in their times. The terracotta figurines from the recent excavations at Rajghat (cf. Pl. XI) and Ahichchhatra present a feast of beauty to the eye and the best female heads skilfully finished appear like lyrics expressed in clay. They are remarkable, firstly, for the pleasing variety of coiffure, and secondly, for paintings in lines and colours still preserved on some of them. Traces of painting were found also on terracottas found at Bhita, and so painted terracottas seem to have been not uncommon. The colours usually used were red, pink, yellow and white.

Finally it may be observed that much of the terracotta work of the Gupta period is imbued with the spirit of true art prevailing at the time. It can rightly be claimed for the Gupta artist that he adorned whatever he touched. The vision of Bāṇabhaṭṭa that the four quarters in his age appeared as if beautified by clay modelling (*pustamayaiva chakāśire kakubhāh*) seems to have been based on the reality of quantitative production of works of art in clay and stucco.

5. Painting.

The art of painting reached its perfection in the Gupta age. It appears that training in painting formed a necessary item in the cultural make-up of the Gupta citizen and that every cultured man and woman tried to attain excellence in it during

---

twisted in short crisp ringlets (*Raghu*, VIII, v. 53). Female toilet experts (*Prasādhikās*) used scented powder and paste to secure the effect of spiral twisting. Another style consists of hair combed in the form of peacock's feathers, sweeping on the two sides of the central parting (referred to by Kālidāsa as *barha-bhāra-keśa* and by Daṇḍin as *barhi-barhāvali* and *līla-mayūra-barhi-bhaṅgi-keśapāśa*).

our age. In Sanskrit dramas and romances portrait painting appears as a frequent motif, either as a diversion for the love-sick party or as a means of uniting it to its object of love.

The few paintings in the Bedsa caves noticed by J. Dubreuil have been assigned to the third century A.D. Except for them pre-Gupta work in painting is almost unknown. The most celebrated examples of Gupta painting are preserved in the wall frescos of the Ajanta caves in Hyderabad, the Bagh caves in Gwalior State, the Sittannavasal temple in Puddukkottai State and in the rock-cut chambers at Sīgiriya in Ceylon.

Originally the majority of the caves at Ajanta were embellished with paintings, but now they have survived in only six *viz.* Nos. I, II, IX, X, XVI, XVII. Caves IX and X show the earliet specimens of Indian painting (*c.* 1st century B.C.), after which for about 300 years there is a gap in our evidence. There was a remarkable revival in the Gupta age, when most of the famous frescoes in caves Nos. I, II, XVI and XVII at Ajanta were painted.

As regards the technique of these pictures, the surface for the paintings was prepared in a very simple way. Pulverised rock, cowdung, earth and chaff were mixed and the resultant composition was thoroughly pressed on the rather porous surface of volcanic traprock. The surface was then levelled with a trowel, and after it was dried, the drawings in bold outline were directly done by the artists in red ochre (*dhāturāga ālekhana*). The colours were also simple. Red ochre, yellow ochre, indigo, lapis lazuli, lamp black and chalk were used very effectively. There was no attempt at modelling, though at times shading was done by dotting and crosslines. High light at times was added on the ornaments or nose to give them prominence.

The master painters of Ajanta were in love with nature. The flowering trees, quietly flowing streamlets and the roaming denizens of the forest have received unqualified appreciation from them. The elephants and monkeys, deer and the hare are represented with utmost sympathy. They are not mere animals to the Indian mind but part and parcel of the pattern of creation which the artist, the philosopher and the intelligent citizen, all alike learnt to understand sympathetically.

A broad and comprehensive outlook on life inspired the painters to greet the whole world as part of their *repertoire*. In the words of Bāṇabhaṭṭa the *mural* paintings made manifest the whole universe (*darśita viśvarupa*) as it were and this epithet conveys most appropriately the comment of a contemporary critic. In the words of Rothenstein : "On the hundred walls and pillars of these rock-carved temples a vast drama moves before our eyes, a drama played by princes and sages and heroes, by men and women of every condition, against a marvellously varied scene, among forests and gardens, in courts and cities, on wide plains and in deep jungles, while above the messengers from heaven move swiftly in the sky. From all these emanates a great joy in the surpassing radiance of the face of the wold, in the physical nobility of men and women, in the strength and grace of animals and the loveliness and purity of birds and flowers ; and woven into this fabric of material beauty we see the ordered pattern of spiritual values of universe."

The subjects of these paintings are three-fold, relating to decoration, portraiture and narration. The decorative designs include patterns and scrolls (*patrāvalī*), figures of animals, flowers and trees. Their variety, according to Griffiths, is infinite, carried into smallest details so that repetition is very rare. Graceful figures of fabulous creatures and mythological beings, such as Suparṇas (with a human bust joined to the body of a bird), Garuḍas, Yakshas, Gandharvas, Apsarasas, have been used to fill spaces.

Of the portraits the central figures are those of the various Buddhas and Bodhisattvas. Incidents from the life of Gautama Buddha are freely painted. The great Bodhisattva Padampāṇi

Avalokiteśvara in cave I (Pl. XII) shows the highest attainment in the way of figure painting. We may recognize it as the very acme of Asiatic pictorial art. The narrative scenes are mostly from the Jātakas, which had been already popularised by the sculptors.

The paintings in cave XVI date from about 500 and are slightly earlier than those in the cave XVII. The scene known as the 'Dying Princess'[1] in cave XVI has received unstinted praise from Griffiths, Burgess and Fergusson. "For pathos and sentiment and the unmistaken way of telling its story this picture, I consider, cannot be surpassed in the history of art. The Florentine could have put better drawing and the Venetian better colour, but neither could have thrown greater expression on it". In cave XVII we find a considerable amount of work of the narrative style still preserved, and the cave has been called literally a picture gallery illustrating some of the most engrossing episodes in the birth, life and death of the Buddha. The art is more graphic and less charming. The 'Mother and Child' group (Pl. XIII) in cave XVII is undoubtedly a very attractive specimen of Ajanta art. The scenes of a hunt of lion and black buck, and of elephants in cave XVII are exceptionally fine work. According to Mrs. Herringham these pictures are composed in a light and shade scheme which can scarcely be paralleled in Italy before the 17th century and the posing and grouping are curiously natural and modern.

The paintings of cave I and II are the latest of the series and they may be assigned to about the early seventh century. The special merit of individual figures in cave II consists in clever drawing which shows the artist to have apparently gone out of his way to invent specially difficult poses. The woman standing with her left bent up (Pl. XIV) and the swinging

[1] This scene really represents the final episode of the *Shaddanta Jātaka*, where the queen dies of remorse when she sees the tusks of the noble elephant, who was her husband in the previous birth.

figure of lady Irandatī are very pleasing. A large picture in cave I (Pl. XV) probably shows the Indian king Pulakeśin II receiving an embassy from the Persian king Khusru Parvez.[1] This event must have taken place between A.D. 626 and 628. Several Bacchanalian groups in cave I show connection with the great embassy picture. These seem to illustrate Khusru and his queen Shirin drinking together. The faces, the drapery and other articles are clearly of Persian influence.

The paintings at Bagh in Malwa represent only an extension of the Ajanta school and in variety of design, vigorous execution and decorative quality seem to have ranked as high as those at Ajanta. The majority of them are of a secular nature. In two of the groups the subject is extremely gay, illustrating the performance of the *hallīśaka*, a musical dance, acted by a troupe of women led by a man. They are elaborately dressed, singing and dancing with considerable freedom. These paintings may be assigned to the middle of the sixth or the seventh century.

The paintings in the cave temple Sittannavasal (*Siddhānām vāsa*) in Pudukkottai state, although executed in the time of Pallava Mahendra-varman, deserve notice here, as they are in the best traditions of the classical art as found in Ajanta. The ceiling of the cave contains the representation of a *padma-vana*, a magnificient lake with geese, fish and buffaloes frolicking among lotuses in bloom and bud, which some youths are shown gathering. The figures are drawn with great care and delicacy of feeling. The best paintings here are those of a king and his queen, and of two dancing nymphs, *apsarasas*, whose exquisite grace and elegance are extremely pleasing.

The paintings in the galleries of a rock-cut citadel perched upon the summit of a tower-shaped hill 600 feet high at Sīgirya in Ceylon consist of a procession of noble ladies, richly attired

[1] This is, however, denied by many scholars who believe it to be representation of a Buddhistic scene (JBRS. XXX, 185 n).

and profusely adorned, proceeding to the Buddha temple, attended by their maid-servants carrying the materials of worship. The painters have given us only half of three-quarter length portraits, and their work is of high merit. Whether they were natives of Ceylon or immigrants from India we do not know.

The paintings of our age show the art at its best. The assurance and delicacy of lines, the brilliancy of colours, the richness of expression informed with a buoyant feeling and pulsating life, have rendered this art supreme for all times.

6. General Estimate.

The above brief survey of the various aspects of the Gupta art must have shown the reader that its characteristic features are refinement or elegance, simplicity of expression and dominant spiritual purpose. *En ensemble* these characteristics give Gupta art an individuality, which has remained unchallenged so far. In the first place this art is marked by refinement and restraint, which are the signs of a highly developed cultural taste and aesthetic enjoyment. The artist no longer relies on volume to give an impression of grandiose, but focuses his attention on elegance which is not lost in the exuberance of ornaments. The keynote of his art is balance and freedom from the dead-weight of conventions. The dictum is at once apparent if we compare the standing life-size figure of the Gupta Buddha of Yaśadinna with the colossal standing Bodhisattva in the Sarnath Museum, both from Mathura and in red sandstone. The exuberance and whirpool movement of Amarāvatī marbles yielded place to an aesthetic sobriety in the treatment of drapery, ornament and other elements of decoration.

Whatever emerges from the hands of the Gupta artist appears perfectly natural; there is no place for over-elaboration. This work is not the product of the craftsman's mechanical skill, but the result of the discriminating taste of a true artist who is conscious of his self and is master of his technique. The art creations become real samples of *lalītakalā*, a term met with for the first time in Kālidāsa (*Raghu*, VIII, v. 67).

Another characteristic of Gupta art is the concept of beauty for which we have the very appropriate term *rūpam*, used again by the same great poet. The men and women in this art-loving age applied themselves to the worship of beautiful form in many ways. But aesthetic culture did not weaken the strong structure and stamina of life or bedim its supreme objective by yielding to the riotous worship of the senses. Art was worshipped in order to deepen the consciousness of the soul and awaken it to a new sense of spiritual joy and nobility. Kālidāsa, the supreme genius and poet of this age, has expressed this attitude of life devoted to beauty in a sentence addressed to Pārvatī, the goddess of Personal Charm, by her consort Śiva: 'O fair damsel, the popular saying that beauty does not lead to sin is full of unexceptionable truth'[1] *The path of virtue is the path of beauty*—this appears to be the guiding impulse of life in the Gupta age. To create lovely forms and harness them to the needs of higher life—this was the golden harmony that made Gupta art a thing of such perpetual and inexhaustible attraction.

This leads us to another distinguishing feature of Gupta art, namely its profound religious and spiritual appeal, its basic inspiration from a higher source investing it not only with great charm but also with universal significance. The epic of the life which the master artists painted on a colossal scale in the caves at Ajanta has become for all times the standing commentary on the grand ordered patterns of good and evil manifesting themselves in each individual's life and also the whole world. The painted forms of gods and sages, of kings

---

[1] *Yaduchyate Pārvati pāpavṛittaye na rūpamityavyabhichāri tadvachaḥ. Kumāra*, V, v. 36.

and counsellors, of queens and attendants, embellished with personal charm and majesty, present to the eye the choicest expressions which spiritual reality can assume in coming down from the divine to the human plane. It seems as if art's function was to visualise the ideal of *Anuttara-jñānāvāpti*, so often declared as life's supreme goal in the written records of the age. Religion, however, did not impede the free development of art on the purely aesthetic side. In the narrative paintings of Ajanta charming and delicate scenes from contemporary life are inserted freely. Scenes of home and palace life, toilet and sports, festivities and processions have converted these paintings into a record of permanent value and beauty.

Another distinguishing feature of Gupta art is its simplicity of style and felicity of expression by which great ideas take a concrete form in a natural and easy manner. The technique and subject of art were blended in a characteristic harmony. The outer form and the inner meaning are knit together like body and mind. In the words of Kālidāsa this fusion of the inner and outer elements is like the coalescence of Thought and Speech in a manner as natural and perfect as the union of Pārvatī and Parameśvara in the ideal Ardhanārīśvara form. The concise formula of "knit like Word and Sense" (*Vāgarthāv-iva-sampṛiktau*) represents the ideal of harmony and synthesis achieved in this period in many spheres of thought and life, and not the least in the domain of art.

The above survey of the main characteristics of Gupta art will show that it is but natural that there should be a general agreement among scholars and art-critics that it represents ancient Indian art at its best. It is its strength and the dominant position at home that was the real secret of its inspiring vitality abroad. The honourable position, which the Gupta art occupied in India, infused it with such power and prestige as enabled it to mould the art traditions of the greater part of Asia. Transplanted in new environs beyond the borders of India with its inherent vigour and richness of contents, this art brought into being the cultural empire of Greater India whose immortal glories have been unearthed from the waterless deserts of Central Asia and the fertile islands of the east. The conventions of fresco painting especially found a congenial home in Central Asia and China, and were received with enthusiasm by many foreign races which had come under the influence of Buddhism and which looked for inspiration of India in the matter of culture, religion and literature.

SELECT BIBLIOGRAPHY

CHAPTER I

THE PUNJAB, SINDH AND AFGHANISTAN

(*c.* 180 A.D. to *c.* 450 A.D.)

1. Banerji, R. D. Notes on Indo-Scythian Coinage (*JASB*, NS. IV, 81-96).
2. Cunningham, A. Later Indo-Scythians. London, 1893-94. (Reprinted from the Numismatic Chronicle).
3. Herzfeld, E. Paikuli : Monument and Inscription of the Early History of the Sassanian Empire. 2 Vols. Berlin, 1924.
4. ———— Kushano-Sassanian Coins (*MASI.* No. 38). Calcutta, 1930.
5. Martin, M. F. C. Coins of the Kidāra Kushāṇas (*Num. Suppl.* XLVII, 23-50—*JRASBL.* III). Calcutta, 1957.
6. Parruk, F. J. Sassanian Coins. Bombay, 1924.
7. Smith, V. A. Catalogue of Coins in the Indian Museum, Calcutta. Vol. I. Oxford, 1906.
8. Whitehead, R. B. Catalogue of Coins in the Punjab Museum, Lahore. Vol. I. Oxford, 1914.

CHAPTER II

NEW INDIAN STATES IN RAJPUTANA AND MADHYADESA

1. Allan, J. Catalogue of the Coins of Ancient India (in the British Museum). London, 1936.
2. Altekar, A. S. New Nāga Coins and the Identity of Bhavanāga (*JNSI.* V. 21-26).
3. ———— Some Alleged Nāga and Vākāṭaka Coins (*JNSI.* V. 111-34).
4. ———— Nandsa Yūpa Inscriptions (*EI.* XXVII).
5. ———— Maghas of South Kośala (*Journal of the Ganganatha Jha Research Institute*, Allahabad, I, 149-60).
6. Cunningham, A. Archaeological Survey of India, Reports, II. Simla 1871.
7. ———— Coins of Mediaeval India. London, 1894.
8. Jayaswal, K. P. History of India, 150—350 A. D. Lahore, 1933.
9. Motichandra. Hoard of Kauśāmbi Coins from Fatehpur (*JNSI.* II. 95-108).

10. Pargiter, F. E. Dynasties of the Kali Age. London, 1913.
11. Smith, V. A. Catalogue of Coins in the Indian Museum, Calcutta. Vol. I. Oxford, 1906.

CHAPTER III

THE ŚAKA RULERS OF WESTERN INDIA

1. Acharya, G. V. Hoards of the Coins of the Western Kshatrapas (*Num. Suppl.* XLVII, 95 ff—*JRASBL.* III). Calcutta, 1937.
2. Altekar, A. S. Was Jīvadāman a Mahākshatrapa more than once? (*JNSI.* I, 18-19).
4. ——— Inter-regnum in the reign of Mahākshatrapa Rudrasena (*JNSI.* VI).
4. Bhandarkar, D. R. Kshatrapa Coins from Sarvania (*ASR.* 1913-14, 227-4).
5. Parruk, F. J. Sassanian Coins. Bombay, 1924.
6. Rapson, E. J. Catalogue of the Indian Coins of the Andhra Dynasty, the Western Kshatrapas, etc. (in the British Museum). London, 1908.

CHAPTER IV

EASTERN DECCAN

1. Gopalachari, K. Early History of the Andhra Country. Madras, 1941.
2. Jouveau Dubreuil, G. Ancient History of the Deccan. Pondicherry, 1920.
3. Krishna Rao, B. V. History of the Early Dynasties of Andhradeśa, *c.* 200-625 A. D. Madras, 1942. (Not very reliable in respect of details).
4. Raychaudhuri, H.C. Political History of Ancient India (4th edn.). Calcutta, 1938.
5. Sircar, D. C. Successors of the Sātavāhanas in Lower Deccan. Calcutta, 1939.
6. Subramanian, K. R. Buddhist Remains in Āndhra and the History of Āndhra between 225 and 610 A. D. Madras, 1932.

CHAPTER V

THE VĀKĀṬAKAS

1. Allan, J. Catalogue of the Coins of Ancient India (in the British Museum). London, 1936.
2. Altekar, A. S. Some Alleged Nāga and Vākāṭaka Coins (*JNSI.* V, 111-34).

3. Altekar, A. S. Were the Vākātakas defeated by the Guptas in *c.* 350 A.D. ? (*IC.* IX, 99-106).
4. Aiyangar, S. K. The Vākāṭakas and their Place in the History of India (*ABORI.* V, 31-54).
5. Jayaswal, K. P. History of India, 150-350 A. D. Lahore, 1933.
6. Krishna, H. Mysore Archaeological Survey Report, 1929, pp. 197 ff.
7. Mirashi, V. V. Vākāṭaka Inscription in Cave XVI at Ajanta (*Hyd. Ar. S.* XIV). Hyderabad, 1941.
8. Pai, G. Genealogy and Chronology of the Vākāṭakas (*JIH.* XIV, 1-26, 165-204).
9. Pargiter, F. E. Dynasties of the Kali Age. London, 1913.
10. Smith, V. A. The Vākāṭaka Dynasty of Berar in the 4th and 5th centuries (*JRAS*, 1914, pp. 317 ff).

LIST OF INSCRIPTIONS (CHAPTERS II, III and V)

Abbreviations :—B—Buddhist. Br—Brahmanical. C—Cave. CII—Corpus Inscriptionum Indicarum. CP.—Copper-plate. P—Pillar. R.Y.—Regnal year. S—Stone. Ś.E.—Śaka Era. V.E.—Vikrama Era.

MĀLAVAS AND YAUDHEYAS

Serial No.	Year	Find-place	Reference
1.	282 V.E.	Nandsa Yūpa	*EI.* XXVI (in present).
2.	428 V.E.	Bijaygadh Yūpa	*CII.* III. 251.

MAUKHARIS OF BADVA

1.	295 V.E.	Badva Yūpa	*EI.* XXIII, 42.
2.	—	Badva Yūpa	*EI.* XXIV, 251.

MAGHA KINGS

The era is assumed to be the Śaka era; for other views see Chap. II.

		BHIMASENA	
1.	52 Ś.E.	Ginja	*EI.* III, 306.
		BHADRA-MAGHA	
2.	81 Ś.E.	Kosam—S	*EI.* XXIV, 253.
3.	86 Ś.E.	Kosam—S	*EI.* XVIII, 160.
4.	87 Ś.E.	Allahabad Museum	*EI.* XXIII, 245.
5.	87 Ś. E.	Allahabad Museum	*EI.* XXIII, 245.
		SIVA-MAGHA	
6.	—	Kosam—S	*EI.* XVIII, 159.
		VAISRAVANA	
7.	107 Ś.E.	Kosam—S	*EI.* XXIV, 146.

BHIMA-VARMAN

Serial No.	Year	Find-place	Reference
8.	130 Ś.E.	Kosam—B	*IC.* III, 177.

WESTERN KSHATRAPAS

RUDRA-DAMAN I

Serial No.	Year	Find-place	Reference
1.	72 Ś.E.	Junagadh—S	*EI.* VIII, 36.
		JIVA-DAMAN I	
2.		Junagadh—S	*EI.* XVIII, 339.
		RUDRA-SIMHA I	
3.	103 Ś.E.	Gunda—S	*EI.* XVI, 233.
4.	—	Junagadh	*EI.* XVI, 239.
		RUDRA-SENA I	
5.	122 Ś.E.	Mulwasar	*Bhagnagar Inscr.* p. 2.
6.	127 (6 ?) Ś.E.	Jasdan—P	*EI.* XVI, 236.
		RUDRA-SIMHA II	
7.	228 Ś.E.	Watson Museum	*Watson Museum Report* for 1919-20, p. 7.
8.	232 Ś.E.	Mulwasar—S	*Bhavanagar Inscr.* p. 23.
		SAKA SRIDHARA-VARMAN	
9.	241 Ś.E. (?)	Sanchi Museum—S	*JAŚB.* XIX, 341.
		A DISTANT DESCENDANT OF CHASHṬANA	
10.	—	Mewasa—S	*Watson Museum Report* for 1923-4, p. 12.
		MAHADEVI PRABHUDAMA	
11.	—	Basarh clay seal	*ASIR.* 1913-4. p. 136.

VĀKĀTAKAS—MAIN BRANCH

RUDRA-SENA I

Serial No.	Year	Find-place	Reference
1.	—	Deotek—Br	*POC.* VIII, 613.
		PRITHVI-SHENA I	
2.	—	Nachne-ki-Talai-S	*CII.* III, 234.
3.	—	Ganj—S	*EI.* XVII. 13.
		PRABHAVATI-GUPTA AND THE HEIR-APPARENT DIVAKARA-SENA	
4.	13 R.Y.	Poona—CP.	*EI.* XV, 30.

PRAVARA-SENA II

Serial No.	Year	Find place	Reference
5.	2 R.Y.	Kothuraka—CP.	*EI.* XXVI, 155.
6.	13 R.Y.	Belora—CP.	*EI.* XXIV. 265.
7.	18 R.Y.	Chammak—CP.	*CII.* III, 236.
8.	18 R.Y.	Siwani—CP.	*CII.* III. 243.
9.	19 R.Y.	Riddhapur—CP.	*JASB.* XX, 56.
10.	23 R.Y.	Indore—CP.	*EI.* XXIV, 52.
11.	23 R.Y.	Dudia—CP.	*EI.* III, 258.
12.	23 R.Y.	Tirodi—CP.	*EI.* XXII, 167.
13.	27 R.Y.	Pattana—CP.	*EI.* XXIII, 81.
14.	—	Belora—CP.	*EI.* XXIV, 260.
15.	—	Patna Museum—CP.	*JBORS,* XIV, 465.
16.	—	Mānsar—CP.	*Nagpur University Journal,* No. 3, p. 20.

PRITHVI-SHENA II

17.	—	Balaghat—CP.	*EI.* IX, 267.

NAME OF THE KING LOST

18.	—	Drug—CP.	*EI.* XXII, 207.

A PRIVATE VAKATAKA RECORD

19.	—	Amaraoti—S	*EI.* XV, 267.

VĀKĀṬAKAS—BASIM BRANCH

VINDHYASAKTI II

1.	37 R.Y.	Basim—CP.	*EI.* XXVI, 137.

DEVA-SENA

2.	—	India Office—CP.	*NIA.* II, 176.

HARI-SHENA

3.	—	Ajanta—C.	*Ayd. Ar. S.* XIV.
4.	—	Ghaṭotkacha—C.	*ASWI.* IV, 138.

NAME UNKNOWN

5.	—	Ajanta—C.	*ASWI.* IV, 129.

NALA DYNASTY

BHAVATTA-VARMAN

1.	11 R.Y.	Rithpur—CP.	*EI.* XIX, 100.

SKANDA-VARMAN

2.	12 R.Y.	Podagadh—S	*EI.* XXI, 153.

ĀBHĪRAS AND TRAIKŪṬAKAS

ABHIRA KING ISVARA-SENA

Serial No.	Year	Find-place	Reference
1.	9 R. Y.	Nasik	*EI.* VIII, 88.
		TRAIKUTAKA KING DAHRA-SENA	
2.	207 Chedi era	Pardi—CP.	*EI.* X, 51.
		TRAIKUTAKA KING VYAGHRA-SENA	
3.	241 ,,	Surat—CP.	*EI.* XI, 219.
4.	245 ,,	Kanheri—CP. B.	*JBBRAS.* V, 32.

CONNECTED INSCRIPTIONS

BHARA KING BHAGADATTA

1.	—	Pauni—S	*EI.* XXIV, 11.
		KING SIVANANDI	
2.	—	Padam Pawaya—S	*ASIR.* 1915-6, p. 107.

CHAPTERS VI—XI

A. Original Sources

I. Inscriptions

1. Fleet, J. F. Corpus Inscriptionum Indicarum. Vol. III (Inscriptions of the Early Gupta kings and their Successors). Calcutta, 1888.
2. Sircar D. C. Select Inscriptions bearing on Indian History and Civilisation. Calcutta, 1943.

A complete list of inscriptions bearing on the history of this period is given at the end of this bibliography. Important articles concerning their interpretation are given under 'References' against each.

II. Coins

1. Allan, J. Catalogue of the Coins of the Gupta Dynasties and of Śaśāṅka king of Gauḍa (in the British Museum). London, 1914.
2. Smith, V. A. Catalogue of Coins in the Indian Museum, Calcutta. Vol. I. Oxford, 1906.

V. A. Smith's articles on the Gupta Coinage (*JRAS*, 1889, pp. 1-158; *JRAS.* 1893, pp. 77-148; and *JASB*, LXIII, 164-209), though somewhat out of date, may still be consulted with advantage.

III. Traveller's Accounts and Foreign Works

1. Beal, S. Sā-yu-ki Buddhist Records of the Western World, tr. from the Chinese Hiuen Tsang. 2 Vols. London, 1906.
2. ———— Life of Hiuen Tsang by the Shaman Hwui-li. London, 1911.

3. Chavannes, H. Mémoire Composé a l'époque de la grande dynastie T'an sur les Religieux Eminents qui allerent chercher a loi dans les pays d'Occident, par I-tsing. Paris, 1894. A summary of this work, in English, is given in the Introduction of Beal's tr. of *Life of Hiuen Tsang*).
4. Legge, J. H. Record of the Buddhistic Kingdoms, being an account of the Chinese monk Fa-hien's Travels. Oxford, 1886.
5. Takakusu, J. A. Record of the Buddhist Religion as practised in India and the Malay Archipelago, by I-tsing. Oxford, 1896.
6. Watters, T. On Yuan Chwang's Travels in India. 2 Vols. London, 1908.

IV. *Literary Works*

1. Āryamañjuśrīmūlakalpa, ed. by T. Ganapati Sastri. Vol. III. Trivandrum, 1925.
2. Devī-Chandragupta.
3. Kaumudīmahotsava.
4. Pargiter, F. E. Dynasties of the Kali Age. Oxford, 1913.

B. Modern Works

I. Historical Texts

1. Banerji, R. D. Age of the Imperial Guptas, Benares, 1933.
2. Basak, R. G. History of Northern-Eastern India. Calcutta, 1934.
3. Dandekar, R. N. History of the Guptas. Poona, 1941.
4. Jayaswal, K. P. History of India, 150-350 A. D. Lahore, 1933.
5. ——————— Imperial History of India. Lahore, 1934.
6. Raychaudhuri, H. C. Political History of Ancient India (4th ed.). Calcutta, 1938.
7. Seletore, R. N. Life in the Gupta Age. Bombay, 1943.
8. Smith, V. A. Early History of India (4th ed.). Oxford, 1924.
9. Upadhyaya B. Gupta Sūmrājyakā Itihās (in Hindi). 2 vols. Allahabad. 1939.

The books of Jayaswal and Saletore are of little use. Most of Jayaswal's theories have been rejected by scholars and Saletore's chapters on Political history are full of mistakes. The best treatment of the Gupta period will be found in Dr. Raychaudhuri's book. The two works by R. D. Banerji and R. N. Dandekar contain useful information, but are less reliable in respect of details.

II. Select Articles

1. Aiyangar, S. K. Studies in Gupta History (published as Supplements to *JIH.* V & VI).
2. Altekar, A. S. Attribution of Chandragupta-Kumāradevī type (*Num. Suppl.* XLVII. 105—*JRASBL.* III). Calcutta, 1937.
3. Bhandarkar, D. R. Identification of the Princes and Territories mentioned in the Allahabad Pillar Inscription of Samudragupta (*IHQ.* I, 250).
4. Bose, S. K. Studies in Gupta Palaeography (*IC.* IV, 181, 325).
5. Das Gupta, N. N. On the Successors of Kumāragupta I (*B. C. Law Volume*, p. 617).

6. Ganguly, D. C. Early Home of the Imperial Guptas (*IHQ*. XIV. 532).
7. Heras, J. Relations between the Guptas, Kadambas and Vākāṭakas (*JBORS*. XII, 455).
8. Jayaswal, K. P. Kalki (*IA*. XLVI. 145).
9. Majumdar, R. C. Successors of Kamūragupta I (*JASB*. NS. XVII, 249).
10. Saraswati, S. K. Gold Coin of Budhagupta (*IC*. I, 691-92).
11. Sen Gupta, P. C. Gupta Era (*JRASBL*. VIII, 41).

Articles on the historical data of *Kaumudīmahotsava* and *Devī-Chandragupta* have been enumerated in footnotes.

LIST OF GUPTA INSCRIPTIONS

Abbreviations :—B—Buddhist Image. Br—Brahmanical Image. C—Cave. CP.—Copper-plate. J—Jaina Image. P—Pillar. S—Stone.

(Unless otherwise stated the year refers to the Gupta Era. The object on which the inscription is engraved is mentioned after the find-place.)

SAMUDRA-GUPTA

Serial No.	Year	Find-place	Reference
1.	5	Nālandā—CP.	*EI*. XXV, 50; XXVI, 135.
2.	9	Gaya—CP.	*CII*. III, 254; *IC*. X, 77; XI, 225.
3.	—	Allahabad—P	*CII*. III, 1; *IHQ*. I, 250; *JBORS*. XVIII, 207; *JRAS*. 1935, p. 697; *EI*. XXII, 35.
4.	—	Eran—S	*CII*. III, 18; *JIH*. XIV, 27; XIX, 27.

CHANDRA-GUPTA II

Serial No.	Year	Find-place	Reference
5.	61	Mathura—P	*EI*. XXI, 1; *IHQ*. XVIII, 271; *ABORI*. XVIII, 166.
6.	82	Udayagiri—C	*CII*. III, 21.
7.	88	Gadhwa—S	*CII*. III, 36.
8.	93	Sanchi—S	*CII*. III, 29.
9.	—	Mathura—S	*CII*. III, 25.
10.	—	Udayagiri—C	*CII*. III, 34.
11.	—	Basarh Clay Seals (Govinda-gupta)	*ASR*. 1903-4, p. 107.

KUMARA-GUPTA I

Serial No.	Year	Find-place	Reference
12.	96	Bilsad—P	*CII*. III, 42.
13.	98	Godhwa—S	*CII*. III, 40; cf. also pp. 264, 267.
14.	106	Udayagiri—C	*CII*. III, 258.
15.	113	Dhanaidaha—CP.	*EI*. XVIII, 347.

Serial No.	Year	Find-place	Reference
16.	113	Mathura—J	*EI.* II, 210.
17.	116	Tumain—S	*EI.* XXVI, 115.
18.	117	Karamdanda—Br.	*EI.* X, 71.
19.	120	Kulaikuri—CP.	*IHQ.* XIX, 12.
20.	124	Damodarpur—CP.	*EI.* XV, 129.
21.	128	Damodarpur—CP.	*EI.* XV, 132; XVII, 193.
22.	128	Baigram—CP.	*EI.* XXI, 78.
23.	129	Mankuwar—B	*CII.* III, 45.
24.	—	Gadhwa—S	*CII.* III, 39.
25.	—	Basarh Clay Seals (Ghaṭotkacha-gupta)	*ASR.* 1903-4, p. 107.
		SKANDA-GUPTA	
26.	136-8	Junagadh Rock	*CII.* III, 56.
27.	141	Kahaum—P	*CII.* III, 65.
28.	141	Rewa—P	Summary of Papers (Part II), 12th Or. Conf. p. 39.
29.	146	Indore—CP.	*CII.* III, 68.
30.	—	Bhitari—P	*CII.* III, 52.
		GOVINDA-GUPTA AND PRABHAKARA	
31.	V.S. 524 (467 A.D.)	Mandasor Fort Wall	*ASR.* 1922-23, p. 187.
		NARASIMHA-GUPTA	
32.	—	Nālandā Clay Seal	*MASI.* No. 66, p. 65.
		KUMARA-GUPTA II (OR III)	
33.	154	Sarnath—B	*ASR.* 1914-5, p. 124.
34.	—	Bhitari Seal	*JASB.* LVIII, 89.
35.	—	Nālandā Seal	*MASI.* No. 66, pp. 66-7; *IA.* XIX, 225.
		BUDHA-GUPTA	
36.	157	Sarnath—B	*ASR.* 1914-5, p. 125.
37.	159	Paharpur—CP.	*EI.* XX, 61.
38.	163	Damodarpur—CP.	*EI.* XV, 134.
39.	165	Eran—P	*CII.* III, 88.
40.	—	Damodarpur—CP.	*EI.* XV, 138; *IC.* V, 432.
41.	—	Nālandā Seal	*MASI*, No. 66, p. 64; *IHQ.* XIX, 119, 272.

(An unpublished inscription of Buddha-gupta on a pillar at Benares is referred to in *IHQ.* XIX, 123).

OTHER GUPTA KINGS

Serial No.	Year	Find-place	Reference
42.	—	(Successor of Pūru-gupta) Bihar—	*CII.* III, 47; *JBORS.* XIX, 377; *IC.* X 170.

Serial No.	Year	Name of the King	Find-place	Reference
43.	169	—	Nandanpur—CP.	*EI.* XXIII, 52
44.	—	Vishṇu-gupta	Nālandā Seal	*EI.* XXVI, 235; *IHQ.* XIX, 119.
45.	188	Vainya-gupta	Gunaighar—CP.	*IHQ.* VI, 40.
46.	—	Vainya-gupta	Nālandā Seal	*MASI.* No. 66, p. 67; *IHQ.* XIX, 275.
47.	191	Bhānu-gupta	Eran—P	*CII.* III, 91; *EI.* XXII, 16; *IHQ.* XIX, 143.
48.	224	—	Damodarpur—CP.	*EI.* XV, 142; XVII, 193, fn. 1.

INSCRIPTIONS OF CONTEMPORARY RULERS AND DYNASTIES

Serial No.	Year	Name of the King	Find-place	Reference
49.	461 (V.S.)	Nara-varman	Mandasor—S	*EI.* XII, 315; XIV, 371.
50.	474 (V.S.)	Nara-varman	Bihar Kotra—S	*EI.* XXVI. 130; *JBORS*, XXIX, 127
51.	480 (V.S.)	Viśva-varman	Gangdhar—S	*CII.* III, 72.
52.	493 and 529 (V.S.)	Bandhu-varman	Mandasor—S	*CII.* III, 79; *IC.* III, 379; IV, 110, 262, 361; VI, 110, 339. *S. K. Aiyangar Com. Vol.* p. 69.
53.	156	Hastin	Khoh—CP.	*CII.* III, 93.
54.	163	Hastin	Khoh—CP.	*CII.* III, 100.
55.	191	Hastin	Majhgawan—CP.	*CII.* III, 106.
56.	198	Hastin	Navagram—CP.	*EI.* XXI, 124.
57.	199	Saṁkshobha	Betul—CP.	*EI.* VIII, 284.
58.	209	Saṁkshobha	Khoh—CP.	*CII.* III, 112.
59.	—	Hastin and Sarvanātha	Bhumara—CP.	*CII.* III, 110; *IHQ.* XXI, 137.
60.	174	Jayanātha	Karitalai—CP.	*CII.* III, 117.
61.	177	Jayanātha	Khoh —CP.	*CII.* III, 121.
62.	191	Sarvanātha	Sohaval—CP.	*EI.* XIX, 129.
63.	193	Do.	Khoh—CP.	*CII.* III, 125.
64.	197	Do.	Do.	*CII.* III, 132.
65.	214	Do.	Do.	*CII.* III, 135.
66.	—	Do.	Do.	*CII.* III, 129.

(For the era used in Nos. 60-65, cf. *EI.* XXIII, 171; Bh. List, p. 159 fn.)

Serial No.	Year	Name of the King	Find-place	Reference
67.		Chandra	Meharauli—Iron P	*CII.* III. 139.
68.	1 (Regnal)	Toramāṇa	Eran—S	*CII.* III, 159.
69.	15 (Regnal)	Mihirakula	Gwalior—S	*CII.* III, 162
70.	—	Yaśodharman	Mandasor—P	*CII.* III, 142, 150; *IA.* XVIII, 219;
71.	589 (V.S.)	Yaśodharman	Mandasor—S	IA. XVIII, 219; XX. 188.

CHAPTER XII

SOUTH INDIA

A. Original Sources

Inscriptions—Detailed references are given in the Chapter.

B. Modern Works

1. Gopalachari, K. Early History of the Andhra Country. Madras, 1941.
2. Gopalan, R. History of the Pallavas of Kāñchī. Madras, 1928.
3. Jonveau Dubreuil, G. Ancient History of the Deccan. Pondicherry, 1920.
4. Minakshi C. Administration and Social Life under the Pallavas, Madras, 1938.
5. Moraes, G. M. Kadambakula. Bombay, 1931.
6. Rice, B. L. Mysore and Coorg from Inscriptions, London, 1909.
7. Sircar, D. C. Successors of the Sātavāhanas in the Lower Deccan Calcutta, 1939.

CHAPTER XIII

HISTORY OF CEYLON

A. Literary Sources: Pali

1. Dāṭhā-vaṁsa, ed. & tr. by B. C. Law. Lahore, 1925.
2. Dipavaṁsa, ed. & tr. by H. Oldenberg. London, 1879.
3. Hatthavaṇagalla-vihāra-vaṁsa, ed. by James d'Alwis.
4. Mahāvaṁsa, earlier portion of the chronicle by Mahānāma, ed. by W. Geiger (P. T. S.). London, 1908. Tr. by the same (P. T. S.). London, 1912.
5. Mahāvaṁsa, the more recent portions of the chronicle also known as the Cūḷavaṁsa, ed. by W. Geiger (P. T. S.). London, 1925. Tr. by the same (P. T. S.). London, 1929.
6. Mahāvaṁsa : Chaps. 1-36 tr. by G. Turnour and 37-100 tr. by L. C. Wijesinha. Colombo, 1909.

A. Literary Sources: Sinhalese

1. Attanagalu-vaṅsa, ed. by M. Kumāraṇatuṅga. Colombo, B.E. 2466.
2. Daḷadāpūjāvaliya, ed. by K. M. Perera. Colombo, 1893.
3. Daḷadāsirita, ed. by E. S. Rājasekhara. Colombo, 1920.
4. Nikāya Saṅgraha, ed. by D. M. de Z. Wickremasinghe. Clombo, 1890. Tr. by C. M. Fernando with an Introduction by W. F. Gunawardhana. Colombo 1908.
5. Pūjāvaliya, Chap. 34 ed. by M. Medhaṅkara Thera and tr. under the title, 'A Contribution to the History of Ceylon' by B. Gunasekara, Colombo, 1895.
6. Rājāratnākaraya, ed. by Simon de Silva. Colombo, 1907.
7. Rājāvaliya, ed. by B. Gunasekara. Colombo, 1911, Tr. by the same Colombo, 1900.

B. Modern Works

1. Codrington, H. W. History of Ceylon. London, 1926.
2. Pridham, C. Historical, Political and Statistical Account of Ceylon and its Dependencies. 2 vols. London, 1849.

C. Archaeology, Epigraphy, Numismatics and Art

1. Archaeological Survey of Ceylon. Annual Reports, 1890-1939. Colombo.
2. Archaeological Survey of Ceylon. Memoirs, I-IV. Colombo.
3. Ceylon Journal of Science, Sec. A., I & II.
4. Codrington, H. W. Ceylon Coins and Currency in the Memoirs of the Colombo Museum. Colombo, 1924.
5. Coomaraswamy, A. K. History of Indian and Indonesian Art. London, 1927.
6. Epigraphia Zeylanica, I-IV.

The following inscriptions published in *EZ.* have a special bearing on the period dealt with in this chapter :

1. Peramaiyān-kuḷam Rock Inscription of Vasabha—*EZ.* I. 66-73.
2. Pālu Mākichchāva Rock Inscription of Gajabāhu I—*Ibid*, 208-11.
3. Jetavanārāma Slab Inscription of Kaniṭṭha Tissa—*Ibid*, 252-59.
4. Thūpārāma Slab Inscription of Gajabāhu I—*Ibid.* III, 114, 19.
5. Runävälisäa Pillar Inscription of Buddhadāsa—*Ibid.* 120-26.
6. Two Rock Inscriptions at Vihāregala—*Ibid.*, 163-69.
7. Tōṇigala Rock Inscription of Sirimeghavaṇṇa—*Ibid.* 172-88.
8. Kataragama Inscriptions—*Ibid.* 212-25.
9. Anurādhapura Slab Inscription of Khudda Pārinda—*Ibid.* IV, 111-15.
10. Nāgirikanda Rock Inscription of Kumāradāsa—*Ibid* 115-28.
11. Habāssa Rock Inscription—*Ibid.* 213-17.
12. Vessagiriya Rock Inscription of Sirināga II—*Ibid.* 218-22.
13. Rock Inscription of Goṭhābhaya at Timbiriväyu—*Ibid.* 223-28.
14. Vallipuram Gold plate Inscription of the reign of Vasabha—*Ibid.* 229-37.
15. Fragmentary Inscription from Jetavanārāma, now in the Colombo Museum—*Ibid.* 246-52.

7. Muller, E. Ancient Inscriptions in Ceylon. London, 1883.

D. Select Articles in Journals

1. Geiger, Wilhelm. Konigsnamen in den Brāhmi Inscriften Ceylons, Festschrift für M. Winternitz zum Siebsigsten Geburtstag, pp. 313-21. Leipzig, 1933.
2. Levi, Sylvain. Les Missions de Wang Hiuen-Tse dans l'Inde (*J.A.* 1900, pp. 297 ff & 410 ff). The portion relating to Ceylon has been translated into English by J. M. Seneviratne and published in the *Journal of the Royal Asiatic Society, Ceylon Branch*, XXIV, 74 ff.).
3. Paranavitana, S. Gajabāhu I and Mahallaka Nāga, their relationship, (*JRAS, CB.* XXX, 452 ff.).
4. Smith, V. A. Inscriptions of Mahānāma at Bodhgaya (*IA.* XXX, 192-97).

CHAPTER XIV

THE ADMINISTRATIVE ORGANISATION

The chapter is based mainly upon facts collected from inscriptions and coin-legends, to which reference has been made in footnotes. The following are additional sources :

1. Benerji, R. D. Age of the Imperial Guptas. Benares, 1933.
2. Bloch, T. Excavations at Basrah (*ASR.* 1903-04, pp. 81-122).
3. Bṛihaspati-Smṛiti (GOS LXXXV). Baroda, 1941.
4. Legge, J. A. Record of the Buddhist Kingdoms, being an account of the Chinese monk Fa-hein's Travels. Oxford, 1886.
5. Nārada-Smṛiti (*SBE.* XXXIII). Oxford, 1889.
6. Saletore, R. N. Life in the Gupta Age. Bombay, 1943.
7. Upadhyaya, B. Gupta Sāmrājya kā Itihās (Hindi). Allahabad, 1939.
8. Yājñavalkya-Smṛiti. Bombay, 1918.

CHAPTER XV

THE COINAGE

1. Allan, J. Catalogue of the Coins of Ancient India (in the British Museum). London, 1936.
2. ———— Catalogue of the Coins of the Gupta Dynasties and of Śaśāṅka, King of Gauḍa (in the British Museum). London, 1914.
3. Altekar, A. S. New Nāga Coins and the Identity of Bhavanāga (*JNSI.* V, 21-27).
4. ———— Some Alleged Nāga and Vākāṭaka Coins (*JNSI.* V, 111-34).
5. Cunningham, A. Coins of the Indo-Scythians. London, 1888-92. (Reprinted from the Numismatic Chronicle).
6. ———— Later Indo-Scythians. London, 1893-94. (Reprinted from the Numismatic Chronicle).
7. ———— Coins of Mediaeval India. London, 1894.
8. Martin. Coins of Kidāra and Later Kushāṇas (*Num. Suppl.* XLVII, 23-30—*JRASBL.* III). Calcutta, 1937.
9. Motichandra. Hoard of Kauśāmbī Coins from Fatehpur (*JNSI.* II, 95-108).
10. Rapson, E. J. Indian Coins. Strassburg, 1898.
11. ———— Catalogue of the Indian Coins of the Andhra Dynasty, Western Kshatrapas, etc. (in the British Museum). London, 1908.
12. Smith, V. A. Catalogue of Coins in the Indian Museum, Calcutta. Vol. I, Oxford, 1906.

CHAPTER VI

COLONIAL AND CULTURAL EXPANSION

I. Insul-India

1. Chaterji, B. R. Indian Cultural Influence in Cambodia. Calcutta, 1928.
2. Majumdar, R. C. Ancient Indian Colonies in the Far East :
Vol. I. Champā. Lahore, 1927.
Vol. II. Suvarṇadvīpa. Pts. 1 & 2. Dacca, 1937-38.
3. ———— Kambujadeśa. Madras, 1944.
4. ———— Hindu Colonies in the Far East. Calcutta, 1944.

II. Eastern Turkestan and China

1. Bagchi, P. C. Le Canon Bouddhique en Chine. Vol. I. Paris, 1927.
2. ———— India and China. Calcutta, 1944.
3. Chakravarti, N. P. India and Central Asia. Calcutta.
4. Ghoshal, U. N. Ancient Indian Culture in Afghanistan. Calcutta.
5. Stein, A. Ancient Khotan. Oxford, 1907.
6. ———— Serindia. Oxford, 1921.
7. ———— Innermost Asia. Oxford, 1928.

CHAPTER XVII

INTERCOURSE WITH THE WESTERN WORLD

1. Charlesworth, M. P. Trade-route and Commerce of the Roman Empire. Cambridge, 1921.
2. Kennedy, J. Early Commerce with Babylon (*JRAS.* 1898, pp. 250 ff).
3. Priaulx, Osmond de Beauvoir. Indian Travels of Apollonius of Tyna and the Indian Embassies to Rome. London, 1873.
4. Rawlinson, H. G. Intercourse between India and the Western World Cambridge, 1916.
5. ———— Foreign influences in the Civilisation of Ancient India (*JBBRAS*, XXIII, 217 ff.).
6. Sastri, K. A. N. Foreign Notes of South India. Madras, 1939.
7. Smith, V. A. Graeco-Roman Influence on the Civilisation of Ancient India (*JASB.* LVIII, 107 ff.).
8. Tarn, W. W. Hellenistic Civilisation. London, 1930.
9. Warmington E. H. Commerce between the Roman Empire and India. Cambridge, 1928.

CHAPTER XVIII

SOCIAL AND ECONOMIC CONDITIONS

This chapter is based mainly upon the data collected from inscriptions to which references have been given in the footnotes. The following are additional sources :

1. Altekar, A. S. Position of Women in Hindu Civilisation. Benares, 1938.
2. Bloch, T. Excavations at Basarh (*ASR*. 1903-04, pp. 81-122).
3. Bṛihaspati-Smṛiti (GOS. LXXXV). Baroda, 1941.
4. Nārada-Smṛiti (*SBE*. XXXIII). Oxford 1889.
5. Saletore. R. N. Life in the Gupta Age. Bombay, 1943.
6. Sewell, R. Roman Coins found in India (*JRAS*. 1904 pp. 591-637).
7. Upadhyaya, B. Gupta Sāmrājya kā Itihās (Hindi). Allahabad, 1930.
8. Warmington, E. H. Commerce between Roman Empire and India. Cambridge, 1928.
9. Yājñavalkya-Smṛiti. Bombay, 1918.

CHAPTER XIX

RELIGION AND PHILOSOPHY

The portion dealing with the religious condition is mostly based upon the data collected from contemporary inscriptions.

1. Bhandarkar, R. G. Vaishṇavism, Śaivism and other minor Religious Systems, Strassburg, 1913.
2. Burgess & Indraji. Inscriptions from the Cave Temples of Western India. Bombay, 1881.
3. Das Gupta, S. N. History of Indian Philosophy, 3 vols. Cambridge, 1932-40.
4. Farquhar, J. N. Outline of the Religious Literature of India. Oxford, 1920.
5. Laṅkāvatārasūtra, ed. by D. T. Suzuki, London, 1932.
6. Legge, J.A. Record of the Buddhistic Kingdoms, being an account of the Chinese monk Fa-hien's Travels. Oxford, 1886.
7. Radhakrishnan, S. Indian Philosophy. Vol. II. London, 1940.
8. Raychaudhuri, H. C. Materials for the Study of the Early History of the Vaishṇava Sect (2nd ed.), Calcutta, 1936.
9. Suzuki, B. L. Outlines of Mahayana Buddhism. London, 1907.
10. ——————— Mahayana Buddhism. London, 1938.
11. Tattvārthādhigama-sūtra of Umāsvāti, ed. by J. L. Jaini. Arrah.
12. Upadhyaya, B. Bhāratīya Darśana (Hindi). Benares, 1942.
13. Vidyabhusana, S. C. History of Indian Logic. Calcutta, 1921.
14. Winternitz, M. History of Indian Literature (Eng. Tr.). Vol. I, Calcutta, 1933.

CHAPTER XX

EDUCATION, LITERATURE AND SCIENCES

1. Altekar, A. S. Education in Ancient India (2nd ed.). Benares, 1944.
2. Āryabhaṭīyam of Āryabhaṭa, tr. by Clarke. 1930.
3. ——————————— tr. by P. C. Sen Gupta (Journal of the Department of Letters, Calcutta University, XVI, 1927).

4. Buhler, G. Indian Inscriptions and the antiquity of Indian artificial Poetry (Eng. tr.) (*IA*. XLI).
5. De, S. K. Sanskrit Poetics, London, 1925.
6. Dutt, B. B. & Singh, A. N. History of Hindu M..thematics. 2 vols. Lahore, 1935-38.
7. Dutt, B. B. Bakhshali Manuscript (Bulletin of the Calcutta Mathematical Society, XXI, 1-60).
8. Edgerton, F. Pañchatantra Reconstructed. 2 vols. New Haven, 1924.
9. Hoernle, A. F. R. Bower Manuscript. Calcutta, 1893-1912.
10. Kane, P. V. History of Alaṁkāraśāstra, being a preface to Sāhityadarpaṇa. Bombay, 1923.
11. Kaye, G. R. Hindu Mathematics, Lahore, 1889.
12. ——————— Hindu Astronomy. Calcutta, 1924.
13. ——————— Bakhshali Manuscript. Calcutta, 1927.
14. Keith, A. B. History of Sanskrit Literature. Oxford, 1928.
15. ——————— Sanskrit Drama. Oxford, 1928.
16. Macdonell, A. A. History of Sanskrit Literature, London, 1913.
17. Mirashi, V. V. Kālidāsa (Marathi), Nagpur, 1934.
18. Pusalker, A. D. Bhāsa—a Study. Lahore, 1940.
19. Ray, P. C. History of Hindu Chemistry, etc. Calcutta, 1887.
20. Sen Gupta, P. C. Hindu Astronomy (Cultural Heritage of India, III. 341-77).
21. Thibaut, G. & Dvivedi, S. Pañchasiddhāntikā of Varāhamihira.
22. Thibaut, G. Astronomie, Astrologie und Mathematik. Strassburg, 1899.
23. Varāhamihira, Brihatsaṁhitā, Ratnagiri, 1874.
24. ———————, ——————— with the commentary of Bhaṭṭotpala. Benares, 1895.
25. Winternitz, M. Geschichte der Indischen Literature 3 vols. Leipzig, 1909-22.

CHAPTER XXI

ARCHAEOLOGICAL REMAINS OF THE GUPTA PERIOD

For the sites and remains described in this chapter references may be made to the following :

1. Archaeological Survey of India, Annual Reports, 1902-03—(in progress).
2. Archaeological Survey of India, Reports (by Cunningham). 23 vols.
3. Archaeological Survey of India, Memoirs.
4. Archaeological Survey of India, New Imperial Series.
5. Archaeological Survey of India, Reports of Circles.
6. Archaeological Reports of Baroda, Gwalior, Hyderabad, Jaipur, Mysore and other Indian States.

CHAPTER XXII

FINE ARTS

1. Agrawala, V. S. Handbook to the Sculptures in the Mathura Museum. Mathura, 1939.

2. Agrawala, V. S. Guide to the Archaeological Sections of the Provincial Museum, Lucknow. Lucknow, 1940.
3. ———— Rajghat Terracottas (Journal of the U. P. Historical Society, July, 1941, pp. 1-8).
4. Banerji, R. D. Age of the Imperial Guptas, Benares, 1933.
5. Brown, Percy. Indian Architecture, Buddhist and Hindu. Bombay, 1942.
6. Codrington, K. de B. Ancient India from the Earliest Times to the Guptas. London, 1926.
7. Coomaraswamy, A. K. History of Indian and Indonesian Art, London, 1927.
8. Cunningham, A. Archaeological Survey of India, Reports, Vol. X.
9. Griffiths, J. Paintings in the Buddhist Cave Temples of Ajanta. 2 vols. London, 1896-97.
10. Herringham, Lady. Ajanta Frescoes. London, 1915.
11. Saraswati, S. K. Temple Architecture in the Gupta Age (Journal of the Indian Society of Oriental Art, VIII, 1940).
12. Smith, V. A. History of Fine Art in India and Ceylon. Oxford, 1911.
13. ———— Indian Sculpture of the Gupta Period (Ostasiatische Zeitschrift. III, 1915).
14. Subramaniam, K. R. Buddhist Remains in the Āndhra and the History of Āndhra between 225 and 610 A.D. Madras, 1932.
15. Vishṇudharmmottaram, sections translated by St. Kramrisch. Calcutta. 1928.
16. Vogel, J. Ph. Buddhist Art in India, Ceylon and Java. Oxford, 1936.
17. Yazdani, G. Ajanta. Pts. 1 & 2 London, 1930-33.

INDEX

Abbreviations used are—

auth. (author); *chief.* (chieftain); *dynst.* (dynasty); *feud.* (feudatory); *gov.* (governor); *grt.* (grant); *ins.* (inscription); *isl.* (island); *kg.* (king); *lit.* (literature. All texts are included in this); *loct.* (locality, general term for geographical regions); *mk.* (monk); *mt.* (mountain); *nav.* (navigator); *off.* (officer); *p.* (poet); *peo.* (people); *pl.* (copper plate); *prc.* (prince); *q.* (queen); *r.* (river); *sac.* (sacrifice); *sch.* (scholar); *t.* (teacher); *trb.* (tribe).

PLATE I

Kanishka III, Vāsudeva II, Scytho-Sassanian, Later Scythian, Kidara Kushāṇa, Mālava, Yaudheya, Bhavanāga.

PLATE II

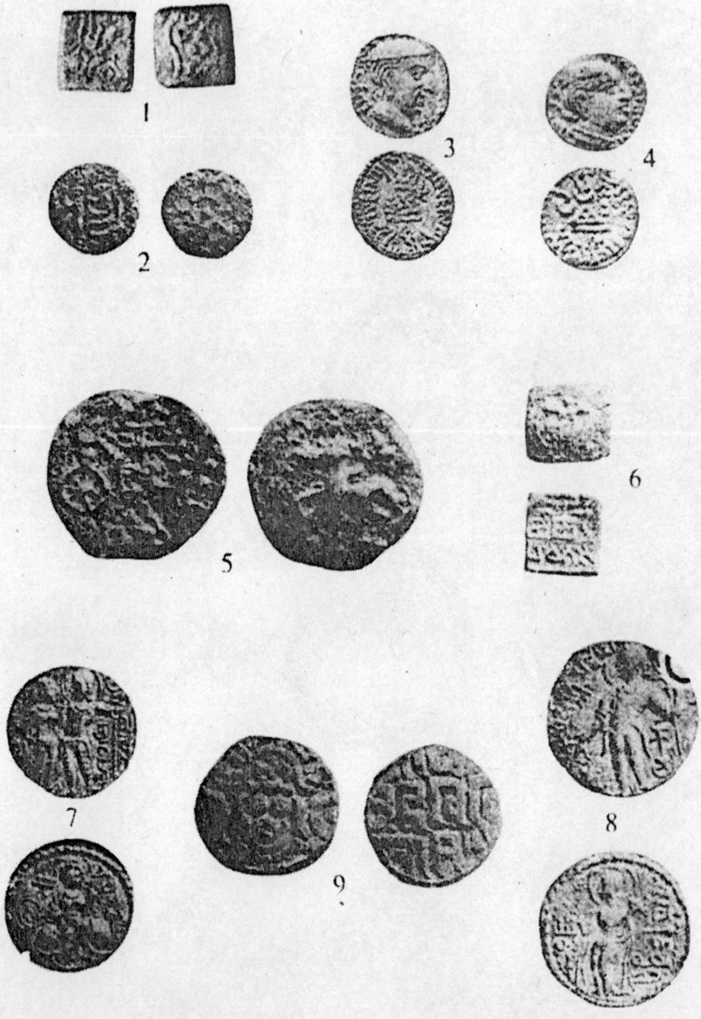

Vīrasena, Achyuta, Jīva-dāman, Lankey Bull, Pavata. Chandra-gupta I. and Kumāradevī, Samudra-gupta—Kācha. Muhammad bin Sam.

PLATE III

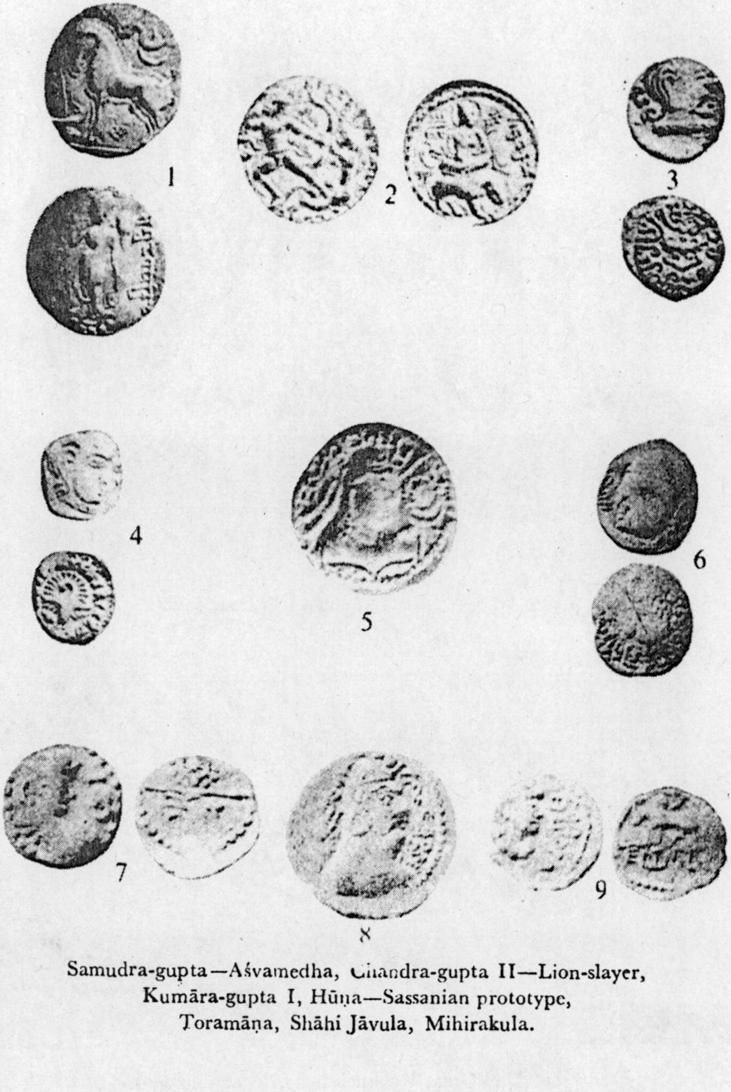

Samudra-gupta—Aśvamedha, Chandra-gupta II—Lion-slayer, Kumāra-gupta I, Hūṇa—Sassanian prototype, Ṭoramāṇa, Shāhi Jāvula, Mihirakula.

PLATE IV

1. Scene from Buddha's Life, Amaravati.

2. The Great Renunciation, Nagarjunikonda.

PLATE V

1. Scythian Warrior, Nagarjunikonda.

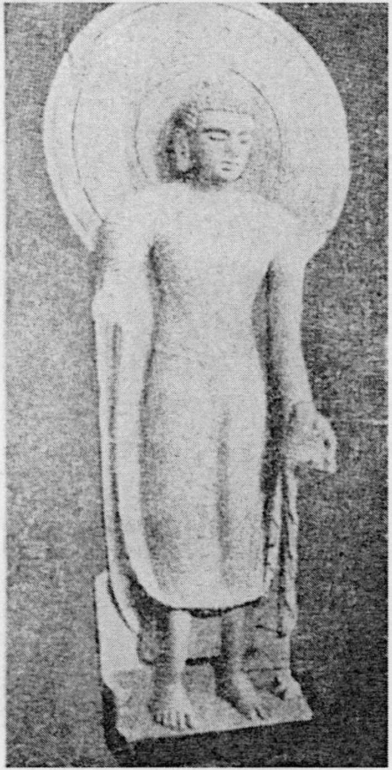

2. Buddha, Mathura. (*Courtsey Mathura Museum*)

3. Buddha (Copper), Sultanganj.

PLATE VI

PLATE VII

1. Mukha-Linga, Khoh.

2. Vishnu, Mathura.

PLATE VIII

1. Anantaśayana Vishṇu. Daśāvatāra temple, Deogarh.

2. Nara-Nārāyaṇa, Daśāvatāra temple, Deogarh.

(Copyright, Archaeological Survey of India)

PLATE IX

1. Kalpalatā motif, Gharwa.

2. Doorway, Daśāvatāra temple, Deogarh.

(*Copyright, Archaeological Survey of India*)

PLATE X

Facade of Chaitya hall. Cave XIX. Ajanta.

PLATE XI

1.

2.

3.

4.

Terracotta figurines, Rajghat Benares.

PLATE XII

Avalokiteśvara. Ajanta.

PLATE XIII

Mother and Child, Ajanta.

PLATE XIV

Lady with the left leg bent up,
Ajanta,

PLTE XV

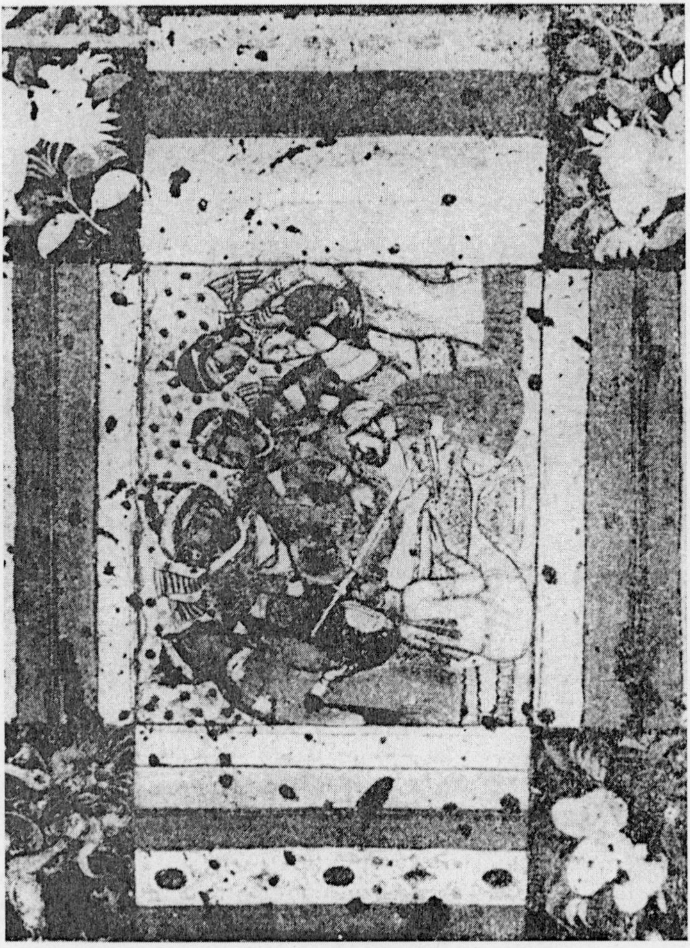

Persian Embassy (?), Ajanta.
(Courtesy Department of Archaeology, Hyderabad).